HISTORY OF ROME

HISTORY OF

ROME

MICHAEL GRANT

CHARLES SCRIBNER'S SONS
New York

Library of Congress Cataloging in Publication Data
Grant, Michael, 1914–
   History of Rome.
   Bibliography: p.
   Includes index.
   1. Rome—History. I. Title.
DG209.G75   1979   945'.632   78–12966
ISBN 0-684-15986-4

Designed by Jacques Chazaud

1 3 5 7 9 11 13 15 17 19 H/C 20 18 16 14 12 10 8 6 4 2

Printed in the United States of America

CONTENTS

List of Illustrations

List of Maps
and Tables

FOREWORD

The Romans are difficult to assess today. They employed force; yet what they accomplished by the use of it has never been equaled. For Rome conferred, indeed imposed, upon the Mediterranean area and upon vast hinterlands on three continents, a unity that these regions had never known before. And will they ever regain it? So far they have not.

But that is by no means all. For although Rome forms part of a larger Greek-Roman story, it possessed a potent individuality of its own. The notion, which is still sometimes aired, that Roman culture was merely an imitation of its Greek models is outworn and misguided in almost every field. On the contrary, in the literary and visual arts alike, as well as in law and the governmental sciences, Rome's achievement was of singular originality and distinction.

Ancient Rome is also unparalleled among the great communities of the Western world because it lasted for so long. No other occidental civilization or major political unit has so far rivaled its millennial duration. For the historian it is infinitely useful that this continuously evolving society should be available for his investigation at every phase of its growth, vigorous existence, and eventual transformation.

The Roman experience is useful for two reasons. First of all, it is wonderfully worthwhile to attempt to recreate this unique phenomenon just as it was, leaving our own modern concerns out of the matter altogether. The study of such an exciting and distinctive historical process is amply justified, purely and simply on its own account. Yet at the same time this interest takes on a new dimension when it is remembered that we ourselves, whether we like it or not, are Rome's heirs. In a thousand different ways, the Romans are permanently and indestructibly woven into the fabric of our own existences. They lived through many events and developments that resembled, prefigured, and caused what has happened, is happening, and may happen in the future to our own communities and our own selves.

The circumstances and backgrounds, it goes without saying, are in some respects radically different. But to conclude that people today cannot profit from this ancient history, that Rome is unable to communicate to us any relevant lessons or warnings—to use that old-fashioned phrase—is a mistake. For the past is deeply and unavoidably engrained in our own lives. It is therefore plain common sense to turn this inescapable possession to our advantage. For it can show us the good and bad and strange things of which humanity has proved to be capable, and is therefore capable still; and besides, as the philosopher George Santayana pointed out, those who cannot remember the past are condemned to repeat it. We admit that, when faced with a decision in our personal lives, we are habitually guided by the recollection of things that we ourselves have done or experienced at an earlier stage of our own lifetimes. But why limit this to our lifetimes? Why assume that we cannot also learn from the experiences and decisions and achievements and mistakes of those who have lived before?

First, then, Rome should be studied entirely on its own account, and every endeavor should be made to extract its own peculiar quintessence, regardless of any guidance it may have to offer to ourselves. Yet, at the same time, nothing will be lost, and perhaps much gained, by seeking analogies with our own experiences as well. For both these reasons, the effort to find out as much as we can about this unique segment of world history needs no further justification.

However, the task of pursuing such an aim is far from easy. This is mainly for two reasons—which at first sight seem to contradict each other. To begin with, the ancient sources, literary and archaeological alike, are often tantalizingly inadequate and uninformative. A great many of the documents that once existed have been lost, and those that survive are often enigmatic, biased, and neglectful of many matters that we should dearly like to know about. And yet the second reason why this task is so difficult is because the quantity of this material, however unsatisfactory, is nevertheless so colossal, which is hardly surprising since it encompasses a thousand eventful years.

There are, of course, countless modern histories of ancient Rome, and to many of them I owe a profound debt. Yet they have not prevented me from persisting with this new attempt, because however far it will fall below the greatness of the theme, I believe there is room for another book on this subject at the present time, one of approximately this size and scope, one that will take into account, insofar as this can be done, the researches, discoveries, and insights contributed by scholars in recent years.

But, given all this material, what principles of selection and omission ought to be adopted? First, would it be better to write a narrative story, or divide the book according to subjects? Both approaches seem equally necessary. Narrative history may be unfashionable, but a history of Rome makes no sense without it. If it is nothing but narrative, however, it will miss some of the major developments, so it will be necessary to pause from time to time to discuss matters in greater depth. Among these matters for discussion will be social, economic, literary, and artistic topics, and an effort will be made to relate these to the multiracial Roman Empire as well as to Rome itself. For those who want additional names, details, and comments, I have provided supplementary material in the notes. The most difficult task is to establish an appropriate balance between different epochs. In particular, it is important not to neglect noncentral periods that were vital to Rome's growth or transformation, even though the quantity of trustworthy evidence available about them is sometimes relatively small.

And what about our moral judgments? Are the Romans "good" because of all their positive achievements or "bad" because of their unmistakable brutalities? One cannot keep moral judgments out of it altogether because, as Cicero pointed out, it remains *objectively true,* in spite of debatable marginal cases, that some sorts of behavior are good, and others bad, and no vicissitudes of taste or special circumstances can make them otherwise. But when we pass on to intellectual judgments, for example, concerning the political wisdom or unwisdom of actions taken by this or that personage, the historical task becomes more delicate still. It is easy enough to sit in one's study, and perhaps never leave it, and pronounce that Scipio or Caesar or Marcus Aurelius acted sensibly or otherwise; yet chair-borne hindsight of this kind can never be based on a knowledge of all the circumstances and facts. Nevertheless, modern historians owe it to their readers to stand up and be counted and express a certain number of personal views. True, this may turn out to reveal less about ancient times than about the historian's own environment and the prejudices it has instilled in him. However, if some of these perconceptions are consciously held, so much the better, because then at least they will be under some control. But other unconscious preconceptions, despite all vigilance, will creep through as well.

This is another way of saying that we cannot claim to be as objective as we would like to be. Like others, I have tried, and no doubt without as much success as I should have wished. But at least one result of this attempt, which I believe to be good, has been the conclusion that I cannot subscribe to any unitary, all-explaining theories of Roman history. There is too much of it, and it is too varied for any single, dominant theme to be conceded a monopoly. Just as attempts to find any *one* cause for what is described as Rome's Decline and Fall are doomed to failure—as one might surely expect when so elaborate an institution is concerned—so, too, all overall explanations of its earlier development, including theories of inevitable cycles, are doomed to failure because there are always too many loose ends. Perhaps if one were dealing only with political history one could write it around the single guiding theme of imperial unity, and approaches to this unity and failures to achieve it. But in the wider field of the whole civilization of the Roman World, there is no single formula that will cover Fabius Maximus and Catullus and Plotinus, for they are so totally different—manifestations of a fabulous diversity and richness. If I have succeeded in giving even a hint of this richness in the present book, I shall be pleased.

I owe acknowledgments to the following: Professor Fergus Millar and Messrs. Duckworth and Co. Ltd., and to Professor R. M. Ogilvie and Fontana Paperbacks and the Harvester Press, for allowing me to see copies of their books, *The Emperor in the Roman World* and *Early Rome and the Etruscans* before publication; and to Mr. Edward de Bono and Messrs. Weidenfeld and Nicolson for permission to reproduce a passage from their volume, *The Greatest Thinkers.* And I want to thank Miss Christine Sandeman and Mrs. Susan Loden of the same firm for all the work they have done to prepare the book for the press. I also appreciate greatly the constructive encouragement I have received from Mr. Charles Scribner, Jr., the helpful editing of Miss Edith Poor and Miss Helen McInnis of Charles Scribner's Sons, the many valuable suggestions provided by Mr. Palmer Bovie, and I record with very great gratitude the help my wife, Anne-Sophie, has given me at every stage.

MICHAEL GRANT
Gattaiola, 1978

HISTORY OF ROME

I.
ETRUSCAN
ROME

Preceding page:
Wolf with Romuius and Remus

1
Rome and Etruria

Italy and Rome

I taly's central position in the Mediterranean is a call to self-assertion, suggesting many promising opportunities if and when its population is capable of grasping them. For instead of forming a barrier between the eastern and western reaches of the sea, the country serves as a link between them, open to maritime channels on either side. Moreover, the curiously elongated shape of the peninsula provides, next only to Greece, the longest coastline in Europe. There is a mile of shore for every fifty-nine square miles of land, whereas Spain, for example, has only one for one hundred and forty-five square miles. Besides, Italy is significantly placed in relation to the continental lands to its north. It is far enough removed from them to escape many of their turmoils, yet near enough to gain a share of whatever cultural advances are in the making.

At least three-quarters of Italy's territory consists of hills. They rise into the harshly ribbed vertebrae of the Apennines which dominate the whole land, curving down from the northwestern seaboard to the eastern, Adriatic coast, and then back again to Italy's toe. Yet there are also plains at the foot of this mountainous mass; they provide convenient inland corridors, and for the most part enjoy a relatively temperate and humid climate, which in early times opened up possibilities of agriculture on a scale that no other Mediterranean country had ever before been able to attempt. In comparison with other parts of the world, and particularly with the little, less bountiful plains of Greece, these regions seemed welcoming indeed.

The greatest of the plains is the Po Valley in the north between the Apennines and the Alps. However, that region, known to the Romans as Gaul this side of the Alps (Cisalpine Gaul), is part of the continental landmass rather than of the peninsula itself, and throughout more than half the period covered by this book it was not yet regarded as part of Italy at all. Yet in the south, too, even more fertile districts are to be found, especially along the west coast which was more attractive than the east because its mountains are not so steep and recede further from the sea. On this shore there was above all the Campanian plain, centered around the Gulf of Cumae (Bay of Naples), and to its north the two hundred and thirty-mile stretch of lowland Latium; and then, north of Latium, there was Etruria, separated from it by the river Tiber, which, although smaller than the Po, is the largest river of peninsular Italy and possesses the most extensive drainage area.

Descending from the central massif, the Tiber becomes navigable in its lower reaches, like so many other rivers of the world on which important, durable settlements have likewise been founded. And fifteen miles from the Mediterranean, or twenty for those traveling on its stream—far enough to provide warning of maritime raiders, but near enough to give it ready access to the sea—was the lowest of the river's feasible crossing points: at Rome. This crossing, close to an island in the river, linked together the lowest stretches of firm ground on either bank, at the point where the Tiber turns and breaks through a low range to the marshy coastal plain before debouching at the only possible harbor for many miles in either direction.

It was a crossing of vital importance since it coincided with the most convenient of the few longitudinal routes of Italy, a route that provided the main line of communications along the whole of the western and more populous flank of the country. Moreover, like London and Paris, the site commanded easy progress not only across the river, but along its course as well. Both upon its waters and by the road that lay beside it there was access to precious, rare salt pans on the shore, and inalnd the continuation of the same road up the Tiber valley led by fairly easy passes into the central regions of the land.

Once the inhabitants of Rome became strong enough, they would be able to dominate these vital passages in all directions. However, this potentiality was a challenge and a peril as much as an advantage. People at an important junction are as likely to reap suffering as profit, and the men and women who came and lived here were open to aggression from all sides and needed all the protection they could get.

They got it from the cliffs on which they planted their settlements, for the river lay in a deep trough at this point, and the settlers came to live on the hills and hillocks above its southern bank. These heights were between a hundred and three hundred feet above sea level—a series of flat-topped spurs projecting, more sharply than now, towards the Tiber and safely raised above the floods to which its valley was exposed. Ravines, former tributaries of the river, divided the hills from one another and to a lesser extent from the main plateau of the hinterland as well.

The site of Rome enjoyed a good water supply at all seasons and was within easy reach of fertile soil. It had seen human occupation, at least at sporadic intervals, from a very early date. The skull of a single-tusked elephant that lived some two million years ago has been found in its alluvial sands, and the soil beneath a suburb has yielded a Neanderthal man's skull more than thirty thousand years old. Other discoveries include the flint and copper implements of people who lived in the place early in the second millennium before our era.

Not long afterwards, in about 1600 B.C., men and women with unfamiliar customs made their appearance in Italy. They buried (inhumed) the bodies of their dead, practiced a seminomadic pastoral economy, and made excellent bronze work and decorated pottery. These settlers are described as representatives of the "Apennine culture" because they lived on either side of that range, to its north in the valley of the Po and to its south in Etruria, which extended down as far as Rome's river, the Tiber. Contrary to the view that prevailed until recently, the Etruscan sector of the culture probably developed more rapidly than the other. Moreover, from ca. 400 B.C. onwards this culture gained strength on the south bank of the Tiber too and left traces inside Rome itself, where objects that belonged to them have been found on the low ground near the river upon the site of the *Forum Boarium* or Cattle Market—to which they may have been transported from a neighboring hill.

It is possible, though not certain, that the men and women who lived on the site of Rome at that time were already speaking the Indo-European speech that later became Latin and Italian. And there is also quite a likelihood that from the time of these Bronze Age settlers onwards habitation continued without a break: in other words, the city that exists today was founded by the middle of the second millennium B.C.

A new phase, archaeologically better documented, began early in the last millennium B.C. when new groups of migrants gradually moved to this location. These were the descendants of men and women who had probably been settled for some generations in the area later called Latium and now the southern part of Lazio, a roughly triangular, well-watered country consisting of rolling plains furrowed into gullies and undulating folds. Some thirty miles deep and sixty miles long, Latium extended from the borders of Campania as far north as the Tiber and the site of Rome. Before 1000 B.C. the populations that had established themselves in this region had apparently been joined by immigrants of mixed origins coming by sea from the Balkans in small, isolated, pioneering groups.

Whatever may have been the case with their predecessors, these settlers probably spoke a primitive dialect related to Latin. They engraved bronze skillfully but supplemented this talent by a growing familiarity with the use of iron, a knowledge they had acquired along the sea routes from the Aegean. In contrast to their predominantly pastoral forerunners, they ploughed the soil with light ploughs and did not bury but burned (cremated) their dead. They form one of the mainstreams of Iron Age history. But another, too, became increasingly apparent, for Latium also contained people, coming perhaps originally from southern Italy, who like the Bronze Age people of the previous millennium did not cremate their dead but buried (inhumed) them. This element gradually became dominant in Latium and greatly increased its prosperity.

One of the nuclei of these Latin communities was the Alban Mount (Monte Cavo), thirteen miles southeast of Rome. Its peak was a natural fortress some three thousand feet in height, dominating a semicircle of cone-shaped hills. The Alban Mount was a former volcano that had ceased to be active in about the fourth millennium B.C. By that time, however, its eruptions had guaranteed the future wealth of the area by covering the marshy clay plain for miles around with layers of new soil containing phosphates and potash. This mixture, with the addition of decaying leaves from the forest of fir, pine, chestnut, and beech that still covered the territory, made the sodden clay especially fertile when it was drained.

By the early years of the first millennium, the settlement of the Alban area and of Latium was nearing completion, and nomadism was finally giving way to intensive cultivation. It was at this juncture that the Iron Age settlers moved in to Rome. Groups of shepherds and farmers gradually moved across from the Alban region until they came to the Tiber and built their huts upon the Roman hills, which were particularly attractive because they provided communication with Etruria beyond the river. First of all—the latest archaeological discoveries indicate a date during the tenth century B.C.—groups of these people settled on the level summit of the isolated and well-protected Palatine Hill and in the marshy, moatlike valley of the Forum, which lay between the Palatine and the Quirinal, Esquiline, and Capitoline Hills. Next, in the ninth and eighth centuries B.C. more immigrants came and settled on the Quirinal, guarded by steep ravines on three sides; and then others established themselves on the Esquiline as well. The precipitous Capitoline and the Caelian, rising northwest and east of the Palatine respectively, also received inhabitants in an early period, though at what stage cannot yet be determined.

And these people not only dwelt on the hills and the Forum that lay between them, but they also deposited the remains of their dead near their dwellings. Cremation and inhumation, the two types of interment characteristic of the two groups of Iron Age settlers, are both found. The cremators dug small, deep, circular pits within which they placed large globular jars that had stone slats as lids. Inside the jars were urns in which the burned

Cremation urn in the form of a hut. Later eighth century B.C.

ashes of the dead person were laid. Often the urn was a little model of one of the huts in which the people themselves lived—a design that seems to have originated in Latium. As for the inhumers, they buried the bodies in hollowed-out logs or rough stone sarcophaguses, which they laid in long rectangular pits or trenches sometimes lined with stones. Cremation and inhumation are sometimes found side by side on Roman sites and even, on occasion, in such close proximity that graves of the two kinds actually cut into one another. But whether the practitioners of these two customs differed from one another in race we cannot say. All that it is safe to conjecture from these first Iron Age cemeteries at Rome is that the two groups, whoever they were, gradually mixed and amalgamated both with each other and with whatever sparse populations they already found living on the hilltops when they arrived.

Rome, according to the traditional belief, was founded in 753 B.C. But the date is wholly mythical—too late for the first regular settlements and too early for the time of true urbanization. It is worthwhile to note how this fictitious date came to be fixed. In the first place, the city's period of monarchic rule was widely, and probably correctly, believed to have come to an end in the last years of the sixth century B.C. To fill the preceding period, later Romans could muster the names of only seven kings of varying authenticity. To accommodate these seven kings, and the more or less legendary events associated with them, it seemed necessary to suppose that their reigns had covered two or three hundred years, which, working back from their expulsion shortly before 500 B.C., fixed the foundation of Rome in the ninth or eighth century.

And so one later historian favored 814 B.C. for this foundation—on an entirely erroneous principle, because his only aim was to synchronize the event with the origin of Rome's later archenemy Carthage, which was believed to have been founded at that date. Another writer preferred 748–747 instead—on the equally fallacious grounds that this provided a convenient period of exactly four hundred years before a recorded celebration of the Secular Games, a religious festival that marked periods of time, often centuries, and had been celebrated, it was believed, in 348 B.C. However, an alternative date for the foundation, favored by another ancient historian, was 751—the move from 748–747 being made to permit the interpolation of certain names that this author wished to insert in the list of annually elected consuls. And then a writer of the first century B.C., Varro, needing two more years for the same sort of reason, fastened upon 753 instead. That, ultimately, became canonical, but it is as wholly speculative and unsound a date as any of the others.

Thus, when we seek to reconstruct the early history and chronology of Rome, its abundant patriotic and partisan myths and legends have to be distrusted. And yet these, unfortunately, are the only literary materials that we possess for all these early centuries before any reliable historical facts are available. The myths are immensely important because they tell us what later generations of Romans believed about their country and how their minds worked. But to find out what actually happened in early days we are compelled, for the most part, to have recourse not to these stories but to archaeological excavation; and the record that this provides for us is sometimes entirely different from the stories told by the mythographers.

The Etruscan City-States

Another example of the same difficulty is provided by Rome's Etruscan period. Rome was at one time, as archaeological evidence reveals, a largely Etruscan city. Its myths do not deny that this was so. Yet the strange love-hate attitude that later Romans exhibited towards the Etruscans (and that is apparent, for instance, in many passages of Virgil's poetry) reflects such great discomfort about this period of foreign domination, far back in the past though it was, that most of the salient facts are obscured and can only be partially recovered by painstaking archaeological research.

In the first place, this tells us, and is telling us in ever greater detail year by year, who the Etruscans were. Their city-states flourished in the seventh and sixth centuries B.C. in a homeland that roughly corresponded with what is now southern Tuscany and northern Lazio, covering a highly varied territory stretching two hundred miles from the Arno to the Tiber and inland as far as the Apennines. The Etruscan people inhabiting this region called themselves "Rasenna" and displayed an art with pronounced oriental characteristics. Their splendid gold jewelry, for example, and the architectural themes and techniques that they employed to spectacular effect (preserved nowadays, when their cities have otherwise scarcely survived, mainly in grandiose rock-cut tombs) were strongly reminiscent of the near east—to some extent Asia Minor, but also the coastlands of Syria and Phoenicia (Lebanon) and historic Mesopotamia and Assyria beyond them.

Now similar trends were also apparent in the art of Greece during its "orientalizing" phase which was precisely at the time of the greatest Etruscan art. Orientalizing tendencies had first begun to pervade Greece late in the eighth century B.C. because the country's isolation, following its so-called Dark Age during the convulsions at the beginning of the millennium, was beginning to come to an end. The virtual monopoly of eastern Mediterranean trade, which had passed during the previous chaotic period from Mycenae and other places in Greece to the Semitic cities of Tyre and Sidon in Phoenicia, was at this time challenged once again by the Greeks. Greek ships, as well as those of the Phoenicians, began to bring home objects of eastern trade and workmanship, thus causing oriental motifs to flood into Greek art. The lead was taken by the maritime isthmus city of Corinth, whose artists, as well as those from its offshoots or colonies on either side of the Adriatic, extensively painted eastern themes on their vases. In these polychrome paintings, new patterns of animals and winged monsters replace the former geometric designs. This representational, illustrative type of art had long been familiar in Syria and Egypt and Assyria. But in Greece the introduction of such tendencies proved epoch-making, releasing novel

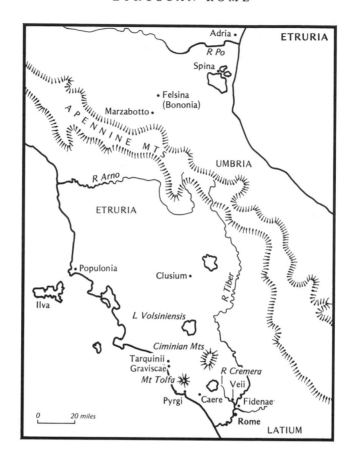

creative forces and endowing the rising civilization with a new and distinctive personality.

And Greece in turn played a great part (though not necessarily, as we shall see, the only part) in conveying the new orientalizing influences to Etruria, both directly from the mainland and indirectly through the colonies of Magna Graecia in south Italy. Etruria became one of the chief export markets of the Greeks, whose painted vases filled with amber, tin, lead, and luxury goods, flooded into the country. The Etruscans employed immigrant craftsmen from Corinth and its colonies, and Etrusco-Corinthian pottery dominated the local markets from ca. 600 B.C. when a Greek-speaking community made its appearance at Gravisca (Porto Clementino), the port of the Etruscan city of Tarquinii (Tarquinia).

Etruscan art absorbed this Greek influence thoroughly. Yet the result seems strangely different and individual, just as Etruscan society, too, is in many ways alien from the Greek (for example, in its strange mixture of intense religious feeling with brutal physical force, and in the prominence it accorded to women, almost unparalleled in western lands until the present century). At its more pedestrian levels, the art of Etruria merely resembles an off-beat provincial variation of Greek art, such as could be found in other fringe areas of Hellenic culture in Europe and Asia. At its best, on the other hand, it achieves authentic, imposing originality.

The most typical features of Etruscan temples, their lofty platforms and roomy colonnaded porches, are clearly un-Greek. Moreover, an Etruscan statue like the Apollo of Veii (Veio, ca. 500 B.C.), though largely Greek in shape and manner, displays an un-Greek gross and forceful abundance of life, and an unclassical treatment of detail. These are partly the artist's own contribution, but they are also based on an apprehension of the eastern past that was more direct among the Etruscans than among the Greeks, for the orientalizing tendency is unmistakably sharper and deeper in Etruria. And this must have been the result of links with the near east so strong that they are best explained (with due respect for strenuous modern proposals to the contrary), not merely by indirect contacts with that area through trade with orientalizing Greek cities, but also by the supposition that the Etruscans' leading men possessed oriental affinities and connections because they themselves had originally been of eastern origin. This tradition was believed by them and accepted by the Greek historian Herodotus, who regarded the Etruscans as immigrants from Lydia in Asia Minor. It is true that the origin of the Etruscans is not the most important thing about them; what is important is the way in which their independent city-states developed in Etruria. Nevertheless, their origin remains of some interest; and the likelihood that they originated from some region of the near east—whether Lydia or elsewhere—is demonstrated not only by the artistic echoes and parallels, but also by other evidence. For example, their belief in revealed religion and in specific methods of divination seems to go back to that part of the world. Moreover, their mining of metals was highly reminiscent of Asia Minor and regions beyond.

They exploited this activity on a scale that, by ancient standards, was prodigious. Indeed, it was the copper available locally to the people of coastal Populonia, from which they could make bronze, that evidently first brought these adventurers to the country and, supplemented later by extensive iron, gave them their huge prosperity and the weapons to maintain it. Moreover, their success was further guaranteed by extremely effective agriculture that made use of sophisticated methods of drainage and soil conservation recalling the techniques of Mesopotamia. And there is epigraphic evidence of eastern connections too, since inscriptions from the Aegean island of Lemnos reveal that its people spoke a language resembling Etruscan. (And Thucidydes believed that the Etruscans had once lived there.)

We can read the twenty-six characters of the alphabet used by the Etruscans, which they developed from the letters employed by Greek colonists in southwestern Italy. However, our fifty bilingual inscriptions in which Etruscan is juxtaposed with another language unfortunately fail to disclose the nature of this tongue, or even to show whether it forms part of the Indo-European stock to which Greek and Latin belong. But that now seems on the whole improbable, a conclusion which suggests that the language of the Etruscans, like so many of their institutions, came from the east, thus confirming the view that they themselves, or their governing class, were likewise of eastern origin.

If so, it may be supposed that in the years around 700–675 B.C.—at a time when Asia Minor and the lands beyond it were suffering from especially troubled conditions—a succession of small bands of immigrants from some unidentifiable eastern territory, following perhaps in the wake of reconnaissances by earlier traders, arrived upon the shores of Etruria. Running their ships aground on the flat, gray-black beaches, they seized the hill spurs nearby, fortified them with wooden palisades, and established upon them in due course the powerful city-states that we know as Etruscan. They did so with the collaboration, willing or forced, of the peoples whom they found already in residence there; for, despite the sudden upsurge suggestive of a new cultural element, there is also a strong measure of archaeological continuity on the sites. Indeed, the whole trend of modern research insists that they should be seen in the context of their Italian forerunners and neighbors.

The Etruscans owed to their eastern forebears, as well as to the Greeks when they subsequently got to know them, a marked talent for urbanization, and this was encouraged by the compulsion, imposed by Italy's geography, to cluster together on the relatively few sites that were eligible and attractive. And so the Etruscans created their cities, first near the coast, and then on inland sites towards the middle course of the Tiber. Traditionally there were twelve such communities in Etruria, though it is hard to draw up a complete list for any given time, and archaeology has revealed a number of townships far exceeding that total. But twelve was the approximate number of their major city-states.

In spite of traditions that there had once been a single king over the whole country, each of these cities seems to have been fully independent of all the rest. Once a year (at least in later times) they sent delegates over their excellent roads to a joint gathering at the shrine of the divinity Voltumna, which has not yet been identified but was probably not far from Lake Volsiniensis (Bolsena). Yet the political initiatives that this loose cult union attempted were apparently rare and generally ineffectual. True, its member cities no doubt maintained shifting patterns of alliances with one another. But they had grown up in physical isolation, kept apart by the wooded and hilly country that surrounded them. In consequence, each city usually tended to act on its own.

And indeed these states were not only independent but also highly individual and distinguished from each other by sharp political, social, and cultural differences—almost as great perhaps as those that distinguished, say, Athens, Corinth, and Sparta in Greece. This point, too rarely appreciated, is of major importance to early Roman history, for Rome was influenced at most significant junctures not by the Etruscans as a whole, but by this or that Etruscan city-state. Owing to the inadequate state of our sources, we cannot always say which of these cities exercised such effect at any given moment. But obviously, to a large extent Rome is likely to have been most greatly influenced by the southern communities, which lay so close to the Tiber. They were Tarquinii (Tarquinia), Caere (Cerveteri), and Veii (Veio), only forty, twenty, and twelve miles distant respectively from Rome. These south Etruscan cities, standing on their hilltops in close proximity to the coast, were livelier and more cosmopolitan, more open and receptive to Greek and other foreign contacts than their middle and north Etruscan counterparts, which lay beyond almost untouched forests in the interior. And so it was they, Tarquinii, Caere, and Veii, that developed a particularly brilliant and prosperous culture in ca. 670–630 B.C. and supplied the formative stimulus and inspiration that transformed Rome from a huddle of hut villages into a city.

Earliest Rome

By the early seventh century B.C., the communities on the several spurs of the Palatine, Esquiline, and Caelian had joined together at least for religious purposes and perhaps politically as well. The unit they now formed was the *Septimontium* or Seven Hills (different from, and smaller than, the later Seven Hills of Rome). Then, perhaps in Ca. 625–620, the low-lying area later known as the Forum was systematically drained, and it was probably at this juncture that Rome's Great Drain, the *Cloaca Maxima,* was dug through it—at first in the form of an open trench. Thus the Forum was able to start its long career as a meeting place and market for the unified Roman hills. Within another quarter of a century, the momentum quickened still further. The Forum, and the Sacred Way that connected it with the other quarters of the town, received their first permanent pavements, and the Forum Boarium (Cattle Market) near the river was also regularly laid out.

And it was at about the same time that a further decisive step was taken towards the unification of the city. For now the northernmost spurs, the Quirinal and Viminal, joined the growing community. Before long, the expanded township began to make use of the rocky Capitoline as a common citadel. Whether the earlier, smaller amalgamation, the Septimontium, had only been for purposes of common worship or had been more comprehensive, this new and larger Rome of the Four Regions as it was called was a completely unified entity, its boundaries marked with a sacred furrow by a bronze ploughshare drawn by a white bull and white cow.

It still cannot be proved for certain that these developments were directly due to the example or counsel of Rome's Etruscan neighbors, but this seems highly probable. The appearance of such rapid internal changes, accom-

The Great Drain (Cloaca Maxima), by which the Forum was drained in eighth century B.C., entering the Tiber (its vault dates from about the time of Augustus). Above it is the Cattle Market (Forum Boarium), including a round unidentified temple ("of Vesta") of second/first century B.C., reconstructed under Hadrian.

panied, as excavations show, by the transformation of a purely domestic economy into a community of professional handicrafts, suggests that some such powerful external agency was at work. Moreover, contacts between Iron Age Latium and southern Etruria were nothing new; they had been taking place from the mid-eighth century onwards, and Rome had participated in them almost from the start, progressively assimilating its material culture to that of Etruria. And it is in the last quarter of the seventh century B.C., at just about the time when the Forum was drained, that the first pottery and metalwork from the nearby Etruscan cities of Caere and Veii begin to appear at Rome. The place is evidently on the way to becoming an Etruscan town.

2
The Etruscan Monarchy

Etruscan Rome

What interested the Etruscans about Rome in the first place was not its attractions but its position on the way south to the uniquely inviting land of Campania. For behind this same coast, starting ninety miles beyond Rome, lay the Campanian plain, incredibly favored by nature. Traversed by two rivers and fanned by moist winds, this territory of spongy volcanic earth enjoyed relatively mild and short winters. Moreover, its soil, retaining enough of the abundant seasonal rainfall to resist three months of summer drought, became capable of producing in some districts as many as three grain crops every year, in addition to a catch-crop of vegetables as well.

But the Greeks reached Campania before the Etruscans, for in the eighth century B.C. Greek colonists, attracted by the fertility of the area—as well as by the possibility of trading with Etruria—chose Cumae, on the coast just northwest of the gulf named after it (now known as the Bay of Naples), for their settlement on the mainland of Italy. Cumae became a great center for the sale of grain and the diffusion of Greek influence over the greater part of south Italy and Sicily, known to the ancients as Magna Graecia for this reason. But before 600 (or perhaps a good deal earlier, according to some interpretations) the travelers, or armies, from certain Etruscan city-states made their way into Campania, and founded—or refounded—the leading city of the fertile lowlands, Capua (Santa Maria Capua Vetere), seventeen miles north of Neapolis (Naples). From Capua the Etruscans began to extend their domination over the greater part of the Campanian plain, though they did not succeed in controlling Cumae itself.

Whether they had first come to Campania by land or by sea cannot be determined. But in any case they rapidly found it desirable both to create a land route to these new southern dependencies and to possess harbors on the way to them as well. That brought them into Latium, which lay between

Campania and themselves; so that during the seventh century many leading Latin towns became subject to Etruscan city-states, at least to the extent that these city-states controlled their communications and imposed ruling classes upon them. And above all, it was the Etruscans who stimulated an enormous development of Latium's agriculture, introducing, after the model of their own country, a system of irrigation based on drainage channels *(cuniculi)* about five feet deep and two or three feet wide. Because the surface loam was very precious and needed to be saved, rainwater had to be poured into the channels with great speed. Cut into the volcanic soil over almost the whole Latin plain stretching northwards from Campania and southwards from Rome, they made it practicable for this potentially fertile region to be cultivated with unprecedented intensity—and the entire territory rescued from the marsh, just as the Dutch later reclaimed their lowlands from the sea.

It was impossible for the Etruscans to hold Latium without also taking Rome which lay between Latium and themselves. The town was on their very borders, and its river crossing was essential for their access to the Latin plain. There was also the added attraction of Rome's proximity to the salt pans at the mouth of the Tiber (first exploited on its north bank), since salt was essential to the Etruscan cities and they could not obtain it from any other source.

These then were the reasons why Rome came under Etruscan influence. As we saw in the last chapter, when discussing the stages of its urbanization, the decisive period of that process seems to have been the last quarter of the seventh century B.C. Nor was it long before influence took the form of overt political control, and Rome, as its own subsequent writers were obliged to admit, came under the rule of an Etruscan monarch.

Early Roman Religion

What sort of a place did he find? Above all else, it was a religious community. The Romans had from the earliest period cherished a powerful, pervasive, and peculiar religion. Centuries later, Cicero praised their continuing conviction that everything is subordinate to divine rule and direction. Roman religion was based on mutual trustfulness *(fides)* between the divine powers or gods, on the one hand, and men and women on the other. The trust accorded by the gods, and their benevolence—what was called the peace of the gods *(pax deorum)*, a balance of nature in which divine powers and human beings worked in harmony—could be secured by meticulous ritual and not so much, as more recent religions would maintain, by good moral behavior, since for centuries there was no very prominent moral element in Roman religion. Nevertheless, this idea of the divine peace indirectly exercised a moral influence, since the respect that it induced for vows made to the gods was extended, in the course of time, to vows made to other human beings as well.

Yet the individual human being was not what mattered in the religion of the Romans, for they saw this as a group affair, not a matter for individuals. And indeed the same applied to the whole of Roman life, in which individuality was submerged in family, clan, and state. As in other ancient Indo-European-speaking communities, the family or household, and the clan *(gens)* or group of households, were of overriding importance. The head of the family *(pater familias),* any male citizen who had no living ancestor in the main line, was absolute; there is nothing, perhaps, in any other known culture quite as extreme as this long-lasting patriarchal assertion. Although the *pater familias* might call in, by custom, a council of male relatives, and although he habitually left the running of his house to his wife, it was he who monopolized all rights. In the home, his word was literally law—and so long as he remained alive, his sons never came of age.

Thus he controlled, among much else, domestic cult, which played a mighty part in daily life. The household deities were worshiped every day and at every meal, and no important family event could take place without securing divine approval. Whether domestic or communal worship came earliest is disputed; but in any case the latter was a magnified version of the former. Vesta, worshipped by her Vestal Virgins, beside the Forum, in her round straw hut which later became a temple, was the hearth goddess of the Roman state. But she was equally prominent in family cult as well, symbolizing the solidarity of the home as well as the nation.

Roman religion possessed no sacred writings except invocations and prayers, and its priests were not a caste set apart, but men following secular careers. Yet it was nonetheless real for all that. "To understand the success of the Romans," declared the Greek historian Dionysius of Halicarnassus at the turn of our era, "you must understand their piety." The gods were national, invisible, potent citizens of whatever country they favored, and the Romans, duly performing manifold observances towards them, believed that they favored Rome.

Yet these powers that inspired their awe and reverence, which is what *religio* meant, were regarded as mysterious and unknowable, and for a long time were scarcely seen as personal beings. In the earliest times, the Romans, like many other Italians, lacked the Greek taste for seeing their deities in personalized anthropomorphic form, so that the temple of Vesta contained no image at all. They also in those early days lacked the desire to clothe their gods and goddesses in a mythology. Instead, they were inclined to see divine force, or divinity, operating as pure function or act, both in human activities like opening doors or giving birth to children and in natural phenomena, such as the movement of the sun and stars and the seasons of the soil.

Yet this impersonal concept was already becoming gradually modified from a very ancient date, when Greek ideas first began to come in, both directly and through the medium of Etruria. For example, Vesta, even though she lacked a statue, was the same, etymologically and by assimilation, as the Greek Hestia. And Mars, the first god recognized by the Romans (and by other Italians too) as chief of all the divinities, was identified with the Greek Ares. Nevertheless, Roman religion retained its independence because its deities remained somewhat different from those of the Greeks. Mars, for example, was not entirely a war god like Ares, since he was rather the protector of the whole people, in agriculture as well as war. Indeed, he shared an ancient sanctuary in the Forum, known as the Regia, with the power of fertility, Ops Consiva. The first cult building on the Regia site, replacing earlier huts and burials, was a stone-founded and stone-walled precinct dating from the later seventh century B.C. It contained a monument of which the purpose is still unknown; perhaps it was dedicated to Mars. As the name Regia suggests, early Rome was a monarchy. The word comes from *rex* ("king") and the Regia was therefore, in all probability, the building in which the king had his residence.

The Structure of the Earliest Roman State

That Rome had originally been ruled by kings was unanimously asserted by its subsequent historians. Before Etruscan rule began, there had already been, according to this tradition, four non-Etruscan monarchs. Most or all of these four names are either of dubious historicity or downright fictitious —notably the alleged city founder Romulus, which just means "the man of Rome." Yet the memory that Rome had been a monarchy was authentic and is confirmed by the survival of the royal title *rex* into later times, after the kings had gone, when it came to be borne by a priest known as the *rex sacrorum*, "king of religious affairs"—residing, as the early monarchs had apparently resided, in the Regia. We know practically nothing about the most ancient phases of this kingship except that, as the survival of the *rex sacrorum* suggests, it included religious duties. The office, perhaps, was not necessarily hereditary or adoptive, but elective, as in the city-states of primitive Greece.

From the beginning, so later tradition maintained, the Roman state was divided into three units known as tribes *(tribus)*. Some scholars suggest that this division represented a racial distinction, corresponding to three different components in the original Roman state; but this is uncertain, and they

Inscription in early Latin recording ritual law and "a King" (rex) beneath the Black Stone (Lapis Niger) in the Forum Romanum (550-500 B.C.).

may instead have been groups of clans without any clear ethnic differentiation. In any case, the threefold division is likely to have been made in the first place in order to facilitate military and financial censuses of the people. The names of the three tribes are Etruscan, and this could mean either that they are Etruscanized designations of units that had already existed under different names before the Etruscan monarchy, or, alternatively, that they were new institutions that the Etruscan monarchy first brought into existence. The latter is the more natural interpretation; and if we accept it, these tribes may reasonably be ascribed to the earlier times of Etruscan influence, perhaps towards the end of the seventh century B.C.

The three tribes were subdivided into ten *curiae* or wards (from *co-viria,* gathering of men), each comprising a number of clans or groups of families (once again, not necessarily differentiated by race); a similar kind of organization seems to have existed in other Latin towns, and perhaps in Etruscan communities as well. It was upon these *curiae,* and upon the tribes into which they were grouped, that the earliest recognizable Senate was based, for it contained three hundred members, that is to say thirty from each *curia* and one hundred from each tribe. These senators were selected by the kings from the *patres familias*—the heads of the clans and of their component families—and were known as *patres conscripti;* how freely they debated under the monarchy we cannot tell. The *curiae* also met together in a body to form the earliest Assembly Rome possessed, the *Comitia curiata.* Probably this merely ratified decisions that had been made by the king, perhaps after he had consulted with the Senate, though when a king died, the Assembly may have played a part in electing his successor. The curial system also seems to have been the basis of Rome's most primitive military organization. This comprised an army or legion *(legio)* of three thousand infantry and three hundred cavalry, that is to say, one thousand and one hundred respectively from each of the tribes, and one hundred and ten respectively from each *curia.*

Owing to the Etruscan tribal nomenclature on which these developments are based, it is possible that they ought to be synchronized with the fifth name on Rome's traditional king list, for he was Etruscan and brings us to firmer ground since he represents the Etruscan takeover of Rome, which is a historical fact. Roman legend tells that this first of the city's Etruscan kings succeeded peacefully to the throne—though such a tradition may be merely a patriotic device to scotch the idea that Rome had ever been forcibly subjected to foreigners. His name was said to be Tarquinius Priscus (i.e., the Elder, in contrast with his son Tarquinius Superbus, who became king later), and his origin was attributed to one of the earliest Etruscan cities, Tarquinii, on a high plateau not far from the sea, forty miles northwest from Rome. Some have felt that this homeland was invented for him by later historians because the record of a Roman monarch named Tarquinius so obviously recalled the name of the place—and the Tarquins really came from Caere, which was closer to Rome and more intimately connected with it; moreover, the mausoleum of their family had been discovered there, with their name "Tarchna" Latinized as "Tarquitius." But the name is not uncommon, and it seems better not to abandon the view that the Tarquins came from Tarquinii.

The traditional dates of Priscus's reign are 616–579 B.C., and here tradition harmonizes for the first time with the findings of archaeology, which ascribe the decisive stages of Rome's urbanization to the last quarter of the seventh century. The Etruscans may, then, have established political control of the city at precisely that time; though some would argue, instead, that their monarchy only started in ca. 575. But it is not at all certain that the legends are right when they tell of *two* Etruscan kings of Rome bearing the name of Tarquin. There may have been more than two; or there may have been only one, retrospectively subdivided into two so as to attribute good deeds to the first, and bad, tyrannical deeds to the second (Superbus meaning "the arrogant"), under whom the monarchy was believed to have come to an unlamented end.

It was apparently in this Etruscan period that the rulers of Rome quit their earlier royal residence in the Regia and established themselves instead, and built a citadel, on the precipitous, defensible Capitoline Hill, while their followers settled between the Capitoline and Palatine in "Etruscan Street," the Vicus Tuscus. Moreover, excavators' reports of the destruction in ca. 600 of small towns including Politorium (Castel di Decima) ten miles south of Rome may bear witness to a territorial drive by the Etrusco-Roman monarchy in this direction.

How Etruscan did Rome now become? Opinions differ. As inscriptions show, there was a Latin-speaking population under an Etruscan-speaking ruling class. Nevertheless, it has been argued recently that there was deep interpenetration and fusion between the two ethnic and linguistic groups, and that Rome did, at this time, turn into a more or less homogeneous Etruscanized city. Support for this view from later Roman historians cannot be expected because it would have been unacceptable to the national pride. Yet to a certain extent at least, that is what must have happened, for the later institutions of the Romans still continued to embody highly important Etruscan features. Their religion contained much that was Etruscan, including the calendar. Their mythology, too, when they came to have one, owed much to the same source; for example, the adoption of Aeneas as Rome's precursor, perpetuated by Virgil who was himself partly Etruscan, is traceable back to the city's occupation by that people among whom Aeneas was revered.

Moreover, whereas the Etruscans had taken their alphabet, with modifications, from Greece, either directly or through the medium of the Greek city of Cumae in Campania, the Romans then proceeded to borrow their own, after further changes, from their Etruscan neighbors and overlords. That is why, like the Etruscan alphabet, it is short in vowels and redundant in the C, K, and Q group, and the letterforms of the earliest Latin inscriptions bear the same witness to Etruscan origins. And from the same source once again came much Roman ceremonial, and the names of families and localities, and many architectural achievements (gateways, bridges, arches, designs of houses), numerous styles and themes of pictorial art, and highly developed agricultural methods.

True, most of these borrowings, except for the last, had little effect on the illiterate, impoverished majority of the population of the region, who had to live as always not far from the borders of bare subsistence. But at all higher levels the influence of the Etruscans was deeply pervasive, which is scarcely surprising since it was only due to them that Rome had become a city at all.

"Servius Tullius"

Midway in the Tarquinian regime, and, to be exact, between the suspect pair of Tarquins, legend inserted the mysterious king Servius Tullius. The dates given for his reign are 578–535 B.C., but they are entirely unreliable, and indeed this monarch is more richly encrusted with fictitious myth, if possible, than any of the kings who supposedly came before or after him. Servius Tullius was said to be a Latin, although a rival theory declared him to be Etruscan. But his name is Latin, and he is best thought of as a member of the native population that dated back to pre-Etruscan times. However, he apparently pursued the development and expansion of Rome on the lines of his Etruscan predecessor; and indeed, he was credited with a thorough overhaul of the institutions of the Roman state. Many object that the reforms attributed to him, like so much else in the historians' account of the kings, ought instead to be assigned to a date perhaps as much as two centuries later. Yet these measures are appropriate to the stage of evolution that the community seems to have reached in his day, and may be discussed at this point.

What happened was that the three original tribes of Rome were replaced by twenty-one new ones, four in the city and seventeen in Rome's rural appendages. These new tribes represented local, geographical divisions, and the urban tribes correspond with the Four Regions of Rome, which seem to have been established slightly earlier, in about 600 B.C. Even if it is not quite certain that the three earlier tribes had been instituted for census reasons, this was surely the purpose of Servius's twenty-one new ones: they were basic units for raising levies and collecting taxes. As for the rural tribes —of which the geographical delimitation remains uncertain—sixteen out of the seventeen of them were known, at least in later historical times, by the names of families that were eminent at Rome, and it is possible that these names go back to Servian times. Nevertheless, if this was so, the choice of such designations was not much more than a sop to the aristocracy, for the novel insistence on a territorial residential basis meant a diminution of family loyalties and enabled the enfranchisement of Etruscan and other immigrants who lacked these allegiances and reserved their allegiance not for any family but for the monarch.

Moreover, under the same king, or at least at the same period, a completely new military system was inaugurated, according to which the size of the army was doubled to six thousand and based no longer on the *curiae* or the tribes but on sixty "centuries" of one hundred men each.

This change had highly important effects both of a political and of a military nature. On the political side it meant that the Assembly of *curiae,* the *Comitia curiata,* was replaced for most practical purposes by a new Assembly of centuries, the *Comitia centuriata.* This made for greater efficiency since the curial system, having been based on wards, had proved unadaptable to an expanding city; for example, it cannot have worked well when citizens moved, and it was ill adjusted to dealing with individual immigrants. After the monarchy was over, it would become the official duty of the *Comitia centuriata* to elect chief magistrates and to decide on peace or war. What powers it already possessed under the kings we cannot tell, and although they were broader than those previously enjoyed by the *Comitia curiata,* they were probably still not large. It seems likely that only the king or his nominee decided what measures should be brought before the centurial Assembly, and that when this was done it could only accept or (less likely) reject them without debate. In other words, the *Comitia centuriata* was a useful organ of the monarch's authority and might have some say in state decisions, but still was not a particularly democratic institution. Besides, the ruler tried to eliminate alternative loyalties by making these assemblymen, in their capacity as soldiers, take the oath to himself.

Moreover, there was no question of "one man, one vote." Voting was not by heads but by groups, and the procedure was so organized that the richer groups were predominant. The new army on which the centurial Assembly was based consisted of property owners graded according to wealth. On this basis, the infantry were divided into five classes, of which the first and richest provided no fewer than eighty of the one hundred and ninety-three centuries of voting units, while those, richer still, who could pay for horses, provided another eighteen—so that the wealthy or relatively wealthy filled more than half of the total number of centuries of which the Assembly was constituted. Here then was a political system in which, while birth was no longer the dominant consideration, it had given place not to democracy but to property ownership.

This manning of the new army by property owners, men rich enough to provide their own arms and armor, directly echoes changes in military organization that had been occurring elsewhere, first in Greece and then in Etruria. From about 750 B.C. the Greeks had begun to develop heavy infantry equipment, partly under Assyrian influence and partly through contact with the metalworkers of central Europe. And thereafter, more

Bronze-fitting on Etruscan war chariot from Monteleone showing two combatants heavily armed and armored in the Etruscan style. (550-530 B.C.).

completely from about 675, Greek military history had shown a slow and piecemeal adoption of this sort of equipment—round shield, defensive metal body-armor, and thrusting spear—with the tactical corollary that these heavily armed soldiers (hoplites, from *hopla,* "arms") fought in a closely knit line or phalanx. They were all men who possessed sufficient property of their own to equip themselves with the full array of this personal armor. Then from about 650 B.C. the hoplite shield began to appear in Etruria too, as archaeological finds and vase paintings reveal, and during the course of the sixth century the full set of hoplite arms came into standard use among the Etruscans.

And so this military innovation arrived at Rome as well. Its attribution to Servius Tullius, or at least to the general period during which he appears to have ruled, finds confirmation from an Esquiline tomb of the early sixth century B.C. in which was discovered a bronze shield like those adopted in the hoplite reforms of Greece and Etruria. Such were the arms of the men who provided Rome with its greatly enlarged reservoir of recruits, who were to achieve such astonishing military triumphs in the years to come. And each spring before setting out to war, they sat and deliberated in the *Comitia centuriata* and endowed it with a military *esprit de corps;* it was the Roman Army in Assembly, orderly obedience its second nature.

This was then, to a large extent, a middle-class army, containing the men whom the prosperity of Etruscan Rome had encouraged to flourish. But it was also still an aristocratic army to the extent that the land-owning noble clans, being the richest section of the population, continued to play a prominent part in the manning of the infantry. And the eighteen centuries of cavalry (*equites,* "knights"), who formed the richest group, no doubt also consisted chiefly of nobles. Yet the reforms of the middle-class hoplite infantry gradually deprived these horsemen of a dominant role in military operations, though it may be conjectured that they remained the personal bodyguard of the kings.

Servius encircled at least the northern part of his city of the Four Regions with a rampart. This was not what is now known as the "Wall of Servius Tullius," which encircles the larger area of later Rome and does not go back further than the fourth century B.C. Yet surviving remains of another earthwork can be attributed to a considerably earlier date than the wall since they are partly built over sixth-century tombs and were found to contain a fragment of Athenian pottery datable, at the very latest, to ca. 470 B.C. and perhaps to a period two or even five decades earlier. Traditionally, as we have seen, Servius died in 535, but there is no firm basis for that exact date, and the earthen defense-work may reasonably, if conjecturally, be ascribed to him, not only on the somewhat vague grounds that he was believed to be the builder of such a wall in ancient times and that this

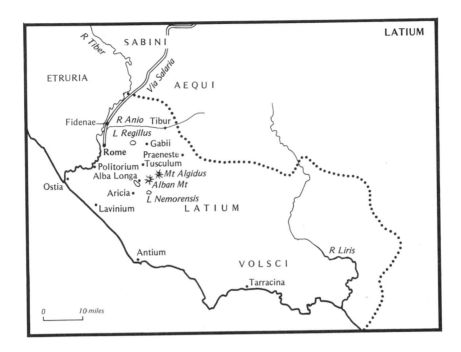

tradition fits in with his general measures to extend Rome's strength, but also because similar ramparts were being built at other Latin and Etruscan towns at about the same epoch. The Roman earthwork was apparently rather more than twenty-five feet high, with a ditch in front. It was erected on the vulnerable open plateau on the north side of the town, from the Quirinal along the brow of the Viminal towards the northern end of the Esquiline, so as to block the heads of the valleys leading from the interior of Latium to Rome.

A rapidly devoloping city-state like Rome was certain to inspire many enmities. Moreover, Servius, as we have seen, appears to have been a Latin, an interloper in the line of Etruscan kings, and thus a provocation to a number of his neighbors. Yet he also seems to have been an expansionist in the Etruscan tradition, for although our sources are obscure and tendencious, it may well have been in his time that Rome emerged as the leading power of northwestern Latium. The dominant feature of this land, the Alban Mount (Monte Cavo), had become a common religious sanctuary for the Latin communities around. It was devoted to the sky-divinity Jupiter —*Diou-pater,* "the bright one"—at first simply an impersonal power of the heavens manifesting itself in different ways, a power worshiped in common by the Indo-European-speaking peoples and some of their predecessors and here known as Jupiter Latiaris. On the slopes of the mountain was the town of Alba Longa (Castel Gandolfo), famous in Virgil's legend as the parent city of Rome, although this is unconfirmed by archaeology. Whether Alba Longa founded other towns of Latium as further legends recount, and if so, how many, must remain equally uncertain. But its headship of a loosely knit league of Latin towns from about the tenth century B.C. onwards, when it began to control the main inland route to the south, deserves acceptance. The towns of Latium, being grouped in inward-looking fashion around a plain, were readily inclined to form associations of this kind, of which there seem to have been several; and Alba Longa, on the slopes of the revered Alban Mount, was eminently suited to take the lead of one of them.

However, Alba Longa was only about twelve miles from Rome, and with aggressive monarchs on the Roman throne a clash was bound to come. It came, and Rome won. Legend ascribes the victory to a pre-Etruscan king of the city, and archaeology confirms that the balance of power between the Albans and Romans was already beginning to shift from the ninth or eighth century B.C. But the final eclipse of Alba Longa, and of other towns of northwest Latium as well, may be regarded as forming part of a general Roman expansion at about the time of Servius Tullius, during the sixth century. There is no reason to doubt the tradition that after the decisive confrontation, some of Alba's leading families soon came to Rome and were admitted to its aristocracy, and that other Albans were settled upon the Caelian hill.

Etruscan war chariot from Monteleone.

Reconstruction of an Etruscan temple as described by Vitruvius.

And while extending their rule in this northwesterly direction, the Romans of this epoch also seem to have expanded the same distance southwestwards as far as the coast, and to have established the port of Ostia at the mouth of the Tiber—beyond Politorium which had already been reduced earlier—in order to exploit the adjoining salt beds. This event too was attributed by tradition to an earlier king but once again may tentatively be ascribed to the time of Servius Tullius. It is true that archaeological evidence on the site of Ostia itself has so far totally failed to reveal any settlement whatsoever dating back to the time of the kings. But this may be only because the settlement in question was located outside the later Roman harbor town, on ground that has not yet been fully explored. The "regal" Ostia probably existed.

And Rome's first wooden bridge, the Pons Sublicius replacing the island ford, may well belong to the same time as this first Ostia. For when the salt had been collected at the river mouth, it was hard work to convey it to the city by river, which meant taking it upstream. This was, it is true, sometimes done with the aid of tow ropes, but cargoes also frequently had to be transported by land, along the left bank. The Romans needed the bridge to move the salt across the Tiber, to their Etruscan purchasers and others beyond.

Servius Tullius, if such innovations are to be attributed to him personally, again had the outside world in mind when he added an appendage to Rome of the Four Regions. This he did by building an important temple on the Aventine Hill which lay just beyond the city's boundaries to the south. It was a shrine of Diana—"the bright one" like Jupiter, and at the same time a goddess of forests who helped women by giving them children. It had been believed until recently that Servius, by constructing this temple, was deliberately superseding a similar, widely frequented, cult of Diana near the Latin town of Aricia, in an old volcanic crater valley at the foot of the Alban Mount sixteen miles southeast of Rome. But now this view needs modification since, although the Aventine shrine cannot yet be completely reconstructed, archaeologists have offered reasons for believing that its Arician counterpart was probably the later of the two. Nevertheless, the Aventine shrine may well have been intended, if not to eclipse Aricia, at least to attract dispossessed immigrants from its territories and other parts of Latium, and that could well be why it was located outside the boundaries of the city. Evidently it enjoyed considerable prestige in the area, since its regulations, we learn, were accepted by other Latin towns, for example, Tibur (Tivoli).

But the inspiration for the Aventine cult may have come not from Latium but from Greek cities whose federal worships Servius Tullius was seeking to imitate. And, in particular, his model is likely to have been Massilia. This great and influential port on the southern coast of France, founded in ca. 600 B.C. (under the name of Massalia) by Greek seafarers from Asia Minor, had come to dominate the Mediterranean shores from southern Spain to where the border between France and Italy exists today. Its settlers had borrowed and imported the worship of their goddess Artemis from its world-center at the ancient Greek city of Ephesus (Selçuk) on the coast of Asia Minor—and with this Ephesian sanctuary the Roman cult of Diana, who was early identified with Artemis, possessed a manifest connection. For the Aventine shrine of the goddess was the possessor, perhaps from the outset, of a statue of the many-breasted type that was peculiarly characteristic of Ephesus; very probably the Romans obtained it from Massilia. At all events, its introduction to Rome represented a decisive step, a more decisive step than earlier cults of Mars and other deities, towards the personal, anthropomorphic interpretation of gods and goddesses.

The importation of this statue of Artemis-Diana is significant for another

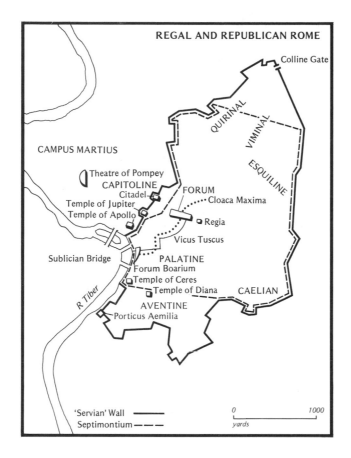

REGAL AND REPUBLICAN ROME

Colline Gate

QUIRINAL

VIMINAL

ESQUILINE

CAMPUS MARTIUS

Theatre of Pompey
CAPITOLINE
Citadel
FORUM
Temple of Jupiter
Cloaca Maxima
Temple of Apollo

Regia

Vicus Tuscus

Sublician Bridge
PALATINE
Forum Boarium
Temple of Ceres
Temple of Diana
CAELIAN

R Tiber

AVENTINE
Porticus Aemilia

'Servian' Wall ———
Septimontium – – –

0   1000
yards

reason. It confirms that early Rome did not obtain all its Hellenic influences through the medium of Etruria but derived some of them directly from the Greeks who were struggling with the Etruscans for the dominance of the western Mediterranean. This is confirmed by the geographical situation of the Aventine temple, standing guard over the river wharves of the Tiber, which formed a center for Greek (as well as eastern) traders very early on. And below the northwestern end of the Aventine stood a very ancient altar (the Ara Maxima) which tells the same story. It was dedicated to Hercules, who was identified with the Greek god of traders, Heracles, and the location of his altar at that spot meant he was to preside over these commercial activities.

But another, even greater, new Roman shrine was more Etruscan than Greek. This was the temple of Jupiter the Best and Greatest, and of Juno and Minerva, on the Capitoline Hill, beside the citadel where

Silver *denarius* of Augustus (16 B.C., moneyer C. Antistius Vetus),
celebrating Tarquinius Superbus's treaty with the Latin town
of Gabii (FOEDVS *Populi Romani* CVM GABINIS)

the Etruscan kings resided. According to tradition the two Etruscan
monarchs Tarquinius Priscus and his son Tarquinius Superbus, who
reigned before and after Servius Tullius respectively, each played a part
in the foundation of the temple. Priscus dedicated it and got the work
started, and Superbus completed its construction. But the involvement
of Priscus may only be a retrospective fiction designed to ascribe the in-
ception of this great project to the "good" monarch rather than to his
"bad" disgraced son; the truth of the matter probably is that the temple
was entirely due to the initiative of Superbus. If so, then it belongs to
the very end of the Etruscan monarchy, traditionally placed in the last
years of the sixth century B.C. The temple was, for the most part, in the
Etruscan manner, with a terracotta statue of a fully personalized Jupiter
executed by a famous Etruscan sculptor.

Jupiter the sky god was called Best and Greatest, said Cicero, because he makes us prosperous, but also because, under Etruscan influence, he was now the successor of Mars as the principal god of the Romans. When he first began to assume this function, at a somewhat
earlier date, he had still been associated with Mars and with another
antique Italian god Quirinus, the god of the Quirinal Hill; they formed
a triad or trinity. But now the triad were Jupiter, Juno, and Minerva.
The names, in these forms, were Italian, but they had Etruscan (as well
as Greek) counterparts, and the linkage of these three divinities is
Etruscan. It was a grouping that may have been seen in other parts of
Rome already. But it was here that it became famous, on the Capitol,
where the trinity was worshipped in a shrine divided into three sections
(cellae), such as are also found at other Etruscan centers.

But the most significant feature of the Capitoline temple was its extraordinary size and grandeur. It had a deep, Etruscan porch of three
rows of six columns, and a row of free-standing columns down each
side (not found in smaller Etruscan temples). It measured one hundred

Brass medallion of Antoninus Pius (A.D. 138-61) celebrating the legendary defense of Rome's bridge (Pons Sublicius) by Horatius Cocles against Lars Porsenna of Clusium.

and eighty feet in width and over two hundred feet in length, as its six-teen-foot-high stone platform, so characteristic of Italian as opposed to Greek temples, reveals. Much of this still survives, though little more of the original structure is now to be seen. These huge dimensions made it, as far as we can tell, the largest temple of its time in the entire Etrus-can sphere; not many exceeded its size even in Greek lands. And al-though in the Etruscan fashion the superstructure was only made of wood, the building was of marvelous splendor, colorfully decorated with lavish paint work and many monuments, including a statue of the god by Vulca of Veii.

The Fall of the Monarchy

And then, perhaps almost immediately after the dedication of this glittering temple, the Etruscan monarchy of Rome, in the person of Tarquinius Superbus, fell from power. Superbus had made a treaty with strategic Gabii (Castiglione) ten miles to the east, the site of abundant recent archaeological discoveries; he had also apparently planted garrisons a good deal further afield. But in the end he was overthrown. The traditional date of his expulsion, 510 B.C., must be regarded with grave suspicion because that is also the year in which the last tyrant of Athens was expelled from his city, and Greek historians could not resist inventing the coincidence.* But Tarquinius Superbus probably fell not more than three or four years afterwards, and a rival theory that the Etruscan monarchy at Rome did not end until the 450s has gained little support.

In other parts of Italy too, including Etruria, monarchies were losing their grip and collapsing in these last years of the sixth century B.C. Moreover, it was a period when the Etruscan city-states in Latium and Campania were generally in retreat, hard-pressed by their enemies the Greeks. In particular, Aristodemus of the Greek city of Cumae, the bitter rival of the city-states of Etruria, in 529 had repulsed Etruscan and other attackers in the marshes and woods north of his native city. Nearly twenty years later

Etruscan relief from Chianciano showing battle scene. Fifth century B.C.

---

*The Table of Dates on page 516 synchronizes some of the major events in Roman and Greek history.

he may have helped the Latins to defeat Etruscan forces once again, this time at Aricia, a victory which, according to one interpretation, enabled him to become the autocratic ruler of his home town. The first of these engagements weakened Etruscan power in general and probably helped, in the long run, to undermine Tarquinius Superbus. The second clash seems to have taken place shortly after Superbus's expulsion and to have made it more difficult for him (or for any other Etruscan) to seize control of Rome ever again.

Incidentally, this second battle also gave the town of Aricia, which had helped in the successful fight, the temporary headship of a loose religious and perhaps also political confederation, such as Alba Longa had possessed in earlier years. The preeminence of Alba had been based on the worship of Jupiter Latiaris, and Aricia's was founded on its shrine of Diana overlooking Lake Nemorensis (Nemi), to which reference was made above. Alba Longa had succumbed to the Romans; but this time Rome, its monarchy fallen, was no longer in a position to oppose or suppress the Aricians, who were therefore able to exploit their cult of Diana, deliberately seeking to outbid the Roman shrine of the same goddess on the Aventine. Nor did Aricia have to worry too much about possible encroachments from other Etruscan-dominated cities either, since Rome was not the only Latin town where the Etruscans had lost their authority, or were rapidly losing it. Their defeat at Aricia was part of a general collapse of their rule over wide areas of Latium. Latins and hill tribesmen profited from the Etruscans' troubles and moved in across their lines of communications; other Latin cities in addition to Aricia were recorded as conducting successful rebellions— Etruscan power in Latium was broken. Moreover, archaeologists have now shown that the life of certain towns in Etruria itself now came to an end at about the same time.

Such then was the fall of Rome's Etruscan rulers. However, despite the equal misfortunes of their compatriots in other parts of Latium, and in Campania as well, they did not, during the troubled years that followed, accept their ejection by the Romans as final. In the first place, Tarquinius Superbus tried, unsuccessfully, to engineer his own return. And Lars Porsenna of the inland Etruscan city-state of Clusium (Chiusi), acting independently of the Tarquins for he was by no means their friend, marched eighty miles southwards upon Rome and attacked it in a sudden raid. Moreover, contrary to the patriotic legend enshrined in Thomas Macaulay's *Lay of Horatius,* defender of the Sublician bridge, it appears that Lars Porsenna actually captured the city and held on to it for a time, until the setback at Aricia (in which his son commanded the defeated army) compelled him to leave.

Etruscan bronze helmet dedicated at Olympia by Hiero I of Syracuse to celebrate his victory over the Etruscans and Carthaginians off Cumae in 474 B.C.

Nor was Porsenna the only Etruscan adventurer who briefly forced his way into the disorganized towns; indeed, some of these raiders were even able to settle with their troops inside the boundaries upon the Caelian Hill. So Rome had good reason to remain highly apprehensive of continued and renewed raids from Etruria, which lay so close. And such raids, from time to time, continued to occur, while inside the city, too, Etruscan influence still remained strong. Nevertheless, no really serious attempt was made by any of the Etruscan states to recover Rome or Latium, or even the greater lost prize of Campania beyond. Indeed, the latter country became even more manifestly irrecoverable after Syracuse, the greatest Greek city in Sicily, had subjected the Etruscans (and their Carthaginian allies) to another defeat off Cumae in 474 B.C.

Yet their lack of perseverance in the south did not by any means signify that this remarkable people was exhausted. The reason, strangely enough, why they were willing to turn away from Campania and Latium was that certain of their city-states were, at this very period, launching a massive fresh drive in the opposite direction, north of the Apennines in the region that the Romans later called Cisalpine Gaul. The Etruscan city-state that took the initiative was Clusium, and the main center of this northern sphere of influence was Felsina (Bologna), refounded on the site of an ancient town; Marzabotto, seventeen miles to its southwest, gives us a unique picture of what an ancient Etruscan city looked like; Virgil was descended from Etruscan forebears who had founded Mantua; and the Greek ports of Adria (Atria) and Spina on the mouths of the Po are shown by excavations to have possessed substantial Etruscan trading communities—the enmity between Greeks and Etruscans, which was so vigorous on the west coast of Italy, apparently being absent. This new, northern enterprise of the Etruscans, though it survived long enough to bring writing and civilization to continental Europe, did not last for more than a hundred years. But for the time being it increasingly absorbed all their energy and attention. As far, therefore, as the menace from Etruria was concerned, Rome found itself able to enjoy a respite.

II. THE UNITY OF ITALY AND ROME

Preceding page:
The College of Vestals fleeing Rome after capture by the Gauls, from a painting
by Hector Le Roux.

3

The Unification of Italy

Rome's Hostile Neighbors

The worst of the grim difficulties that descended upon the Romans after the fall of the Tarquins still remain to be described. For, although the Etruscan menace soon declined for the time being, the city continued to suffer from an abundance of other enemies eager to take advantage of its diminished position. In consequence, the greater part of the two centuries that now followed witnessed constant, uphill fights against each one of them, in turn, or often simultaneously; sometimes they were fights upon which the very survival of Rome depended.

In the first place, its immediate neighbors and relatives, the Latins, once the power of the Etruscan Tarquins was removed, immediately became recalcitrant. For it was at about this time that the legend-encrusted town of Lavinium, near the sea sixteen miles from Rome, threw off its allegiance to the Romans and asserted its claims as common sanctuary of a group of Latin coastal towns. This union, or league, conflicted with Roman interests, and in ca. 496 a memorable battle was fought beside the volcanic depression of Lake Regillus (Pantano; now drained). Regillus belonged to the territory of Tusculum (near Frascati) which, in conjunction with the Arician League, took the military lead in resisting the Romans. However, in the engagement that followed, Rome's heavy armed infantry, supported by its mounted knights (equites), proved superior to the old-fashioned Latin cavalry and won a decisive victory. As a result, the Romans incorporated in their own religion two deities who had been worshiped in Tusculum since very early times—a borrowing characteristic of their religious practice, intended to transfer and attract to themselves the power and following of the divinities of defeated states. The twin gods thus acquired after Regillus were Castor and Pollux, the Greek Dioscuri—horsemen who were believed to have helped the Romans magically in the victorious battle and who from now on became the patrons of the cavalry or knights of Rome.

But the battle may not have been as decisive as the legends of the Romans subsequently reported, since soon afterwards they made a treaty with the Latin towns on a basis not of superiority but of equality. Rome was only to provide the combined army with its general when its turn to do so arrived; on this understanding the treaty provided for reciprocal support in war against common enemies from the neighboring hills. And it probably also stipulated mutual recognition of private rights—a foretaste of the sensible, statesmanlike measures that were destined, in later years, to take the Romans step by step to imperial power. But they had no such power yet; otherwise they would not have agreed to such an equally balanced arrangement. Nevertheless, this was not equality with each and every Latin city individually, since Rome made its treaty with these communities jointly and as a whole. This implied that the Romans, though no longer forceful enough to dominate Latium as they had under the Etruscan monarchy, were still sufficiently strong to be recognized as the equal of the principal Latin cities combined.

And before long the balance began to tilt further in favor of the Romans. The first sign of their superior pretensions came in about 415 B.C. when they were entrusted with the organization of the Latin festival on the Alban Mount. And very soon afterwards, profiting by a quarrel between Aricia and another Latin city, Ardea (a primitive port), Rome moved ahead further by signing treaties with at least one, and perhaps both, of them *separately* and with Lavinium as well. This did not mean that it now considered that these towns, or any one of them, had now become its equal; it meant instead that it was prepared to flout the Latin League by making private arrangements, advantageous to itself, with any one of the league's individual members with which it desired to associate in this way. This was a foretaste of further Roman encroachments to come. But, for the most part, the equilibrium was still not openly upset.

This relative harmony with the Latins was imperatively needed since the menace from the Apennines, to Latins and Romans alike, was severe. Their remote valleys, deep glens, and high plateaus fostered isolated shepherd communities, speaking Oscan which was an Indo-European relative of Latin. These pastoral peoples, living tough lives wholly lacking in Mediterranean amenities, greatly coveted Latium's access to the sea, superior fertility, and winter pastureland. And so, for a century and more after the downfall of the Tarquins, they attacked the Latins and Romans and engaged in many fluctuating seesaw struggles for the critical mountain passes.

The tribes that led these persistent onslaughts were the Volsci and Aequi. The main threat came from the Volsci who had come down from the heavily forested central Italian mountains during the sixth century B.C. and had established themselves in the middle reaches of the Liris (Garigliano) valley in southeast Latium, which provided the main inland route down into Campania. Then, tempted by the maritime plain, they moved right up to the regions southeast of the Alban Mount, on the very doorstep of Rome's Latin allies. From 494 B.C. onwards these Volsci looted and raided Latin and Roman territory almost every year. They weakened only after Rome, in about 377, had captured their coastal stronghold Antium (Anzio), the only really useful port of Latium, protected by a promontory from the northwest winds. Nevertheless, Antium was then lost by the Romans again and had to be recaptured in 338 when the ships the Volsci had based on the port were captured. This was the termination of their independent existence. As time went on, they succumbed gradually to Romanization and almost ceased to exist as a separate entity.

The highland Aequi also came down from the hills, compelled by the overpopulation of their meager slopes northeast of Rome. In about 484 they captured and fortified Algidus, a narrow strategic pass on the east side of the Alban Mount, through which passed the inland Via Latina, for many years the only road from Rome to the south. Then, for fifty years or more, sometimes allied with the Volsci or others, they waged unceasing strife against the Latins and Romans. At last, however, in about 431 they were dislodged from Algidus, retiring gradually to their central Italian fastnesses, where they too, within the course of the following century, were eventually Romanized—by virtual extermination.

The chief interest of these petty, repetitive, and for many years inconclusive wars against the Volsci and Aequi lay in the invention by the Latin League in the 490s, or even before, of *federal Latin colonies.* These were not whole territories like Britain's "colonies" in North America and elsewhere, but were towns, with tracts of cultivable land around them—settlements of farmer-soldiers, to whom newly acquired or recovered lands were allotted on lease or by freehold gift. These colonies, somewhat resembling in this respect the *kibbutzim* of modern Israel, were intended to provide potential Latin bases against external enemies and to influence local life in favor of pacific agriculturalism. At first they were established on the eastern borders of Latium, and the next century and a half witnessed the foundation of fourteen such settlements in these and other regions. Although the strategic points at which they were established were no doubt selected by the Latin League only after consultation with Rome, these were Latin and not Roman foundations, and the Roman citizens among their settlers had to forfeit that status and become citizens of the Latin League instead. It was not until a good deal later that the Romans borrowed for themselves this fruitful idea that was to play such an immense part in their future development of Italy.

The enemies against whom the Latins and Romans joined forces also included the Oscan-speaking Sabines, who lived in independent Apennine hilltop villages north-northeast of Rome. Once again they had long coveted the superior resources of the plain of Latium. In later Roman tradition they were famed for their courage, strong morality, and religious devotion. In due course some of them adopted a rudimentary urban life, notably at sites whose strategic location revealed their desire to secure a supply of Ostian salt—a desire that was highly distasteful to Rome, which had made a treaty with Gabii to keep them at bay. However, only a very few years after the start of the Roman Republic, one of the leaders of the Sabines, Attus Clausus, was so eager for a share of Rome's amenities that, with the agreement of its authorities and presumably of its Latin allies as well, he moved his whole clan of four thousand or more relatives and supporters to Roman territory, where he settled them and became the founder of Rome's great Claudian clan (ca. 505 B.C.). Similar Sabine origins were later claimed by other Roman clans and families as well. At first, however, Roman hopes that by admitting these immigrants they had scotched the menace of the Sabines were disappointed, because their raids continued almost without intermission. In about 496 B.C. the raiders reached the city's ramparts, and about thirty-six years later their successors even briefly occupied the Capitoline citadel itself before an army from the Latin city of Tusculum helped to eject them.

Then in 449 Rome defeated the Sabines severely, following this up, as it liked to do, by assimilating a Sabine god Sancus under the name of Dius Fidius who was given the significant function of watching over oaths and treaties and good faith between nations—a matter presided over by priestly officials (fetiales) who, by proving that all Rome's wars were just, exercised from this time onwards an excellent effect upon Roman morale. Thereafter, during the next one hundred and fifty years, hostilities with the Sabines diminished and vanished, and the amalgamation of the two peoples was gradually accomplished, to a large extent because of the mutual advantage of transferring sheep between summer (Sabine) and winter (Latin) pasturage.

It had been a major piece of good fortune to Latium and Rome (helped on by able diplomacy) that these hostile Volscian, Aequian, and Sabine neighbors were too poorly organized ever to unite effectively against them, for that could have meant the reduction to impotence of Latins and Romans alike. And this was all the luckier, as far as Rome was concerned, because the gravest of all the threats to its existence came, at the very same time, from yet another and all too familiar source—Etruria just across the Tiber.

Victory over Veii

The termination of the Etruscan kingship in Rome had been followed by a period of confusion during which, in addition to all the other enemies of Rome, Etruscan adventurers made raids upon the city, sometimes successfully; and yet, at the same time and despite the ejection of the monarchy, Etruscan influence in Rome itself continued to linger on. In the end, the peril proved greater than the influence, for one Etruscan city-state, Veii, was intolerably close, only twelve miles away. This extremely short distance between the two places meant that neither could ever feel safe from the other. Veii was powerful and its geographical position extremely strong. It was situated on a steep, sheer plateau and surrounded on three sides by a moat of running water, including, beneath the eastern end of the citadel, the River Cremera (Valchetta) which went on to flow into the Tiber five miles north of Rome.

Originally, like Rome, a group of hut villages that amalgamated into a single Iron Age settlement, Veii had become by 600 B.C. not a symbiotic Etruscan-Italian community, such as Rome seems to have been, but a purely Etruscan city, and a city whose wealth and culture, during the century that followed, contributed greatly to the rising prosperity of Etruscanized Rome, which was linked to its territory by the Sublician Bridge. These extensive possessions of Veii were guarded by a ring of bulwark colonies and peripheral bases fed by roads for heavy-wheeled traffic leading in every direction—including the direction of Rome. Furthermore, Veii excelled in the Etruscan techniques of cultivation and irrigation and supplied agricultural exports over a wide area.

In comparison with the various hill tribesmen who subjected Rome to harassment, it found these powerful, advanced people infinitely more formidable rivals. Given such extreme proximity, their competing demands for markets, land, and coastal salt were bound to lead to serious clashes and had probably done so as early as the seventh century B.C. For the Tiber was a highway that had to be controlled either by Veii or by Rome; in the long run, no compromise was possible.

In the later 480s, the recently established Roman Republic had been mainly controlled by the clan of the Fabii. They were traditionally connected with Etruria and owned land towards Veii; in consequence they were recognized by their fellow Romans as the defenders of the Etruscan frontier, which they guarded with a private army of their own. So it was now against the threat from Veii that the Fabii threw this semifeudal force into the field. At first the hostilities amounted to little more than an exchange of cattle raids, but by setting up a blockhouse near the Cremera, to command the stream and adjoining roads, the Fabian clan transformed this minor skir-

Etruscan warrior supporting wounded comrade.
Bronze finial of candelabra. Early fifth century B.C.

mishing into open warfare. But in the disastrous battle of the Cremera that ensued (ca. 476–475), three hundred members and dependents of the Fabii perished, and the blockhouse was destroyed by the enemy. The whole west side of the Tiber was now impregnably in the hands of the Veians, and they may even have occupied the Janiculum Hill which rose above its bank and looked straight across at Rome.

But next, after the Etruscans' crushing defeat by the Greeks in 474, Veii felt it advisable to make a truce with its Roman neighbors across the river, undertaking to deliver grain and money. Then, after the middle of the century, the balance of power continued to shift in Rome's favor, and it began to prepare for a final showdown. One of the principal bones of contention was the town of Fidenae (Castel Giubileo) on the south (Latin) bank of the Tiber just opposite the spot where the Cremera joins its larger stream. This place was the first station on the salt road *(Via Salaria),* and the hill on which it stood controlled the lowest river ford above Rome. So Fidenae was a highly strategic post, which neither Veii nor Rome was willing to allow the other to possess; and it apparently changed hands more than once, first in earlier times and then in the first part of the fifth century B.C.

In about 444, the Romans seemed aware that a major war with Veii lay ahead. They now made a radical change in their government, replacing the two annually elected consuls (instituted at the beginning of the republic) by three (later six) army officers with consular power *(tribuni militum consulari potestate),* an arrangement that was retained for most of the next eighty years*; the character and rank of these officials show that military needs were the primary consideration. And in the following year a new magistracy, the censorship, was created. Its two joint occupants, men of very senior status, were to be elected for eighteen months every four years in order to make up and maintain the official list of citizens. Once again the primary purpose was military, for the censorship was intended to facilitate recruitment, which had become a complicated matter owing to the property-holding qualifications required for those serving in the army.

Fortified by these preparations, the Romans now felt ready to move against Veii, and they were all the more eager to do so because they themselves were suffering from famine and pestilence and stood in urgent need of new land. So in about 435 or 425 they passed to aggressive action and once again occupied Fidenae. An appeal directed by Veii to the Etruscan confederation met with no response. This was a significant proof of the country's lack of unity, which was to prove suicidal. Its immediate result

---

*For a slightly earlier intermission in the consulship, when the consuls were temporarily replaced by *decemviri,* see p. 75.

was to prompt the Veians to strengthen their natural defenses against likely Roman attacks. Wherever possible, the cliffs on which the city stood were cut back to make them more precipitous, and around other parts of the 480-acre periphery an earthen rampart with a stone breastwork was constructed.

The occupation of Fidenae by the Romans meant full-scale war; it was probably the most fateful of all the wars they ever fought since their very existence depended on the outcome. It was they who took the initiative, and they placed Veii under siege. The fighting, conducted with unprecedentedly large forces, seems to have gone on intermittently for at least six or seven years, though perhaps not for the ten described by tradition. In the end, the Romans succeeded in advancing on the northward side of the walls and occupying the only neck of territory that offered level access to the city. Now this piece of land happened to contain one of the agricultural drainage tunnels that irrigated the whole of this territory; coming in from the open country it passed under the walls and thus entered into Veii itself. This tunnel, then, the Romans cleared, using it to move a small body of men into

Handle of Etruscan bronze chest from Praeneste (Palestrina): soldiers carrying a dead comrade. Fourth century B.C.

the middle of the enemy city, which in this way fell into their hands. The hero of the day was Camillus, who, despite the mythical nature of many of his alleged exploits, nevertheless emerges as a partially historical figure, the earliest the republic can offer. Shortly before the siege began, he had compelled the Romans to adopt continuous military service, without intermissions for harvesting, and he had introduced regular pay; and it was he who carried the campaign to its triumphant conclusion.

The Romans severely damaged and partly destroyed the captured stronghold, razing its defenses and turning out many or all of its inhabitants. This elimination of a city-state's independent existence was a sinister innovation in Rome's military history and a sign of the critical gravity of the war. In keeping with the religious solemnity of their victory, the Romans, as on other occasions, took over the defeated enemy's patron deity as their own, establishing her cult on the Aventine Hill just outside the walls of their own city. She was Juno, who was already worshipped as an associate of Jupiter on the Roman Capitol but at Veii enjoyed an independent and magnificent cult, with the special title of Regina, the Queen. As in other parts of early Italy, she stood for vitality and youthfulness and thus for political and military strength; and from now onwards she would no longer watch over Veii but over Rome.

The downfall of this first great Etruscan city to succumb to the Romans was a turning point, for not only did it remove an enormous, hampering obstacle to their progress, but it almost doubled the size of their territory as well. The newly conquered lands, linked by the excellent Etruscan road system, were distributed as individual allotments to Roman citizen-farmers, without very much consideration being given to the Latin confederate cities, which were shown by this largely Roman victory to be outmatched, both singly and corporatively, by the victors. Moreover, Rome's fame was spreading to new lands. After the victory Camillus dedicated a war memorial, a golden bowl, in Apollo's oracular sanctuary at Delphi in Greece. As an intermediary in this enterprise he probably employed the Etruscan city-state of Caere, which alone of nearby cities had close connections with Delphi; it had failed to help its neighbor and compatriot Veii in the siege. And so the triumphant Romans began to appear in a wider context than Italy, among the nations of the world.

The Gallic Invasion and its Aftermath

However, a formidable setback was on the way at the hands of the Celtic Gauls. Celtic-speaking peoples, in the eighth and seventh centuries B.C., had moved out of central Europe as far as Spain and Britain, and then during the fifth century, they gradually crossed the Alps and expelled the Etruscan settlers from most of northern Italy which was henceforward known as "Gaul this side of the Alps," or Cisalpine Gaul. Some of the Celts who spread through Europe lived peacefully and even luxuriously; and they developed a lively, swinging, swelling art, based principally on the free use of contemporary Greek and Etruscan models but also echoing eastern influences, notably from Scythia (south Russia). But the Gauls who swarmed into the valley of the Po were more warlike. They had developed a frightening, if somewhat barbaric, military organization, including cavalry with iron horseshoes—an innovation in ancient warfare—and infantry carrying finely tempered, slashing broadswords.

In about 387–386 B.C., under their king Brennus, thirty thousand of these immigrants drove southwards from the Po valley into the Italian peninsula itself, in the hope of acquiring additional land and plunder. Learning of this move, the Romans may have sent a reconnaissance force to the inland Etruscan city of Clusium (Chiusi), which the Gallic force was threatening. At all events, the Gauls decided to abandon their attack on Clusium and moved rapidly down against Rome itself. Only eleven miles from the city, beside the Tiber's little tributary, the Allia (Fossa della Regina), they were confronted by an army of ten thousand to fifteen thousand Romans. Whether some Latins, too, formed part of these troops is uncertain; but in any case it was the largest force Rome itself had ever put into the field. However, in the battle that followed, the Roman phalanx of heavily armed, spear-carrying soldiers was rushed by the much faster cavalry and infantry of the Gauls and outreached by their swords. The Roman army was routed, and most of its soldiers plunged into the nearby stream and were drowned. The blackest of all days in the history of Rome left it wholly without any men to defend it.

Brennus and his men marched on and three days later arrived at the city, which, with the possible exception of the Capitol, they proceeded to overrun, setting its buildings on fire, as a layer of burned debris at the edge of the Forum still shows today—broken roof tiles and carbonized wood and clay. Rome had fallen to its first barbarian conquerors, something that was not to happen again for eight hundred years. The Romans never forgot this horrifying and humiliating event, and, like their successful siege of Veii a few years earlier, it brought them to the attention of the outside world for it attracted the notice of Greek historians. Yet the Gauls were soon bought off and departed because they had received news that their own lands in the north were threatened by external foes. And henceforward, despite the occasional raids that they still launched into the peninsula, the Gallic peoples lacked the stability to offer a permanent threat.

In this crisis, the Romans owed a debt to their surviving Etruscan neigh-

Funeral stele from Felsina (Bologna) showing journey to the underworld (center) and combat between Etruscan horseman and Gallic (Celtic) footsoldier. End of fifth century B.C.

bor, the city-state of Caere. It was situated on the edge of bare downland a mere twenty miles from Rome, very close to the sea where it possessed three little ports. The Caeritans had gained great wealth and importance both from their metalworkings and their widespread Greek and oriental connections. It was these links that had enabled them to confer substantial commercial and cultural benefits upon Rome during its monarchy, including the vital use of its ports. And then, later, they had acted as intermediary with the pan-Hellenic shrine of Delphi in the celebration of Rome's victory over Veii—a victory that they themselves had helped to bring about by failing to support their own besieged compatriots, with whom they had long been on bad terms. Now, during the invasion by the Gauls, they had helped Rome once again, not only by giving refuge to the sacred objects from its temples, but also by exerting military pressure to hasten Brennus's departure. They were glad to help the Romans because Greek threats and raids that menaced their own seacoast meant that they needed Roman assistance in their turn.

Responding to this friendly attitude, Rome seems to have granted Caere a novel, privileged status (ca. 386?). This *hospitium publicum,* as it was called, entitled its people to come to Rome on terms of equality with Rome's own citizens in matters of private jurisdiction, and to enjoy freedom from local taxes, as Romans would likewise at Caere. This proved a historic formula because Rome later extended it, with adaptations, to many other cities also. For the present, however, this understanding was intended to safeguard the new frontier line that the conquest of Veii had enabled the Romans to push forward into Etruria. Nevertheless, in ca. 353, Caere had the temerity to reverse its friendly policy, joining its sister-state of Tarquinii in objecting forcibly to what was by now a too painfully manifest inferiority to Rome. But the rising was soon brought to order, and the Caeritans were forgivingly accorded a hundred-year truce.

After the onslaught of the Gauls the Romans no longer considered their city sufficiently protected by the old earth rampart of Servius Tullius. So in 378 B.C. they erected a massive new wall, one of the great defensive works of the age; the large portions of it that can still be seen today bear the erroneous name of the "Wall of Servius Tullius." It was made of volcanic stone from recently captured Veii and planned by contractors whom masons marks show to have been Greeks. More than twelve feet thick and twenty-four feet high, the new wall enclosed a larger area than the previous rampart, including the historic Seven Hills of Rome: the Palatine and Caelian, and the adjacent and independently fortified Capitol; the whole of the Esquiline, Quirinal, and Viminal Hills to the north (which had only partly been included in the old perimeter); and the newly included Aventine to the south, together with the adjacent Circus Maximus where chariot races were held. This fourth-century wall encompassed an area of over one thousand acres. This meant that the new Rome possessed by far the largest perimeter of any city in Italy, being more than twice the size of recently demolished Veii and more than four times the dimensions of Caere. A prominent part in the creation of the wall is likely to have been played by Camillus, who had been the hero of the siege of Veii and who later, after the grave setback of the Gallic invasion, led the Romans into a rapid and vigorous recovery.

The Romans
in Latium and Campania

But Rome's major problem now was its Latin confederates. Between these ostensibly equal partners, the pendulum had already begun to swing in the direction of the Romans before the fifth century was half over, and then, after the conquest of Veii, their monopoly of the conquered farmlands had emphasized their growing superiority rather crudely. Under the shock of the subsequent Gallic invasion, however, Rome decided to display tact to the Latins by giving them, after all, a share in the settlement and defense of the newly conquered Etruscan lands, in which, accordingly, two Latin colonies were planted.

Yet the sentiments of the cities of the Latin confederacy towards Rome were deteriorating. They had not, it is true, been disloyal for the most part during the Gallic invasion, since they had been just as alarmed as the Romans, but several of the largest Latin towns now began to prefer independence to their Roman alliance. Thus in 381 the citizens of Tusculum, although wholly surrounded by Roman territory, seemed on the verge of hostile action. But at this juncture Rome successfully wooed them with an offer of incorporation into its own state and full Roman citizenship into the bargain. This was a fruitful new idea for the future—a Latin city had been given all Rome's privileges and transformed from a Latin into a Roman community, while nevertheless retaining its own city organization and self-government.

Significant, too, was the whole concept that Roman citizenship could be extended in such a way; Athens and Sparta and Corinth had never effectively learned such a lesson, and a Greek monarch later noted that this sort of arrangement was a peculiar source of Rome's strength, providing invaluable numerical superiority over its successive enemies. In the previous century no city or individual would have found it attractive to change Latin for Roman status. But now that the Romans were stronger than the Latins, feelings had changed. For one thing, possession of Rome's citizenship was a safeguard against arbitrary violence on the part of its officials; and the local aristocracies of the Latin towns were not averse to such mergers since they often possessed intimate links with their Roman counterparts already. Indeed, the Tusculan nobles adapted themselves so enthusiastically to the new order that they henceforward supplied Rome with numerous consuls —a greater number, over the course of the years, than any other single city.

In 366 the consuls, now definitively revived after eighty years of intermittent military government, were given a junior colleague, the *praetor,* to relieve them of much civil jurisdiction so that they could have a freer hand for the warfare that still seemed likely to lie ahead. For hostile attitudes to Rome were now spreading among the Latin communities. One of their leading malcontents was Praeneste (Palestrina). This princely ancient town, on the Apennine spur dominating a major road to Campania, had formerly been an important outpost of the Etruscans, who gave it a lavish prosperity rivaling that of the cities of their own homeland. And the place also possessed a great shrine and oracle of Fors Fortuna, the bringer of increase, from which Rome had derived its cult of that goddess. During the fourth century B.C. the Praenestines may have remained outside the Latin League; at any rate they relished the growth of Rome so little that they sided with its Volscian enemies and even employed Gallic mercenaries to fight against its troops.

Another unsatisfactory Latin city from the Roman point of view was the no less antique Tibur (Tivoli), eighteen miles from the city. Like Praeneste, this town dominated an important road, from its high hill above a Tiber tributary, and it became a powerful member of the Latin League, surrounded by several dependent communities. During the fourth century, however, it appears to have engaged in frequent skirmishes against the Romans and may even have severed relations with them altogether. But in 358 Rome succeeded in reimposing the old treaty upon this and other Latin cities, probably on less favorable terms involving a measure of military control.

The Romans also took a decisive step by extending their sphere of influence into Campania. Its leading town Capua (Santa Maria Capua Vetere), thirteen miles inland, was the second city in all Italy, enriched by the great fertility of the region and destined to become famous for its skillful working of bronze. It had been the capital of an Etruscan empire in Campania during the seventh and sixth centuries B.C., but thereafter its Etruscan rulers were replaced by the Samnites. Descended from the Sabines and speaking a form of Oscan akin to theirs, these rough hill-men, of whom more will be said shortly, had come from fortified strong points high up in the center of the peninsula. As their population increased, they began to covet the productive Campanian lowlands, and not only Etruscan Capua but Greek Cumae fell into their hands (ca. 438–421). Before long, these Samnite immigrants controlled a league of Campanian cities, readily absorbing the Greek and Etruscan flair for business and becoming a distinct Campanian nation, less warlike than their invading forebears. In about 343, the members of this confederation, threatened by fresh waves of invasions from Samnium, took the fateful step of appealing under Capua's leadership to the Romans. Thereupon Rome, in the hope of agricultural benefits, decided to make its entrance into this large, rich area and responded to the Campanian appeal, an event that set up a whole series of chain reactions affecting much larger areas.

At first, however, things did not go smoothly for the Romans since their army mutinied at having to fight so far afield (342). Moreover, Capua soon regretted its appeal to them and sided with the Latins instead—who had now become openly hostile to Rome. The Latins had interpreted the Roman intervention in Campania as a menacing attempt to encircle them, and, when the operation seemed to be failing, they felt encouraged to ask the Roman government for a full restoration of their own previous parity and equality. These proposals were sharply rejected, and war between Rome and the Latins soon followed.

It was one of the bitterest wars the Romans ever had to fight—and the first in which they can be seen to have employed a well-planned, long-term strategy. This eventually brought catastrophe to the Latins and their Campanian allies, whose cavalry, fighting poorly, suffered a heavy defeat at Trifanum, not far from Capua. At this point, the Campanians made a separate peace with Rome, which proceeded to assert control over the northern part of their country. And then over the next two years, the Latin cities, too, were obliged to submit, one after another.

When the fighting had ended, the Latin League was broken up (338). It had lost the struggle because its members were too disunited. A very long epoch had come to an end—the day of the Latins was done forever, except as a component of Roman power.

But Rome now showed a gift for conciliatory organization that no important states of the ancient world, including those of the otherwise cleverer Greeks, had ever displayed before. The Romans dealt with the defeated Latins not in a spirit of vindictiveness, which would have defeated its own purpose, but with cool common sense; and it dealt with them not by imposing any overall, bureaucratic solution, but by making piecemeal arrangements with each individual city, as the facts of every separate case seemed to require.

In the first place, Aricia and three other places near Rome were granted full Roman citizenship like Tusculum nearly half a century earlier. Roman territory was thus expanded to forty-five hundred square miles, with a

population of at least a million. Secondly, Tibur and Praeneste, although deprived of some land, retained formal independence, and their earlier alliances with Rome were confirmed. Thirdly, the other ancient Latin cities, while likewise permitted to retain their former status, were allowed treaties only with Rome and not with each other; and Rome granted the male inhabitants of this category of city a new sort of right, citizenship without franchise *(civitas sine suffragio)*. This was, in effect, a partial, halfway Roman citizenship, by virtue of which the men of these places, while not normally given the "public" right to vote in Rome's elections (which they could in any case rarely have exercised since they lived too far away), were granted "private" rights, notably the right to enter into contracts with a Roman according to Roman law *(commercium)* and the entitlement to marry a Roman without forfeiting inheritance of paternity rights *(conubium)*. This idea, apparently developed from the guest-right privilege granted to Etruscan Caere some forty years earlier, was tried out first on the member towns of the Campanian League and a Volscian group; and only then, after these experiments, was it extended to the Latin cities and later to the Sabines as well.

It was an ingenious and not unattractive arrangement. Admittedly, it was imposed on a unilateral basis by the dominant Romans, who unlike their partners were free to enjoy their own civic rights in *all* the cities with which they were associated. Furthermore, these communities had to follow Rome's foreign policy and were also obliged, in the event of war, to raise and pay a quota of troops for "mutual defense"—which meant, in effect, the service of Rome's needs, though it was assumed that these would coincide with their own. Yet these soldiers were allowed to serve in their own cities' contingents, under commanders of whom half were their own compatriots; and the Romans avoided the Greek error of imposing standing garrisons. Indeed, except in times of crisis, they had little cause to make demands or interfere, secure in the knowledge that the Latin cities were ruled by landed nobilities allied with their own. Nor did these communities have to pay the tax on property *(tributum)* that fell upon Roman citizens in times of emergency.

For a long time, therefore, this halfway Roman citizenship escaped the slur of inferior status, and it worked. The outstanding political acuteness of the Romans enabled them to get the balance right. Their aim was to maintain control over the Latins and others without offending local feeling; and that, as the relative contentment of these associates amply demonstrated, is what they for the most part achieved over a prolonged period of time. Indeed, Latium from now on was so closely and inseparably knit together with Rome that Virgil could later write of the Latins, in addition to the Romans, as the rulers of the world.

Among the Latin "colonies" established during the previous century and a half, seven were authorized by Rome to retain special privileges, but the rest, like other Latin cities, received the novel halfway status. Henceforward, there was an ever-growing number of such colonies, which were effective bulwarks of empire carefully located so as to guard the possessions of Rome and its associates from external enemies and prepare the way for future forward leaps.

Typical of these new Latin colonies was Cales (Calvi, near Capua), which now became a center of Roman authority in Campania. Plots of land at this settlement were allotted to more than two thousand families—Latin, Roman, and Campanian settlers. Far distant from the capital by the colonizing standards of the time, Cales became a pattern for future extensions of "Latinity"—which now meant Roman power. Another somewhat later

The walls of the ancient Latin colony of Signia (Segni).
Probably fourth century B.C.

foundation of the same type, Cosa (Ansedonia) on the mid-Etruscan coast
(273 B.C.), shows not only the earliest known Roman harbor but the remains
of capacious cisterns, a neatly rectangular street plan modeled on Greek
urbanism in south Italy and Sicily, the remains of a voting place for the
annual elections of local officials, and strong polygonal walls with eighteen
towers and three main gates. For it was upon these Latin colonies that the
task of defense chiefly fell, and they were planned to form an iron ring
around Rome's remaining enemies in central Italy.

But a further and at first secondary, though in the long run more durable,
instrument of power invented in the later fourth century B.C. was the purely
Roman colony, including no allies among its settlers but Roman citizens
only. Colonies of this type were once again placed at skillfully selected,
strategic vantage points; for example, all the earliest foundations of this type
were planned on the sea, to serve as coast guard stations. These Roman
colonies were always linked directly to Rome by a solid and continuous
stretch of Roman territory, which meant that they needed fewer defenders
and could therefore operate with a much smaller quota of settlers than their

Latin counterparts. Rome did not want to send too many potential fighters so far afield, and in any case, there were not all that many families willing to go to such places, where their metropolitan citizen rights hardly seemed to count any longer. So these Roman colonies comprised only three hundred families each—only a seventh as many as there were to be at their large Latin counterparts such as Cales.

One of the very first Roman colonies, sent out perhaps a decade or so before the final downfall of the Latin League, was at Ostia, beside the mouth of the Tiber. Ostia had probably first been taken control of by the Romans some two centuries earlier, but now a more determined effort to occupy the place was made. One of these groups of three hundred Roman citizen-families was sent to settle in a rectangular fort of five acres, designed like a camp with two geometrically planned intersecting main streets and a strong stone wall that three hundred male settlers could man if they stood six feet apart. The colony's primary function was to defend the Tiber mouth from maritime enemies and pirates, thus saving Rome from the necessity of maintaining a permanent fleet, which is still wanted to avoid. But although there was scarcely a harbor at the mouth of the delta-forming river, Ostia also regulated trade, supervised the collection of salt, exacted the payment of customs, and stored grain and other foodstuffs that could then go on by road or river up to Rome.

Twenty-seven miles further down the coast, Antium too, after its final capture from the Volscians in 338 B.C., was given a Roman colony, apparently augmented by native settlers; and in 317, in response to complaints, the place was granted autonomous local government like the Latin colonies, thus establishing a new and permanent precedent for these much smaller Roman citizen foundations. Thirty-eight miles lower down again, at the remotest extremity of Roman territory, a third maritime Roman colony was established in 329 at another former Volscian town, Tarracina (Terracina), each settler being allotted one and one-third acres of land. By 218 B.C. the number of coastal Roman colonies had risen to twelve, and by this time there were more than that number again maintaining guard over river crossings, exits from mountain passes, and road centers. They were all potential sites for army bases and were often resented by their neighbors, so that the colonists had good reason to remain loyal to Rome.

Altogether, if we include not only the two types of colony but individual allotments outside colonies as well, sixty thousand holdings were established between 343 and 264 B.C., so that the area thus occupied was multiplied threefold, to a total of some fifty thousand square miles; and the settlers who manned them provided a mighty contribution not only to agriculture but to defense—and further aggression.

The Samnite Wars

Outstanding among the enemies whom these colonists had to confront
were the Samnites, warlike peasants and herdsmen who lived in unwalled
villages throughout the landlocked valleys and gray limestone uplands of
the Apennines. The Samnite nation in this central Italian homeland was
divided into four large tribes which were linked together in a loose but
sometimes militarily effective league and which sent delegates to a federal
assembly. In the middle of the fourth century B.C. these Samnites were
Italy's largest political unit, possessing twice the territory and population
of the Romans.

It was pressure of population, with inadequate agricultural land to feed
it, that had brought some of their compatriots down into Campania. But
now the separate confederacy which they formed in that country had been
overwhelmed by Rome; and this the Samnites who had remained in central
Italy could not tolerate. The Latin colony of Cales also provoked them, and
so did another established in 328–327 at Fregellae (Opri) on the river Liris,
(Garigliano), which was their border with the Romans. So the Samnites
now took advantage of internal dissensions at one of the chief cities of
Campania, the ancient Greek foundation of Neapolis (Naples), to occupy
it with a garrison—which the Romans drove out, thus precipitating the long
and complicated Second, or Great, Samnite War (327–304).

Its first important campaign, in 321, inflicted upon the Romans their
worst defeat for over sixty years, the entrapment and humiliating surrender

Relief of walled hill-town from Avezzano.

of a whole army at the Caudine Forks, east of Capua. After this disaster they were obliged to evacuate Cales and Fregellae and stopped fighting altogether for five years. Moreover, on the resumption of the fighting, the Samnites won further victories, which culminated in an alarming incursion into Latium itself. Yet in the end they could not prevent Rome from refounding the two Latin colonies they had lost and settling five others as well—further fetters upon Samnite expansion.

Rome also created a potent new instrument of warlike policy by building the Via Appia (Appian Way) traversing the one hundred and thirty-two miles from Rome to Capua, mostly across the coastal plain. The more ancient Via Latina, following an upper inland route, was uncomfortably vulnerable to attacks from Samnium, to which the new Via Appia was not exposed. The forerunner of so many other Roman roads on three continents, weapons of peace as well as war, this "Queen of Roads" was constructed, as far as possible, on a straight course, with bridges or paved fords to carry it across rivers, while viaducts spanned marshy territory. By such means, the Second Samnite War was eventually won by the Romans. Their success left their enemies firmly excluded from southern Italy and much inferior to the victors in land and population alike.

But a Third Samnite War (298–290) was still to follow. In 296 the Samnite commander broke out northwards to join forces with a frightening combination of anti-Roman allies—Gauls, Etruscans, and Umbrians. But while the Etruscans were kept at home by a diversion, the Roman army won an important battle at Sentinum (Sassoferrato) in the Apennines. It was one of the most northerly points that their soldiers had ever reached, and never before had so many been engaged. But the victory was not decisive, because hostilites still continued for another six years. Fortunes varied, but finally the territory of the Samnites was penetrated by the Roman forces and ravaged from end to end, so that they had to give in.

Rome's success in this war decided the whole future fate of peninsular Italy. It had been a ferocious, patient struggle, in which the Samnites had clung to valley after valley with dogged determination. But the Romans had learned to exploit their interior lines in order to split the enemy into isolated blocks, and the Latin colonies that they had continued to found served the same purpose of dividing the central Italian tribes one from another. And so the enemy were gradually worn down, and driven up the hills away from their winter pastures.

In the process, the Roman army had become a good deal larger than before. It was now subdivided into two legions. Each legion was a masterpiece of organization, more mobile than the Greek phalanx which had served as the original model, because a legion contained an articulated group of thirty smaller units (maniples), each of which could maneuver and

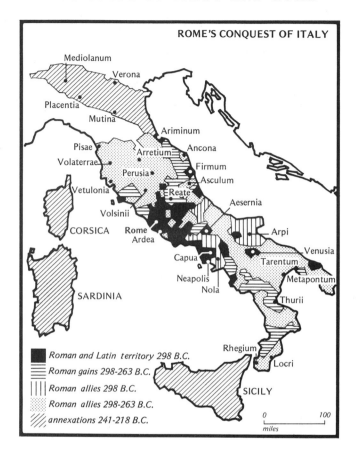

ROME'S CONQUEST OF ITALY

Mediolanum
Verona
Placentia
Mutina
Ariminum
Pisae
Ancona
Volaterrae
Arretium
Firmum
Perusia
Asculum
Vetulonia
Reate
Volsinii
Aesernia
CORSICA Rome
Ardea
Arpi
Venusia
Capua
Tarentum
Neapolis
Nola
Metapontum
Thurii
SARDINIA
Rhegium
Locri
SICILY

■ Roman and Latin territory 298 B.C.
≡ Roman gains 298-263 B.C.
|||| Roman allies 298 B.C.
∷ Roman allies 298-263 B.C.
/// annexations 241-218 B.C.

0   100
miles

fight separately on its own, in rough mountainous country as well as on the plains, either in serried ranks or open order, thus combining compactness with flexibility. Moreover, every maniple was formed into three lines, each of which could advance in turn through the line ahead, replacing it and enabling it to draw back for rest and replenishment. This new manipular legion, tested to the utmost against the Samnites, was to prove the key to Rome's future success.

Earlier in the century, the Roman state had begun to provide standard weapons and equipment, an important stage towards the creation of a professional army. And so, all legionaries wore helmets, breastplates, and leg guards (greaves) and carried swords; and thrusting javelins had been superseded by javelins for throwing, more than six feet long, half wood and half iron. This new weapon had probably been introduced during the Samnite wars. Those campaigns, coming on top of the Romans' ceaseless hostilities with so many of their neighbors during the previous two centuries and more, had forged their army into a terrible weapon. It was perfectly suited to the dour perseverance that characterized the citizens of Rome, enabling them to respond so efficiently to each successive external threat—real or imagined since, as their sphere of interests continually widened, it was hard to know whether the threats were authentic or imaginary. However, the Romans were so amply fortified by their religious leaders with the belief that all their ways were just that they could never suppose that the military measures they were taking might be morally wrong. And that being so, as the great Greek historian Polybius noted, they were generally not reluctant to employ force when they felt that force was needed.

They were also capable of atrocious cruelty. But what made the Romans so remarkable was the combination of these unpleasant traits with a talent for patient political reasonableness that was unique in the ancient world. They had displayed this gift before, and now they showed it once again; for in spite of all Rome's raw wounds from the recently ended hostilities, the defeated Samnites were offered the same treaty terms that had been proposed to them at the end of the previous (second) war. Rome's treaties with other states were either "equal" or "unequal." But the latter formula, explicitly stating the inferiority of the other party, was increasingly becoming the choice the Romans preferred, and it was this type of "agreement" that was accorded the defeated Samnites. In 280 the Romans also made treaties with seven Etruscan cities in order to make them part of the defense system against the Gauls—similar arrangements were made in more distant parts of Italy as well.

Such treaties, intended for peoples not close or reliable enough to be accorded the half citizenship of the Latins, were an integral and essential part of Rome's Italian system and explain why its dependents and subjects were regularly known as "allies" *(socii)*. Yet, as the treaties entered into by the Romans were bilateral, their allies were not normally permitted to be allies with one another as well; in this sense, there was no confederacy in Roman Italy. Like the Latins, these other allies had to provide troops if requested, and when their treaties with Rome were "unequal," the requests were likely to be somewhat more peremptory. Yet their aristocracies, even if somewhat less close than the Latin nobilities to the Roman governing class, were generally known personally to its members and regarded by them with sympathy; and this sort of friendly link with municipal leaderships was Rome's blueprint for its imperial future. The Romans protected the rulers of these allied towns from internal revolutions and left them alone to rule their own peoples according to their own laws and with a minimum of conformity; and the peoples in question could be reminded that, without having to pay taxes to Rome, they were securing from it protection and peace. Besides, from about 289 B.C., drawing on their extensive spoils of Italian bronze, the Romans developed from earlier experiments a coinage to meet the common commercial and industrial needs of the area. In this, as in other respects, association with the Romans proved beneficial rather than restrictive.

On the whole, Rome found it advisable, and was encouraged by its religion, to keep its bargains with its allies, displaying a self-restraint, a readiness to compromise, and a calculated generosity that the world had never seen. And so the allies, too, had little temptation to feel misused. The proud Samnites, it was true, had lost a considerable amount of their land to Roman settlers, and among them disaffection still continued to linger beneath the surface. But they were only a few out of a grand total of one hundred and twenty Italian communities with which Rome, in due course, formed perpetual alliances. After the end of the Samnite wars a network of such agreements was extended across the whole of central Italy.

The whole Roman approach was empirical, working from precedent to precedent according to each individual case, the relationship with every community in turn being considered on its own merits. This complex multiplication of differing agreements seems like a classic example of the cynical principle "divide and rule." And so it was. But like the earlier understandings with the Latins, it was reckoned and weighed out so acutely, with that instinctive, hard, practical Roman genius for common-sense statecraft, that the system, unlike any of its partial Greek models, proved successful for generation after generation. That was how the Romans accomplished their first major historical achievement, the creation of Italy. They could speak on behalf of the country and claim to represent it as no other ancient city-state had ever before been able to be spokesman for the territories it had brought under its control. And so, as we shall see, when a major military crisis arose later in the century, Rome was able to muster nearly four hundred thousand Roman and allied troops—and even under supreme pressure most of them would still remain conspicuously loyal.

4

The Class Struggle

The Early Republic

During these one hundred and seventy years of almost incessant fighting, the Roman community had found itself racked by the gravest internal disturbances it was to experience for many centuries to come.

When the Etruscan dynasty of the Tarquins was overthrown shortly before 500 B.C., tradition maintained that the headship of the state had immediately passed from the expelled monarch to a pair of consuls elected every year. Efforts have been made in modern times to dispute this view and speak of an interim period lasting for some decades, or even for a century and a half, in which there was indeed a new republic, but a republic governed initially not by two such annually elected functionaries but by a single one chosen, with subordinates, for one or two years at a time, on the analogy of certain Etruscan cities that were likewise moving at this time from regal towards republican government. But this is somewhat unlikely. Certainly there was provision in the Roman constitution for the nomination of a single, autocratic dictator in an emergency—but only temporarily, for a period of six months at most, and never in any continuous succession. It seems therefore that we must instead accept the strong tradition, based on the lists *(Fasti)* which purport to record all these appointments, that maintained that there were pairs of top officials from the beginning of the republic; though for one hundred and fifty years or more, these pairs were probably not yet called consuls but praetors, from *prae-ire,* "to march ahead" or "precede."

However, let us, for the sake of convenience, describe the two colleagues as consuls from the beginning. The character of consular office was significant and contradictory because it sharply combined supremacy and limitation. The consuls were supreme in that each of them was invested with absolute *imperium,* the administrative power conferring command of the army and the interpretation and execution of the law. In Rome, therefore, unlike modern Britain, the center of political gravity lay not in the legislative but in the executive, and this executive was not "responsible" to the community or Senate or Assembly from day to day, but "representative," limited only by law. In these respects the United States of America is somewhat closer than Britain to ancient Rome—whose ideas it deliberately borrowed—in that the power of the American president, despite sharp modern disputes on the subject, is likewise limited by nothing but the law. In ancient Rome, however, the "magistrates," as these officials were called, as well as the relatively few lesser magistrates added later on, were subject to fewer limitations than the president of the United States. (To take a single example, they enjoyed immunity from prosecution while in office.) This state of affairs corresponded with the Romans' marked respect for lawful public authority and their inherited, disciplined conviction that it ought to be obeyed. And this large power vested in the executive obviously gave it a greater possibility of getting things done. But on the debit side, the situation, though it admittedly did not silence criticism of the consuls, inhibited the development of democracy in any modern Western sense.

Yet although responsible to no one, and limited only by the law in the exercise of their duties, the consuls nevertheless were subject to two practical restrictions. In the first place, they were elected for only a single year. And, secondly, being a pair, they were subject to one another's vetoes. Since the power of each was all-pervading, neither one could prevail over the other; if they disagreed, it was understood that the colleague who was against action could veto his fellow consul who was for it. The retention of a negative veto of this kind was not altogether inadvisable since the annually elected consuls might be stupid or incompetent, or arrogantly obstinate. Yet they also possessed the inherited training of their class, which very often produced a remarkable spirit of consensus and an attitude of selfless sacrifice to the needs of the community as a whole. The consuls also possessed the opportunity, generally if not always advantageous, of being able to consult the other representatives of their own experienced clique, since these were their fellow members of the Senate.

The members of this body, which retained its numerical strength of three hundred for nearly half a millennium, had naturally gained more say in affairs after the monarchy was expelled, an act in which they surely played a substantial part; and from that time onwards they allowed officials and other notables to join the heads of the families who had formerly monopolized their ranks. The Senate possessed no executive powers. But it advised the elected magistrates on domestic and foreign policy, finance, and religion, and counseled them on legislative proposals as well—though it was generally willing enough to give a free hand to these officials, who were their fellow senators and belonged to the same clans and families as themselves. And the consuls on their side, despite their extensive constitutional powers, were likely enough to defer to the Senate's advice for the same reasons— and also because the brief annuality of their own office made them vulnerable after it was over. Besides, the senators were endowed with redoubtable prestige due to their positions and family traditions and achievements. The Latin word for this prestige, *auctoritas,* conveyed a very urgent call for respect and deference, and the individual *auctoritas* of each senator combined to form a corporate influence that, in a county dependent to an exceptional extent on collective endeavors, remained strong enough to survive all the growing pains of the republic and keep on guiding its policies for centuries.

That is not, of course, to deny that there were dissensions within the ranks of the Senate itself. No doubt there were, at all periods. Yet for a very long time there was nothing resembling a divergence of party programs. It was rather a matter of shifting networks of personal and collective associations, as clans, families, or sometimes individuals combined temporarily with one another in rival groups. But any disagreements that thereby arose did not greatly inhibit the effectiveness of the early republican Senate as a whole, even in the face of a whole host of foreign and internal oppositions and problems.

Since the Senate remained in law purely advisory, it was not the body that elected the consuls year by year. This was the Assembly of Roman citizens *(comitia centuriata),* which had received its shape, it was said, from King Servius Tullius. However, this assembly had been weighted from the beginning so that the centuries of the well-to-do possessed far greater voting power than the poor. Moreover, candidates for the consulship were proposed to the Assembly *by the senators,* from their own ranks. The Assembly, it is true, enacted laws, declared war and peace, and conducted trials. Yet the senators, with their superior prestige and wealth, controlled its votes on all such occasions. In many respects, therefore, the legal appearance of democracy was sharply corrected by what in fact happened.

The Greek historian Polybius, keenly studied and followed by the makers of the American Constitution, looked back from the second century B.C. and enormously admired the Roman state for the internal equilibrium that, despite all its problems, it had maintained over so many hundreds of years; and this he ascribed to Rome's system of mutual automatic balances and checks between its legislative, executive, and judicial branches. Yet the equilibrium to which he devoted this praise rested on a quaint cluster of unspecific, impalpable, illogical customs and conventions that were called into play empirically and pragmatically as each successive situation de-

Silver *denarius* of P. Licinius Nerva (113/112 B.C.) showing
two voters in the Assembly with an attendant.

manded. Indeed Polybius himself appreciated this, pointing out that the
system had developed "not according to a theory but through frequent
conflicts and practical crises." Yet there was not any authentic "balance"
at all, since the Assembly's formal power so greatly exceeded any power it
possessed in reality.

This curious gulf between fact and appearance was created by one of the
most important factors in Roman life, which continued to influence it
profoundly for centuries. This was the institution of *clientela.* Roman society was a structure composed of powerful *patroni* and their dependent
clientes. The client was a free man who entrusted himself to the patronage
of another and received protection from him in return. The client helped
his patron to succeed in public life and furthered his interests by every
means in his power, and in return the patron looked after his client's private
affairs and gave him financial or legal support.

Such mutual arrangements are not unparalleled in other societies, but the
Roman institution was remarkable for its all-pervasiveness and binding
cogency. *Clientela* was hereditary; it was also heavily charged with feeling
and emotion. A man was supposed to rate his clients even before his own
relations by marriage. A law of the mid-fifth century B.C. damns and curses
any patron who behaves fraudulently towards his client. *Clientela,* it is true,
was probably not enforceable by legal sanctions. But that was immaterial
beside the powerful quasi-religious force it had attained by long and universally respected custom. The keynotes of this force were *fides,* mutual good
faith—worshipped as a goddess, according to tradition, from the dimmest
early past—and *pietas,* the dutiful respect owed to patrons just as it was
owed to parents, fatherland, and gods.

Here was another reason why the Assembly, for all its impressive demo-
cratic-sounding "powers," could never be a truly democratic body. Not
only were its richest members in possession of disproportionate voting

power, but those assemblymen who lacked wealth were, for the most part, clients of rich men and senators in whose favor, therefore, or in favor of whose friends and relations, they were in duty bound to cast their votes in the annual elections to state offices. On the credit side it might be said that a poor client's relationship to his patron, based on inescapable ties of good faith, gave his life a meaning and security that poor people in other countries have frequently lacked and still lack today. Nevertheless, *clientela* acted as a powerful brake on democratic development and indeed helped to prevent it from ever taking place.

Patricians and Plebeians

For one thing, this relationship between patrons and clients reflected the basic division of Roman society, existent when the republic started or earlier still, between patricians and plebeians *(plebs)*. After the beginning of the republic, as we have seen, although the Senate was apparently not increased in size, it came to include not only heads of families *(patres familias)* but other prominent personages as well. And since these were very often the sons, descendants, or relatives of the *patres familias,* they became known because of this relationship as *patricii.*

The patricians exercised power not only through their clients but by virtue of a monopoly, hallowed by custom, of inherited religious rights, including the administration of major cults and the power to consult the gods *(auspicia),* as well as the control of law and the calendar, which were both religious in character. During the fifth century B.C. some fifty-three patrician clans *(centes)* are known—less apparently than there had been under the kings, though some names may be lost—comprising a closed body of not more than one thousand families. At the outset of the republic there was a small inner ring of especially powerful patrician clans, notably the Aemilii, Cornelii, and Fabii. And to these were added, after their immigration from Sabine territory, the Claudii as well.

However, these patricians comprised less than one-tenth of the total citizen population of Rome, and possibly not more than one-fourteenth. The remaining large majority of the inhabitants (apart from a number of slaves, a normal feature of ancient societies) were the plebeians, and the sharp political and social distinction that separated them from the patricians was the outstanding feature of early republican social history. To some extent *clientela* kept the plebeians happy, since their patrons were obliged by insistent moral sanctions to give them help. But although all clients were plebeians, not all plebeians were clients; immigrant traders, for example, were left out in the cold. Besides, the most that a patron could do, or was willing to do, was not always enough to prevent discontent. For one thing, the plebeians were completely excluded from influential positions, including the consulships, and initially from membership in the Senate. This was a point that irritated the more powerful and prosperous of the plebeians—who alone among that order could afford the costs of holding office, so that it was they who were often seen leading movements of plebeian protest. To this extent, successive Roman attempts at social reform or revolution were merely the endeavors of the influential men at the top of the plebeian class to climb to higher status, sometimes with the support of this or that opportunistic patrician.

But there was a great deal more to the internal disturbances of the early republic than that. While exclusion from office was only frustrating for the prominent plebeians at the top, the remaining plebeians, who covered a very wide spectrum ranging right down to the bottom of the "free" social scale, did not want power so much as rescue and protection from the abuses of power that were being committed by others. Many of these men had suffered grievous impoverishment from the abrupt fall in Rome's prosperity and resources after the expulsion of the Etruscan monarchs. When this happened, the city had sunk right back to the status of a purely agrarian community operating at a low subsistence level; and what with the active competition offered by their Latin allies, and harassment from enemies on every side, there just was not enough tolerable soil available, on the small territory of the early republic, to give everyone a living. Besides, much of this territory was public land *(ager publicus),* inaccessible to the plebeians; and even if one of them did possess land of his own, he very often had to go and fight in one of the unceasing frontier wars, and when he came back, his farm had gone to ruin in his absence.

In these conditions, crippling grain shortages occurred time after time. They brought famines, and to ward them off, the Romans founded a temple of the grain goddess Ceres (ca. 496 or 493). The worship of Ceres was essentially a cult of the plebeians. It was borrowed from the Greek city of Cumae, where her Greek counterpart Demeter was one of the leading divinities. This Greek origin was significant since the Roman temple was located beneath the Aventine Hill, in an area near the Cattle Market and the river wharves that was a center for Greek traders. And it was to the Greeks that the poor of Rome, as of other places, looked for ideas of democracy—and sometimes for ideas of popular, plebeian-based, one-man rule, for which would-be autocrats allegedly made three separate bids at Rome during these early years of the republic. The economic situation in the fifth century was grim, due not only to the shortages and famines but to the shattering epidemics that came in their wake. And in the hope of removing these further terrible accompaniments to all their internal and external troubles the Romans continued their religious borrowings by taking over the great Greek healing god Apollo, in whose honor they built a temple in about 431 B.C.

As a result of the disastrous agricultural situation, a large number of plebeians fell desperately into debt. All debt legislation of the ancient world, in which rates of interest were very high indeed, seem to us alarmingly stringent; and the Roman laws were no exception. Worst of all, if a man could not pay his debts, and had exhausted other means of raising money, he had only his own body left to pledge, and so he became, on default, not indeed precisely a slave but a "man in fetters" *(nexus)*, whose position amounted in practice to very much the same thing: a chattel and prisoner reduced to inherited serfdom to his creditor, with little hope of ever recovering his lost freedom again. In the first century of the republic, as very often later, debt was a crucial and catastrophic problem. Indeed, it must be regarded as the chief reason for the bitter hostility that now developed between the plebeians and their patrician governing class; for it was the state authorities' unjust and arbitrary enforcement of the laws of debt that caused the plebeian indignation and sense of grievance to reach the boiling point.

Yet the patrician government could not do without the plebeians, since those of them who possessed the requisite property qualifications were needed as soldiers; and this consciousness that they were indispensable encouraged the plebeians to resort to collective protests. Since trade unions and general strikes had not been heard of, their protests took the form of secessions. *Secessio* signifies their "retirement" from the rest of the Roman community, in the sense of a literal physical departure. To suggest that all the recorded secessions were threats that were never carried out is unconvincing, since the tradition to the contrary is too persistent. What we are told is that the plebeians, or a proportion of them, moved away from the city—presumably with their families—to one of the hills beyond its periphery, a remarkable example of organized collective bargaining that virtually created a temporary state within a state and split the nation in two. What is more, the plebeians were reported to have made withdrawals of this kind no fewer than five times during the first two and a quarter centuries of the republic. It is true that since later historians made a practice of inventing duplicates and mirror images of recent events and inserting them into their picture of the distant, little-known past, there probably were not as many as *five* of these secessions. Nevertheless, to reject all but the last of them is still unduly sceptical. It seems reasonable to accept, tentatively, the very earliest secession as well, since the new social and economic problems at the outset of the diminished, embattled republic must have been acute.

What seems to have happened, then, on the first of these occasions (494 B.C.) was that a body of plebeians marched up the Aventine Hill, which was still outside the walls of Rome at this time and belonged, as we have seen, to an area frequented by Greek traders familiar with democratic ideas. And once there, following an old Italian formula, the plebeians all swore to one another a corporate oath of mutual support. Their secession, followed by this oath, proved effective because, in order to prevent the nation and the army from disintegrating, the patrician authorities felt obliged to grant their main request. This demanded the creation of a small number of functionaries to represent plebeian interests. These tribunes of the plebeians or of the people *(tribuni plebis),* as they were called, would have the duty of interceding against the acts of any state official in order to protect plebeians from execution, arrest, or molestation—including a takeover by their creditors. The tribunes, who thus became the defenders of the plebeians just as patrons were obliged to defend their clients, did not draw their power from any law —they were not state officials or magistrates—but derived it from an oath sworn by the plebeians to safeguard their inviolability, any infringement of which would provoke a curse and incur pain of death. The first holders of these tribunates were plebeians of substance and ambition. Their office was a strange and unprecedented institution with a long, varied, and fateful future, during which it sometimes contrived to protect the private rights of its constituents—though not always, and it never succeeded in making Rome into a democracy.

Shortly after the establishment of the tribunate, a quarrel developed about the land owned by the state *(ager publicus).* The patricians preferred to maintain this public ownership, which enabled them to settle on such territory and treat it as their own, while the plebeians on the other hand wanted it to be distributed among themselves. While this dispute was still under way, constitutional agitation in 471 obliged the state authorities to agree to the establishment of a special Council of which the members were to be exclusively plebeians *(Concilium plebis).* It was the task of the *tribuni plebis* to summon this Council, tribe by tribe, to meetings at which the annual elections of their own successors took place, various kinds of measures *(plebiscita)* were moved and passed, and lawsuits and trials of certain categories were conducted. This existence of the plebeian Council created what seems to modern students an almost ludicrously complicated state of affairs according to which, in addition to the *Comitia centuriata* and its semiobsolete predecessor, *Comitia curiata,* there was now what amounted virtually to a third Assembly. But the *Concilium plebis* was not, initially, an official organ of the Roman state, since it was only about two centuries later that its enactments came to be accorded equal validity with the laws. Until then, they were merely expressions of the plebeians' will and intent and were noted as such by the government—which generally found it advisable to accept them.

The Twelve Tables

All this was being done against a background of famine, pestilence, and savage frontier warfare against numerous enemies. In these desperate circumstances, the plebeians, who bore the brunt of the miseries and the fighting, felt more discontented than anyone else, out of the conviction that every privilege that they had so far attained was merely formal and that nothing substantial had been done to relieve their social and economic miseries. Nor did they really know, legally speaking, how they stood, since the laws were not written down and were interpreted by the college of priests *(pontifices),* who at this time were all still patricians. It was this issue that played a dominant part in the plebeians' next demands—and these demands became so violent and pressing that in 451 B.C. the normal appointments to consulships were temporarily suspended and a commission of ten patricians, the *decemviri,* under the chairmanship of Appius Claudius, was appointed to write down a collection of laws. The product of their labors was enacted by the Assembly of the centuries as a statute and openly published for all to examine as had never been done before, on tablets that were set up in the Forum: the Twelve Tables. The original tablets were destroyed in the invasion by the Gauls some sixty years later, but considerable and apparently typical portions of the texts have come down to us in scattered and often reedited quotations by later authorities.

In demanding that such a step should be taken, the plebeians were inspired by the Greek ideas they had heard around the Aventine and its wharves, for the establishment of a code of laws as a means of political compromise was an expedient very familiar to the Greeks. Indeed, tradition maintained that before carrying out their work the decemvirs had made a journey to Athens—which is unlikely, though they may have visited the Greek cities of southern Italy and Sicily or at least studied their procedures. True, whether the Twelve Tables ought to be regarded as displaying any extensive or specific Greek influence at all is far from certain, especially as they do not constitute a Greek-type code but are a mosaic of varied, incomplete provisions. However, much that we find in them is attributable in a general way to Rome's contacts with Greek thought, directly and through Etruria, over the previous one hundred one hundred and fifty years.

The surviving excerpts and adaptations of the Twelve Tables constitute by far our most precious information about Rome of the fifth century B.C. Their field is the civil law, the law regarding the rights and duties of Roman citizens *(cives Romani)* and the relation of one citizen to another—which continued to be the only law Rome had for many centuries. The contents of the tables form a strange mixture of widely ranging principles and minor details, of private, public, and criminal law, of rules about matters ranging from communal hygiene to personal safety. What is quite clear, however, even from the somewhat modernized Latin in which these regulations have come down to us, is that the men who originally framed and drafted their short, gnomic sentences were hard practical thinkers who were able to express themselves in terse, plain, and almost painfully exact language and who already possessed in full measure that unparalleled talent for precise legal definition that is one of Rome's greatest gifts to humanity.

The impact of the Twelve Tables upon later generations was enormous. After their disappearance in the Gaulish invasion they were meticulously reconstructed and remained legally valid. Indeed, they were traditionally seen, with a measure of respectful exaggeration, as the source of much or most of the whole body of Roman law; and for century after century they retained a dominant position in the education of every Roman citizen.

This massively triumphant subsequent career of the Twelve Tables might lead us to conclude that the efforts of the decemvirs who drew them up had been successful. Paradoxically enough, however, their initial publication of the tables was extremely badly received—by the very plebeians for whose benefit the entire exercise had been conducted. For the decemvirs had not, to any significant extent, regarded it as part of their job to introduce into their compilation any new measures to improve the plebeians' lot. On the contrary, their duty, as they interpreted it, was merely to reduce to visible statute form the most important regulations of the already existing customary law, with only insignificant additions or adjustments. By carrying out this task, and thereby publishing abroad the more socially significant and controversial of the rules that had hitherto been known only to the patricians, they believed they had done quite enough to satisfy plebeian demands —and that they could, therefore, in the interests of the patricians, safely evade having to do anything more. But plebeian contentment was not forthcoming.

Nevertheless, we who scrutinize the tables today find it impressive that a people at such a relatively early stage of development were so clearly able to disentangle law from religion, deriving the sanction of their legal pronouncements not from any divine or wholly or partly legendary lawgiver, as so many of their predecessors in other places had done, but rather from a sense of justice and equity, still narrow yet already strong. The Twelve Tables also show a surprisingly precocious clarity of conception in dealing with contract and property. And they proposed, as we saw earlier, a death penalty for any patron who cheated his client—though that, like the rest of these provisions, was presumably nothing new.

Moreover, in the measures regarding marriage, archaism is not untempered by liberalism. In the earliest days Roman matrimony granted every husband the power of *manus,* which bestowed on him the same rights over his wife as his status as father of the family also gave him over their children. But a slight weakening of the husband's authority was already sanctioned by the Twelve Tables, according to which his wife, after she had reached the age of twenty-five, retained possession of her own property. This right, it is true, was still subject to formal control by father or guardian (according to the type of marriage), and the Twelve Tables gave a mother no right of succession to an intestate son. However, despite such official limitations, the *mater familias* enjoyed, by custom, great respect and influence, being required to supervise, for example, the education of her young children. On the lips of men, it is true, there was much stress on women's place and duties in the home. But women lived and went out and about with a liberty that far exceeded the conditions of their Greek counterparts and instead recalled the freedom enjoyed by the women of Etruria. The Twelve Tables give some idea of how far this movement towards emancipation had gone. By another law of the tables, a wife could avoid her husband's legal control by passing three nights each year away from his house. In due course there also developed free marriage, based on mutual consent, which gave the husband no authority over his wife.

Up to a point, too, though the details are much disputed, the tables safeguarded a Roman citizen's capital rights, for they confirmed that the only court that might hear a capital charge and impose a death sentence was the *Comitia centuriata*—which at least meant that he could not incur this peril from any other court. But that might not be particularly comforting, especially as summary capital jurisdiction by officials was not ruled out. Nor was the ferocious severity of the law of debt sufficiently mitigated. It was all very well adding, as was done, that the execution of a court order against debtors must be delayed for thirty days and that the creditor must feed them adequately and not overload them with chains. But it was not yet made clear that there must always be a court order before the creditor took forcible action; and above all the bitter fact remained that he was still eventually permitted to take his debtors over as permanent serfs. Moreover, the very fact that the tables defined these and other already existing social hardships, far from improving the atmosphere as had been hoped, meant that when people saw in writing all the rules and sanctions that had been imposed on them and were still in force, they felt appalled.

Social Appeasement

The decemvirs therefore failed to win the approval of the plebeians, as indeed the legends surrounding their endeavors faithfully recall, though they add numerous melodramatic embroideries. The decemvirate continued into a second year of office, during which a veto on intermarriage between patricians and plebeians was apparently confirmed. But then the decemvirs fell from power, and the normal succession of consulships was restored. Their downfall was achieved by a second secession in 449, once again, it would appear, to the Aventine, which had been allocated to them as agricultural or building land some seven years earlier in an attempt at conciliation under pressure. The years 449 and 447 also witnessed legislative measures in favour of the *plebeians* that strengthened and confirmed certain of their existing institutions; but these were exaggerated by later historical tradition because the fall of the decemvirs seemed, retrospectively, such an important and progressive landmark. Then, in 455, the ban on intermarriage between patricians and plebeians may have been lifted. Or more probably—since the patricians, backed by their clients, continued for years to fight every position foot by foot—this was only an attempt to remove it, which did not prove successful. This conclusion is suggested by the continuing decline in the number of patrician families who carried their persistent distaste for intermarrying to the lengths of class suicide.

In the following year the succession of consuls was temporarily broken when groups of army officers were appointed instead. This was primarily for military purposes (p. 49). But the new system, which continued not merely for a year or two like the earlier substitution by decemvirs, but for nearly eighty years (with interruptions), also served the cause of the plebeians, who were able to gain an occasional place among these military officers, a place that they had not yet succeeded in gaining among the consuls. But the most prominent member of the new leadership was the winner of the war against Veii, Camillus, who was a patrician.

Towards the end of Camillus's career, however, the consulate was restored; and after a prolonged struggle two tribunes of the people, Licinius and Sextius, reelected, it was said, for as long as ten years (376–367), at last carried a proposal that one of the consuls could henceforward always be a plebeian. Very soon, individual plebeians were attaining positions of great and long-lasting political power; and only twenty-five years after the Licinian-Sextian measure, the inclusion of a plebeian among every pair of consuls became obligatory. The censorship, too, (p. 49) became accessible to plebeians by 351 at the latest, and in 339 it was decreed that one censor must always come from their ranks. The effect of these changes was to create a new ruling class, no longer an entirely patrician aristocracy but a nobility consisting of those men, patrician and plebeian alike, whose ancestry had included consuls or censors or dictators—which is what the term "noble" came to mean. And within the next century plebeian clans such as the Marcii and Decii and Curii, in addition to those who had come from Tusculum and elsewhere, succeeded in establishing themselves among the leaders of this new oligarchy of nobles.

Plebeians of lesser rank were aided by the creation of a new office of state, the praetorship, in 366. This "urban praetor" was to undertake legal and other civilian functions in order to leave the two consuls free for military duties. But this intervention also helped the plebeians since the interests of the underprivileged were benefited by the successive praetors' yearly "edicts." Higher officials of the Roman state were accustomed to proclaim by edict, on annual appointment to their office, the major policies that they proposed to follow as its occupants. Among such edicts those of the praetor, owing to his legal responsibilities, were of special significance for the development of private law, and ultimately they became even more important than the Twelve Tables and the source of a great deal of later legislation. It was true that like other senior functionaries, praetors were merely supposed to apply regulations that were already in force rather than institute new ones; but in fact their edicts formulated a multitude of new rules and improvements adapted to the increasing complexity of society. They included many remedies for unfairness and abuse and were guided, subject to a certain latent and not always conscious class bias, by tolerant flexibility and massive fairness, the "equity" of which the Twelve Tables had already shown signs.

Nevertheless, such improvements only became apparent over the years. For the time being, even if the annexations of Veii and its territory meant that more land was now available, many people remained in the grim clutches of poverty and debt. Licinius and Sextius tried to do something about this by providing that the interest that a debtor had already paid should be deducted from the amount of debt he still owed. Although the tribunes added, in order not to distress creditors too much, that this balance must then be repaid in annual installments within a period not exceeding three years, their proposal was by ancient standards radical; it reminded conservatives of alarming demands for a clean slate that had become a feature of Greek city-states. For such reasons, these relief enactments evidently remained ineffective, for we hear of no fewer than four further endeavors to mitigate debt hardships within the course of the next fifty years. There was even an attempt to veto borrowing on interest altogether (ca. 342). Its aim was to prevent hardships and abuses; but it must also have made it much more difficult for impoverished people to secure the loans they wanted.

Licinius and Sextius also established limits on the amount of land that could be owned by any one person. This was intended to appease the land hunger of the poor and to make sure that they secured an adequate share of conquered territories; but the measure seems to have become a dead letter before long. Nevertheless, the endeavors of these two tribunes of the people, dim figures though they are, to ease the conditions of the plebeians, were unprecedented and impressive—the most important internal reforms since the foundation of the republic. And it was fitting, though perhaps still overoptimistic, that in the crisis year of their principal measures Camillus vowed a temple to Concord, thus echoing the ideal and desideratum often invoked by Greek cities, under the name of Homonoia, in order to end their internal disharmonies.

The next decades witnessed further perceptible advances in social progress and unity, so that Rome went into its decisive struggle against the Latin cities (Chapter 3) with a reasonable degree, if not of concord, at least of public acquiescence. Whatever the deficiencies of the system from a democratic viewpoint, it proved of decisive importance for the future that Rome, convulsed by these social dissensions at the same time as it was attacked by foreign foes on every side, had prevented the internal strife from reaching suicidal proportions; it was thus given a free hand to suppress each of its foreign enemies in turn, vastly expanding its territory and resources in the process.

Yet in the acute emergency of the Second and Great Samnite War (327–304 B.C.), fresh measures of social appeasement still seemed urgently necessary in order to ensure that Rome's plebeian soldiers continued to fight. The most far-reaching step was taken by the consul Poetelius, probably in 326 B.C., shortly after the beginning of the war. As we have seen, there had already been many measures designed to relieve the position of debtors earlier in the century; but the reforms of Poetelius, although obscure to us today, were apparently more comprehensive and effective. True, the supposition that he altogether abolished the ancient custom by which a debtor could be sold and become the permanent hereditary bondman of his creditor seems unlikely. Yet he improved on the Twelve Tables by insisting that in all circumstances a court judgment was necessary before this extreme step could be taken. He may also have enacted that loans could be made on the security of the property of the borrower instead of his person; and that creditors, therefore, must be prepared to accept whatever property debtors offered as a payment. Although this was not the end of the problem, since it was destined to recur even more urgently within not many decades, these measures were evidently far more important for most Romans than any military or political developments of the day and almost significant enough to justify the later enthusiasm of the historian Livy, who declared that the legislation of Poetelius inaugurated a new era of liberty for the Roman plebeians.

Of outstanding importance, too, though scarcely less enigmatic, are the social reforms introduced shortly afterwards by the first of all Romans who can be regarded as a historical personage, Appius Claudius, censor in 312 B.C. Appius Claudius, known as Caecus ("blind")—which he became in his old age—must have been a remarkable man. For one thing, he was the writer of a series of pungent moral sayings in verse, thus becoming the first known personage in Latin literature. Furthermore, during his censorship he inaugurated two mighty engineering and building traditions by constructing, first, the precursor of Rome's aqueducts, the Aqua Appia, which brought water from the Sabine hills to the city in an underground tunnel (including one mile of overground conduit), and, secondly, the Via Appia or Appian Way which was to play an active part in the strategy of the Second Samnite War.

Moreover, although himself a patrician, Appius Claudius employed his censorship to increase the part played by the plebeians in public life. A desire to secure their effective service in the armies fighting the war may have also been in his mind. But his principal aim was to further the interests of a class disqualified from army service, the landless urban population— whom no previous reformer had ever tried to help. Appius's intention was probably to avoid discontent and turbulence on the home front; but at any rate, whatever his motives, he helped these city poor. In the long run, his efforts on their behalf enjoyed some success; from then on the plebeian Council felt a special responsibility for this section of the population, though the effects of his reforms were by no means conspicuous immediately, since some of them were rescinded only eight years after they had first been enacted.

As censor, Appius Claudius also admitted the sons of former slaves (freedmen) to the Senate, a step that even many centuries later would still have seemed revolutionary and was in fact reversed by the consuls of the following year. More lasting in its beneficial effects on the plebeians was a further development that Appius appears to have instigated in 304 B.C. by a calculated indiscretion. This was the publication by his secretary, Cnaeus Flavius, who had become a state official, of a manual of correct forms of legal procedure. Despite the disclosure of laws in the Twelve Tables, the knowledge of these technicalities had hitherto still remained a monopoly of the patrician college of priests *(pontifices)*. But now their publication made them available to future generations of lay jurists. This event, and the powerful opposition it aroused in conservative circles, created an atmosphere of perilous tension; and Flavius, the perpetrator of the courageous deed, like Camillus before him, dedicated a shrine to the spirit of Concord. It was probably no coincidence, or at least part of the same series of progressive events, that a law of 300 B.C. gave all citizens the right to appeal *(provocatio)* against capital sentences imposed by any official; another law of the same date made half the membership of the *pontifices* plebeian.

In 298 the third and last Samnite War began, and it lasted for eight years. The ferocious struggle ended in victory, but also in financial exhaustion. The plebeians of middle rank serving in the army had done so, like many before them, at the cost of the prosperity of their farms, which often fell into decay, so that despite the Poetelian law, they fell heavily into debt. So restless did they become, and so grave was the consequent friction, that in accordance with the constitution a dictator, Quintus Hortensius, was appointed (287 B.C.) as a temporary expedient to meet the emergency.

What economic measures Hortensius took, we are not sure. But it is at least known that he passed a law of a constitutional nature in favor of the plebeians, providing that the resolutions of their Council, the *Concilium plebis,* should have the force of law and be binding upon the whole community, patricians and plebeians alike, without the need for the National Assembly, the *Comitia centuriata,* or Senate to concur. Thus a right that had been claimed for more than one hundred and fifty years was conceded, and the decisions of the plebeians were now every bit as valid as those of the executive. At very long last, the struggle between the orders had ended. The Roman people, acting through the Assembly, had already been sovereign at a much earlier date in the eyes of the law, but not in reality. Now, when the plebeians' measures had gained full legal acceptance—and for the next century and a half these enactments provided the greater part of Rome's legislation—it might seem that the people's sovereignty had been brought to completion; and the Hortensian law that produced this result has sometimes been hailed as the triumph of democracy.

But that it was not, for three reasons. In the first place, whatever measures Hortensius may have taken to clear up the debt situation did not prove permanently effective, any more than the enactments that had gone before them, so that democracy in the economic and social fields was still out of reach and sight. Secondly, the plebeian Council, though it could on occasion be swayed by agitators opposed to the establishment, was normally controlled by its richest members just as thoroughly as the National Assembly was. And, thirdly, the Council's guiding spirits, the tribunes of the people who possessed the power of vetoing the actions of all Roman magistrates, were cleverly won over by the other side. This happened by gradual stages. First—the dates are uncertain—they were allowed to sit in the Senate and listen to debates. Next, they received the right to put motions to the Senate. And finally, and this had happened before the end of the century, they were even authorized to convene the Senate and preside over its sessions. None of this was unacceptable to the tribunes themselves, for they were often men who wanted to pursue official careers. This they were finally in a position to do, now that Rome possessed a dominant nobility composed of plebeians as well as patricians.

If things had gone the other way, and the tribunes of the people had continued to develop their formal powers of obstruction, the whole machinery of government might well have been paralyzed—and that, at least, was a result that their transformation from protesters into henchmen of the government prevented. Yet, from the standpoint of the oppressed plebeians, this development signified that the struggle between the orders, though won in a formal sense, had in other and more important respects been lost. It proved harder for the poor, henceforward, to find champions, for the new sort of progovernment tribunes placed their vetoes at the disposal of the Senate instead—and the Senate was glad to use them for its own purposes, not only in order to keep their fellow plebeians down, but also to prevent ambitious state officials from getting out of hand.

By ancient and modern standards alike, the Roman class struggle had been impressively peaceable. True, it had not been quite as "reasonably" conducted as patriotic ancient historians later maintained; the threats of secession, for example, were open blackmail. Nevertheless, the struggle had at least been carried on for all these long years with a minimum of physical violence and through due process of law. Its termination has been called by some the high-water mark of the republic's political achievement. Yet, instead, it has been found disappointing by revolutionary or liberal historians, who look for continuous social progress and do not find it here. However, its absence is hardly surprising given the highly conservative character of the Roman people—patricians and plebeians alike—whose whole society depended fundamentally upon *clientela,* and ancestral tradition, and the habit of obedience to authority, group, and community. Besides, this system, patched together by what may seem to us a peculiar and unsatisfactory series of compromises, at least passed the pragmatic test because it worked. Indeed, it continued to work, with relatively little change, for at least as long as any politico-social system has ever worked in the history of the Western world. And in the process, despite all its manifest faults, this system enabled Rome to face its mortal enemies with an imposingly united front such as few modern states could display today.

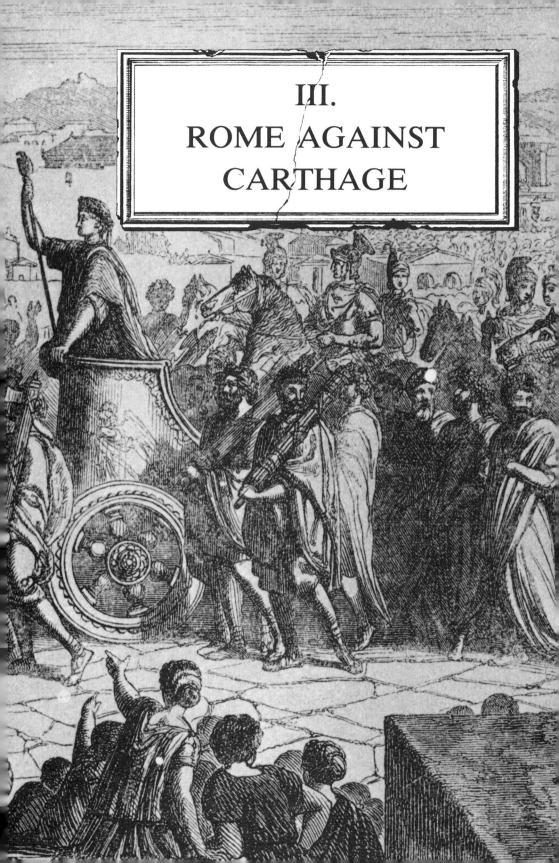

III.
ROME AGAINST CARTHAGE

5

First Wars against Foreign Powers

The Invasion of Pyrrhus

The Greek cities, which so abundantly filled southern Italy and Sicily that they were described as Magna Graecia, did not have much to do with the Romans before 300 B.C. But the end of the Samnite wars brought the territory of Rome's subject allies far down towards the south, within easy range of some of these Greek towns. The most important of them on the mainland was Taras, the Roman Tarentum, now Taranto on the gulf of that name. Tarentum lay astride an isthmus, between a shallow protected bay and a tidal lagoon, and possessed an almost impregnable citadel. Larger than Rome in the early third century B.C., the city based its great prosperity on the wool from its winterland, dyed with purple from the murex mussels in the city's harbor. From this port, the safest and most spacious on any Italian coast, the dyed wool was profitably exported to Greece and elsewhere, and so was grain, another product of the Tarentines' considerable and fertile inland possessions. They were governed by a democracy that, although somewhat aggressive, displayed relative stability by Greek standards. They possessed the largest fleet in Italy and an army of fifteen thousand men, but since their expansionist tendencies were not matched by military talent, they often supplemented this force by hiring mercenaries. The duty of these was to protect the frontiers of Tarentum from its Lucanian neighbors (related to the Samnites) by keeping them in a state of semidependence.

The Tarentines had an old agreement with Rome, according to which the latter undertook not to send ships into their gulf which they regarded as their own sphere of influence. Nevertheless, an eventual confrontation looked inevitable after Rome in 291 B.C., during the last days of the Samnite wars, founded a Latin colony of exceptionally large dimensions at Venusia (Venosa), near the far end of defeated Samnium. Surrounded on three sides by deep ravines, and dominating the most considerable river of southern

Italy from its lofty ridge, Venusia was primarily designed by the Romans to split off the Samnites from their Lucanian neighbors. But it was also fewer than ninety miles from Tarentum, whose ruling democratic party regarded its establishment as a strong provocation; Rome seemed to be deliberately setting itself against the freedom of the Tarentines to extend their possessions in southern Italy any further.

This growing tension came to a head in 282 when the Greek city of Thurii (Terranova di Sibari), on the southern side of the Tarentum gulf, was attacked by Lucanian raiders and appealed to the Romans; and they, after hesitation, responded and duly sent a fleet to place a garrison in Thurii. Tarentum regarded this as a clear breach of the agreement not to send ships into its gulf, but the Romans considered that this agreement had become obsolete through lapse of time. Such were the misunderstandings, often genuine enough, that continually accompanied Rome's half-conscious imperial advances from this time onwards.

The Tarentines sank the Roman fleet, killing its admiral; and they drove the offending garrison out of Thurii, jeering at the bad Greek spoken by Rome's envoys. They also applied for help, as was their custom, to a Greek military adventurer, in this case King Pyrrhus of Epirus just across the Adriatic. Pyrrhus, who claimed descent from Alexander the Great, was one of the foremost of the minor rulers and rent-an-army generals who had proliferated since Alexander's death half a century earlier. Accepting the invitation from Tarentum, he proclaimed that he would put an end to the Roman power threatening the liberty of the western Greeks. Then he set sail for south Italy, taking with him twenty-five thousand mercenaries, the most highly esteemed professional soldiers of their day, many of them veterans of extensive military experience. And so the Romans had to prepare for the first battles they had ever fought against a Greek army and a Greek state.

The basis of Pyrrhus's force was a phalanx of twenty thousand men. In battle, lined up in depth, they displayed a front that bristled with the heads of their long lances, as impenetrable as a barbed wire entanglement; and their task was to hold the Roman army while their cavalry on the wings turned its rear or flank. Pyrrhus also brought with him a contingent of twenty, frightening, Indian war-elephants, which he used not frontally like tanks as was the custom, but laterally, so that they could join the horsemen in attacking the enemy's flanks.

His first battle against the Romans was fought at Heraclea (Policoro), a coastal colony of Tarentum lying to its west. The legions stood up well to Pyrrhus's phalanx, which proved somewhat unwieldy. But his elephants routed the Roman horses—which could never have faced these animals untrained—and then charged the flank of the legionaries, putting them to flight, though at a heavy cost of Epirote as well as Roman lives. Thereupon, joined by Samnites and Lucanians, the king marched right on up into Latium; but in the disappointing absence of further defections to his cause, he soon decided to fall back again. In the next year, with a larger force, he won another of his costly victories, known henceforward as "Pyrrhic," in a battle near Ausculum (Ascoli Satriano) in northern Apulia. The Romans resisted his phalanx for a whole day, but on the following day, with the help of his elephants, he forced them back, though they avoided total disaster by regaining their fortified camp. At this point, Pyrrhus made an offer of peace, demanding little more than freedom for Tarentum and its allies. But at the instigation of the aged Appius Claudius the Blind, the proposal was turned down, for he saw a great future for the Romans in southern Italy. And he also believed that they should never treat with an enemy while he was still faring reasonably well.

Next, in autumn 278, Pyrrhus moved on to Sicily; probably he had always intended to do this, seeing the island as a base for further Mediterranean conquests. Once again, he scored military successes—and once again they were without any definitive result. So, three years later, he returned once again to the Italian mainland. There he engaged a Roman army at Beneventum (Benevento) in western Apulia, formerly a Samnite town. But the result of the battle went against him, or was at best inconclusive and damaging, because the Romans had by now discovered that elephants, if wounded by javelins, got out of control and could be made to trample their own soldiers. After this engagement, Pyrrhus's force had been reduced to only one-third of its original size. In order, therefore, to avoid being caught between two Roman armies, he felt obliged to draw back to Tarentum. And from there, before long, he evacuated Italy altogether and returned to Greece, where he was killed two years later at Argos by a tile thrown down from a housetop by a woman.

Pyrrhus was a clever tactician but lacked persistence and long-term concentration, embarking on too many mutually inconsistent projects and oscillating between excessive hopefulness and gloom. Moreover, although in south Italy and Sicily the Romans were fighting farther from their homeland than he was, his excellent Greek professional army was no match for the combined military resources of their astutely unified and abundantly populated allies and colonies. The outcome of the war had effectively demonstrated that the Greek states of south Italy could no longer stand against Rome; and in 272 the Tarentines accepted the alliance that was proposed to them. The Romans were becoming conscious of their imperial responsibilities; it was probably in this decade that some south Italian mint, so far unidentified, produced the first silver coinage to be issued in their name, followed in about 269 by issues minted at the capital itself.

Heavy bronze *as* (I = the unit) of Rome, 269-266 B.C. Helmeted heads of Roma (above, right).

And so, within four generations after the lowest point in Rome's fortunes, the whole of peninsular Italy down to the southernmost regions had come under their control. Moreover, this victory won by the republic in its first war against a Greek army had been noted in the wider Greek lands of the east, where Pyrrhus's defeat was rightly seen by perceptive observers as a portent of things to come. For the first time Rome was recognized, among these nations, as a powerful military state; and one of the great successor kingdoms of Alexander, Egypt of the Ptolemies, now proceeded to establish diplomatic relations with its government, by a treaty negotiated in 273.

Carthage

Rome's war with Pyrrhus had also brought it into much closer contact than ever before with the largest western Mediterranean power, Carthage in north Africa, in the country that is now Tunisia. And from now onwards the problems threatening the peaceful coexistence of the two powers rapidly multiplied.

During the later eighth century B.C., when most Mediterranean trading was in the hands of the Semitic Phoenicians living on the coastland of Lebanon, one of their leading cities, Tyre, founded an offshoot on these shores far to its west, calling it the "New City" of Carthage (Kart-Hadasht). Probably the proximity of purple beds contributed to the selection of the site. But it was also well chosen, like other foundations of the Phoenicians, so as to safeguard vital points along their western maritime lifelines. In this chain, Carthage was of exceptional importance because of its position at the narrow waist of the Mediterranean. Situated on a peninsula in the recesses of the Gulf of Tunis, it was well protected from the interior by steep hills; and among its several beaches a long, narrow bay behind a small headland provided a spacious and sheltered port, later amplified by two artificial harbors, half a mile from the citadel hill.

For three-quarters of a century Carthage was simply a colony of Tyre, but from then onwards, apart from nominal and decreasing ties, it became an independent republic. By the early third century B.C. its population was three times that of Rome. Its inhabitants, allowed a share of the city's commercial profits, were content to remain sluggishly nonpolitical, while the government owed its stability and strength (much admired by the

Greeks) to the small, tenacious, cautious, money-making ruling class which —despite keen internal jealousies—exercised control like the directorate of a big commercial company. These rulers were served by a navy and an army largely composed of Africans and mercenaries, since it was considered advisable to exempt the Carthaginians themselves from military service, so as to leave them free to conduct their trading. Under this regime, by 650 B.C., Carthage had taken over and greatly enlarged the old Phoenician trading posts and settlements all around the western Mediterranean. And they created many new posts too, selecting, like their predecessors, carefully spaced-out anchorages on offshore islands or promontories or river estuaries with suitable sheltered beaches.

Above all, like their fellow Phoenicians before them, these Carthaginian seafarers urgently wanted metals. Now the country best able to provide these was Spain. But to sail due westwards in that direction without any intermediate stopping places would have incurred all the hazards of an unwelcoming north African coast and a hostile current, so they needed bases upon the islands on the way. A particularly vital link in this chain was western Sicily, where Carthage assumed leadership of the already existing Phoenician colonists, establishing its main base at Panormus (Palermo), which commanded a superb harbor and fertile hinterland. Greek attempts to dislodge the settlers were unsuccessful, and henceforward for three hundred years it remained the firm policy of the Carthaginians to retain this Sicilian foothold. In Sardinia, too, they inherited and developed at least four ports, confirming their power in the region by a naval victory over their Greek rivals off Corsica (ca. 535). The possession of all these island bases also enabled them, for a time, to keep the Greeks away from Spain, their principal objective, where Carthage was consequently able to take over and develop important Phoenician settlements at Malaca (Málaga) on the Mediterranean and even on the Atlantic coast at Gades (Cádiz), which had easy access to the southern Spanish mines.

Moreover, the Carthaginians' strong points in Sardinia gave them access to a second important source of metals also, namely, Etruria. In their victorious naval battle against the Greeks off Corsica, they had been allies of the Etruscans, and they even had a share in two of the ports of Etruscan Caere. At one of them, Pyrgi, bilingual Etruscan and Phoenician inscriptions have been found. The other was called Punicum—the Latin for "Carthaginian".

And meanwhile they were extremely active in Africa as well. Among their leadership, there was a traditional difference of opinion about the relative merits of maritime and continental ventures, and at different times both policies resulted in large extensions of their influence in Africa. By sea, the west coast of the continent was explored as far down as Sierra Leone.

And the land empire established by Carthage in north Africa was larger than that of any previous Mediterranean state, only Egypt excepted. Despite the deserts adjoining its territory, Tunisia has large alluvial pockets rich in natural phosphates and highly productive of wheat, vines, olives, and fruit, all of which the Carthaginians cultivated with unprecedented skills, recorded in famous agricultural handbooks. By the fifth century B.C., they had taken over and developed the entire twenty thousand square miles of this plain—thus enabling Carthage to push westwards into Algeria and Morocco and open up a land route into the interior of Africa.

The First Punic War

It was only a matter of time before this empire came into conflict with the new Mediterranean power of the Romans. Carthage was only one hundred and thirty miles across the strait from Sicily, and its settlements at the harbor of Etruscan Caere were barely thirty miles distant from Rome; moreover, at that city itself there is also likely evidence for early trading by the Carthaginians. Indeed, they were believed, perhaps correctly, to have signed an agreement with the Romans at about the time of the foundation of the Roman Republic; it seems to have confirmed Carthage's monopoly of the western Mediterranean, but to have guaranteed Italian coast towns against its attacks. Another treaty is datable to 348 B.C. and it was renewed in 279, this time because the Carthaginians shared Rome's hostility to Pyrrhus.

Once he had left Italy, however, relations between the two powers sharply deteriorated. The breaking point came when the local ruling group at Messana (Messina), situated on the straits separating Sicily from the Italian peninsula, invited the Carthaginians to occupy their city and help them suppress the internal and external opponents of their regime; and the invitation was accepted. But this upset the Greek cities of south Italy that had now become allies or dependents of Rome, since they saw Carthaginian domination of the narrows as a menace to their own safety and prosperity.

Silver shekel of Carthage. Early third century B.C.

When, therefore, the men in charge of Messana changed their minds and appealed to Rome instead, and the south Italian cities added their own urgent persuasion, the Roman government accepted the challenge (264); the Senate had been hesitant but was overruled by the Assembly, which wanted plunder. So war became inevitable. Its ostensible aim was to decide the future of Messana; the huge ramifications of the hostilities that this was going to involve could not be foreseen.

For this First Punic War, which side was to blame? Surely both. Rome had pushed its territories forward to a point where supposed threats directed against themselves or against their allies by this neighboring great power could all too easily be made into a pretext for a clash; while at Carthage, too, there was a powerful element that would stop at nothing to secure more trade. Had its leaders in 279 received an informal Roman assurance of a free hand in Sicily? Perhaps they had, and perhaps this was what had prompted Carthage to intervene at Messana. But in any case it and Rome were so divergent in culture, so mutually uncomprehending, that differences were almost impossible to bridge over by diplomatic methods.

So, Rome as well as Carthage having responded to Messana's appeal, the Romans successfully transported two legions across the strait to occupy the Sicilian city, and the Carthaginian admiral who had failed to stop them was crucified by his own government. But the focal point of this initial phase of the First Punic War was the Greek city-state of Syracuse, on the east Sicilian coast. The most populous city in the Greek world, Syracuse stood on the side of a deep bay; the bay was partly closed by its island-citadel, which was joined to the rest of the city by a mole and dominated the entrances to active ports on either side. The Syracusans were the leaders of a flourishing mercantile society and issued a particularly spectacular silver coinage to serve their commercial operations.

It was for protection against the king of Syracuse, Hiero II, that Messana had initially appealed to the Carthaginians, and it was in order to thwart his expansion that they had accepted the appeal. It is therefore surprising to find that Hiero, at the outset of the First Punic War, entered into an alliance with Carthage against Rome. For, even apart from what had happened at Messana, this was a strange decision for a Sicilian Greek and a Syracusan, brought up to regard Carthage as the enemy. Yet Hiero must have believed Rome to represent, ultimately, an even greater peril than the traditional Carthaginian foe. However, driven back by a strong Roman military offensive, he almost immediately went into reverse and sought for peace with the Romans after all. They responded prudently, requiring an indemnity and perhaps tribute, but conceding him a fifteen-year alliance and the control of thirty miles of territory. He remained Rome's loyal ally until his death forty-eight years later, and a new institution had come into being: the foreign "client" kingdom, beyond the frontiers of the Roman state, but its dependent—an extension of the custom according to which, in the Roman community, individual clients depended on their individual patrons.

In spite of further victories in the following year, the Romans rapidly came to the conclusion that the limited war they had originally launched would settle nothing and that a satisfactory peace could be achieved only by driving the Carthaginians out of Sicily altogether. Yet this could not be done unless they had a navy—which they did not possess and never had possessed on any substantial scale. So they now proceeded to construct a fleet from virtually nothing, built of the timber that Italy provided in far greater quantities than Carthage. This enterprising decision to challenge the naval supremacy of the Carthaginians, who had been sending ships as far as Sierra Leone before the unseamanlike Romans knew anything about nautical matters at all, was the most extraordinary feature of the war. It lasted for no fewer than twenty-three years, and for the greater part of this time the Romans were maintaining a fleet of more than two hundred warships.

In 260 B.C. they began by constructing a flotilla one hundred and forty strong. The ships they built, modeled on one they had captured from the Carthaginians, were massive quinqueremes; this was the standard type of war vessel of contemporary Greek states, carrying marines and a crew of three hundred sailors, divided into groups of five to an oar, of whom only one or two had to be skilled. In order to frustrate the superior naval dexterity of the enemy by making the sea fights as much like land battles as possible, the Romans equipped their craft with "ravens" *(corvi)*. These were boarding bridges or gangways tied to the mast with a rope and hinged, or more probably slotted, so that they could be released and let drop on the enemy's decks. Fixed underneath the *corvus* was a heavy iron spike or beak which crashed through the planks of the Carthaginian ship, thus holding it fast for boarding by the marines.

Equipped with these instruments the Roman fleet embarked on the second phase of the war, which witnessed the largest naval engagements that the Greco-Roman world had ever seen or would ever see again. The first of these clashes was at Mylae (Milazzo) off the northeast coast of Sicily. The ravens worked well, and fifty enemy ships were destroyed (260); but the Romans did not yet possess the nautical knowledge to follow up their success. Then, four years later, off Cape Ecnomus in southern Sicily (near Licata), they won the most grimly contested naval battle ever fought in ancient times in western waters. After the warships in the Roman center had moved forward and become perilously enveloped, those on the wings managed to extricate them by determined grappling and boarding, and the enemy was very badly mauled.

This victory inaugurated the third phase of the war, for it threw the north African shores wide open to the Romans. Their general, Regulus, made an unopposed landing and advanced to within a single day's march of Carthage itself. Then, seeing that the Carthaginians were harassed by a rebellion in the interior, he seized the opportunity to offer them peace. But his terms were so stringent that the fighting continued: and the Carthaginians now made good use of a Spartan mercenary leader, Xanthippus. In spring 255, the two armies clashed in the Bagradas (Medjerda) valley. There Regulus's force, punctured by the enemy's elephants and encircled by their cavalry, was annihilated, and he himself was taken prisoner. A Roman fleet came to retrieve the situation and won a preliminary victory, but was unable to rescue him; and on the way home, it was wrecked by a storm and lost more than two hundred and fifty ships.

After these disasters the attempt to invade north Africa was abandoned, and the war entered its fourth and last phase, in which the Romans, with one new fleet after another, renewed their attempts to gain victory in Sicily. This new period began well for them with the capture of Panormus, which confined the Carthaginians to the western tip of the island. Nevertheless, hostilities dragged on for another thirteen years—to a large extent because of the Romans' further enormous, exhausting losses from storms, due to the inexperience of their admirals. Eventually however, with the aid of a forced loan from its richest citizens, Rome raised yet another fleet; but this time the ships were lighter quinqueremes, without the *corvi* which had proved perilously top-heavy. The Romans were nearly exhausted, and this was the very last fleet they could ever have afforded to raise; but it proved successful. With its help, they completed the investment of the main surviving Carthaginian strongholds in western Sicily, and then they won an easy, total naval victory near the offshore Aegates (Egadi) Islands. Thereupon Carthage was forced to accept peace (241); and soon afterwards, fittingly enough, the unit of the Roman bronze coinage began to display a ship's prow as its design.

The Greek historian Polybius called this prolonged war the fiercest and bloodiest struggle that had ever been fought; both sides had lost appalling numbers of men and ships. Although the Romans could call on the services of sailors and shipbuilders from Greek south Italy and Etruria, in every branch of expertise and tactics, especially engineering, the Carthaginians were still superior. And yet they had lost. They had lost partly because of the grave initial failure of their commanders to prevent the Romans from crossing into Sicily. It was true that the Roman command system, too, was faulty because the consuls were very often incompetent to manage a fleet, and besides, one of them was recalled home every year to preside at the annual elections and was accustomed to take his army with him—half the total Roman force. But every Carthaginian general suffered from an even more intractable dilemma: if he was defeated, he might be crucified by his government; and if he won, it suspected his future intentions so deeply that reinforcements often failed to reach him. Besides, that government was deeply divided within itself, with the major landowning group far less interested in the war than in developing the continental territory of Africa. For these reasons, the Carthaginian generals could never deliver the final blow and had to settle for a war of exhaustion. But in that sort of fighting they proved to be at a disadvantage against Rome, since their mercenaries lacked any patriotic incentive to fight; the Roman legions were manned by men who belonged to a political system that had been welded into an effective unity.

Defeated Carthage was not yet removed from the face of the earth. But it was forbidden to send ships into Italian waters ever again and was compelled to pay a large indemnity over the next ten years. And, above all, it was obliged to evacuate Sicily altogether. The Romans felt that they must take it over in order to forestall an eventual return of the Carthaginians, which would have threatened Italy once more. And Rome was eager to lay hands on the abundant Sicilian grain. So with the exception of Hiero II's state of Syracuse and a few other cities, which remained officially independent as client allies, the Romans now proceeded to annex the whole of the island. In order to recoup their war losses and cover the expenses of the administration, they borrowed Hiero's efficient and famous tax system in order to levy direct taxation or tribute in the form of tithes (a tenth part of the crop). Even though most of Sicily was now part of their own territory, they decided that its people, being foreigners unfamiliar with Roman ways —and only mediocre soldiers—should commute the military service required of other subjects and allies by paying tax instead.

This annexation of Sicily was a fateful step, for it brought the Romans outside Italy, of which the island was not in ancient times a part, and gave them their first overseas province. An entirely new and lasting stage in Roman history had begun—the epoch of imperialism outside the mother country. It was appropriate enough that some forty years later a Latin poet named Naevius, who came from near Capua, chose this war among all others as the theme of his epic glorifying the power of Rome.

Yet it was unfortunate for the Romans that their first province had belonged to Carthage. In annexing this island, Rome also took over the Carthaginian mercantile idea that such possessions were intended to be a source of profit, of which the provincial governor could take his share. In 227, it was decided that this official should be an additional praetor appointed each year for the purpose. But, as the term *provincia* (sphere of military command) indicates, the Romans evolved no specific theory of provincial administration, merely prolonging wartime conditions in amended form and providing the governor with only a very small staff. Indeed they did not envisage the province as a unit at all. Instead, it remained a group of city-states that enjoyed various different relations with the Romans, but in general, although paying them direct taxation were themselves permitted to levy indirect taxes from their own subjects. In addition, the Sicilian province, like other provinces after it, included a fair amount of public land confiscated by the Roman state, which then very often leased it out to the cities or their inhabitants.

The loss of Sicily, then, was the gravest of the damages imposed on the Carthaginians after their defeat. Yet such losses, though enormous, were still less serious than new disasters in which they found themselves involved in the very next year after the First Punic War had come to an end. At this juncture twenty thousand of their mercenary troops who had been brought back to north Africa broke into violent mutiny because their pay was in arrears. Then this polyglot mass of warriors, from more than half a dozen different peoples, proceeded to declare themselves an independent state, issuing a wide range of separatist coins; and they marched inland upon Carthage itself. Moreover, at the very same time, the subject races of the African hinterland likewise seized the chance to take up arms against their oppressors. It was not until after more than three years of this Mercenary ("Truceless") War, comprising the most savage fighting and most inhuman atrocities ever recorded, that the mercenaries were finally annihilated.

Now, during these convulsions, the Romans, who had so recently been the enemy of Carthage but were now bound to it by an agreement, came readily to its assistance; they regarded the mercenaries in Africa as an

Base silver double shekel of the Libyan rebels against Carthage in the Truceless War, 241-238 B.C. Head of Zeus; bull.

international danger threatening to unleash general anarchy. But when immediately afterwards in Sardinia the fellow soldiers of these rebels broke into revolt against the Carthaginians and appealed to Rome (238), it became clear that the attitude of the Roman government had radically changed. It now proceeded to send troops to the island's southwestern coast to help the dissidents—and to seize control of the Carthaginian fortresses. Carthage could do nothing, and the Romans went on to annex Sardinia and Corsica, just as they had annexed Sicily earlier, adding insult by demanding a further indemnity.

Whatever explanations were offered at the time, this forcible annexation of Sardinia and Corsica was the act of a nervous bully and showed that the famous Roman "good faith" was nonexistent, or at least was regarded as inapplicable to non-Italians. Nor was the annexation justified on economic grounds, since, although use was made of Sardinia's grain, little was done to develop its important mineral resources for a long time to come. Rome was acting out of pure opportunism, seizing the chance to guard against a possible resurgence of warlike feeling at Carthage—a shortsighted measure since in fact their aggressive action did everything possible to revive such emotions among its Carthaginian victims. The two islands were made into a second, single Roman province, whose people paid a tithe like the Sicilians' and a new praetorship was created (227), once again, to supply the province with annually appointed governors. The only comfort for Carthage, a small one, was that although the people of Sardinia, who were of mixed non-Italian stock, were greatly despised by the Romans, it took the Roman authorities well over a century to pacify the mountainous interior of this newly acquired territory.

6
The Changing Roman World

An Age of Innovations

In a bid for popularity, designed to keep up morale at the outset of the First Punic War, the government of Rome had introduced an institution of horrifying brutality that retained an enormous following throughout the whole of the subsequent history of the city: the gladiatorial combat—a national sport and a psychological safety valve. It is possible that duels of this kind were an invention of the Etruscans, who had employed them in the first instance as religious ceremonies involving the sacrifice of war prisoners to the spirits of their own fallen warriors; and then they kept the contests on for amusement, recording them on grave urns of the third century B.C.

Earlier, however, than any Etruscan artistic representations of such fights are Samnite wall paintings depicting them, which date from not long after 400. It may well, therefore, have been from Samnium rather than Etruria that Rome learned to stage these entertainments; indeed, for a long time the Romans themselves regarded "gladiator" and "Samnite" as synonymous terms. But, if so, there were probably intermediaries in this borrowing, namely the Samnite settlements in Campania, in whose chief city Capua (long renowned for its leadership in this grisly activity) appeared early paintings of armed, helmeted gladiators scarred by wounds and dripping with blood.

In any event, in 264 B.C. similar fights were first seen at Rome. At a funeral in the Cattle Market in that year, two sons of the dead man exhibited three simultaneous gladiatorial combats—a figure that was to rise, within the next half century, to twenty-two such contests staged on a single occasion. The ferocious cruelty of these sports betrays the existence of a powerful streak of sadism in the ancient Roman and Italian character.

But if the First Punic War was the occasion for this sanguinary innovation, it also witnessed, paradoxically enough, many novel humanizing influences derived from the Greek world. The ties linking Rome to that world went back hundreds of years, but they had remained somewhat tenuous, and the Romans had remained more or less immune to the profounder effects of Greece. The war, however, provided many new contacts with south Italy and Sicily and brought from those parts a considerable number of Greeks, who contributed an influx of Greek culture.

For example, Greek works of art were shown at Triumphs in 272 and 264. And then Livius Andronicus, a Greek or half-Greek who had come as a prisoner of war from the principal Greek city of south Italy, Tarentum, opened up altogether new ground. He seems not only to have become the first, or one of the first, teachers of Greek literature at Rome, but also, though little of what he wrote has survived, to have virtually invented Roman poetry as well. Adjusting the clanking Latin tongue to Greek verse forms, he wrote tragic dramas based on classical Athenian models; and one of them was performed, by a remarkable innovation, at the Victory Games of 240 B.C. He also wrote an adaptation of Homer's *Odyssey* into Latin, which, although his style was by later standards somewhat craggy, evidently displayed considerable skill. With Livius, two thousand years of Latin literature had vigorously begun—and it had begun on a characteristic note, combining Greek influence and inspiration with the very different Latin language and the Roman, Italian ethos that it reflected. In other words, the Greek world had created the climate in which those who wrote Latin found themselves able to develop their own unquestionable originality.

Advances in Roman Law

The period of the First Punic War also produced two landmarks in the evolution of Roman law. The first started from what seemed an insignificant happening. In 253 B.C. the chief priest *(pontifex maximus)* Titus Coruncanius—the first plebeian to hold that office—commenced the practice of admitting his students to his legal consultations; and perhaps he admitted members of the general public as well. This step carried further forward the reform of fifty-one years earlier by which the publication of the forms of judicial procedure had broken the monopoly of such knowledge previously enjoyed by the college of priests. This disclosure had created a new need to interpret the law, and now, therefore, Coruncanius began the training of the first men who would serve as Roman lay jurists *(iurisprudentes)*.

These personages, whose long line was thus inaugurated, did not usually practice as advocates (this was left to professional orators), but were advisers, teachers, writers, and public figures. They exercised their legal influence at every point, counselling praetors and other officials and judges, assisting individual citizens in a wide variety of matters, and giving answers *(responsa prudentium)* on questions of law submitted for their attention. The best of them responded to these queries with a combination of steadying legality and liberal equity—a Roman blend that appeared also in the court decisions that bore their mark. In these secular lawcourts it became established over the years that legal rules could not be laid down merely by the arbitrary act of the public officials who presided over them—men not likely to be learned in the law. So the jurists sat in on the trials and judgments and made their own vital contribution. In court and out of it, they had to ask themselves what was implied in the ordinary informal acts and happenings of everyday life, and what the normal effect of these happenings would be; and on these conclusions they ruled. The gradual public recognition of their rulings as valid and efficacious was one of the lasting triumphs of Roman civilization.

Since they were not advocates, the detachment of these lawyers from the practical results of any lawsuit raised their pronouncements above mere partisan biases. True, working from customs, precedents, and experience as they did, this famous objectivity, like that of other, non-Roman legal personages before and after them, was sometimes limited, whether they realized it or not, by the feelings, attitudes, and aims of the oligarchy to which they belonged. This is why so much of Roman law is concerned with maintaining the rules of private property. Nevertheless, it was these jurists who directly or indirectly built a huge part of the imposing structure of Roman law. Their interpretations, revisions, and enlargements of the Twelve Tables and other statutes and praetors' edicts, and their legal formulations of many customs that had never been formulated before, advanced Rome's previous legislative creations at innumerable points. And so the jurists became the central figures of Roman law for many successive generations, during which time they did much to create the way of life that the Western world has followed ever since.

Other far-reaching legal developments originated from a further event of the First Punic War: namely, the establishment in 242 B.C. of a second praetorship at Rome to supplement the much older city praetorship established in 366 B.C.* This new official was the *praetor peregrinus* (ca. 242). It was his task to deal with legal cases in which at least one of the contestants was a non-Roman *(peregrinus)*, that is to say, either a foreigner or a

---

*The praetors appointed to govern Sicily, and then Sardinia–Corsica, added a third and fourth to the total number.

subject of Rome who did not possess Roman citizenship—a category that would soon display continuous increases in size, corresponding with each successive overseas annexation.

The concept behind this new peregrine praetorship had never found legal expression before, because hitherto Roman law, as formulated in the Twelve Tables and other legislative pronouncements, had all been civil law *(ius civile)*, and as such had dealt exclusively with the relations between one Roman citizen *(civis)* and another. Foreigners were, strictly speaking, without rights. The new post of the *praetor peregrinus*, therefore, represented a major enlargement of this previously nonecumenical Roman viewpoint, extending it, in due course, to wider issues of many kinds—the sort of issues, inevitably, in which the constructive, equitable methods of the rising lay jurists were relevant and helpful. So the law that the peregrine praetor administered might be described as civil law with its more formal parts omitted; stress was laid on its universal implications rather than narrowly national aspects.

The creation of this new office also contributed largely to the evolution of one of the most potent and effective ideas that the Romans ever originated. This was the "law of nations" *(ius gentium)*, the history of which,

Bronze statuette of Etruscan peasant ploughing (the figure of Minerva is a subsequent addition), sixth century B.C.

involving various changes of meaning, has extended right up into our own times. In the period when the term first began to be formulated, during the later third and second centuries B.C., it defined those portions of the Roman law that were open to citizens and noncitizens alike: that is to say, those branches with which the new peregrine praetor was concerned. Both his office and the concept of the *ius gentium* that it helped to develop evolved out of the growth of commercial, social, and political relations between Rome and other states.

Legal ideas of this sort were not altogether new to the world. Other ancient nations also, although they likewise had originally thought in terms of a law applicable only to their citizens, had evolved rough-and-ready codes for the benefit of their traders; and besides, from early times onward, specific treaties between one Greek city-state and another had sought to guarantee the mutual protection that these commercial interests required. And then Rome, too, although not directly copying Greek influences, had proceeded along somewhat similar lines when it granted its subject allies a sort of half citizenship that conferred trading and matrimonial rights. But now, in addition, as the peregrine praetorship continually extended its scope, many questions of marriage, status, and succession, and points relating to contracts for sale and hire and work and services, gradually received legal definition in relation to noncitizens even if they possessed no such special allied rights at all.

Later jurists attributed the obligatory force of this application to "the law of nations." In employing this concept, they were making the large assumption that it rested on some corpus of legal principles that was universally acceptable. In consequence, as more time passed, *ius gentium* came to be elevated into a philosophical ideal of "natural law" interpreted as a set of precepts valid everywhere in the world. Later still, the ramifications of the term became even more immense since it was held to signify the various rules governing relations between states—rules which are now grouped together under public international law.

This *ius gentium* was stimulated and rendered inevitable by the peregrine praetorship; and then it was further developed by provincial governors. It demonstrated that a body of law could be established upon a foundation acceptable to the members of different peoples and races at any and every phase of social, economic, and political evolution; and so it brought the laws of the Romans nearer to universal applicability than any others that have ever been devised, and it uniquely displayed their genius for social organization. Above all, *ius gentium* was redolent of common sense, which is, indeed, characteristic of Roman law as a whole. Its exponents, like English lawyers later on, were often reluctant to specify the principles that guided them. Yet a Roman jurist was boldly prepared to offer generalizations, not

Bust of Gallic warrior. Third century B.C.

indeed for their own sake, but in order to solve each specific set of problems that had to be confronted, thus striking the shrewdest balance between theory and practice and having the best of both. Moreover, the great majority of these generalizations have never, in all the intervening centuries, been discredited or discarded—and in most cases not even reformulated, since they had been set out by the Romans, from the first, in carefully thought-out language of a clarity and sharpness that could not be improved upon. Roman law was much superior, in precision and substance alike, to the legal systems of the Greeks, in spite of their rich jurisprudence.

Nevertheless, law is one thing and litigation is another, and even the Romans found that perfect fairness in regard to the latter was hard to come by. Despite the impressive laws and concepts the ancient Roman lawcourts *(iudicia publica)* were called on to put into effect, it would be unrealistic to see their processes in too rosy a light. They were still, in the second century B.C., more or less improvised, being formed as the occasion arose. Besides, these courts, like the people who worked for them, consciously or unconsciously served the ruling class; furthermore, there was no real professional tradition of impartial justice and no organized police to enforce it, any more than could be found in any later Western country until well after 1800. Roman litigants also experienced many vexatious delays, though even the twentieth century A.D. still has its share of these. And the limits of free speech and free political action would have seemed to us excessively narrow. Nevertheless a great proportion of Rome's available intellectual power and subtlety, throughout the whole millennium of antiquity, was poured into the development of its law, and since then it has continued to have a history lasting for two further millennia. Moreover, in the course of that prolonged period, it has often seemed that the whole principle of order as a bulwark against chaos, indeed the very survival of civilization itself, depended upon the maintenance of the legal structure the Romans left behind them.

The Challenge of Flaminius

In the last chapter it was pointed out that the Roman class struggle had ended in formal victories for the plebeians, but that these ostensible successes were, in practical fact, converted into a victory for the nobility instead—not indeed the ancient patrician class, but the new nobility of those men, patricians and plebeians alike, who belonged to families that could boast at least one consulship at some time in the past. In this new order, the plebeian Council *(Concilium plebis),* which had now gained full validity for its decisions, played an effective and essential part. Yet the poor possessed very little say in those decisions since they were formulated by nobles —and besides, the Council's membership, like that of the National Assembly *(Comitia centuriata),* was dominated by the middle class of substantial peasants.

This middle class included many men who, like the poor, were clients of dominant noble patrons. Other members of this same intermediate category, however, were sufficiently independent to stand up, from time to time, for the underprivileged. Thus, on one notable occasion in the 230s they directly challenged the wishes of the nobility in the interests of those who were impoverished and landless. The clash originated from an event that had taken place half a century earlier, in 283 B.C.: Rome's annexation from the Gauls of the Ager Gallicus, the Adriatic coastal district south of the Po. Yet this territory, together with the area that lay north of the river,* had never been made part of Italy. Apart from the foundation of a Roman and a Latin colony, Rome had made extremely little use of its lands, initially because there had been no demand for them. Yet later the situation had

---

*Cispadane and Transpadane Gaul respectively, the joint components of Cisalpine Gaul.

Statuette of Gaul found near Rome.

changed, because the First Punic War produced ex-soldiers who had seen their farms gone to ruin while they were away on active service and who therefore demanded to be given new land to replace what they had lost. As a result, during the difficult decade that followed the conclusion of the Carthaginian war, there was intense popular pressure for the breakup of the Ager Gallicus into small, individual allotments.

The agitation was led by a tribune of the people, Gaius Flaminius, a "new man" outside the patrician-plebeian nobility. But the senators, who held valuable leaseholds in this region, objected to any such distributions; where-upon Flaminius, with the aid of other "new" gentry whose public careers he agreed to assist, carried the proposal through the plebeian Council over the heads of the protesting Senate. This high-handed action was believed to be without precedent in recorded Roman history; Flaminius had disclosed the secret that policy could, against all tradition, be made outside the Senate. What he had done was censured by later conservative historians since it set the precedent, a century later, for a whole mass of other agrarian measures. Indeed, during that future period there were no fewer than forty such proposals, which in some cases were much more revolutionary in character than Flaminius's bill and were blamed for the downfall of the republic. More radical writers, on the other hand, believed he had struck a valuable blow against oppression.

However at this juncture a new generation of Gauls was threatening to avenge their defeat of half a century earlier, which had led to the loss of those Adriatic lands. In consequence, Flaminius's proposed distribution of the Ager Gallicus was denounced by his Roman opponents as a gratuitous act of provocation against the Gauls because it introduced substantial

Roman cultivation (centuriation) around Lugo near Ravenna. The large divisions measure about 800 yards square.

Roman manpower into this delicate border area. In 225, therefore, a coalition of Gallic tribes sought to remedy this situation by violent means, launching an army of seventy thousand with powerful cavalry and war chariots, in an attack that penetrated deep into the peninsula. But at Telamon (Talamone), halfway down the Etruscan coast, this force, while retreating in order to store its plunder in safety, was hemmed in between two Roman armies; and in the subsequent engagement the Gauls, fighting back to back, were almost annihilated. Never again did an army of their people cross the Apennines, though the Romans never forgot the first terrible onslaughts of these naked warriors, with their flashing gold necklaces and bracelets.

Flaminius did not hold a command at the time of the victory, but he succeeded, in spite of his nonnoble background, in winning a consulship in 223. And after that, he marched north—regardless of a senatorial order to come back to Rome—and led the first army ever to cross the Po, the precursor of later expeditions that would eventually transform this area into a populous and flourishing part of the Italy from which it had so long been excluded.

7

The Invasion by Hannibal

Carthaginians in Spain

I t was not the Gauls, however, who offered the gravest menace to Italy in the 220s B.C., but once again the Carthaginians. This time the threat came from the armies they maintained in Spain. Their dominant position in that peninsula was a new phenomenon, or rather the revival of an old one, for Carthage had earlier possessed a Spanish coastal empire. During the middle years of the third century B.C., when it lost the First Punic War and was expelled from Sicily and Sardinia and Corsica, it had also, under pressure from Greek Massilia (Marseille) which competed for the western Mediterranean ports, been deprived of almost the whole of its former Spanish dominions until finally little more than Gades (Cádiz) and the Straits of Gibraltar remained in its hands. But after putting an end to the ferocious mercenary revolt, the Carthaginians achieved a startling revival and, employing their subject lands in Algeria and Morocco as stepping stones, soon proceeded to build up a Spanish empire all over again. The agents of this recovery were the most able family Carthage ever produced, the house of the Barcids. In spite of determined political opponents, they had gained an impressive position at home, and now they settled themselves for several decades in Spain, establishing a hereditary line of semi-independent governors.

The first of the family to set himself up there was Hamilcar Barca, who had played a distinguished part in the First Punic War, when he earned substantial credit for the resistance that postponed his side's defeat. Next, when the war was over, and when he had again fulfilled a leading role in the suppression of the rebellious mercenaries, he was authorized by his government in 237 B.C. to proceed to Spanish waters; his task was to recapture territories and resources in compensation for the loss of Sicily and the other islands. His successes in Spain were impressive. Starting from Gades, he reconquered most of the southern and eastern regions of the

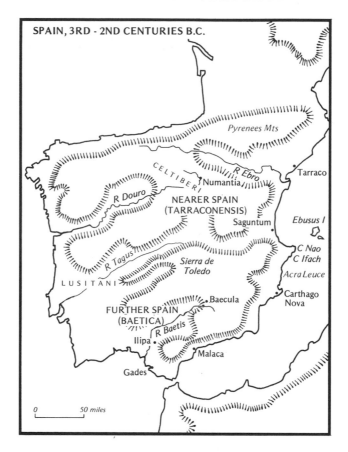

SPAIN, 3RD - 2ND CENTURIES B.C.

Pyrenees Mts

CELTIBERI

R Ebro

Numantia

Tarraco

R Douro

NEARER SPAIN
(TARRACONENSIS)

Saguntum

Ebusus I

R Tagus

C Nao
C Ifach

LUSITANI

Sierra de
Toledo

Acra Leuce

Baecula

Carthago
Nova

FURTHER SPAIN
(BAETICA)

R Baetis

Ilipa

Malaca

Gades

0   50 miles

country as far north as Cape Ifach and Cape Nao, halfway up the coast;
and near the limits of this occupation, beside lands that recalled the most
fertile territories of north Africa, he established a port and capital at Acra
Leuce, the White Promontory (Alicante). Already the Spanish territories
he had occupied were larger and richer than those the Carthaginians had
ruled before; and the Spaniards, men of mixed Celtic and Iberian stock
famous for their physical endurance, provided him with a new army—the
best Carthage had ever possessed throughout its history. The finely tempered Celtic swords that these soldiers carried were products of the immensely rich mines the conquests included. A share in the revenues from
these mines went to Hamilcar's political enemies at Carthage and induced
them not to obstruct him.

In 229, however, he was drowned. His son-in-law Hasdrubal, who succeeded him, moved his headquarters further south, in order to be near his

Silver double shekel of Spanish mint showing Hamilcar Barca as Melkart-Heracles (237-228 B.C.).

home base. The site he chose, Carthago Nova or New Carthage (Cartagena), stood on a peninsula commanding one of the best harbors in the world; and it was protected from the interior by a lagoon, though a valley provided access to the abundant silver mines its townsmen exploited. Yet although Hasdrubal had selected this more southerly capital, he pushed the frontier of the new Carthaginian Spain a long way to the north, advancing to the banks of the River Iberus (Ebro), halfway up to the Pyrenees. And he also expanded his conquests deep into the interior, arranging a coordinated series of alliances and treaties, such as the Greeks who had settled in the same country had never succeeded in achieving.

Then Hasdrubal was murdered (221) and the command passed to his brother-in-law Hannibal, the son of Hamilcar Barca who had originally brought him out to Spain. Hannibal pushed still further inland as far as the

Silver double shekel of Carthago Nova (Cartagena) showing Hannibal as Melkart-Heracles (221-218 B.C.).

River Douro and beyond the Tagus; and his diplomatic methods earned him considerable popularity among the Spaniards. However, one coastal town south of the Ebro, Saguntum (Sagunto), decided to resist him. With the Romans, on the other hand, this place was more friendly, and indeed, under the direction of an anti-Carthaginian party, it may have formed some sort of alliance with them. At all events, it was to Rome that the Saguntines now appealed—perhaps not for the first time. And Rome, its war party led by the Aemilii and Scipios, took the fateful step of responding favorably. Before long its delegates were on their way to Hannibal at Carthago Nova in order to transmit the Senate's command that he should keep his hands off Saguntum. A peace party at Carthage was in favor of complying, but Hannibal rejected the ultimatum and pressed on with the blockade of Saguntum, which fell to him (219) after a savage eight months' siege. The Romans angrily ordered the Carthaginian government to hand Hannibal over to them—a demand that was predictably turned down. Debate in the Senate about what should be done next was keen and bitter; but finally the Roman envoy told the Carthaginians that their refusal to surrender Hannibal meant war. The curtain was now going up for the most terrible of all Rome's struggles and the most far-reaching in its results—the Second Punic War (218).

Saguntum in Spain, of which the capture by Hannibal in 219 B.C. precipitated the Second Punic War.

The rights and wrongs of the war are hard to determine since much hinges on an obscure treaty that Rome had made with Hasdrubal in 226. According to the Greek historian Polybius, it was agreed, at this meeting, that the Carthaginians were not to cross the River Ebro in arms. This was a point on which Rome must have been eager to insist, in order to calm the apprehensions of Massilia, which was its long-standing ally and an ally of Saguntum as well. This Greek city, as it had shown by its hostility towards the earlier Carthaginian empire in Spain, had long been anxious for the safety of its own trading stations on the east coast; and it still possessed Spanish outposts north of the Ebro. Moreover, there was a second and more direct reason why Rome did not want the Carthaginians to cross the river. This was because of the fear that they might march right up the Pyrenees and across them, traverse the south of France, and move down into Cisalpine Gaul (north Italy), where they could help the Gauls against Rome. And it appears that in 226 Hannibal agreed to the urgent Roman stipulation that he should not march north of the Ebro. But he would never have consented to such a restriction unless the Romans, at the same time, had agreed that they themselves would not interfere south of the river—at Saguntum, for example. There must, therefore, have been a second clause in the Ebro agreement to this effect.

But, if that was so, how did the Romans justify their subsequent breach of the understanding? Probably on the grounds that the treaty of 226 had been negotiated with Hasdrubal himself on a personal basis only and had never been ratified by the Carthaginian government. And that may well have been the case. Nevertheless, the real, underlying motive of the Romans' action, as so often in their subsequent history, was a profound suspicion of the foreigner—in this case, of Hasdrubal's successor Hannibal, whom they suspected of planning a major campaign across the Ebro. As to his own attitude, he must have known that his siege of Saguntum, whether it violated a formal Carthaginian treaty with the Romans or not, involved a serious risk of war against them. The legend, which may be true, was that his father had once made him swear eternal hatred towards the Romans. But, in any case, he evidently felt determined to avenge his country's defeat in the First Punic War, and Rome's perfidious behavior after it had ended. And he believed that the new Spanish empire his family had won, rich in minerals and warriors, gave him his opportunity to carry out these plans of vengeance and reversal.

The Victories of Hannibal

But the Romans, too, were confident in their human resources, and so now they declared war. They intended to send forces to Spain via the land route and Massilia and to send them to the north African homeland of Carthage as well.

However, both these designs were forestalled by Hannibal's audacious decision to invade Italy. This came as a surprise to Rome, which knew he had constructed no fleet. But instead he made for Italy by the difficult land route. He took with him, on the final stage of the march, some forty thousand men, comprising well-trained, Carthaginian-officered Spanish infantry and excellent African (Numidian) cavalry, with thirty-seven elephants. And he confidently hoped to augment this army on arrival in north Italy by winning over anti-Roman Gauls and Rome's Italian subject allies; in this way he would be able to cut off the vast reservoir of Roman-Italian manpower before it could ever be drawn upon.

In April 218 B.C., brushing aside native opposition, he transferred his army across the Rhone, and then in the early autumn he crossed the Alps. The mountains were treacherous going because of premature falls of snow, but Rome's belief that they would stop an army from getting through proved mistaken. Nevertheless, when Hannibal came down into the Po valley, he had only twenty-six thousand men left, and the Senate's generals hoped to wear him down by a series of delaying actions. But they were almost at once defeated in two successive battles, on a northern and then a southern tributary of the Po. First, on the River Ticinus (Ticino), where they tried to engage Hannibal's tired army before it could recover, a skirmish between advance guards displayed his cavalry's superior speed, equipment, and training so clearly that the Romans fell back across the river to the Apennine foothills. There, on a rough, snowy December day their commanders, instead of staying on the higher ground as they should have done, were induced by a feigned Carthaginian flight to order their forty thousand legionaries to wade across the swollen waters of the River Trebia (Trebbia), and attack him. But the morale of the Roman soldiers was low because they had had no breakfast, and in the morning mist an ambush from the reed beds took them by surprise in flank and rear, so that they were overwhelmed and only a quarter of their numbers escaped the subsequent massacre.

And so already, within only two months, Hannibal had overrun the whole of northern Italy, with the isolated exception of two newly founded Latin colonies at Placentia (Piacenza) and Cremona, which stood firm. It was true that he had lost most of his elephants; and the help he received from the local Gauls was not all he had hoped for. Yet as a result of his victories, he was able to increase his force to a total strength of fifty thousand. And now, from his new north Italian base, he believed the time had come to incite Rome's Italian allies to revolt. Meanwhile at Rome itself, the more prosperous among the plebeians, who controlled their own Council and the National Assembly, were infuriated by the bungling that had lost them the north Italian lands they had fought so hard to win; and their appointment of the reformist "new man" Flaminius to a second consulship in 217 was a criticism of the Senate's conduct of the war.

Flaminius tried to block the Carthaginian army's southward advance, but early in the year they evaded him by breaking through an unguarded Apennine pass; and then they pressed on through marshy country, in such rough conditions that Hannibal, riding on the sole surviving elephant, lost the sight of an eye through exposure to the icy cold. However, as he ravaged Etruria and seemed to be making for Rome, he drew Flaminius after him and on a foggy April morning trapped his army in a defile between the hills and Lake Trasimene. Surrounded on all three sides, most of the soldiers of two Roman legions were killed, and Flaminius himself was among the fallen. This victory presented Hannibal with an open, undefended road to Rome itself. However, he did not take the opportunity. This was partly because the total destruction of Roman power might not have been in his own country's interests, for it would only have introduced rival powers from the eastern Mediterranean to fill the vacuum. But in any case, he lacked good siege equipment; and in its absence, the walls of Rome could not be breached by any attacker, especially without a supply base nearby. And no such base existed because, to Hannibal's acute disappointment, not

View of Lake Trasimene, where the Romans were disastrously defeated by Hannibal in 217 B.C.

one single town of central Italy defected to his side. Rome's system of colonies and allies stood this searching test with admirable firmness.

So Hannibal swerved aside from the city and instead decided to seek allies in the southern part of the peninsula, which, for the most part, was non-Italian and un-Romanized. As he marched through Campania and Apulia, relying on their grainlands for food and on their ports for contact with Carthage, his army was shadowed by a veteran Roman general, Fabius Maximus, now dictator. Fabius's reappointment had been arranged, with the concurrence of the Senate, by the unusual procedure of election in the Assembly, since one of the consuls who should have nominated him was dead and the other was cut off from the city. Fabius was a Roman of the old and canny type, and the strategy he now put into effect avoided risking his hastily recruited new armies in any further pitched battles—a policy that earned him the nickname of Cunctator (Delayer)—while instead he cut off the enemy's supplies by devastating the surrounding countryside. But this policy of caution and destruction was understandably hated by many Romans and Italians and lost him the popular support that had brought him to power.

In the following year, therefore, the generalship was removed from him and bestowed on two inexperienced consuls, who were entrusted with the largest army Rome had ever put into the field; they were placed in joint command of the force as consuls had never been before, since it had hitherto been the custom for each to command his own separate army. In a supreme effort to end the war at a single blow, they accepted battle on a smooth open plain near Cannae, a small fortress near Italy's heel. Hannibal had provoked them to this by seizing the place, which contained a valuable depot of stores; and then he chose an open plain for the battle to show the Romans they had nothing to fear from reserves. Believing that their numerical superiority would tell, they attacked, and Hannibal allowed his convex crescent or échelon to become concave under the pressure of their center. But the prevailing hot sirocco wind blew blinding clouds of sand into the faces of the Romans, and they found themselves caught in a pincer movement by the enemy's light troops on either flank and cavalry in the rear. Wedged tight in these hopeless conditions, the Roman army, after savage resistance, was almost wholly destroyed. This battle, the bloodiest defeat Rome ever suffered, provided an unprecedented example of a smaller force successfully enveloping a larger one on both sides, a tactic that required perfect coordination and was admired by the German general von Schlieffen and studied in the First World War in 1914.

One of the consuls was killed in action, but the other, although a nominee of the Assembly and consequently blamed for everything by later conservative historians, received a courteous reception at Rome from his fellow senators who thanked him for not despairing of the republic—for in the city, despite this catastrophe, morale remained indomitable. Indeed, even before the end of the very same year, under a government now unquestioningly left in the hands of the Senate, Rome's terrible losses were already more than made good by further recruitment, so that Hannibal's victory had failed to repair his numerical disadvantage. Moreover, in order to avert further disastrous pitched battles, Fabius's strategy was seen to have been good after all, and was revived; the Roman armies were divided into a number of small forces distributed at vital points, like a pack of dogs circling around a lion. Yet Cannae had led, at last, to some of the defections Rome had feared—not, indeed, among its subject allies in the center of the peninsula, but in the geographically remoter and culturally more alien areas of south Italy and Sicily, where the vitally important cities of Capua, Syracuse, and Tarentum all successively went over to the invader (216–213). These desertions, and above all the defection of Capua, gave Hannibal sorely needed men, weapons, bases, and supplies. Nevertheless, by a series of mighty sieges, conducted by double cordons of troops supplied with the most scientific equipment, all the rebellious towns were gradually won back again, Capua and Syracuse in 211, and Tarentum in 209.

In 213 or 212, despite all these troubles, Rome emphasized its status as a major power by issuing for the first time, on a large scale, its historic silver coin the *denarius* which provided a much improved means of meeting the state's financial needs. Nor was it of any avail, in 211, for Hannibal to advance to the outskirts of Rome itself. Accompanied by an escort of cavalry, he rode slowly around the walls on his black horse, watched by the inhabitants on the walls. At that very moment, as it happened, the site of his camp, three miles away, came up for auction in the city—and was duly sold at a normal price. Nothing could have shown him more clearly that the Romans, in spite of all the disasters they had suffered at his hands, were still determined to survive and win.

The Scipios in Spain

Because of the remarkable dramas of Hannibal's Italian invasion, the Second Punic War is often looked at as a war fought primarily on Italian soil, with a secondary sphere of operations in Spain. But the Spanish campaigns fought during the same years were a deciding factor in the outcome of the war. Although the Romans had failed to keep Hannibal from crossing the Pyrenees and marching on Italy, they nevertheless succeeded in preventing his younger brother Hasdrubal Barca, whom he had left behind to rule Carthage's Spanish empire, from sending him any reinforcements. This they did by making the fateful decision to fight an active war in Spain itself, despite all the crises that they were undergoing in their homeland.

Rome's Spanish armies were commanded, for the first seven years of the war, by two men named Scipio, the father and uncle of the great Scipio Africanus. In spite of initial offensives by Hasdrubal Barca, the Scipios gained a number of successes that enabled them to gain control of the Mediterranean seaboard of the country, moving gradually southwards along its coast until in 211 they captured Saguntum, the original bone of contention, which they then made preparations to use as a base for further advances. Because of these setbacks Hasdrubal Barca failed on several occasions in attempts to break out across the Pyrenees. Moreover, successive drafts of recruits, who would have been very useful to Hannibal's Italian campaigns, had to be diverted from north Africa to his brother's Spanish army instead. Yet the diversion of these troops, which gave such an invaluable breathing space to the hard-pressed Romans in Italy, caused the downfall of the Scipios in Spain, for in 211 both the brothers were successively defeated and died in battle.

The Carthaginians were now able to take back the regions they had lost south of the Ebro. Yet they did not cross the river. After their losses of Capua and Syracuse in the same year, they did not feel confident enough to tackle the defenses, somewhat feeble though they were, that the Roman survivors of the Scipios' defeats had erected along its banks. Moreover, as soon became clear, Rome had by no means finished with Spain. In 210 the Assembly, at last reemerging from the timidity imposed by its earlier failures against Hannibal, induced the Senate to acquiesce in the appointment of a new and surprising general to command the Spanish armies. This was Publius Cornelius Scipio (later Africanus), son and nephew of the commanders who had perished in Spain the year before. Publius Scipio was only twenty-five. He had therefore held none of the senior offices regarded as necessary prerequisites for such an appointment. Yet he was not untried in war, and his exploits had inspired the conviction that he was the right man for the job.

Once in Spain, he reverted to the attacking strategy of his father and uncle. He chose as his target the enemy headquarters and arsenal at Carthago Nova. While assaulting the town from the land side, he profited by a squall, which had blown up and lowered the level of the lagoon, to send his troops through the shallow waters and scale the fortifications that were undefended on this side—and by this means the whole of Carthago Nova fell into his hands (209). In the following year, he marched into the interior of the country and engaged Hasdrubal Barca's smaller army at Baecula (Bailén) on the upper Baetis (Guadalquivir). Compelled to fight quickly because he feared the arrival of enemy reinforcements, Scipio divided up his

Bronze coin of Carthago Nova showing head of Scipio
Africanus after he captured the city in 209 B.C. Horse
and palm tree (Carthaginian types).

main force and, using his light troops as a screen, fell on the enemy's flanks.
This striking demonstration of a novel flexibility in Roman tactics, which
showed how carefully Scipio had studied Hannibal's Italian victories, won
him the battle.

Yet Hasdrubal Barca escaped and at last got out of Spain altogether,
taking an unexpected land route around the western extremity of the Pyrenees and proceeding onwards to Italy, with the intention of joining his
brother Hannibal there. His escape transformed the battle of Baecula from
a tactical victory into a strategic defeat. And Scipio did not try to pursue
him. Probably his orders from Rome did not allow him to; but even if they
did, he was right not to make the attempt—since, if he had done so, he
would have exposed himself in difficult country too far from his base and
would thus have risked losing Spain altogether; and besides, he would never
have caught Hasdrubal Barca in any case. As it was, the departure of
Hasdrubal Barca's army insured final Roman success in the Spanish campaign. This was scaled by a huge battle in 206 against his successors, fought
at Ilipa (Alcala del Rio, near Seville). Here Scipio introduced a sophisticated variation into his outflanking tactics by reversing the usual battle
order and moving his light auxiliaries from the flanks to the center of his
line. This meant that the men now located on the flanks were his best troops,
the legionaries; it was they who now found themselves entrusted with the
encirclement of the enemy force, and they carried out their task triumphantly. This time, the victory was conclusive. Many native princes abandoned their alliances with Carthage. And by the end of the year, it had lost
its Spanish possessions forever.

And so these most valuable portions of the Iberian peninsula had fallen
into the hands of Rome, which annexed them and converted them into two
new provinces: the eastern coastal strip of Nearer Spain, and beyond it,
Further Spain (Baetica) comprising the southern coast and the valley of the
Baetis (Guadalquivir). Eight years later, the Roman government appointed

Denarius of Osca (Huesca) in Spain, minted from local
silver for the payment of tribute. Second century B.C.

two new praetors to administer these territories. A five percent tribute was
imposed on grain, resembling the taxes earlier instituted in Sicily. But
otherwise, the pattern was different, for it seemed practicable in this more
warlike country to add the duty of military service, so that the country's
manpower resources could provide auxiliary units to supplement the legions. Moreover, the Romans developed and expanded Carthaginian mining in the country, which was rightly said to overflow with metals; at
Carthago Nova alone, the capital of the Nearer Province, the silver mines
subsequently employed as many as forty thousand workers at one time. And
so a fixed sum in silver was levied on the population in addition to the
tribute.

In 206 Scipio established a new town named Italica (Santiponce, near
Seville), where his veterans were given grants of land. Although Italica was
not granted colonial status, the foundation of such an Italian-style community overseas established a novel and far-reaching precedent. The purpose
of the place was to serve as a fortress against the tribesmen who dwelt in
the hinterland, for in this fierce country the Romans still had an immense
military task ahead—which took them two hundred years to complete. So
it is doubtful if even the large revenue they soon found themselves able to
collect sufficed to pay for the costs of occupation. Yet at least the Carthaginians had been expelled from this enormously important and strategic
territory.

The Triumph of Scipio Africanus

Nevertheless, the events that had led to their expulsion seemed, at first,
to bring them certain compensating advantages, for the removal of Hasdrubal Barca's army from Spain was Hannibal's gain in Italy. And it came at
a very appropriate time. For in spite of their successes in south Italy, the
Romans were almost at the end of their resources. In 209, twelve Latin
colonies out of the existing thirty had declared their inability to supply any
more troops, or the money to pay for them. They had been bled white and

could fight no more. Moreover, Etruscan cities, too, were beginning to be disaffected. And now the arrival of Hasdrubal, fulfilling hopes that Carthage had been cherishing for eleven years, caused alarm throughout Italy. After crossing southern France and the Alps unopposed, he descended into the Po valley, where new Gaulish recruits raised his numbers to thirty thousand. Then the two Carthaginian brothers moved towards one another, intending to join forces.

Meanwhile the Romans, after mobilizing massively yet again, and in spite of their exhaustion, had an army in the north of Italy and an army in the south. At this juncture they benefited from a great stroke of luck: captured dispatch riders of Hasdrubal revealed to them that his meeting place with Hannibal was to be in Umbrian territory. On receiving this news, the southern Roman commander Gaius Claudius Nero, leaving a force to watch Hannibal, undertook a rapid six-day, two-hundred-and-forty-mile march up the Adriatic coast to the Umbrian river Metaurus (Metauro). On the following morning Hasdrubal heard a double bugle call from the camp of the Romans, which told him that their two armies had united. This meant that he was outnumbered by at least ten thousand men. In a desperate attempt to slip through and join forces with his brother, he moved up the Metaurus valley after nightfall. But he lost his way in the dark and was overtaken among the gorges and slippery crags, and died fighting—and almost all his men died with him.

For the first time during the entire long period of the war, the Romans had won a pitched battle in their homeland, and the end of Hannibal's occupation of Italy was now only a matter of time. He learned what had happened when his brother's head was hurled into his camp. Then he withdrew into the mountains of Italy's toe and stayed there, without emerging, for another four years.

Bronze coin perhaps of Arretium (Arezzo) in Etruria, planning rebellion against Rome in 209/208 B.C. (or to herald arrival of Hasdrubal), with pro-Carthaginian type of elephant.

When two of these years had passed (205), Scipio, fresh from his Spanish victories, was elected consul and asked the Senate for permission to invade Africa and attack Carthage directly. The senators were very reluctant, since they still felt apprehensive of Hannibal's continued presence in Italy and were anxious not to impose further burdens on the allied towns. But when Scipio appealed over their heads to the Assembly, promising vengeance on the Carthaginians for all the sufferings they had inflicted, the Senate gave way, somewhat grudgingly. That is to say, it agreed that, whereas Sicily was to be his province, he could also sail to Africa if the interests of the state required it, with two legions in addition to whatever volunteers he could collect. He recruited seven thousand of them, thus bringing his total army up to thirty thousand, and with this force landed in north Africa some twenty miles from Carthage (204). There he was joined by a neighboring prince Masinissa, ruler of part of Numidia (eastern Algeria), who had changed sides along with his excellent cavalry.

In the next year Hannibal returned from Italy, his fifteen-year-long invasion at an end. His early victories in Italy had temporarily silenced his political opponents at home. After the loss of Capua, however, they had begun to be much more vociferous. And now, finally, Carthage had begun negotiations for peace with the Romans and the discussions had reached an advanced stage. Nevertheless, Hannibal was still able to persuade his government to break these talks off. Thereupon Scipio moved inland to sever the enemy capital from its agricultural supplies, and in 202, near Zama, seventy-five miles from the city, the final battle of the war was fought. It was not a real climax because the eventual outcome of the campaign could be in no doubt. But it achieved great fame owing to the caliber of the rival commanders—and before the engagement, the two men had a famous meeting about which nothing is known, except that it was unproductive.

When the battle began, neither side succeeded in outflanking the other, for both were by now thoroughly familiar with tactics of this kind. But the issue was decided by the horsemen of Rome's new Numidian allies, who broke off their pursuit of the enemy's cavalry wings and fell on their rear, achieving total victory. There were few Carthaginian survivors, but Hannibal was one of them. He recommended to his government that peace should be made immediately, and this was done. The terms were less favorable than they would have been in the previous year if negotiations had not been suspended. The indemnity to be paid by the Carthaginians was doubled; their fleet was limited to ten ships instead of twenty; and Masinissa, who became king of all Numidia, was rewarded with part of their western borderlands. And finally, they were forbidden, henceforward, to engage in any war without the prior consent of Rome.

They had already lost Spain, and now they had ceased to be a major power and would never become one again. So the Romans had victoriously completed the most decisive single phase of their rise to domination. The Second Punic War had made it certain that they would remain in control of the entire western Mediterranean region for many hundreds of years to come. For the West, therefore, with the possible exception of the struggles of the twentieth century A.D., the Second Punic War proved to have been the most momentous war of all time.

But victory had only been won by feats of unprecedented endurance. In spite of initial disastrous defeats, the Italian dominion built up with such patience by Rome had, on the whole, resisted the temptation to defect, fully justifying the Roman system. Even in the gravest peril Roman and Italian morale and discipline had stood firm, leaving memories of this supreme test which later writers were never tired of recalling. The solid virtues of many Romans and Italians, working together as loyal, obedient partners within a tradition built up over many generations, had prevailed and won the day.

They won partly, as the historian Polybius says, because no comparable cooperation was to be found among the enemy's mercenaries, who were exploited by their bosses much worse than the Romans exploited the Italians and in consequence lacked the same incentives to loyalty. And another reason why the Romans and Italian soldiers won was because there were more of them. Moreover, their numbers were greatly increased because the property qualification formerly required before a man could become a legionary had been reduced, so that much poorer men could now be called up at public cost. These "proletarians," as they were called (from *proles,* "offspring," since children had hitherto been the only contribution they were able to make to the state), were recruited between the ages of eighteen and forty-six and served in the legions for an average of seven years, so that the old city militia was turning into something like a professional army.

The men who had officered this new army gave close, hard attention to technical innovations in soldiering, of which Scipio Africanus was the principal author, first in Spain and then in north Africa. His achievements show the careful attention he paid to the tactics that Hannibal had displayed in Italy, and how he even improved on them. He also drilled his army in tactical methods, based on Rome's experience of small-unit hill fighting during the Samnite wars. The knack was to allow the three lines of the maniple (of which there were thirty in a legion) to act more or less on their own. Yet there were occasions when the independent action of these three lines, or even of the maniple itself, risked excessive dispersion, and so Scipio also experimented in Spain with a unit combining three maniples, the cohort, which provided greater cohesion but at the same time still allowed greater flexibility than the larger legion itself. There were improvements in the construction of the throwing javelin. But the legionaries were also armed with the heavy, excellently made, Spanish cutting swords, which became their most important weapon.

The career of Scipio, on whose initiative all this was done, revealed that the times when all Roman leaders were almost anonymous, brief-tenured representatives of a team had begun to come to an end. Scipio was a new phenomenon. It was symbolical that he was the first of Rome's generals to be known by the name of the country he had defeated—Africanus. He was also the first to enjoy so long and close a relationship with his army, during the unprecedented ten years when he held high command at the Assembly's wish. His final triumph raised him to the most powerful position any Roman general had ever possessed, pointing manifestly, as later historians noted, to the eventual emergence of other commanders who would use such powers to become autocrats. But Scipio himself did not do so; probably he never thought of doing so, for the time had not come for such thoughts.

Yet already there was something special and distinctive about him. He was a man and a general of rare imagination and initiative—which he employed in the skillful management of men. Sympathetic to the growing influx of Greek culture, he was not afraid to show an un-Roman love of splendor and display, which was deplored by senatorial opinion but pleased ordinary people; on the coins of captured Carthago Nova his own portrait seems to appear, which was something that had never happened to a Roman before, though individual portrait busts in bronze and marble began to come into their own in this century. And Scipio appears to have possessed that mystical assurance of a direct, personal line to the gods which is always so formidable and infuriating a feature in a statesman or soldier. Such convictions made Scipio impatient of petty Roman restraints. Yet at the same time, he also had a keener sense of humor than most Romans. And in a war scarred by many atrocities, he was unusually kind to his defeated enemies. He was an unfamiliar sort of Roman, replacing traditional prudence by a novel individualism, a spirit of adventure.

The enemy Hannibal was a greater general even than his father Hamilcar, and greater even than Scipio, indeed one of the outstanding commanders of all time. That he placed beyond doubt, first, by his initial successes in Italy and the brilliant methods he used to win them, and then by the almost incredibly daring feat of maintaining himself in that hostile, populous country, so far from his home base, for no less than fifteen years. During this period there was ample detailed evidence of his almost unique excellence as a planner and fighter of battles. Employing the Greek device of joint enveloping movements by infantry and cavalry, and adding the Spanish tactics of ambush and lightning attack, he set the stamp of his own personal genius on both these inheritances. And, above all, he was a leader of men so inspired that, throughout all those foreign years, he never experienced a mutiny. This was astonishing since, as we have seen, his multiracial, polyglot armies had little reason to feel allegiance to Carthage—they followed him for himself alone.

It is only as a strategist in the larger sense that the impertinence of hindsight makes it possible to criticize Hannibal. Lack of siege equipment was what caused his ultimate failure; and, even if he could not take this to Italy in the first place, it is hard to see why he could not somehow have secured it afterwards. Moreover, since he needed reinforcements from abroad so acutely and the land route from Spain remained blocked to him for so many years, it seems surprising that he did not challenge Roman naval supremacy by building a fleet—for, after all, the Carthaginian tradition was essentially maritime. But perhaps he was merely realistic in assuming that rivalry with the Romans at sea was out of the question. And maybe, also, he could not persuade his government to construct a fleet for him or underwrite him if he constructed one himself.

In the large sphere where military and political activities merge, this was one of the things that went wrong for him—he did not receive enough backing from the authorities at Carthage. Worst of all, they could not, or did not, send him sufficient reinforcements. It is possible that he miscalculated by supposing that they ever would. And he had made another miscalculation as well. Although his insight into the psychology of the Romans was often keen enough, he proved mistaken in his belief that, after he had won battles, their allies and subjects would defect to him *en masse*. This may have been a deliberate gamble; and so may have been the assumption that such defections, when they occurred, would in the end persuade his government to give him fuller support. But if so, neither gamble came off.

Twenty-nine years old when he came to Italy, Hannibal was a wiry, athletic man, trained to run and box and endure hardship, possessed of an iron self-restraint. He was fanatical and superstitious like most of his countrymen. Yet all the same, not only his talent, but also the integrity of his personal character, caught the fancy of subsequent ages, despite virulent Roman propaganda to the contrary. His final confrontation with Scipio in battle preceded, it was said, by that mysterious meeting, could not fail to stir people's imaginations forevermore. Yet for most of the war it was not only Scipio he had been fighting against but also the corporate strength and endurance of all Rome and its allies. He is one of the world's most noble failures, an altogether exceptional man who took on, in deadly warfare, a nation empowered with rocklike resolution—and that nation proved too much for him. It emerged hardened from the supreme test, and ironically, his most lasting achievement was to confirm and magnify its confidence and power.

IV.
THE IMPERIAL
REPUBLIC

Preceding page:
Two 15th Century Paintings of Scipio Africanus
the Elder. Left: Scipio Africanus and his Accusers;
Right: Scipio Africanus in Retirement at Liternum,
visited by Pirates.

8
"Our Sea"

The Eclipse of the Greek Kingdoms

The happenings of the third century B.C. had brought Rome into forcible contact not only with the Carthaginians but with the Greeks in southern Italy and Sicily. Moreover the same period had inaugurated its relationships with the Greeks of Greece itself, with repercussions upon the whole future history of the Mediterranean, which within a remarkably short time became a Roman lake.

When Alexander the Great (d. 323 B.C.), king of the Macedonians, conquered gigantic territories far to the east, the ancient city-states of the Greek homeland—already brought under Macedonian suzerainty by his father— had still retained their formal independent status but had for the most part faded into relative insignificance. Instead, the important Greek political units of the "Hellenistic" age now beginning were three great monarchies carved out of Alexander's dominions after his death. The rulers of these were: Antigonids in Macedonia; the Seleucids, whose dominions extended from the Aegean to the Hindu Kush; and the Ptolemies, who reigned over Egypt and the lands and seas around it. Upon the peripheries of these vast kingdoms, however, there were other much smaller units. It was with these that Rome first came into collision—and first of all, with the states that were its nearest neighbors.

One of these was Epirus (northwestern Greece), whose king Pyrrhus had unsuccessfully invaded Sicily and south Italy in 280–275 B.C. The next trans-Adriatic state that the Romans encountered was the monarchy of the half-Hellenized Illyrians, who controlled the coast of what is now Dalmatia (Yugoslavia) and expanded southwards into Albania in about 260 B.C. The Illyrians must have been alarmed by Rome's establishment in 246 of a Latin fortress-colony just across the strait at Brundisium (Brindisi), located on two arms of the sea penetrating deeply into the land, and possessing the finest harbor on the east coast of Italy. This was during the First Punic War,

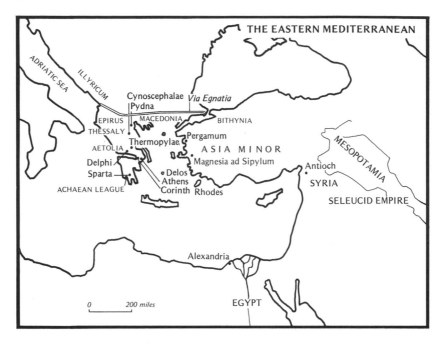

THE EASTERN MEDITERRANEAN

and the principal intention of the Romans was to close the Adriatic to Carthaginian shipping. But the new foundation was likely to restrict the Illyrians as well; and sixteen years later, when Rome demanded satisfaction for their assaults on its envoys and assassinations of Italian merchants, their queen, regent Teuta, a determined and practical ruler, rejected the request.

So the Romans sent troops and ships to bring her to order. This attack, their first direct dealing with a state across the Adriatic, put a stop to Teuta's plans for further expansion and established a Roman protectorate over Greek towns and tribes on the east side of the strait, which had been grateful for this intervention. Then in 220–219 a Greek adventurer in the area, Demetrius of Pharos, tried to exploit, for his own advantage, the Romans' preoccupation with the coming Second Punic War. But he was expelled by their forces and had to flee from his country. Significantly for the future—for others, too, were often to make the same mistake—Demetrius had believed himself to be a free agent, whereas the Romans saw him as their client, on the analogy of the patron-client relationship that played such a large part in Roman society.

Demetrius fled to the king of Macedonia, Philip V, who received him (219). So now Rome, at the outset of Hannibal's invasion of Italy, was directly involved with one of the three major Greek powers, the nearest to Italy. And Macedonia still possessed many of the resources that had led it to Alexander the Great's astonishing victories only a little more than a century earlier. Its territories and dependencies abounded in minerals, timber, grain, and wine. Its peoples, too, were fierce and warlike and could put a large army into the field—even if not as large as the potential strength of the Romans. Besides, Philip V, though impetuous in his political judgments and capable of wanton atrocities, was a successful commander of troops who had raised his country to its greatest power since the time of Alexander, so that he was once again exercising control, directly or indirectly, over most of the southern regions of the Balkan peninsula.

Naturally enough, he regarded the expansion of the Romans, just across the narrows, with the gravest distrust, and these suspicions were confirmed by the experiences of Demetrius that had obliged him to take refuge at the Macedonian court. And then Philip decided that the Romans' crushing defeat by Carthage at Cannae had given him the opportunity to check them; so he concluded a treaty of mutual assistance with Hannibal (215). In fact neither of the two new allies gave any useful help to the other, Hannibal because he was without a fleet and Philip because his fleet could not stand up against Rome's. Moreover, Roman warships now proceeded to appear in the Adriatic and landed men in Greece to foment desultory local hostilities against Macedonian allies and outposts. In 205, therefore, when the victory of the Romans in the Second Punic War was already a foregone conclusion, Philip decided he had better make peace with them for the time being after all. This disillusioned his Greek supporters, without, however, as was soon clear, closing his account with Rome. For one thing, the Romans provoked him by taking over some of the allies who had become estranged from him, notably the Aetolian confederacy in central Greece. This was one of the leagues of city-states that had grown up in recent years as attempted counterpoises to the power of one or another of the large Greek kingdoms, in the present case its neighbor and natural enemy Macedonia; and by now the Aetolians were the dominant power in central Greece. This was the first formal alliance the Romans had ever entered into on Greek soil. It did not last for long, it is true, but long enough to give them a permanent footing in the country.

The worst problem of the three Greek empires, the Antigonids, Seleucids, and Ptolemies, was the debilitating strife and tension that so frequently bedeviled their mutual relations. Philip, still deeply distrustful of the Romans, clearly perceived the perils of these inter-Greek tensions and therefore concluded a secret treaty with his Seleucid fellow ruler. Despite its lack of tight organization the enormous Seleucid monarchy, which had introduced numerous Greek settlers into its Syrian capital Antioch and other cities, was potentially the most formidable of the three great states. More-over, its current ruler, Antiochus III, had earned himself the title of "the Great" because of the vast conquests by which he had pushed his frontier northwards and eastwards in a desire to imitate Alexander, a good measure of whose speed and dash in warfare he had inherited.

In 203–202 Philip combined with Antiochus to make a joint attack upon the third major monarchy, Egypt of the Ptolemies, at that time ruled by a boy-king whose overseas dominions the other two kings now began to divide up between themselves. Governed from its capital Alexandria, the greatest commercial port and cultural center in the world, this Ptolemaic kingdom was run by an unparalleled, highly profitable system of centralized state control; and it presented a particularly tempting target to attackers, owing to its abundance of grain, gold, copper, iron, building stones, and marbles and its monopoly of the growth and export of papyrus.

But this sinister alliance between Macedonia and the Seleucids, designed to eliminate the power of Egypt, greatly disturbed the Greek city-states, which were convinced that the next to suffer would be themselves. Particular alarm was felt by the two principal second-class powers of the time, which were Rhodes and Pergamum (Bergam). The island of Rhodes, just off Asia Minor's southwest coast, was an extremely prosperous mercantile republic with a large and efficient trading fleet. The Rhodians habitually steered their own course in foreign affairs and were mainly concerned to preserve the freedom of the seas from aggressors and pirates, while remaining on good terms with everyone else. In this situation, since their island lay so close to the Asian continent from which the great powers could so easily oppress them, they had welcomed the estrangement that normally existed between the Seleucids and Antigonids. They felt correspondingly threatened by Antiochus's alliance with Philip, whom they detested, in any case, because of his brutal enslavements of defeated populations. In consequence, they now turned to Rome and sought to make it share their anxieties. Further persuasion was added by Pergamum, the civilized capital of another very prosperous second-category state, controlling much of western Asia Minor and deriving substantial wealth from its exploitation of natural resources. The royal house of Pergamum, the Attalids, had broken away from the Seleucid empire in the previous century and were justifiably afraid that it would one day try to take them back again. So their current monarch, Attalus I Soter, took the same line as the Rhodians and joined them in urging Rome to force the Macedonians and Seleucids apart. At the same time both Pergamum and Rhodes started military action against Philip. Their motives were understandable, yet the outcome of their appeals to Rome was to be the collapse, only a few decades later, of the entire international Greek system of which they formed so prominent a part.

It seems possible that until it heard the envoys from these states, the Roman Senate was not aware that Philip and Antiochus had entered into an understanding. In any event, the Pergamenes and Rhodians did not find it too hard to convince them that it existed and was undesirable, for if two of the major Greek powers could make friends with one another in order to attack the third, then it seemed that having eliminated it, they might well feel inclined to combine again to attack Rome as well.

This nervous attitude was significant for the future because it remained the characteristic motive of many of Rome's military moves from now onwards. These actions would often look like naked imperialism, and in a sense that is how they could be described. But they were caused by frightened and often mistaken Roman suspicions, directed afresh at one new foreign neighbor after another following each successive expansion of Rome's sphere of action and influence. Or rather, the suspicions were mainly felt by the upper classes, the Senate and nobility, and it was they who were in favor of fighting the war against Philip. The members of the Assembly, on the other hand, exhausted by the recently concluded eighteen-year-long Second Punic War, at first voted solidly against fighting a new foe. But the Senate's warlike policy prevailed, and an ultimatum was delivered to Macedonia.

It must have been a difficult document to frame, especially for the Romans who habitually tried to describe their wars as just, because Philip had done them no direct injury at all. What they demanded, therefore, was that he should indemnify Pergamum and Rhodes; and they insisted also that he should abstain in future from any hostilities against Greek states. This was a startling piece of interference, implying that Macedonia, one of the three great Greek empires, was, like Carthage, no longer entitled to have any foreign policy of its own; in other words, that it was a client of the Romans, taken unilaterally under their supervision. There had been hints of this doctrine before, in their dealings with the Illyrians, but never before had it been applied to a major Greek power.

Philip rejected the demand as an impertinence, and so Rome's first important war on Greek soil was under way (200). It was a historic clash between the only military powers in Europe. The first two years' campaigns in Macedonia and Thessaly brought little substantial progress. But then it became clear that the Roman commander Flamininus, consul at the age of only twenty-nine, intended to eject the Macedonians from their three principal fortresses in Greece and then drive them out of that country altogether, forcing them to retire to their own homeland.

But Philip decided not to await this attack, since he was aware that a war of attrition would show up his numerical inferiority. Instead, therefore, he himself moved to the offensive, and at the ridge of Cynoscephalae (Dog's

Head), now Karadag in eastern Thessaly, forced a battle upon Flamininus. Philip's right wing charged successfully downhill but was then engaged in the rear by the Romans and routed, and the Macedonian cause was lost. In this first direct conflict between two different military traditions, the new flexibility taught by Scipio Africanus had made the legions more than a match for the tightly packed and relatively immobile Greek phalanx. In its defeat, the future of the east Mediterranean world could be read without too much difficulty, although in this particular battle the Romans had had the better of the ground, so that the major issue of military principle might still be regarded by Greek optimists as open.

Nevertheless, the war was over. After his defeat, Philip was not obliterated by the Romans because they felt they might need him as a bastion against the Seleucids. But he had to give up his fleet and his fortresses and accept the total exclusion of Macedonian influence from Greece. Flamininus filled the vacuum by declaring, at the Isthmian Games in the great mercantile city of Corinth, that the Greek cities were henceforward to be free. This famous Act of Liberation, which could be compared with many similar declarations by Greek monarchs in the past, harmonized with the brilliant young general's respect for Greek culture, since like Scipio Africanus whom he claimed to rival, he was that new type of Roman who felt an inclination to phil-Hellenism. But sentiment, insofar as it entered into the matter at all, coincided with interest, since the pronouncement was also based on that peculiarly Roman interpretation, concerning which we have already had other recent hints, of what "freedom," as applied to such communities, really meant. The Greeks might like to interpret it as complete independence of action. But to the Romans, while it prompted their military evacuation of Greece and ensured its local communities the privileges of self-government, the term was only intended, once again, to mean freedom in the sense of the relationship that a "free" client possesses with his patron. This was to be the cause of many misunderstandings. But it was clearly understood in 167 B.C. by King Prusias II of Bithynia, in northern Asia Minor. As he entered the Senate house at Rome, he fell on his face and cried "Greetings, savior gods!"

Meanwhile, however, the Declaration of Freedom roused the Greeks to such excitement that the birds, it was said, were stunned by the shout of jubilation that arose. This joy was not, however, universal, since Rome's former allies, the Aetolian League, felt none of it at all. Alone of the Greeks, they had given substantial assistance to Rome, and yet because of the general liberation they had been allowed to annex only an insignificant amount of territory as a reward. In their disappointment, they turned to Antiochus and invited him to bring a Seleucid army to Greece so as to drive out what they described as the new despotism of the Romans (193).

At this time Antiochus's relations with the Romans were poor, since they had told him firmly to keep out of Europe. This was a repetition of the overbearing tactics they had employed in dealing with Philip, though it may have been softened on this new occasion by the hint or suggestion that, if he complied, they themselves would not set foot in Asia. Nevertheless, Antiochus ignored their demand, crossing over into European soil and seizing the Propontis (Gallipoli) peninsula in Thrace, which he claimed for himself as territory once owned by his ancestors and belonging by right to the Seleucids as the leading power of the east Mediterranean.

What is more, Rome's ancient enemy Hannibal was now at the Seleucid court. After the Second Punic War, he had led Carthage into an impressive revival; but the Carthaginians had become tired of his strong leadership, and Antiochus allowed him to reside in Seleucid territory. This caused deep suspicion among the Romans; and it was carefully fostered and intensified by the king of Pergamum, now Eumenes II, who deliberately poisoned their relationship with Antiochus just as his father, Attalus, had upset their relations with Philip. This time, in dealing with Antiochus, the Roman Senate did not want war. Yet, as negotiations dragged on, in an atmosphere of increasing tension, it was he who finally lost patience, and he decided to accept the Aetolian invitation. Whereupon in March 192, not content with the corner of Europe he had occupied already, he extended his invasion to Greece itself, although by doing so he made it inevitable that the Senate, for all its reluctance, would send armies to resist him. As it turned out, the Aetolian appeal was imprudent and Antiochus's response to it the height of unwisdom, since both provoked the Romans to further expansion. But he probably felt that they must be stopped now or never.

Despite his vast potential reserves of manpower, Antiochus's conduct of the war found him no match for them. Defeated heavily at the historic pass of Thermopylae (191), he was forced to evacuate Greece. Then, in the following year, the Romans defeated him again, this time at sea. It was the last notable naval victory over a foreign enemy they were ever called upon to win; and its immediate result was that they were enabled to land troops in Asia, which they had never done before. And so came Antiochus's final confrontation with the Romans, a land battle at Magnesia (Manisa) in western Asia Minor (190 B.C.). Scipio Africanus's brother was the nominal Roman commander, but Africanus was there, too, as his adviser; he had remained politically powerful and believed strongly that the Greeks should be protected against Antiochus. On the day of the battle, however, Africanus was ill, and the most heroic part was played by Eumenes of Pergamum. It was he who broke the heavily armored Persian horsemen on the left flank of the enormous army of Antiochus; and then the Seleucid elephants, stampeded by javelins, charged backwards through their own central phalanx, and the Romans had won an overwhelming victory.

Rhodes and especially Pergamum were its chief beneficiaries, while the Aetolian confederacy, which had invited and helped the defeated monarch, was forced to accept a treaty involving the loss of its independence. As for Antiochus, he had to pay the largest indemnity ever demanded by the Romans, and they expelled him from Asia Minor altogether. This, therefore, was one of the decisive wars of ancient times because the Seleucid monarchy, though remaining a continental power in the middle east, ceased forever to be a Mediterranean state—leaving the vacuum to be filled by Rome.

Within only a very short time, therefore, the two most powerful Greek kingdoms had been separately engaged and invaded by the Romans, suffering extremely heavy reverses. Nevertheless, the setback experienced nine years earlier by Philip V of Macedonia had not proved fatal or final after all. In the war that had just been concluded he had fought against Antiochus's Aetolian associates as an ally of Rome, which consequently allowed him to maintain and even partially improve his position.

But then in 179 B.C. Philip died and was succeeded by his thirty-five-year-old son Perseus. He renewed his father's treaty with the Romans, whom he had no desire to offend. But, at the same time, he took numerous steps to strengthen Macedonia's influence among all its neighbors. Moreover, at a time when Greece was plunged into an economic emergency, he showed sympathy to its many bankrupts, declaring an amnesty for debtors. This could be magnified by the ill-intentioned into an act designed to promote social revolution and undermine the Roman arrangements in Greece. Foremost among those who spread this hostile view abroad was Eumenes II of Pergamum, who, not content with his earlier criticisms of Antiochus, still

Silver tetradrachm of the Seleucid King Antiochus III "the Great," defeated by the Romans at Magnesia in 190 B.C.

carried on his father's feud against the Macedonians as well. Indeed in 172, he visited Rome in person in order to denounce Perseus before the Senate. His denunciation was successful, and in the following year the Romans drifted once again into war against Macedonia. The feeble pretext was that Perseus had attacked some border chiefs who possessed ties of friendship with Rome. But the real reason was the anxious fear, among its authorities, that he might make a move to disrupt their entire settlement and policy in Greek lands.

As in the previous Macedonian war, the first campaigns were irresolute and inconclusive. Perseus, though vigorous enough in the field, was too indecisive to take his chances, and the Romans, as often, were slow to get going. But by the fourth year of hostilities, the king had finally been obliged to withdraw from his frontier lines, so that the consul Paullus was able to establish himself on the Macedonian plain itself, where he forced the enemy to give battle at Pydna. At first, the assault of Perseus's weighty phalanx of twenty thousand men drove the Roman legionaries back. But, as the phalanx charged, gaps opened in its line and into these gaps small Roman units insinuated themselves, while others simultaneously enveloped the Macedonian flanks, where their slashing swords inflicted catastrophic losses on the opposing spearmen. The inferiority of the phalanx to the legions had now been demonstrated even more conclusively than before; and the Macedonian army had ceased to exist.

Imperialistic Policies

Perseus surrendered and went on show in Paullus's triumph, and his officials were deported wholesale from the country. Moreover, his monar-

Silver tetradrachm of the Macedonian King Perseus, defeated by the Romans at Pydna in 167 B.C.

chy itself was abolished, and the country was divided into four separate republics. This decision, overriding Macedonian nationhood in the roughest and most sweeping fashion, was momentous, for it was the first time that one of the three great successor states of Alexander had succumbed to total destruction at Rome's hands. The recent shift in the relative strength of Romans and Greeks had been displayed with grim directness. Moreover, the new Macedonian republics found themselves bound by an ominous new principle according to which the "freedom" that they still possessed did not necessarily mean immunity from taxes. Nevertheless, the financial conditions imposed on them were not excessively severe, and at least the Romans had still refrained from straightforward annexations. They were not yet willing to apply to the east the provincial system they had inaugurated in western lands. They lacked the administrative machinery needed to impose such a step and dreaded the responsibility it would involve, still preferring for the time being to act as patrons to client states that remained technically free.

Nevertheless, this was an ominous landmark. Within the space of a single generation the Greek world, hitherto dependent on the balance of power among three large empires, had been irremediably transformed and ruined by the utter defeat of two of those states, one of which had been obliterated; and their place was filled by the Romans who had entered the lands surrounding the Aegean and were there to stay. Furthermore, another significant move was to follow. Immediately after Pydna, a Roman envoy ordered Antiochus III's successor, Antiochus IV Epiphanes, who had captured Alexandria, the capital of Ptolemaic Egypt, to evacuate the city, thus displaying that Rome's conception of its intimate interests now extended to this third major successor state of Alexander as well.

Moreover, owing to the irritable suspiciousness of Rome's leaders there were further tough results of the Macedonian war. Eumenes II of Pergamum, though he had at first been in favor of Rome's hostilities against Perseus, was later suspected by its leaders of having secretly engaged in negotiations with him, a charge that was probably without foundation; but the suspicion was there all the same. And Rhodes, too, worried about the effect of the war on its maritime trade, had certainly had the effrontery, as the Romans saw it, to offer its services to both parties as mediator in the hope of restoring peace. After the fighting was over, both Pergamum and Rhodes felt the Senate's displeasure. As for Pergamum, the Romans started to undermine Eumenes's position in favor of his brother, though they did not persist in this. But Rhodes suffered much more disastrously, since Rome proceeded to convert another island, Delos, into a rival free port, whose rapid rise to commercial supremacy almost completely ruined the trade of the Rhodians. Nor were they any longer in a position to police the seas against pirates—to the eventual great discomfort of Rome itself, which had brought about this result.

Such was the treatment handed out to two loyal, longstanding allies which had momentarily ventured to differ from the Romans about policy. Moreover, others who had actively supported Macedonia were penalized even more harshly by Rome, which perpetrated enslavements in Epirus and massacres in the Aetolian League. At the same time its Achaean counterpart in the Peloponnesus, which had likewise incurred Roman displeasure, had to hand over a thousand detainees who were taken to Italy, including the historian Polybius. All in all, during the first half of the second century B.C. and particularly as a result of these depredations, Greece lost a quarter of all its inhabitants.

In the years that followed, the attention of the Romans was largely focused on a country at the other end of the Mediterranean, namely, Spain. This was, however, nothing new. In the very year in which additional praetors were created to govern the two newly annexed provinces (197), revolts had broken out in each of them, to the south and east of the country. The rebels in both cases received assistance from the warlike, well-armed Celtiberians who lived on hilltops in the northeastern hinterland. Two years later the consul Cato, of whom more will be said later, was sent out to assume the supreme command in Spain; and after extensive operations he succeeded in opening up new lines of communications between the two provincial territories. Yet the Celtiberians still remained defiant; and they were joined by the Lusitanians of Portugal and western Spain. Open hostilities continued at frequent intervals until the father of the famous Gracchi pacified the territory of the Celtiberians in 179, by fighting combined (as was unusual at this time) with friendly approaches designed to win the inhabitants' confidence. For the next quarter of a century his settlement held.

But in this "Wild West" of the empire which invited unscrupulous exploitation, Rome's government was heavy-handed, and in 154–153 both major groups of tribes broke out into rebellion once more; and it was exacerbated by a whole series of murderous breaches of faith by Roman governors over the following years. Moreover, before long a particularly grave situation arose because the Lusitanians found a guerilla leader of genius. This man, a shepherd named Viriathus, for the first time mobilized all their tribes into an effective coalition. Next, by the use of small armed bands skilled in making sudden raids and then vanishing, he began to gain repeated victories against the Romans, penetrating their provinces time after time over a period of five years. Yet he failed to achieve the peace terms he wanted, and finally, as a result of two further acts of perfidy by a Roman general, he came to a violent end (140).

In the meantime, however, the Celtiberians had once again joined the insurgents. Their main base was the hill fortress of Numantia, the key to the upper Douro region, at the junction of two rivers running between deeply cut banks through heavily forested valleys. From Numantia the Spaniards withstood Roman attackers for nearly a whole decade. Finally, after a historic eight-month siege, they were starved out by a force of sixty thousand Roman soldiers under the command of Scipio Aemilianus, Africanus's adoptive grandson (133). Eighty-five years of fighting in Spain were finally over, and the frontier was pushed up to the high tablelands of central Spain and the line of the middle Douro. The Romans had always been interested in the country as a recruiting ground for excellent auxiliary soldiers, and now this much larger territory was available for the purpose. But the Spanish campaigns that at long last achieved that end had been mainly notable for two disastrous features. One was the unusual military incapacity displayed by Rome, which gave its leaders cause for anxious thought. The other was the horrifying manner in which their commanders, one after another, had gone back on their sworn agreements with the Spaniards, a procedure that even some of the most xenophobic senators found impossible to condone.

One reason for Viriathus's early triumphs had been his successful exploitation of simultaneous Roman crises in the Balkans and north Africa in the 140s B.C.

After the last war against the Macedonians, the division of the latter's kingdom into four autonomous but obedient republics had successfully ensured that they should be too weak to do Rome any further harm. But it had also made it certain that they would be too weak to protect themselves; and so it turned out. In 150 a certain Andriscus announced, erroneously, that he was the son of the late king Perseus, and then, meeting only feeble resistance from the republican militias, he successfully reunited Macedonia and revived the kingship in his own person. The Romans had to intervene to expel him and run him down (148).

And at this point they set their sights upon a major revision of policy. Since their previous device of partitioning Macedonia into dependent republics had broken down, the whole concept of encouraging Greek communities to become their "free" but dependent clients—the policy they had been following since the beginning of the century—now seemed ripe for abandonment. It was decided that the principle of direct annexation, which had provided four provinces in the west, must be imported to these ancient eastern regions as well. It had already caused widespread horror when one of the great Greek monarchies, Macedonia, was destroyed in 167; and now there was a further shock when the republics into which that country had been divided were directly annexed by Rome. Within this new province a major road was constructed, the Via Egnatia, following an ancient route all the way from the Adriatic to the northern Aegean. This was the first important Roman road in the East. It linked the Macedonian cities to one another and to Italy and formed part of this new Roman possession's defense system against barbarian incursions from the north.

On Macedonia's southern flank, in Greece itself, the Romans belatedly sent back to the Achaean League in 150 B.C. the survivors, three hundred in number, of the thousand hostages they had deported seventeen years earlier. Not long afterwards, however, they infuriated the members of the league once again by allowing the city-state of Sparta, which the Achaeans had earlier compelled to join their confederation, to terminate its membership. This led to violent anti-Spartan and anti-Roman feeling at the league capital, Corinth, a large industrial harbor and key fortress; and when Roman envoys came to the city they were beaten up. However, Achaean hopes that the Romans were too heavily committed elsewhere to be able to retaliate proved misplaced, since the Roman consul Mummius came down from Macedonia with four legions and captured Corinth (146 B.C.).

By order from his government, the whole place was razed to the ground and all its surviving inhabitants were sold into slavery, while its abundant artistic treasures were shipped off to Rome. This drastic treatment of the city was partly intended as an insurance against social revolution, since the Romans preferred Greek towns to be governed by oligarchies like their own, a preference to which Corinth, dominated by a turbulent proletariat, had failed to conform. But the Romans' brutality was also a demonstration that they would not allow quarreling Greeks to mishandle their envoys and flout their will. Yet, however much Greece had fallen from its high estate, it was a terrible sign of the new times that one of the most ancient and distinguished centers of Greek and Mediterranean civilization should be blotted out of existence in this way.

The Achaean League, too, was abolished, and Greece and its cities, after the installation of suitable local regimes, were amalgamated with the new province of Macedonia and made to pay tribute. The long centuries of Greek independence had been brought to an abrupt and violent end.

And in the very same year the independence of the Carthaginian state, too, was likewise terminated by the Romans, and its ancient capital suffered the same fate as Corinth.

Rome's defeat of the Carthaginians fifty-five years earlier, while eliminating their international power, had not prevented them from making a remarkable recovery, initially under the guidance of Hannibal. They had won back a considerable part of their trade and had employed improved agricultural methods to increase the profits from their African territories. But the fatal impediment to this revival proved to be Masinissa, the violent, ambitious ruler of neighboring Numidia, who held his throne as a client of Rome and was eager to build up his empire. Throughout half a century, following the Second Punic War, Masinissa encroached unscrupulously on Carthage's coastal colonies and wheat lands, while at the same time insuring that Rome failed to arbitrate with any effectiveness to stop him. Finally in 150 the Carthaginians, driven to desperation, took up arms against him, although their treaty with the Romans had forbidden them to engage in independent warfare. And when Masinissa appealed to Rome, the aged Cato insisted repeatedly to his fellow senators that Carthage must be destroyed. Even if its government's resistance to Masinissa's provocation had technically amounted to an infringement of the treaty, Cato's attitude displayed an irrational vindictiveness and jealous fear based on senile reminiscences of his own soldiering against Hannibal. But so harrowing were the memories of that dreaded name that the Senate, in spite of strong opposition, gave in to him, and war was declared.

The Carthaginians, in this hopeless situation, asked for peace. But as Rome repeatedly raised its price, they instead chose to offer a desperate resistance, which continued for four years. It was terminated in 146 by Scipio Aemilianus*, who, after receiving a special appointment from the Assembly in advance of the statutory age, brought the siege of Carthage itself to a successful, bloody conclusion. Its survivors were sold into slavery; the whole city was demolished, and salt scattered on the site so that it should remain barren and accursed forevermore. This was a measure of the traumatic effect Hannibal had exercised on the minds of the Romans. All that remained now was to decide what to do with the African territory that had fallen into their hands. Masinissa had died, and they did not want to give these lands to his sons. And so, instead, as in Macedonia and Greece, they decided on a policy of annexation. Thus, while a number of its cities were allowed to retain nominal independence as Roman clients, the Carthaginian homeland as a whole was converted into the province of Africa, corresponding with the northern part of Tunisia today. The new province possessed immense agricultural wealth. True, it was for psychological rather than economic reasons that this third Carthaginian war had been launched. Yet the African territory won by the Romans as a result was so overwhelmingly rich in grain that it gradually succeeded Sicily as their principal granary.

This ruthless obliteration of Carthage, perpetrated in the very same year as the destruction of Corinth, sent a shudder throughout the civilized

---

*For his later successes in Spain, see p. 142.

Mediterranean world. Roman imperialism could now be seen by all, in its nakedly unconcealed and cynical form. It was a policy that went by the name of the "New Wisdom." And, for all its moral defects, its growing employment had achieved astonishing practical results, for within the space of a few years the Romans had become dominant in almost the whole of the Mediterranean—it was indeed *Mare Nostrum,* Our Sea.

9
The New Society

Senate and Nobles in Charge

The foreign policy of these decisive first decades after 200 B.C., when ferocity and authoritarianism were on the increase all the time, was still directed, except on very few occasions, by the Roman Senate and nobility, that is to say, by those men, patricians and plebeians alike, who numbered consuls among their ancestors.

In the latter part of the previous century, during the Second Punic War, the Assembly had on certain rare occasions asserted itself against the Senate, most conspicuously by insisting upon the appointment of Scipio Africanus, in which the senators prudently decided to concur. But on the whole, the first two Carthaginian conflicts had greatly strengthened the oligarchy's control of affairs. Shortly before these wars had started, the embryonic Roman social revolution had petered out when the tribunes of the people became agents of the nobility instead. And then later on, too, after Hannibal had been defeated, there was a widespread feeling that it was this nobility, operating through the Senate, that deserved the credit for eliminating the gravest danger Rome had ever undergone and gaining for it, in the process, extensive and prosperous new territories overseas. Once won, these provinces came completely under control of the Senate, which, according to a practice that now became normal, appointed as their governors men who had just served as consul or praetor at Rome, a procedure known as *prorogatio*. But this senatorial grip on the expanding empire was only part of a general phenomenon, for as the third century passed into the second, the Senate's control of all Roman policy remained as firm and thoroughgoing as ever before, despite occasional interventions by the Assembly.

This is confirmed by the statistics of elections to the offices of state: "new men," without consular ancestry, remained extremely rare, and government was virtually run by a closed, clublike circle of about two thousand men belonging to fewer than twenty families. Philip V of Macedonia expressed envious amazement at the friendly solidarity among these nobles and senators. True, the career and character of Scipio Africanus had introduced strains into the amicable atmosphere, suggesting that it might not last forever. But so far no substantial deterioration was to be seen.

Indeed, the family of the Scipios themselves was still a living illustration of the system's narrow base. In fewer than a hundred years the members of this single family alone gained as many as twenty-three consulships for themselves. And their surviving epitaphs place overwhelming emphasis not only on public office and military success, but also on genealogical descent as well. These great aristocratic houses kept in their cupboards the wax masks of their ancestors who had held high office. The masks were arranged as a family tree and received religious worship; in family funerals, they were worn by actors engaged to walk in the procession. At such funerals, there

Sarcophagus of Lucius Cornelius Scipio Barbatus (consul 298 B.C.), one of the 23 consuls of the Scipio family (the bust is a later addition).

were speeches in praise of the dead man and his ancestors, and they have provided us, directly or through intermediaries, with much historical information, highly tendencious though it often is.

Tradition, therefore, remained all-important in Roman education, as Cicero was never tired of emphasizing. And tradition implied reverence not only for people of bygone times but also for seniority in the living. Thus, although men could and did hold office fairly young—a praetor at about forty and a consul two or three years later—ex-consuls spoke first in any debate in the Senate, and their experience, which after the wars of the third and second centuries was likely to be considerable, earned deeper respect than ever before.

So, guided by these men, the Senate reinforced its influence and in the absence of any effective counterblast retained a position of virtually irresponsible supremacy, becoming even more exclusive and conservative in the process. And this, as we have seen, displayed itself in an ever tougher foreign policy, based on suspicious, ungenerous, and often unfounded anxieties. Meanwhile, even if the Assembly might occasionally make itself felt, the vast majority of the people, as usual, were content to leave politics to the politicians.

Yet the nobles remained very vigilant against possible unrest, as a curious religious crisis now revealed. During the emergencies of the Punic wars the Senate had several times provided an outlet for popular hysteria by the importation of exciting eastern cults more likely to distract the public from its hardships than the dry Roman ritual could ever have done. Once introduced, the new cults could be toned down and domesticated. But then in 186 B.C. stringent measures were taken to control the emotional, mystic worship of Bacchus (Dionysus). His rites, the *Bacchanalia,* made known by Roman soldiers returning from the east, had spread extensively throughout Italy and were especially common in the south of the peninsula. Conducted by conventicles or secret societies, these practices were believed to be the focus point not only of sexual immorality but also of crime and public disorder. However, the worship had become so deeply rooted that the government saw no possibility of stamping it out. Instead, therefore, they ordered that not more than five persons should be allowed to celebrate the Bacchic cult together, and then only after obtaining the Senate's permission.

The nobility, well aware of the importance of religion to its overall control, at all times meticulously directed and exploited this vital area of social behavior, and one way in which they chose to do so was by declaring undesirable religious practices, like the *Bacchanalia,* to be politically conspiratorial and subversive. Such an attitude, however, was ominous for the future since it produced arbitrary reinterpretations of the law. And what also seemed alarming was the unprecedented scope of the police action by which they enforced these restrictions upon the Bacchic ceremonies throughout allied as well as Roman territory.

The Rise of Latin Culture

In the literary field, too, the nobles and Senate became sensitive about suspected attempts to undermine their supremacy. One of those who suffered was the versatile poet Naevius (b. ca. 270–d. 201 B.C.), a Roman citizen from near Capua. Naevius wrote patriotic works, of which only fragments survive today; they included original tragic dramas about Roman history and legend and a pioneer epic dealing with the First Punic War, in which he himself had served. But in about 204 B.C. he committed some fault for which he was imprisoned and went into exile. Perhaps one reason was that the oligarchy still remembered the offense he had caused over thirty years earlier when he criticized one of the greatest plebeian noble families, the Caecilii Metelli.

Naevius's native ebullience also led him to write comic plays. But here he was outshone by Plautus (b. ca. 254–d. 184). With Plautus, who came from backward Sarsina (Mercato Saraceno) in Umbria, we have already reached the precocious zenith of Latin verse comedy; and twenty of his complete plays (with one incomplete) have survived. His models, like those of his few Latin forerunners, were the sophisticated products of the Greek New Comedy of fourth-century Athens, familiar to many educated Romans now that contacts with Greek south Italy and Sicily had multiplied. Yet Plautus rewrote these plays and made them almost unrecognizable in the process. Not only was he able, by an astonishing *tour de force,* to weld the still gracelessly cumbrous Latin tongue into the meters of the totally different Greek language, but he also wholly abandoned the subtlety of the original Greek comedies in order to give free rein to his own explosive genius for wild, quick-firing, slapstick buffoonery. His success, in the centuries to come, was enormous. And even during his lifetime, although his audiences comprised people at a wide variety of cultural levels, they were prepared to abandon the rival attractions of boxers, dancers, and chariot races in order to come and laugh at what they heard and saw on Plautus's temporarily erected stages.

Moreover, his plays are filled, for all their farcicality, with oblique but telling social criticism. It takes the form of an exuberant inversion of traditional moral standards: a carnivalesque upturning of reverence for parents and matrimonial respectability, and conventional depreciation of women and clients—and especially slaves, to whom he gave much larger roles than they had enjoyed in the Greek New Comedy. Yet Plautus, unlike Naevius, escaped upper-class retaliation. He was careful to claim that his characters and their backgrounds were not Roman but foreign and Greek; so that, superficially at least, it was not Roman institutions at all that were coming under fire.

About fifteen years younger than Plautus was another poet, Ennius (b. 239–d. 169 B.C.), who, like him, avoided getting into any trouble with the rulers of Rome—though he not only wrote moralizing "satire," but also ventured to rationalize the traditional mythology and even Jupiter himself, the national god of the Roman state. Born at Rudiae (near Lecce in southeast Italy), a place where Greek, Latin, and Italian cultures converged and endowed him, as he said, with three hearts, Ennius served as a soldier in Sardinia at the end of the Second Punic War and then on the staff of the Aetolian campaign of 189, subsequently gaining the reward of Roman citizenship. A poor man who enjoyed social life, he was said to have died of gout; but "unless I have gout," he had remarked, "I never write poetry". More industrious, however, than this saying implied, and warmhearted and enthusiastic as well, he was the first professional literary man Rome ever possessed and the first to naturalize Greek literary culture.

This was achieved, above all, by his rough, vigorous, colorful *Annals,* an epic poem following the tradition established by Naevius, in which, momentously adapting the Greek heroic meter—the hexameters of the Homeric poems—he chronicled the entire course of Roman history up to his own day. Only a few hundred lines now survive, but they reveal how he gave distinctive expression to the proud, virile energy and sagacious good sense of the imperial republic of Rome at its best. His compatriots of later generations saw him as the father of Latin poetry, and he exercised a profound effect on subsequent historians and literary critics as well.

Ennius had been brought back to Rome from Sardinia in 204 B.C. by Cato the Elder (b. 234–d. 149) who was born at about the same time as the elder Scipio (Africanus), and although a "new man" without consuls among his ancestors, became one of the outstanding politicians of his time. But they were also embittered rivals, for the comparative harmony that had hitherto prevailed among senators was coming to an end. There had always been, along with the harmony, struggles for office and prestige, in which each great man's claims were vigorously furthered by his clients, but when such diverse personalities as Cato and Scipio were involved, this competitiveness was sharply intensified.

Cato, taking his stand on antique tradition and rallying the support of many conservative landowners of the day, profoundly objected to the excessive personal reverence accorded to Scipio, whom he regarded as a careerist.

Cato also deplored his interest in Greek affairs and debilitating Greek culture (exemplified by his adoption of the Greek practice of close shaving). Ever since the Greco-Roman contacts of the Second Punic War and increasingly after it had ended, Cato saw this Hellenism as an evil influence pervading every corner of Roman life; it seemed to him outrageous when Scipio's brother brought back from the war against Antiochus the first bronze couches, bedcovers, ornate tables, fine cooking, and cabaret girls ever to be seen in Rome. And Cato had his way, for not long afterwards, in 184, he drove both the Scipios out of public life into retirement; and Africanus died soon afterwards.

Cato's election to the censorship of 184 seemed a remarkable achievement for a "new man" and earned him the name of Cato the Censor ever afterwards. It also brought the term "censorious" into our language. The office enabled him to intensify his attacks on Hellenism, and he disguised his own versatile knowledge by inflicting a deliberate pose of boorish ill manners on his increasingly cultivated fellow senators. As censor he introduced numerous measures of moral and economic reconstruction and purification. Among them was the imposition of new taxes on the extravagance he so greatly deplored. They were designed to ensnare his personal enemies but also, in more general terms, were based on a belief, revived at intervals for hundreds of years to come, that sumptuary legislation of this kind could prove effective.

Cato was also opposed to current tendencies towards the emancipation of women, complaining that wives tyrannized their husbands. Since the previous century a much freer form of marriage had become habitual; and the influx of wealth meant that women began to dress and adorn themselves more luxuriously. Moreover, in certain important families, casualties during the wars had wiped out the male line, so that estates came under female control. This brought heavy frowns to the faces of traditionalists, and in 169 a tribune, strongly supported by Cato, carried a bill insisting on the ancient limitation of women's right to inherit. But the law was easily evaded by nominal transfers of property to collusive trustees; and the "guardians" through whom women (except Vestal Virgins) were still legally obliged to conduct public business frequently cooperated with their wards, so that unattached women were, in fact, able to control their own affairs.

They were also permitted to attend public entertainments, and, in the more prosperous households at least, they were taught not only the traditional household skills but also more academic subjects. Thus Cornelia, the daughter of Scipio Africanus, in addition to managing her own estates but presided over a sort of intellectual salon. And women of her rank now played a vital part in political life as well because their marriages formed

Wax diptych: guardian appointed to a woman by Aemilius Saturninus, prefect of Egypt, A.D. 199.

the links in the chains uniting the various groups of political allies; and the important meetings between one politician and another took place in their houses.

Cato's disapproval of Cornelia's father was equaled only by his distaste for enlightened women like herself. Indeed, his whole way of life was based on the single aim of protecting the traditional social values from further contamination. He himself, although he came from farming stock at Tusculum in Latium, had been brought up in the country of the Sabines, to whose traditional harsh discipline and austerity he ascribed what seemed to him the best features in the character of himself and all Romans, including, above all, their courageous endurance and loyal service to the state. This litigious and vindictive, red-headed farmer with the piercing gray eyes was also the epitome of puritanical reaction. But his obsessions were in vain, for although he may have done something, for a time, to reestablish moral responsibility and postpone the lowering of standards, his program could not, in the long run, succeed.

Apart from a work on agriculture, very little of what he wrote has survived. Yet his status as a writer is enormous and secure. The gravest loss is his seven-book *Origins,* a history of Rome. Written in Latin, not in Greek like all its predecessors, it was the first major achievement in this field and virtually inaugurated Latin prose as a literary medium. Yet, despite Cato's distaste for the growing intrusion of Greek education—read a bit of Greek literature, he taught his son, but beware that perverse and corrupting race!—he was prepared to supplement his native Italian trenchancy by certain Greek stylistic features and methods of arrangement; this was scarcely surprising after his patronage of the phil-Hellene Ennius.

Nevertheless, Cato always insisted that the Romans were basically different from the Greeks. In contrast to Greek states, he pointed out, Rome owed its national successes not to a few individuals but to the combined genius of a host of different people living and working together with one another. So great was his distaste for the Scipio-type personality cult that in his *Origins* he actually suppressed the names of great Roman commanders altogether, preferring instead, when describing the Second Punic War, to mention the name of a Carthaginian elephant, Surus. And he correctly identified a very real fault of Roman historiography when he blamed writers for glorifying their own families.

History was closely linked with the government of the Republic—and so was public speaking, at which Cato likewise excelled, exploiting his quick and biting wit to survive no fewer than fifty political prosecutions. This art was the mainspring of Roman public life and education, and, as in his historical authorship, Cato was not entirely immune from Greek influence, in this case the rhetorical "art of persuasion" and the technicalities that it imparted. These influences combined with the urgent practical exigencies of speaking in the Assembly, Senate, and lawcourts to create that most formidable of instruments, Latin oratory, of which Cato was a pioneer exponent.

As orator, statesman, and defender of austere but narrow morality, Cato remained greatly to the fore throughout these years. His foreign policies were predictably narrow, and under the guise of sagacious common sense he sponsored many of the aggressively chauvinistic measures of the epoch, notably the move to obliterate Carthage. At an earlier date, it is true, an equally vindictive proposal to declare war on Rhodes had not met with his approval.* Yet this, we may be sure, was not because of any sympathy with the island's Greek inhabitants, but because (in contrast to his late enemy

---

*Cato had also deprecated the repeated cheating of the Spaniards by Roman commanders. See page 142.

Scipio Africanus) he was opposed to further Eastern interventions, with all the insidious influences they brought in their wake.

In the campaign against Macedonia that had led to the disgrace of the lukewarm Rhodians, one of the youngest Roman officers was Africanus's grandson by adoption, Scipio Aemilianus (b. 185/4–d. 129 B.C.). He indulged even more than Africanus in the new Roman taste for Renaissance-style individualism that Cato so greatly deplored. And time after time, in the years to come, it was to Scipio Aemilianus that the Romans turned in a crisis. It was he, in Cato's old age, who won the Third Punic War (146), and then it was he again who finally defeated the Spaniards (133); and for nearly twenty years of Roman history, although never unchallenged, he remained its key personality and outstanding statesman. He was a man of numerous contradictions, reputedly idle when young, yet formidably active in later years. As a speaker he was excellent, as he had to be; and, although not a brilliant general like Africanus, he was an organizer with plenty of drive. Moreover, despite an ironical wit that was inclined to cause offense, he lavished on his friends and on the general public, when he wanted to impress them, a great deal of personal charm. But what was most important about him was his deserved reputation for decent behavior: he was regarded as a person of integrity in an age that needed this and knew it.

Yet the career of Scipio Aemilianus, though advancing ambitiously from one honor to another, remained curiously negative all the same. For the troubles of his age, the troubles of a city-state that had become within a short space of time the capital of a vast empire, he had no creative solutions to offer. It seems a missed opportunity that this most brilliant man of his age did not supply some of the reforms that he alone might have succeeded in introducing. Yet this negativeness also had its good side, for it meant that he never attempted to break out of the republican system in order to dominate it himself—as, once again, he probably could have if he had tried, and as other men did after him. True, his rabble-rousing exploitations of popular appeal, in defiance of the Senate, were a sinister example to those who came after—and a strain upon the constitution. Yet, like Africanus before him, he was still content to work inside the framework.

An intellectual sympathetic to Hellenism, Scipio Aemilianus had been educated by a variety of Greek tutors and was deeply interested in Greek literature and philosophy, and indeed, although there may not quite have been the "Scipionic circle" of which Cicero later spoke, men who were in touch with him played a large role in the partially Hellenized Roman culture of the time. They included not only Greek men of letters whose philosophy was sometimes stretched to provide or imply an idealistic justification for the emerging Roman commonwealth, but also a distinguished

The family of the Scipios

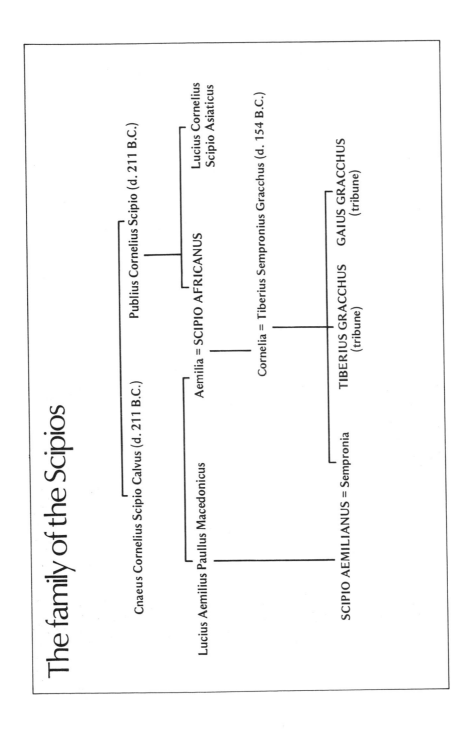

Cnaeus Cornelius Scipio Calvus (d. 211 B.C.)

Publius Cornelius Scipio (d. 211 B.C.)

Lucius Cornelius
Scipio Asiaticus

Lucius Aemilius Paullus Macedonicus

Aemilia = SCIPIO AFRICANUS

Cornelia = Tiberius Sempronius Gracchus (d. 154 B.C.)

SCIPIO AEMILIANUS = Sempronia

TIBERIUS GRACCHUS
(tribune)

GAIUS GRACCHUS
(tribune)

Latin dramatic poet, the short-lived Terence (b. ca. 190–d. 159 B.C.), one of Plautus's successors on the comic stage. As his last name "Afer" indicates, Terence came from northern Africa. He became the slave of a Roman senator, who set him free; and he gained the friendship of Scipio Aemilianus, who was even rumored, probably wrongly, to be part-author of his plays. All six of these survive. They display a constructional skill that left a strong imprint on the future theater of Europe. Their writer is seen to be not only gentler and more contemplative than Plautus, but also closer to his Greek models and therefore farther away from popular taste. Terence depicts his realistic, amoral, young heroes with a fashionable philosophical humaneness beneath which runs an undercurrent of social criticism, more unobtrusive than the running commentary of Plautus but persistent all the same.

This same note recurs in Lucilius of Suessa Aurunca (Sessa) in Campania (b. ca. 180–d. 102), another of Scipio Aemilianus's protégés, who served in his cavalary in Spain. Lucilius turned his exceptional gifts into the channel of satire, of which, in its modern sense, he was virtually the founder. Ennius had written moralizing verses of a mildly satirical kind, but it was Lucilius, as the thirteen hundred somewhat rough, crude lines surviving from his thirty books reveal, who brought his varied and salty mockery to bear upon contemporary life and letters. A rich and well-connected man, he was no friend of those who fell from the social standards he upheld. Yet his sharp, incisive mind and irreverent, exuberant humor cut sharply through the shams and futilities he detected in the contemporary scene. He sensed the wind of change, and even if he did not like it altogether, it found him better prepared than most, and he lived on until the time when it had gained a fuller strength.

Roman Wealth and New Buildings

During these years, an ever-increasing stream of coin and bullion flowed into the Roman treasury from countries overseas. In the year after the brother of Scipio Africanus brought back his immense booty from Asia Minor, the Galatians in the center of that peninsula once again yielded enormous loot (179). Then, in 168, the three-day triumphal procession of the victor of Pydna, Paullus, included two hundred and fifty wagons of spoils and three hundred crowns made of gold. It was a metal that, for the first time, was becoming familiar in Rome, in this form of massive indemnities paid by its defeated foes. And a very large proportion of these new riches found its way into the hands of the senatorial nobility.

The gulf between rich and poor was becoming enormous; and in order to do a little to counteract this trend, the Senate, after Pydna, decided to make an impressive public gesture. Until now, all Roman citizens had been liable to pay the state a direct property tax or *tributum,* which had been levied frequently in emergencies and with particular severity during the Punic Wars. But the Roman public, although prepared to pay indirect taxes (which were not very large), did not consider direct taxation a regular or reasonable part of their obligations as citizens; they would have agreed with Cicero that "it is a statesman's duty not to impose a property tax upon the people"—that is to say, not to impose it upon Roman citizens, for the corollary was that all necessary direct taxation should be extracted from Rome's subjects in the provinces. When, therefore, the Galatian loot was brought back, the Senate repaid to individual Romans a substantial part or even the whole of the tribute that had been levied on them or their families in the Second Punic War. And then, in 167, the plunder seized after Pydna enabled this form of taxation to be abolished altogether, and it was not reimposed for more than a century to come. This was a popular measure that must have done at least something to lessen discontents arising from the increasing disparities of wealth.

Rome already exceeded all the other cities of the Western world in size, and as this influx of foreign wealth continued, its buildings began to assume a monumental appearance. Greek influence was manifest in a new taste for free-standing porticoes and for the basilicas or public halls that replaced the old rows of shops beside the Forum and served as markets, meeting places, and courts of justice. The earliest extant example of an Italian basilica happens to be not in Rome itself, but at the Campanian town of Pompeii (?120 B.C.). It is a large rectangular structure with internal colonnades, which seems, originally, to have possessed a flat wooden roof. The earliest Roman construction of the same type, which has not survived, was the Basilica Porcia (184 B.C.) built by Cato the Censor despite his suspicions of Greece. And other basilicas at Rome followed not long afterwards, in partial imitation.

At a later date, in the first century B.C., these large halls were reconstructed with rounded arches, instead of the rows of flat-architraved columns which had characterized the original basilicas. Although there had been timid earlier attempts at the theme in Greece and Etruria, the arch was a preeminently Roman structural form. It could also be created in isolation from arcades and could even be detached from buildings altogether. The result of the latter process was another typical Roman creation, the freestanding monumental or commemorative arch. Its first recorded examples at Rome, no longer standing today, date from 196 B.C., when two such monuments were erected to celebrate victories in Spain. Later in the century there were others. They were the forerunners of the magnificent imperial triumphal arches that can still be seen in many cities today.

Arched gate of S. Maria di Falleri (Falerii Novi), 241-200 B.C.

These developments in the construction of arches and arcades, and of the curving apses, niches, and vaults which are likewise among the supreme architectural achievements of the Romans, were made possible by the discovery of concrete, the most revolutionary of all their revolutionary structural inventions. Its earliest uses were traditionally attributed to the final quarter of the second century B.C. But recent excavation appears to have ascribed this innovation to a date as early as the first decade of that century. Extensive employment of concrete has been detected in a large market hall and granary beside the Tiber and the Aventine. This is identified, with probability, as the Porticus Aemilia, built in 193 B.C. and restored in 174, though concrete was still not used very widely until a generation or two later.

Adhesives of sand, mixed with lime and water, had been known to Greeks in the previous century. But it was only now that the serious exploitation of such materials began, after the Romans had detected the admirable properties of a material available in the soil, a natural, pulverized, volcanic blend of cinders and clay. It is known as *pozzolana* because of its abundance at Puteoli (Pozzuoli, near Naples), but quantities are also found close to Rome itself. When good, unadulterated lime was mixed with this product in a kiln, the molten mass became an exceptionally consistent and coherent concrete. This was poured over a rubble "aggregate" made from chips of stone, or brick, or pumice, and skillfully graded by weight. The result was a compact, monolithic, almost indestructible mass, extraordinarily resistant to strains and stresses, impervious to water, and exerting no lateral thrust. It could be concealed from the viewer by the surface application of facings of marble or stone, and this was usually done. But the facings were purely superficial and not structurally essential. Gradually, and by a long series of cautious experiments, successive generations of Roman architects would awake to the breathtaking potentialities of this concrete medium and employ it to build their soaring curvilinear marvels of the future.

But meanwhile, until this confidence had been achieved, arches had to be built more cautiously without using the material. Thus in 144 B.C. a praetor built Rome's first aqueduct to include arched high-level sectors of appreciable length, the Aqua Marcia, which supplied the city with water from a source thirty-six miles distant; its channel was lined with concrete, but it remained for future aqueducts to embody the material in their arches. This was only the first stage of a long process of such construction, at the end of which Rome's abundance of running water would be unequaled in its lavishness; nor has any other city ever put it to more spectacular public use, while the provinces, too, would be furnished with aqueducts on a magnificent scale. The Aqua Marcia exemplified the special concern of the Romans of this time for public works of solid, material utility. There was also extensive building of Italian roads; and in Rome itself the streets, although nothing was done to increase their narrow width, were paved with blocks of durable lava from the Alban Mount. The old wooden bridge (Pons Sublicius) across the Tiber, too, was supplemented in 179 B.C. by the Aemilian bridge resting on piers made of stone, to which an arched superstructure was added in 142.

The growing population of the capital, however, was accommodated in lofty, rickety, jerry-built wooden blocks, lacking adequate light, heat, cooking arrangements, or water supply, and subject to frequent destructive fires and floods. For the houses of the rich, on the other hand, wall facings of dressed stone were coming into use. No examples from such an early date survive at Rome itself, but their plan can be recovered from elegant, luxuri-

The Alban Mount and aqueduct of Claudius (Aqua Claudia), painted by
Thomas Cole (1801-48).

ous houses of this and previous periods at Pompeii. The houses presented
plain facades to the street, or let off sections of this frontage space as shops.
The rooms are grouped around a central *atrium,* a blend of courtyard and
front hall which is of Italian, and reputedly Etruscan, origin. It was approached through an entrance passage and covered by a roof containing,
normally, a central aperture. The *atrium* housed the family altar and statues. Beyond it were the living and domestic quarters, which might include
different dining rooms for summer and winter; they were often grouped
around a colonnaded court (peristyle) containing a small garden—though
sometimes the main garden was beyond. Dwellings of this type, which in
some regions of Italy continued to be constructed and reconstructed over
many generations, were notable for their wall paintings, of which the earliest surviving examples go back to about 100 B.C., though they must have
had forerunners. Glazed windows were known but little used except in the
public bathing establishments that developed later on. Although the provision of water was conceived primarily as a public rather than a private
service, the supply directed to the baths and fountains of the towns could

also be siphoned off into leaden pipes leading to the better class of private houses.

Agriculture and Slavery

The wars that transformed Rome by their plunder also brought sweeping social changes throughout Italy. In some areas of the country, the devastations and confiscations during the fifteen years of Hannibal's invasion eliminated many small landholders altogether. And their ruin was also assisted by other factors that continued to operate throughout the Mediterranean

Plan of House of Menander, Pompeii (from third century B.C. onwards); with surrounding houses.

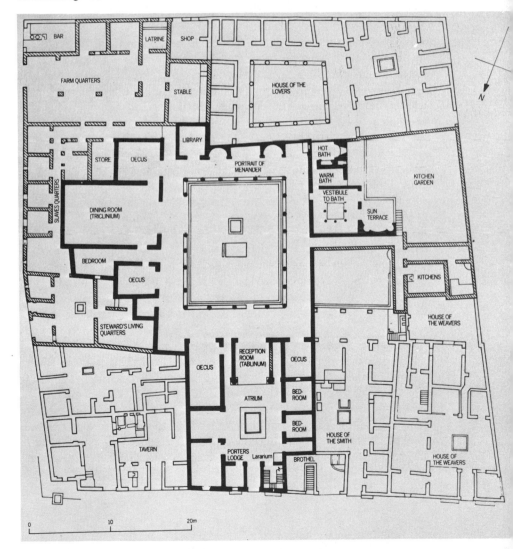

wars of the second century B.C. In this endless succession of foreign campaigns numerous Italian soldier-farmers were killed; and among those who returned, some brought in malaria, which made many areas uninhabitable, and others could not face the prospect of going back to farming and gravitated instead to the war industries of the towns. But above all, whether they returned or not, it was the endless conscription, involving prolonged absence on meager pay, that set the seal on the collapse of their small properties. Every qualified citizen between the ages of seventeen and forty-six was liable to serve for sixteen years, or even twenty years in emergencies. Between 200 and 168 B.C. some forty-seven thousand soldiers were in the field each year; if one included Italians, and south Italian Greeks, the total came to one hundred and ten thousand or one hundred and thirty thousand. Nor were the numbers much fewer thereafter. And all these men were lost to their farms at least long enough for their land to fall into ruin; and very often the decay proved irreparable.

Much of the soil thus vacated passed in due course into the hands of the Roman state, which came to own, by this means, one-fifth of the whole Italian peninsula. Once in possession of such a piece of public territory, *(ager publicus)*, the government could let it out again to private individuals. Those who occupied public land in this way were supposed to pay rent to the state. But its collection was lax, and a large number of the tenants held on to the properties they had acquired without paying any dues at all. A certain number of these fortunate lessees were small holders, but many others were large-scale landowners who either took over single big tracts (later known as *latifundia*) or amalgamated a whole network of medium-sized farms. These were men who, during the foreign wars, had accumulated sufficient money to keep up these great estates or groups of properties and could afford to wait patiently until their endeavors yielded profits. Meanwhile, the ancient legal limitations on the amount of public land any one citizen was permitted to lease were regularly evaded or ignored. So holdings of hundreds of acres became an increasingly prominent feature of the Italian scene; and their wealthy proprietors continued to expand further at the expense of the harassed small holders in the area, by methods ranging from purchases and mortgages to physical violence.

In certain areas of Italy this new phenomenon of the large landowners brought changes in preferred types of agricultural production. The rising populations of the towns offered them an increased market for their crops, and they responded to the challenge by transforming the traditional modest subsistence farming into large-scale, mixed, intensive cultivation for purposes of commercial gain. This cultivation was undertaken with the aid of new scientific methods, such as crop rotation and manuring, new deep-cutting ploughs, and a new systematic selection of seeds. The city of Rome, where people had begun to eat baked bread instead of porridge, still relied on obtaining its wheat from Campania, which also outstripped Etruria as the industrial center of Italy. But in certain other parts of the peninsula, the growing of grain, which had remained the staple crop for so long, at last began to lose its supremacy.

Secondary reasons for this development included competitive importation from the granary provinces and erosion of soil. But, above all, the switch from grain was due to a new preference for other farm products that earned more money. From the middle of the second century B.C. onwards, grapes had become a more important crop than grain, and olives too were in lucrative demand; the ruin of Carthage made Italy the chief wine and oil producer for the West. Vegetables were also important. But the largest agricultural development of the age, especially in southern Italy, was huge-scale farming and breeding of cattle to produce meat, cheese, wool, and leather. These were enterprises that only the biggest estates were able to undertake, since they alone could provide both the upper and lower grazing required for seasonal migration.

We learn about the agriculture of these years from Cato the Elder's treatise *On Farming (De Agricultura),* the earliest Latin prose work to have come down to us intact. To own a mixed ranch, insists this hard-bitten farmer-politician, and to work it scientifically is much the best way to make money. And in this survey, ill-arranged though it is, he provides a vivid picture of the novel enterprises of the day which combined agriculture with commerce, banking, and various kinds of industry. The way to run these estates, Cato maintained, was by making good use of slaves. Enormous numbers of these were now available. Slavery had been a recognized institution since the remotest past. Its large-scale exploitation had been introduced to Europe at an early date by the Phoenicians and then became familiar to the Greeks. Subsequently, as a result of the victorious campaigns of the third and second centuries B.C., slaves flooded into Rome: seventy-five thousand as prisoners in the First Punic War, including twenty-five thousand from Agrigentum (Agrigento); thirty thousand from Tarentum alone, among the numerous captives of the Hannibalic war; huge numbers of Asiatics after the victory over Antiochus III; and one hundred and fifty thousand from Epirus in 167 B.C. They were sold in the great slave markets of Capua and Delos. These enclosures were capable of handling twenty thousand slaves a day. They were kept well stocked not only by the fighting against foreign states but also through kidnappings by pirates, who, ever since Rome's unwise reduction of their enemy Rhodes, had infested the eastern Mediterranean. They were supported more or less secretly by eminent Romans for profit.

Slaves lacked all human rights; and the dramatist Plautus, although expressing himself obliquely, indicated sympathy for their defenseless position in society. Yet household slavery could be relatively humane—and it provided one of the principal channels by which Greek culture came to Rome, supplying the city with its secretaries, teachers, and doctors. In the countryside, on the other hand, slaves fared a great deal worse. Cato estimated that they ought, on the whole, to receive much the same treatment as farm animals, though more careful attention should be devoted to the care and welfare of an ox, which was not so good at looking after itself as human beings. Often these rustic slaves were kept in chains, and when they became too old to earn their keep by working, Cato was prepared to let them perish. Yet he goes on to say that the most efficient principle of management is to treat *both* animals *and* slaves well enough to enable them to work as hard and as long as they can—which meant giving them more food than, for instance, a "free" Egyptian peasant was getting. And Cato was gracious enough to permit his male and female slaves to have sex with one another provided they paid him a fee. Furthermore he lent them money to buy slaves of their own, whom they could train, at his expense, and then sell—very often to himself. And the slave children of his household were suckled by his wife.

Other employers of slaves on the large plantations were as callous as Cato, but less sensible, and subjected them to appalling ill-treatment. As a result, in spite of the danger of death that this involved, many slaves deserted from their masters and went underground. This was one of the reasons why, at certain periods of the second century B.C., the whole structure of the classical Greco-Roman society seemed as if it might crack up and disintegrate. All over the Mediterranean area social strains were acute; and in Italy, in particular, slave disturbances recurred at regular intervals from 198 B.C. onwards.

But the first major crisis erupted in the ranches of Sicily. At the slave barracks of that island, dangerous groups of fellow nationals had been imprudently concentrated; and in 135 their inmates broke out into large-scale rebellion. One of its leaders, a talented, mystical Syrian named Eunus, collected an army of seventy thousand of his fellow slaves, issued coins describing himself as King Antiochus, and seized a very large part of the island, which he held for no less than three years. Finally the revolt was put down with great slaughter. But meanwhile it had triggered off other disturbances in various territories of the east, from which most of the slaves in Sicily had originated. These outbreaks included a formidable rising at Pergamum. Its last monarch had bequeathed his kingdom to Rome (133) precisely in order to avoid that sort of revolutionary development, but in vain. A certain Aristonicus led a nationalistic, popular, Pergamene revolt that attracted and enlisted many slaves, as well as free men, before the Romans were able to suppress him.

Nevertheless, despite all these troubles, it was the slaves who made Italy's agricultural plantations work and prosper, so that the rich became a great deal richer. However, in certain regions of Italy, the effect of this on the "free" rural poor was disastrous. From ca. 181 B.C. the foundation of new colonies, which might have received them, ceased for many years; and not only were they harassed by debt and dispossessed of their small holdings, but on the large estates which had amalgamated and supplanted these little properties, they could not get work. Earlier many poor people had migrated to the cities in order to take up industrial jobs, and now immigrants of a more desperate kind were continually doing the same, but after they had moved in, they still remained jobless and impoverished and ready to make trouble. When they had merely been destitute in the remote countryside, the Roman government, rarely noted for its humanitarianism, might remain unmoved. But their presence as potential rioters in the capital carried worrying political implications that meant that something had to be done.

And there was another even more alarming aspect, this time of a military nature. Recruits to the legions had to have certain property qualifications, which this whole considerable section of Roman manpower, seeing that it had become destitute, no longer possessed—so that now, at a time when Rome needed recruits in many different regions, there was a serious dearth of them. Reforms, then, were seen by many to be imperative, and an attempt to provide them could not be long delayed.

V.
THE FALL OF
THE REPUBLIC

Preceding page:
Participants in Mystery Rites at Pompeii.

10

Reform and
War in Italy

The Gracchi

Tiberius and Gaius Gracchus, young tribunes of the people, now made spectacular attempts to cure the many ills from which Rome and Italy were suffering. They came from the highest nobility; it would have been impossible for anyone but an influential noble to get far with such an enterprise.

During the middle years of the second century B.C. the tribunate had begun to revive some of its earlier powers; certain tribunes were now seen asserting themselves against the Senate. Tiberius Gracchus's brief career came at a time when this revival was under way. He was an idealist. Yet he was also not immune to the characteristic personal hostilities of faction life, since he entertained a private grudge against his cousin and brother-in-law Scipio Aemilianus. However, when Tiberius assumed his tribuneship in 133 B.C., Scipio was still absent in Spain, so the new tribune was able to bring forward a measure although Scipio regarded it as unduly radical. This provided for the creation of individual allotments to be carved out of the extensive Italian public land that had come into the possession of the Roman government since the Second Punic War. Of this territory he proposed to leave only three hundred acres apiece in the hands of the existing tenants, which was said to be the maximum they were allowed to hold by the terms of a long-ignored law; the blow was softened by the allowance of an additional one hundred and fifty acres for every child in the families of these occupants. The rest of the public land was to be distributed in small parcels to poor citizens from Rome. But although the relief of urban poverty may have formed part of Tiberius's intention, his main purpose, against the alarmist background of contemporary slave risings, was to increase the number of free men possessing enough property to qualify them for military service. He was shocked by the growing shortage of such re-

CORNELIA AFRICANI F
GRACCHORVM

Plinth of a statue commemorating Cornelia, daughter of Scipio Africanus and mother of the Gracchi.

cruits, as well as by the ineffectiveness of the Roman army, notably in Spain where he himself had been serving four years earlier.

The measure could not be described as overwhelmingly radical; and Tiberius had the support of many leading men, including his father-in-law, the leader of the Senate, and one of the consuls, as well as the consul's brother who was the richest man in Rome. However, there was also strong opposition to the sort of plans Tiberius had in mind, not only from Scipio Aemilianus who was far away, but from senators who were active in the city itself, and their objections provoked him to pass on to more high-handed behavior. At the suggestion of his advisers he decided to short-circuit obstruction to his bill by presenting it directly to the Assembly, without prior reference to the Senate. This was not illegal and not wholly without precedent: it had been done by Flaminius a century earlier. Yet that had been an exceptional event, and the procedure remained contrary to custom, which played so great a part in Roman politics.

Moreover, when the measure was vetoed by a fellow tribune, Octavius, Tiberius induced the Assembly to depose him from his office. Such a motion was wholly without precedent. However, Tiberius, whose counsellors included Greek philosophers familiar with their own country's doctrines of popular rights, could argue that Octavius's veto, flouting the will of the people, was equally unprecedented—as indeed it was, even if Octavius was technically within his rights. At all events the agrarian bill was now passed. In order to bring it into effect a permanent commission was set up, including Tiberius, his younger brother Gaius, and Tiberius's father-in-law.

The Senate then tried to frustrate Tiberius by withholding any substantial financial backing from the commission. But meanwhile it became known to him, through the channels of his family's hereditary clientships in Asia, that the last king of Pergamum had died and left his kingdom to the Roman people. Thereupon Tiberius proposed, or threatened to propose, that the Assembly should be requested to make part of the enormous revenue from this property available to the colonists the commission was hoping to settle. This meant bypassing the Senate once again; and the suggestion struck a grave blow at senatorial control of foreign and financial affairs, which, although not based on any explicit legal sanction, was hallowed by tradition.

Then, in order to safeguard his legislation against the strong probability of subsequent annulment, Tiberius offered himself for immediate reelection to the tribunate. Now, according to the strict letter of the law, a reelection of this kind, without an interval, was not specifically excluded. It was forbidden for senior magistracies (offices of state), but the tribunate, being an office not of the state but of the *plebs,* was not a magistracy in the technical sense. Nevertheless, the proposed reelection, like Tiberius's way of presenting his bill, was a complete departure from custom. Moreover, as the time for the vote approached, it became clear that he had made too many enemies to win. Under the influence of conservative opinion, people were beginning to suspect that his high-handed actions were directed towards seizing personal, autocratic control of the state. When, therefore, the Assembly began its electoral meeting on the Capitol, a violent quarrel broke out concerning the legality of the proceedings. Physical brawling soon followed, and a crowd of senators and their clients, with an ex-consul at their head, marched on the Assembly and clubbed Tiberius and three hundred of his supporters to death.

It was the first time for nearly four hundred years that blood had been shed in Roman civil strife. Tiberius had not, perhaps, actually broken the constitution; but under provocation he had subjected it to a variety of strains that senators felt they could not endure. Although, therefore, his intentions and reforms were not revolutionary, he had suffered a violent death—and this was a deeply ominous model for the future. In his brief period of activity, Tiberius Gracchus had initiated, for good or evil, something that he surely did not want: the disintegration of the Roman oligarchic system.

Scipio Aemilianus was glad of his death; and the Senate moved into ruthless action against his partisans. Moreover, a number of its members, including Scipio Aemilianus, who had welcomed Tiberius's fate, tried to terminate the activities of the land commissioners. But in this they did not succeed. Friction, it is true, continued, but the efforts of the commission, as inscriptional evidence shows, were actually supported by certain conservatives who hoped for popularity among the poorer Romans and wanted to demonstrate that their opposition had not been directed against the law itself but only against Tiberius's high-handed methods. And so the commissioners were able to carry on with their work; and their achievements even did something to retard the ruin of the small farmers in certain parts of Italy.

Then one of the commissioners, Gaius Gracchus, was elected tribune for 123. He built many myths on the career of his elder brother Tiberius, but his own aims were more far-reaching. Ingenious, subtle, energetic, and passionate, Gaius was a most accomplished orator and used his oratory and diplomacy to win support from any and every direction. His brother had preferred not to abandon "the art of the possible" unless he had to. Gaius had no such qualms. And he was able to improve on Tiberius's record by securing his own immediate reelection to a second tribuneship unopposed. The controversy over his brother's efforts to achieve the same end had apparently led to the eventual admission that this was permissible after all. Indeed, there may have been legislation to that effect during the intervening decade. This, however, is uncertain. And there is also some uncertainty about the distribution of Gaius's measures between his two tribunates. But in all probability a good many of them were put forward during the first of the two years, and almost at its outset.

Gaius began, apparently, by reaffirming his brother's agrarian enactment, supplementing it by a measure providing for the foundation of Roman colonies at centers including Tarentum and Capua and Carthage. The Carthaginian proposal, which perhaps came later than the others, was a complete novelty, since overseas colonization was a Greek idea unfamiliar to the Romans, and many of them found it unwelcome. These colonies, to judge from their locations, were in some cases commercial rather than agricultural, being designed, apparently, for colonists from the urban poor of Rome. Yet Gaius did not cherish the false illusion that all the poor people of the capital could be sent away to become farmer-colonists; and for the benefit of those who remained in the city, he brought forward a law securing the provision of wheat at a reasonable price, which would be insured by an official subsidy. This, too, had been customary in the Greek city-states. But although moderately framed and a far cry from the mass bribery of later legislators, the proposal was seen by conservative Romans as alarming state socialism.

Gaius also arranged for the passage of highly controversial bills concerning the law courts. In 149, as a result of many political scandals, a new court, the *quaestio de repetundis,* had been established to investigate alleged abuses of power by Roman provincial governors, including illegal confiscations and the acceptance of bribes. In the intervening period, however, many such officials had been far too readily acquitted by the courts, since its jurymen, like the defendants, were all senators. In consequence, Gaius Gracchus promoted a measure providing that the juries should henceforward comprise not only senators but knights, that is to say, men possessing the property qualification next below the senators. And then this idea was shelved in favor of a law providing that all the jurymen should be knights without any senators at all.

The rise of the knights had been a major phenomenon of recent years. In ancient times, they had been horsemen of the Roman cavalry, as their designation as *equites* indicated. But when in the third century B.C. this branch of the citizen army was largely replaced by auxiliaries, the knights retained their social position but changed their function, becoming officers in the legions, for example, and functionaries on the staffs of provincial governors. They did not, however, at this stage form a single homogeneous sector of society, being roughly divided into two categories. The first consisted of prosperous landowners, men who resembled senators except that they were slightly less wealthy. The second group, however, engaged in financial operations—from which the senators were officially debarred in the vain hope of insuring that their political functions should remain uncorrupted. These financial knights had a good deal to do. Since Republican Rome virtually lacked a civil service, the collection of public revenues—for instance, indirect taxes (customs dues, etc.) and the income from public land—was habitually contracted out by the state to the highest bidder, who was then at liberty to reimburse himself as profitably as he could. Such bidders were normally knights; they were known as publicans. They also set out to gain contracts for the construction of public buildings and works and the provision of army supplies; and by using the proceeds from such enterprises to buy tax contracts, the knights who engaged in such activities could make impressive fortunes.

Conflicts with the Senate sometimes arose, especially when the *publicani* tried to make too much money from these activities, thus impoverishing the provincials and leaving too little loot for the senators. But until the time of Gaius Gracchus, such attempts on the part of the knightly financiers were curbed without too much difficulty. An entirely new situation, however, was created by Gaius's new court consisting wholly of knights, especially as many of its members belonged to the category whose principal interests were financial. Indeed, his action could be said to mark the beginning of what was later called the Equestrian Order as a separate and significant class of knights in the state, whose interests would inevitably clash with those of the senators, so that the governing cadre of the state would no longer be a homogeneous whole.

Gaius then struck a further blow for the knights in connection with the recently annexed province of Asia, the former kingdom of Pergamum. Tiberius Gracchus had wanted to divert its great revenues for the benefit of his land law. And his brother, too, needed money very pressingly for his expensive schemes for wheat subsidies and colonies. When the territory had first been annexed, tax immunities had been granted to many of its cities, but Gaius now canceled them. Since, however, that still did not bring in enough money, he put the collection of Asian taxes up for auction in the capital, thus granting a monopoly of this highly profitable activity to the tax-farming knights or *publicani.* Gaius no doubt believed that this arrangement would benefit the treasury because of the enthusiasm with which these men would extort the required taxes—since they themselves stood to profit from the operation. Indeed, the immense amounts they now proceeded to gain through his measure greatly encouraged the evolution of the *publicani* into powerful companies. This did a great deal to insure the subsequent growth of the knights into a class separate from and hostile to the Senate.

Finally, Gaius Gracchus tackled a perilously heated question: the status of Rome's Latin and Italian associates or subject allies. Many of them were laboring under bitterly felt grievances that had gradually been accumulating for a good many years. In the previous century, the allies had played a massive part in the winning of the Second Punic War, and after it was over, the time had been ripe for their admission to Roman citizen rights, or at least to some more equal form of partnership. But the Senate had no desire to bestow the Roman franchise on men whose votes it could not control since they lived so far away. So nothing was done to improve their position. On the contrary, from the 180s and 170s onwards, there had been various signs of increased encroachment by Rome. In particular, arbitrary measures had been taken by Roman officials, from whose heavy-handed treatment the allies now felt an urgent desire to seek protection.

Scipio Aemilianus, who had commanded Latin and Italian soldiers in addition to Romans, showed himself to be in favor of the allies' claims. And that was one of the reasons why he had been against Tiberius Gracchus's land law. His opposition was not based solely on plain conservatism; the measure would require many Italian allies to hand over public land they were occupying in excess of the legal limit. They were already upset by their heavy-handed treatment by Roman officials, and this would upset them still further. And that was one of the reasons why, after Tiberius's death, Scipio tried, unsuccessfully, to bring the land commission to an end.

But such efforts, while endearing Scipio to the Italians, made him extremely unpopular with the urban poor of Rome who had hoped to take over public land. And when he died in 129 there were even rumors that with the connivance of his estranged wife, the sister of the Gracchi, some of these angry Romans had murdered him, though such suspicions were probably unfounded.

An effort was made to appease the Italian allies by proposing that they should have a share of the small holdings now to be created out of the public land, but the government refused to allow the commissioners to take this step. In consequence, one of their number, the distinguished commander and scholar Fulvius Flaccus, brought forward an alternative proposal (125 B.C.). What he suggested was that any Italians who wanted Roman citizenship should be given it—which would make them eligible for inclusion in the land distribution—while those who still remained non-Romans should at least become entitled to appeal against oppression by Roman officials. But these ideas, too, came to nothing. However, the Italian question had been well and truly introduced into Roman politics—and the situation was very tense.

Gaius decided that he could not evade the issue; and so in the second year of his tribuneship (122) he put forward a modified version of the proposal of Flaccus, who was now his fellow tribune. According to the new scheme Roman citizenship should be conferred upon all Latins, whereas other Italian communities should be granted the Latin right, which provided that the local civic officials should become Roman citizens. The status was thus a halfway house to the full franchise. But this statesmanlike measure was cunningly outbid by a conservative nominee, Marcus Livius Drusus the Elder, who passed a law providing for the total exemption of holders of the Latin right from capital or corporal punishment by Romans, together with a far more ambitious colonial policy than anything Gaius was proposing. No effort was made to carry this program out. But Gaius had been undermined, and when he went to supervise his new foundation at Carthage, malevolent rumors about the ill-omened site, which had been dedicated to eternal destruction after the final defeat of the Carthaginians, weakened his position still further.

In consequence, when he tried to secure reelection to a third tribunate in 121, he was rejected. And soon afterwards the end came. His political enemies now set out to cancel the Carthaginian colonization altogether; and when his supporters vociferously opposed this, a servant of one of the consuls, Opimius, was killed in a scuffle. Thereupon Opimius persuaded the Senate to pass a declaration of public emergency pronouncing that the government was imperiled and charging the consuls and other high officials "to see to it that the state took no harm." On the strength of this injunction he personally led a crowd of senators and knights in a physical attack on Gaius and Flaccus, who were both killed; and then some three thousand of their supporters were executed after perfunctory trials. The decree that led to these actions, later known as the *senatus consultum ultimum,* was to become a feature of the many disturbed decades that now followed, in which it was regarded by some as a necessary instrument of state and by others as a weapon of illegitimate repression.

Those who held the former view, the conservatives, called themselves the *optimates* (best men); whereas the opposition to emergency decrees was directed by men who were known as *populares,* on the grounds that, following the example of the Gracchi, they were prepared to bypass the Senate in favor of working through the Assembly of the Roman People *(Populus Romanus).* Yet the old system of shifting, personal alliances based on kinship, clientship, favor, and custom continued to exist—even if somewhat shaken by the Gracchan insistence on points of principle; and the *populares* came forward only intermittently in support of particular measures. That is to say, the two groupings never achieved the clear-cut status of opposed political parties in the modern sense. But the rival tendencies persisted and intensified, and this polarization was another of the results of the activity of the Gracchi.

Because of such developments and the further weakening of the structure owing to the new split between Senate and knights, the demolition of the old constitutional system, which had been started involuntarily by Tiberius, accelerated under Gaius. After their deaths, it appeared at first that they had failed. For the time being repression held the field, and their plans seemed to have gone completely awry. But the land commissioners were still not prevented from carrying on with their work, and, moreover, there were soon going to be other *populares* ready to widen the breaches the Gracchi had opened. And so the two brothers left their ineffaceable and permanent mark on the history of Rome, with the result that within a hundred years after their brief careers the republic had fallen apart and was no more.

Marius

Nevertheless, during the final years of the Gracchan crisis the attention of Romans was not exclusively focused on the capital but was also directed towards Gaul across the Alps, into which they were now decisively drawn.

In the previous century their ally in that country, the Greek city-state of Massilia (Marseille), had brought pressure on them to go to war against Hannibal. Now in 125 B.C. Massilia, not for the first time, appealed to Rome for help against another set of enemies, the Ligurian tribes of the French Riviera. The Senate responded and duly suppressed the recalcitrant tribesmen. But in so doing they also came into contact with Celtic tribes of the hinterland and fought against two of them, the Allobroges and the more powerful Arverni (after whom the Auvergne is named); and they heavily defeated each of these in succession not far from the river Rhone in 121. Cnaeus Domitius Ahenobarbus, who won the first of these battles, stayed on and completed the annexation of the whole of southern Gaul, between the Cévennes and the Alps, with the exception of Massilia and its territory, which remained free. A major road, called the Via Domitia after Ahenobarbus, was constructed right across the territory, thus linking Italy by land with Spain, and within the next generation the whole region was converted into a province known as Gallia Narbonensis after its capital at Narbo (Narbonne).

But meanwhile a more serious operation had to be undertaken on the opposite coast of the Mediterranean, in north Africa. There, in the client kingdom of Numidia—flanking the Roman province of Africa—the successor of King Masinissa had died, and Rome divided the country between two young princes (118). One of them was Jugurtha, who had served under Scipio Aemilianus. He was a noted athlete and horseman and a born soldier, whose mask of breezy bonhomie concealed deep resources of calculated cunning and treachery. The Roman partition had given him only the western and more primitive part of the country, and he not only rejected this settlement but also ordered his troops to massacre the Italian residents in Numidia.

Rome declared war on him; but its first two expeditionary forces achieved nothing at all. It was widely believed that Jugurtha, who became known as the lion of the desert, had bribed the Roman generals. This was not, however, necessarily true because they may have been merely inefficient. But in any case, a much more competent general now had to be dispatched (109). He was Quintus Metellus, an excellent disciplinarian, who transformed the demoralized Roman army into a powerful machine. But even he, after two years of successful campaigning, failed to induce his enemy to surrender, and Roman public opinion, not appreciating the difficulties of this desert warfare, secured the appointment of one of his deputies over his head. This was Gaius Marius, a "new man" of middle-class origins from the citizen community of Arpinum east of Rome, who had amassed wealth as a knight and *publicanus* and had built up useful political support. Now, by fomenting the popular discontent against his own chief, he obtained for himself the consulship for 107 and the supreme command. These appointments were made by the assemblies, which overrode the Senate's contrary wishes, thus foreshadowing the overthrow of the oligarchic government during the decades that were to follow.

In order to recruit troops for the war, Marius ignored the property qualifications for military service (which had already been lowered in the Second Punic War) and called up propertyless volunteers on an extensive scale. This inaugurated a period in which volunteer and conscript soldiers alike, on discharge, began to look to their general to use his own power to gain them rewards, since they had no land or money of their own and could not rely on getting any from the Senate, which viewed them with suspicion as potential instruments of sedition. On arrival in Numidia, Marius won impressive successes that showed him to be an exceptional military commander. Yet even so he could not bring about the final defeat of his enemy. In the end, however, Jugurtha was captured through the treachery of an African ally, arranged by Marius's lieutenant Sulla; and the Romans put him to death (104).

Public impatience at the slow course of the Jugurthine War was heightened by alarming developments beyond the northern frontiers. For, despite the establishment of Roman power in southern France (Gallic Narbonensis), the land defenses of Italy had become gravely threatened by two groups of German tribes, the Cimbri and Teutones. Forced to migrate from their homes in Jutland by overpopulation and the encroachments of the sea, these masses of tribesmen spent long years roving along the Elbe and Danube and then, over a period of eight years, inflicted defeats on several Roman armies north and west of the Alps. The culminating setback was a battle with the Cimbri at Arausio (Orange), at which two incapable and quarrelsome consuls suffered Rome's most serious military disaster for over a hundred years (105). Next, the Germans moved on to Spain, still not venturing to invade Italy which was thus granted a respite of three years. During this period, Marius made ready to confront them. Then, fully prepared, he crushed the Teutones in a bloody engagement at Aquae Sextiae (Aix en Provence), where three thousand of his men concealed on high ground won the day by unexpectedly launching an attack on their rear (102). Then, in the next year, he fought a torrid, dusty battle against the Cimbri on the Camp Raudii in north Italy (probably near Ferrara, not Vercelli as supposed), in which shattering casualties were inflicted on them. And that was the end of the German threat.

Yet the war had instilled in the Romans a terror of the northern barbarians which they never again wholly lost. Moreover, it had brought about other consequences also. It had given Marius, elected consul year after year, the opportunity not only to achieve unprecedented power for himself, but also to raise the Roman army's equipment and organization to a new level of efficiency. The *pilum* or thrusting spear which all legionaries carried was now fitted with a wooden rivet that broke on impact so that the enemy could not throw the spear back. There were also important developments in military tactics; in particular, the supersession of the maniple, implying dispersion, by the larger cohort, providing concentration, was now complete. Each cohort contained six centurions of different grades who provided the necessary continuity: men of formidable courage, experience, and initiative, generally promoted from the ranks, who combined the functions and prestige of a modern company commander and a senior sergeant. Each cohort had military standards of its own, and each legion possessed its own silver eagle, the emblem of Rome. Everyone of these units was animated by a new feeling of *esprit de corps:* a feeling, however, that as we have seen, was increasingly directed by these landless volunteers to the commander himself rather than to the state, so that his soldiers became known as "Marius's Mules."

Their dependence upon him was immediately put to the test. After their military service was ended, land had to be found to reward them, in the face of senatorial opposition. To find this land became the task of a popular speaker named Saturninus, for Marius invoked his help, thus revealing the potentialities of an alliance between a thwarted military leader and a demagogue. Elected tribune of the people in 103 and 100 B.C., with some support from the nobility, Saturninus arranged for Marius's veterans to be assigned large allotments in north Africa and then in southern Gaul, while others were settled in colonies in Sicily, Greece, and Macedonia. This overseas colonization was modeled on the policy of Gaius Gracchus, whose system of monthly grain distributions Saturninus also revived.

He innovated by forcing the senators to agree to his program under pain of exile. But the most significant feature of his activity was the violence he organized at meetings and in the streets; this marked the beginning of a new epoch in which such disorders were to become habitual. In this spirit, Saturninus smoothed the way to his own reelection by hiring toughs to murder one of his competitors; and then he had a candidate for the consulship assassinated as well. But by now Marius, consul for the sixth time, had had enough and withdrew his cooperation. In support of the Senate's declaration of an emergency, Marius personally raised an improvised force and

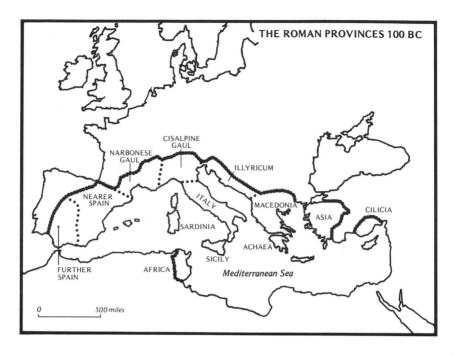

led it into action against Saturninus and his friends, who were arrested and shortly afterwards died by lynching in prison.

This intervention by Marius's soldiery was ominous, for it showed generals of the future they could enlist armies of their own troops and veterans, who were virtually their personal dependents; and they might choose to do this to secure absolute power for themselves. But Marius, although full of ambitions of a more orthodox nature, had no such desire to become an autocrat. He was already, it is true, a portentous and exceptional figure, because no man lacking a consular ancestry had ever before reached such heights. And he adopted a tough, rough manner befitting his self-made career. But he never became the first of the dictator-generals, for their time had not yet arrived. He was rather the last of that series of great commanders, men like the two Scipios, who were still prepared to work within the system. Yet there now followed a period, the opening decade of the first century B.C., in which Marius, having offended both sides in turn, was discarded and played scarcely any part in Roman politics, his heroic foreign wars almost forgotten.

The War With the Italians

It was a time in which the claims of the Italian allies, which had waxed so strong in the time of Gaius Gracchus, were strongly revived, while the Senate did virtually nothing to deal with the problem. These allies had made a full contribution to the fighting against the Numidians and Germans and had expected to benefit largely from the colonial schemes of Saturninus. But the plans had been allowed to lapse, and the numerous Italians who flocked to Rome to riot in favor of their revival had been repressed. That was in 95 B.C.; four years later matters came to a head, when Marcus Livius Drusus the Younger, son of the man of the same name who had opposed Gaius Gracchus, was elected to a tribunate like his father. A person of ostentatious rectitude, the son now proposed a decisive measure granting the full Roman franchise to the Italian allies; and they, in enthusiastic response, proclaimed that he was their patron, and swore an oath declaring that they would be his loyal clients forever. He also claimed, grandiloquently, to be the patron of the whole Senate as well. But neither the senators nor the knights supported his bill, since another proposal he had made, to the effect that the courts should be shared between both of these groups, was satisfactory to neither. And he was also opposed by the urban voters, who did not want to share their privileges with Italians. Nor did the violent gangs, which, like other politicians of this period, he felt constrained to employ, help to inspire confidence in his moderation or diplomacy. His program was rejected, and an assassin fatally stabbed him.

The failure and death of Drusus created feelings of such desperate disappointment among the already disaffected Italians that they now plunged the peninsula into an unparalleled and terrible war (90–87 B.C.). It was known to posterity as the Social War (from *socii,* allies) and sometimes, too, as the Marsian War after one of the central Italian tribes that formed the core of the rebel confederacy.

These peoples, for the most part, wanted full Roman citizenship. But the revolt was also joined by the Samnites and their associates farther south. They still remembered their defeats by the Romans two centuries earlier and increasingly formed much wider aims directed at nothing less than the restoration of their complete independence. Backed by fighting men of excellent quality and experience, the rebels formed a government at Corfinium (Corfinio), a natural center of mid-Italian communications. And there they struck silver coins inscribed with the word "Italia," which was the name they gave to the city. The name was written in the Oscan letters of the old Oscan language of Italy.

The Romans were caught by surprise in the first year of the war, and their

Silver *denarius* of the Italian rebels in the Social (Marsian) War, minted at their capital Corfinium (renamed ITALIA). Soldiers are shown swearing an oath over a pig.

enemies were thus able to maintain the initiative in both the central and southern war zones, failing, it is true, to inflict any crippling blow but pursuing an effective strategy of exhaustion. As for the Romans, for a time they employed Marius as a general, but only as one among others, so that despite successes he soon withdrew in a huff because he had not been granted a special overriding commission. Thereafter they relied on other commanders. And these fought dourly back, helped by the Roman and Latin fortress-colonies, which did not join the rebels and provided the legions with the breathing space they needed. Yet the Romans were increasingly racked by fears that the spread of the rising would threaten their communications with their recruiting ground of Cisalpine Gaul. It may have been made a separate province at this very time so that the area could be given a governor to direct mobilization. If the contacts of the Romans with Cisalpine Gaul were interrupted, they would be hard put to it to find enough troops to place in the field.

The Roman authorities therefore decided, in mid-war, that the major political concessions that they had so catastrophically failed to offer in time of peace could not be delayed any longer. So in consequence one of the consuls of the year, Lucius Julius Caesar, brought forward a bill conferring the Roman citizenship upon all Italians who had remained loyal, as well as on those who had revolted but were now prepared to lay down their arms. This concession halted the impetus of the rebellion, and in the following year the Romans followed it up by measures extending the franchise to every free man south of the Po, while those communities in Transpadane Gaul (the Cisalpine region lying north of that river) that had not gained privileged status already were raised to the halfway Latin status that conferred citizenship on their elected officials. Fighting continued for the next two years on several fronts, but from now on the revolt stood no real chance of success, and in the end the war petered out.

It had been a traumatic convulsion, threatening not only the very existence of Rome's Mediterranean empire but also the survival of the city itself as the center of Italy. In the long run, the results of the rebellion were mixed, for whereas Lucius Caesar's law marked a large step towards the unification of Roman Italy as a nation, it also meant that, when the bulk of Roman citizens could no longer make visits to the capital, the old city-state government had become obsolete. On the short term, the Social War caused ruinous damage around the countryside. It also produced a whole further generation of ex-soldiers who would menace the stability of the state unless they were amply rewarded. And it taught soldiers of the future how to fight against their own comrades on behalf of dubious ideals.

Moreover, the concessions extracted by the Italians during the stress of hostilities proved, on closer inspection, to be inadequate and illusory. They had provided that the new citizens should be restricted to only eight, or at most ten, of the thirty-five electoral tribes, thus insuring that their voting power could always be defeated by the other Roman citizens. This was presumably a last-ditch obstruction by the reactionaries, and in the military crisis of 90 B.C. the Italians do not seem to have fully appreciated the disabilities it imposed on them. But as the war began to draw to an end, this unfairness became a vital grievance.

In 88 B.C., the problem was tackled by the tribune Sulpicius Rufus. He was a friend of the younger Drusus, whose efforts had failed three years eariler; and he was a member of the same circle of wealthy, brilliant young nobles. He was also an orator of incomparable dignity, a master of tragic effects. Relying, then, on these advantages and on devoted groups of armed men parading the streets, Sulpicius put forward a proposal that the newly enfranchised Italian allies should be distributed among all the thirty-five tribes—and he even extended this provision to include freedmen (ex-slaves), who had rarely received any such consideration before, but who might, once included, considerably shift the balance of voting strength. Not surprisingly, Sulpicius's measure encountered the fiercest opposition. So he turned away from his more conservative friends to Marius, who had been skulking disregarded in the wings. And he proposed, in exchange for political help, to secure Marius the supreme command in an important Eastern war.

Silver tetradrachm of Rome's enemy Mithridates VI Eupator,
King of Pontus (120-63 B.C.)

Sulla in the East

This was to be fought against King Mithridates VI of Pontus in northern
Asia Minor—the first of several wars against that monarch, extending over
a period of twenty-five years. A noted hunter, lover, and warrior, Mithridates affected Hellenism but was of Persian descent, and the governing
nobility of his rich country were Iranian or Iranized, providing fine soldiers
from their feudal estates, and especially horsemen. Mithridates had inherited from his father a policy of territorial expansion, and early in his reign,
he himself extended his kingdom with great vigor. The kingdom of the
Cimmerian Bosphorus (Crimea), enormously rich from south Russian
grain, fell under his control, and the Black Sea became almost a Pontic lake.
He thus became an active, aggressive rival of the Romans, whose frontiers
matched his own in Asia Minor.

But Mithridates's attempts to annex the neighboring kingdom of Bithynia, a client of Rome, proved unsuccessful; and Bithynian counterraids
inspired by the Romans caused him such anger that in 88 B.C. he invaded
the province of Asia. And there he caused eighty thousand of its Italian and
Italian-Greek commercial representatives to be massacred by the local city
authorities. He had encouraged Asian debtors to kill their Italian creditors,
and their willingness to comply was a shocking demonstration of Roman
unpopularity. Moreover, such Italian businessmen as survived the holocaust were bankrupted by Mithridates's seizure of the province; and the
debacle was profoundly felt in Rome itself, where the reserves of the treasury, which had been greatly dependent on Asian revenues, fell almost to
nothing.

After thus gaining control of large regions of Asia Minor, Mithridates crossed the Aegean and occupied Athens and other parts of Greece, so that Roman military retaliation became an even more urgent necessity. The supreme command was entrusted to the fifty-year-old patrician Lucius Cornelius Sulla, a man who, after a debauched but financially profitable youth, had distinguished himself in the Jugurthine and Social wars and now assumed the consulship for 88. But the tribune Sulpicius Rufus, by forcible methods, secured Sulla's supersession in the conduct of the Mithridatic campaign by his own new ally, the half-forgotten Marius. However, Sulla, refusing to accept this dismissal, fled to the troops he had been destined to command in Asia Minor (his old soldiers in the Social War) and instead led them successfully in an attack upon Rome itself. It was a fateful moment in history. This was the first march on the capital, the first civil war, and the first clear example of troops acting out of loyalty to their commander to defy the government. Moreover, Sulla created another precedent by declaring Sulpicius (whose legislation was rescinded) to be an outlaw, and Marius another. A price was set on their heads, and Sulpicius was hunted down and put to death. But Marius escaped, amid great perils, and hid in north Africa.

Meanwhile, Sulla left for Greece, where he twice defeated a general of Mithridates and then captured the city of Athens, wrecking its port, the Piraeus. Next, remaining aloof from other Roman troops in the area—whose commanders were opposed to him politically—he crossed over into Asia Minor. But once there, instead of pursuing the fight against Mithridates, he negotiated an agreement with him at Dardanus near Troy (85). Although the monarch was obliged to evacuate his conquered territories and pay an indemnity, the terms were mild for a Roman peace since he secured recognition as ruler of Pontus and a friend and ally of the Romans —the major punishment, instead, falling on the wealthy cities of Asia which had collaborated in the murder of Roman citizens and were now made to pay enormous reparations.

The fact was that Sulla could not afford to expend his troops on prolonging the war, for Rome itself had fallen into the hands of his political enemies. Its government was led, for the next four years, by the patrician Cinna. Like Sulla, whom he now proceeded to outlaw, he had fought creditably in the Social War; and as soon as Sulla had left for the East, he again followed in his footsteps by marching on Rome. Marius, too, came back from his refuge in north Africa to join him and took the lead in political reprisals, comprising by far the bloodiest civilian massacres that Rome had ever experienced. And shortly afterwards, with his mind partly unhinged, he died (86). His brutal ineptitude had given a classic demonstration that military attainments were not always matched by political skill.

Thereafter Cinna's rule became a good deal better than a largely hostile conservative tradition subsequently admitted. He had to grapple with a grave debt problem caused by the convulsions of the past few years. This crisis, reviving a theme dominant in earlier Roman history, had come to a head three years earlier when creditors pressing for repayment murdered a praetor who tried to apply old laws against usury; and the situation was aggravated by Mithridates's occupation of Asia, which caused many of the Italian businessmen he had ruined to recall loans and resort to panic-stricken hoardings of whatever money they could collect, thus withdrawing cash from circulation. But in 86 a radical bill, remitting three-quarters of all outstanding debts, came into force at Rome. The new law was, inevitably, unpopular among that important section of the knights whose financial activities included the launching of loans. But they were appeased by an additional measure directed against another of their grievances: this was a current depreciation of the silver *denarius,* which had meant that the loans they had made in good coin were repaid in bad, with the result that they incurred enormous losses. To meet their complaints, Marius's nephew Marcus Marius Gratidianus initiated a "good money" policy insisting on a sound *denarius,* and unofficial exchange rates were banned. This began to win a good deal of support. But it was cut short because in early 84 a mutiny broke out, in which he himself was killed; and the authority of his successors abruptly dwindled.

11

Reaction and Breakdown

The Dictatorship of Sulla

At this juncture Sulla, outlawed in Rome, openly rebelled and invaded Italy. The disintegrating administration of the city was supported by the Samnites—still smarting from memories of the Social War—and the combined force made a final stand against Sulla outside the Colline Gate of Rome (82). But the outcome was catastrophic to the defenders, and the Samnites fell to a man during the engagement and the butchery of prisoners that followed. Nor were they by any means the only people to be slaughtered, since Sulla organized a mass murder of his enemies that left even Marius's precedent far behind. With the help of a bodyguard of ten thousand men known as "Cornelii," he proscribed and executed a total scarcely short of that same number, including forty senators and sixteen hundred knights. Their lands, too, were avidly confiscated by Sulla, to be given to one hundred thousand of his retired legionaries, settled in numerous large Roman colonies forcibly imposed on the Italian countryside. His nonchalant, devil-may-care manner had always appealed to his soldiers, and now their loyalty in following him against the government was rewarded.

And meanwhile he set about realizing his own highly personal vision of how the nation ought to be reconstructed. For himself he chose the obsolete position of dictator. This office had been incorporated in the earliest republican constitution in order to deal with emergencies; it was not envisaged that its holders would remain in power for more than six months. However, the dictatorship had been abolished at the end of the third century B.C., owing to the fear that it might encourage autocracy. Now Sulla unearthed and revived it for the novel purpose of "making laws and setting up the state"—and with the equally novel absence of any maximum duration, so that he was completely immune from any checks from any quarter. Yet he chose to pass his laws in proper form

Silver *denarius* of Q. Pompeius Rufus
showing his grandfather Sulla as consul.

through the Assembly. And they were numerous. They were also almost uniformly conservative, for Sulla's solution for the troubles of the community, thought out carefully on the advice of his supporting faction, envisaged the restoration of the Senate's flagging authority. There was a certain irony in this because he himself had earlier taken the most decisive step possible to break senatorial power by the naked militarism of his march on Rome. But he was determined that no one else should ever do the same again.

To this end, he decided that one of the principal needs was to break the power of the tribunes of the people, who in recent years had so often challenged senatorial control. Henceforward they were not allowed to move any law whatever without the prior approval of the Senate. Moreover, their veto was abolished in criminal cases and limited in other contexts as well, and they were debarred once they had held office as tribune, from subsequently holding any of the major offices of state, so that the tribunate would cease to attract able and ambitious politicians.

But the most impressive and lasting of Sulla's prosenatorial achievements was the reconstitution of the law courts *(quaestiones)*, of which the number was increased to at least seven, each dealing with a separate range of crimes. Gaius Gracchus had given the original extortion court to the knights, but Sulla excluded them from it altogether, making the *quaestiones* into a senatorial monopoly. However, Sulla was not an enemy of the knights, and this blow was mitigated by the admission of many of them into the Senate, which he doubled in size to six hundred, introducing many of his own Roman and Italian partisans.

The rules governing the Senate's membership were also overhauled. Men who had held the junior office of quaestor were to become senators automatically, though the quaestorship could not be held until the age of thirty and the praetorship not until forty-two, so that the rise of dangerous young careerists would be slowed down. And Sulla, remembering the illegalities of himself and others, took steps to bring provincial governors under firm senatorial control. In particular, they were forbidden to make war outside the province allotted to them, or indeed to depart for any reason beyond its borders, without previous authorization from the Senate or Assembly. One of the principal weapons against those who strayed was a law of treason, *maiestas*—a crime that had been first defined in 100 B.C. and was now handled by one of Sulla's new law courts.

It seemed paradoxical that these measures to shore up the ancient oligarchy should be taken by a man who had revived the office of dictator, and who, moreover, surrounded himself superstitiously with the mystic personality cult of an autocrat. And besides, he lavishly sponsored the vast building activities that traditionally went with this sort of monarchic role, including the construction of the Record Office (Tabularium) of Rome and the rebuilding of the Roman Senate house and of the great precinct of Fortuna at Praeneste (Palestrina), the site of one of his civil war victories. These were projects reminiscent of Eastern princes. Nevertheless, Sulla still stopped short of complete absolutism. Instead, he decided to abdicate from his dictatorship, becoming consul in 80 and returning in the following year to private life in Campania, where he died a year later.

But the memory of this mulberry-faced man, so self-indulgent and yet so energetic, easily moved to laughter and tears, who claimed he never forgot a friend or a foe, remained alive. This was not so much because of his elaborate constitutional scheme. Although he was not blindly intolerant of recent developments, his measures in this field were a putting back of the clock that failed to deal with Rome's essential economic and social problems. Moreover, his assumption that the restrictions imposed on governors and commanders would prove sufficient turned out to be wrong since in the years to come it was they, and not the state, who could mobilize powerful armies and make use of them for their own ends. After all, that was just what Sulla had done himself; and that, in the long run, was why he was remembered, because of the callous horrors of his rise to power. Nor were these recollections of his ruthlessness entirely without good effects, for at least they deterred the Romans from repeating large-scale civil war for thirty years.

The Tabularium (Record Office) begun by Sulla (the upper stories belong to the Renaissance Palace of the Senators).

Painting by Samuel Prout (1783-1852) showing the Tabularium in the background.

Reconstruction of Temple of Fortuna Primigenia, Praeneste (Palestrina).

The Rise of Pompey

The failure of Sulla's constitutional reconstruction was demonstrated without the slightest delay. When one of his former officers, Marcus Lepidus, a man of patrician but liberal family with extensive noble backing, became consul in 78 B.C., he employed his term of office to bring forward an opportunistic program for the restoration of the tribunate, which Sulla had so deliberately weakened. Lepidus staked his chances on a possible mass rising of Italians dispossessed by the proscriptions, in which he himself had amassed a fortune. In 77, supported by another disaffected officer in Cisalpine Gaul, he led a considerable force of Etruscan and other malcontents in a dash for the capital, where an emergency decree was passed by the Senate. His way was barred by an army of the government, and he was defeated at the Milvian Bridge; and shortly afterwards he died.

Far more able was another anti-Sullan, Sertorius, a Sabine who set up an independent government in Spain, where he won over the whole of the eastern seaboard. He also enjoyed widespread support from local tribesmen, among whom his enlightened methods gained him unrivaled popularity, handing on to the future the idea that it might pay after all to treat the provincials decently—and attempt their Romanization. He maintained contact with Lepidus, whose followers to the number of twenty thousand fled to his colors after the collapse of Lepidus's rising in Italy. The men under Sertorius's command swore an oath that if he fell, they would not survive him.

The Senate dispatched an army against them but were forced at the end of 77 to supplement it by sending out substantial reinforcements which they placed under the command of a general only twenty-nine years of age. This was Pompey (Cnaeus Pompeius), who already enjoyed a considerable reputation. His father had been one of Rome's principal officers in the Social War, and Pompey, after serving with him, had built up a strong personal following in central and eastern Italy. When Sulla arrived from the east, Pompey, who was married to his stepdaughter, had joined forces with him. He had then gone on to win victories on Sulla's behalf in Sicily and north Africa, and the dictator had felt reluctantly obliged to grant him a triumph, although according to all the rules he was not even old enough to be a senator. This, then, was the young man who was now sent to Spain against Sertorius. At first, he achieved no result. But finally, Sertorius was murdered at a banquet by his own undistinguished lieutenant, whom Pompey then defeated without difficulty and put to death. In this somewhat unmeritorious fashion he had increased his military renown.

Meanwhile in Italy an event had occurred that inspired great terror among the Romans. It was the last of the series of slave wars extending back to the previous century. But this was a slave war of a special character, because it took place on the Italian peninsula itself and the principal rebels were professional gladiators. The outbreak began at Capua, home of one of the largest gladiatorial schools and barracks. It was led by a Thracian named Spartacus, a man of courage and humanity, who had served as a Roman auxiliary soldier. Slaves of all kinds flocked to join him, and within the space of two years they defeated no fewer than four Roman armies. Spartacus's hope, in conducting these operations, was that his men might seize the chance to break out and make their way across the Alps, after which they could seek their own homelands in freedom. However, they made no serious attempt to carry out these aims, preferring instead to plunder the rich Italian countryside.

Business interests were gravely damaged by their looting; but the military respite it provided was turned to good account by the Roman authorities. They entrusted the command against Spartacus to the ex-praetor Crassus; he was a former subordinate of Sulla, amiable and flattering, easy of access, a talented wire-puller, who had vastly increased his hereditary wealth in the course of the proscriptions. After meticulously training a force of forty thousand men, Crassus attempted in vain to catch Spartacus in the toe of the peninsula but finally cornered and killed him in Apulia, crucifying six thousand of his slave followers along the Appian Way (71 B.C.).

Meanwhile Pompey had been summoned back from Spain to help conduct the operations, and he arrived just in time to take part in the final manhunt, which he and his friends magnified into a major military success, eclipsing the victory of Crassus.

At this point the two ambitious men, each with his own army, might well have come to blows. But Crassus, though a daring financial speculator, was a cautious politician; and Pompey, in spite of many irregularities during his earlier career, showed few signs of openly unconstitutional behavior. Although harboring strong mutual suspicion, they did not clash but instead came to an understanding according to which they would jointly demand election to the consulships of the year 70. Legally speaking, both were unqualified because neither had disbanded his army as consular candidates were required to do, and besides, Pompey, who had not even taken his seat as a senator, was debarred on grounds of his youth. Nevertheless, the Senate had to give way, thus revealing for the attention of future politicians how a resolute combination of ambitious men could frustrate the republic. And so the Assembly duly elected them as consuls.

Setting their disagreements aside, they devoted their year of office to the overturning of Sulla's constitution—a program that gained them considerable popularity, except, of course, in the Senate. Moreover, its members also had to endure the condemnation of one of their colleagues, Verres, whose prosecution for gross dishonesty during his governorship of Sicily was triumphantly undertaken by the rising orator Cicero. In the same anti-Sullan spirit Crassus and Pompey encouraged the censors of the year to expel sixty-four senators. They also supported a bill reducing the senatorial membership of the jury panels to one-third, and a law proposed by Pompey relieved the tribunate of all the restrictions placed upon it by the late dictator. Almost the whole of Sulla's activity in favor of the traditional order was therefore obliterated, and the old flexibility and anarchy of Roman politics had been fully restored.

During the years that immediately followed, Crassus remained content to stay at home, increasing his financial resources and political influence. But Pompey was waiting for a chance to effect some spectacular increase in his military reputation, and the opportunity was not long in coming. It was provided by the scandalous prevalence of Mediterranean piracy. Ever since Rome in the previous century had shortsightedly weakened Rhodes and its naval police force, pirates had been conducting their operations unimpededly, with the connivance of Roman slave-purchasing interests. Efforts by the government to destroy their harbors on the coast of Asia Minor had not proved effective (102), and during the wars of the eighties, their raids had become more and more audacious. Cyrenaica (eastern Libya) had been annexed and made into a new province in order to provide bases against the pirates, but in vain; and now they were directly menacing the grain supply of Rome itself. In 67, therefore, over the heads of the Senate, a tribune put through a bill that entrusted Pompey with the task of suppressing them and conferred on him for this purpose an overriding Mediterranean command, with one hundred and twenty thousand infantry and five hundred ships at his disposal. He carried out this enterprise in an operation of lightning rapidity lasting only three months, during which time he and his officers totally cleared the seas of pirates.

Thereupon another tribune presented a further bill to the Assembly, granting Pompey a general commission to settle the affairs of the Near East, and in particular to terminate the hostilities that were still dragging on against Mithridates VI of Pontus. The bill was made law despite the undiminished reluctance of the Senate, whose dominant position, it was now clear, had virtually ceased to exist. After the peace of 85, Mithridates had rapidly recovered, repelling the officer left behind by Sulla and building up stores of money and supplies, so that when Rome decided to annex adjacent Bithynia in 74, he had marched into that country to forestall them, leaving it garrisoned by a Pontic army. But then the Romans had sent out a general of great ability, a former supporter of Sulla named Lucullus, who expelled the king from Bithynia and even from his own homeland of Pontus (74–70), forcing him to flee to his eastern neighbor and ally Armenia, a country almost new to world history, which had recently become a considerable empire.

Lucullus occupied the Armenian capital; but in 68 his troops refused to carry on. This was partly because he had arranged a reorganization of Asian finances in which Roman business interests had not been allowed to profit as much as they wanted; and at home this had earned him many foes, who played their part in instigating the mutiny in his army. But on the spot, too, the weather conditions his soldiers had to contend with were intolerable, and above all, Lucullus, for all his military talents, was an aristocratic disciplinarian who lacked the ability to get on with the rank and file. In all these unfavorable conditions, his army virtually fell apart. One of the Roman leaders who had accelerated its disintegration from afar was Pompey, an old political enemy, and now it was he who took over the command.

On arrival in the field, he proved outstandingly successful—though his strategic gifts were scarcely put to the test. Mithridates was deserted by his

Armenian allies, so that it was possible to defeat him immediately. He contrived to escape to the Cimmerian Bosphorus (Crimea), but there, faced by a rebellion led by his son, he committed suicide. His fight against the Romans had lasted, with intervals, throughout a quarter of a century. It had been important because it involved them in their most intractable wars of the age. Moreover, these recurrent crises exerted various other impacts on the Roman scene as well. For example, they forced the government to create long-term, semi-independent commands, with all the attendant perils they posed for the central authority. And Rome's continuing involvement with Mithridates, and its outcome, enormously expanded its commitment in eastern lands.

Pompey, after sensationally exploring and opening up the hitherto unknown region of the Caucasus (65), now put into effect a sweeping settlement of the affairs of western Asia, involving an immense amount of detailed planning. Pontus was annexed and united with Bithynia to form a single province. In Syria, the last feeble Seleucid monarch was removed, and his country also, with its great city of Antioch, was taken over and made a province—so that out of the three great successor states of Alexander, Macedonia, the Seleucids, and Egypt, only the last named now remained in a condition of formal independence, although it too was already largely subservient to Rome. In the small Judaean kingdom, where there had been dynastic disputes, Pompey captured the ancient capital Jerusalem, causing great and lasting Jewish distress by walking into the Temple; but a member of the reigning Hasmonaean (Maccabee) dynasty was still allowed to rule, as one of Rome's dependent client-monarchs.

This extension of Rome's ancient *clientela* principle to foreign states was nothing new. But Pompey enlarged its application greatly. The client kings were tied to the service of Rome in order to defend its frontiers and serve as listening posts to the outside world. In return, they were supported by the Romans against internal subversive movements and allowed a free hand inside their own countries. Thus Rome was spared the trouble and expense of administering these territories; and the formula worked well. Only in Armenia, perhaps, was Pompey mistaken in retaining the local prince instead of annexing the country, for he left it as a future bone of contention between the Romans and the powers that lay farther to the east.*

On the site of his victory over Mithridates, he created the new town of Nicopolis, settling a mixed population of veterans, wounded soldiers, and local inhabitants. But that was only one of the forty cities he founded or restored throughout the East, in pursuance of the actively urbanizing tradition of the Greek monarchies. Under upper-class leaderships approved by

---

*First Parthia (p. 218) and then Persia (p. 367).

Rome, the cities, new and old alike, were to provide convenient nuclei, not of Romanization because their culture normally remained Greek, but of Roman political influence and *clientela*.

Pompey's reconstruction of the Near East far exceeded anything of the kind that any Roman had ever performed before, showing him to be an administrator of the very first order. Indeed, although he still had fifteen years to live, this was easily the greatest achievement of his career, massively standing the test of time and forming the basis of all future reorganizations. And the spectacular honors he received from the eastern communities likewise foreshadowed the imperial personages to come. Moreover, his arrangements were immensely lucrative, both to himself and to Rome. As for his own gains, the spoils of war and gifts from grateful or anxious monarchs and cities (he removed many of their tax immunities) made him an even richer man than Crassus—who had hitherto been the wealthiest man of the day—and gave him a larger host of dependents. And his settlement also vastly enlarged the resources of the Roman treasury, raising the annual revenue of the state by no less than forty percent. The triumph at his homecoming was celebrated with unprecedented splendor.

Cicero

While Pompey was away in the East, there had been an uneasy air of suspense at Rome, where people remembered the autocracy Sulla had established when he returned from the same lands. Now they feared that history would repeat itself. Intrigues multiplied, largely prompted by Crassus. He did not act directly against Pompey but financed various needy characters who might work to increase his own personal influence.

One such figure who acquired a good deal of notoriety was Catiline, an impoverished patrician who had supported Sulla but now offered hopes to Sullans and anti-Sullans alike who had become destitute and angry and eager to repair their damaged fortunes. As an undischarged prisoner on an embezzlement charge, Catiline was debarred from becoming a candidate for the consulship of 65, and there were rumors that he and others plotted to murder the men who secured election in his place. He was also disqualified from standing for 64 but was admitted to the competition for 63. At this stage Crassus was apparently still willing to back him; but a wide range of conservative senators, and some of their less conservative colleagues as well, were alarmed by the possibility that he might get in. He seemed to them a flashy and ungovernable person ready for any kind of unscrupulous action that might reverse the setbacks his career had suffered.

In consequence, this large and varied group of worried men banded together to put up a candidate to stand for the consulship against him. The

Marble bust of Cicero.

man they selected was Cicero, from Marius's hometown Arpinum (Arpino). Cicero came of a family that had never provided a consul before, and such "new men" found it notoriously difficult to gain the office; indeed none seem to have done so for the previous thirty years. On the other hand, he was an orator of unique brilliance in a society in which oratory was the major part of politics. He had scored a first-class success in 70 in convicting the corrupt governor of Sicily, Verres; and after that he had backed the assignment of the eastern command to Pompey, who, despite occasional interruptions and reservations, continued to be his favorite statesman from then onwards.

These activities, like his undistinguished origins, might have seemed by no means useful recommendations to the favor of old-fashioned republicans, or even middle-of-the-road members of the Senate. Nevertheless, men of both these categories rallied to his support against Catiline, whom they regarded as a grave threat to social stability. So Cicero duly won the consulship for 63. His colleague was an insignificant character who had privately favored Catiline but was then persuaded not to support his candidacy.

At the elections held in 63 for the consulships of the following year, Catiline made a further attempt to gain office, this time with a program sensational enough to confirm the worst fears, proposing not only sweeping land distribution but a general cancellation of debts. This program was designed to appeal to bankrupt nobles, veterans, and urban poor—indeed, displaced and discontented persons of every sort. But such proposals scared off not only all conservative and moderates, but Crassus as well; and Cicero, who equated debt cancellation with what he considered the worst of all evils, the destruction of private property, helped to secure Catiline's defeat once again. And so now that defeated and disappointed man, estimating that his chances of reaching the top of the tree by legal, constitutional means had vanished forever, began to move outside the law instead and plan the subversion of public order. His intention now was that a force of his discreditable supporters in Etruria, which was full of discontented men ready for violence, should march on Rome in October of this year, 63 B.C.

However, six days before the date fixed for the coup, rumors of its imminence leaked out, and the Senate passed an emergency decree. Nevertheless, in the absence of concrete proof of his seditious intentions, Catiline himself, protected by influential friends, was still left at large in the city and went on plotting revolution. But when Cicero, in the first of his four magnificent Catilinarian Orations, proceeded to unmask and denounce his aims, Catiline felt it advisable to withdraw from the capital and left to take personal command of his followers in Etruria. Rome had become increasingly uncomfortable for him. Cicero had won back a number of his support-

Manuscript of Cicero's book *On the State (De Republica)* on parchment re-used in eighth century A.D.

ers by claiming that Catiline intended to burn the city down; and then by a great stroke of luck he obtained written evidence of Catiline's revolutionary intentions from Gallic envoys visiting Rome. Thereupon Cicero proceeded to seize five of the leading conspirators in the city, including men of very high rank, and obtained the Senate's approval of their execution, which was immediately carried out—on his orders.

The legality of this step was widely disputed. Cicero himself maintained loudly for the rest of his life that his action had been necessary in order to check an imminent rebellion, and that it was warranted by the Senate's concurrence, as well as by their former emergency decree. On the other hand the Senate was an advisory body, not an executive one, so that the deed still remained the responsibility of the consul. And it could be argued against him that this order violated a Roman citizen's right to be tried, and that citizens who were not actually caught red-handed under arms, and were not therefore an immediate source of danger, did not look like the enemies of the state against whom alone such summary treatment would have been justified. It seemed, therefore, that Cicero had acted illegally; and this belief among his compatriots affected much of his future career. But in any case, the Catilinarian plot was not the tremendous crisis from which he claimed, for evermore, to have saved the state, but a relatively minor upheaval. It was only important because of the incomparably eloquent speeches and writings Cicero devoted to it, magnifying and defending his own role.

In the final senatorial debate preceding the execution of the plotters, two statesmen of the future expressed their views. Cato spoke up in favor of Cicero's proposal that they should be killed, and Julius Caesar against it. Cato, the great-grandson of the censor of the same name who had been a leading politician of the previous century, was a man of thirty-two, formidable, inhumanly unforgiving, a heavy drinker, and uncompromising in his opposition to all who appeared not to measure up to the traditional system. Gaius Julius Caesar, five years older, was a patrician linked by marriage ties with Marius and Cinna. After a rather late start in Roman public life, and a period in which his shaky finances were bolstered up by Crassus, he had staged a trial demonstration against senatorial abuses of the emergency decree (63). In the same year he had obtained, at the cost of heavy outlay, the chief priesthood of the Roman state, an office that without interfering with its occupant's political career, was a source of extensive prestige and patronage. At the end of the same year, Caesar was about to become praetor. It was at this juncture that he cast constitutional doubts on the propriety of putting the Catilinarians to death. His opinion did not prevail, but he gained valuable allies among those who were afraid of what such high-handed acts might lead to.

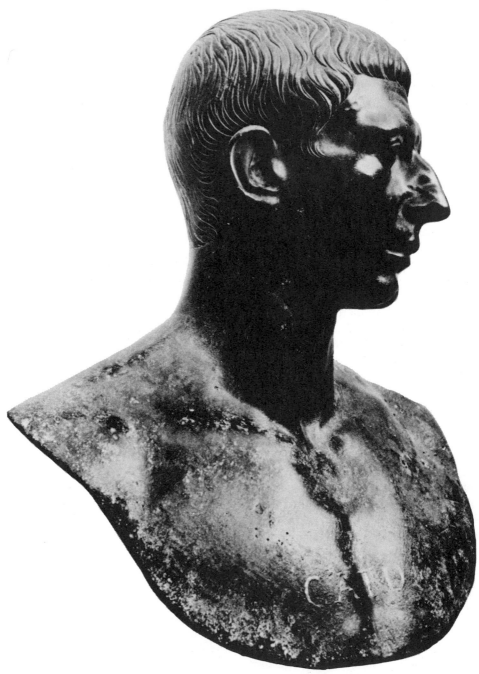

Bronze bust of Cato the Younger.

For the time being, however, Cicero's policy seemed vindicated because Catiline moved into open rebellion at the head of his troops. But now that his friends in Rome had been overwhelmed, he no longer had any hope of marching on the city and instead tried to flee northwards out of the Italian peninsula. But two armies sent by the government, one at either end of the Apennines, caught him in a trap, and he and his followers were destroyed near Pistoria (Pistoia) in January 62 B.C. Cicero was now, for a brief moment, the hero of the hour.

Cicero became famous in later generations and epochs as the most articulate representative of a remarkable upper-class society that pursued a highly cultured and luxurious way of life derived from the immense accretions of wealth by the imperial republic and its leaders. The orator himself possessed a mansion on the Palatine Hill and at least eight houses in the country, some just places of rest as he journeyed from place to place, but others elegantly furnished and adorned by wall paintings, and floor mosaics and housing notable collections of Greek art. Yet, he had not been born to this grandeur and lacked the wealth needed to purchase and maintain all these properties; that is to say, he did not himself possess the means to pursue a successful political career. But he was extremely fortunate to have the close friendship and support of an enormously rich knight and banker, Atticus, who helped him in very many different ways and evidently believed in his political and intellectual aims.

Cicero owed his rise almost exclusively to one single quality. He was one of the most persuasive orators who has ever lived, in an age in which the very core of politics was oratory. The combination of his inborn talents with an elaborate education and training equipped him to speak and write that incomparably eloquent, rotund Latin that persuaded and overwhelmed his listeners in Senate, Assembly, and lawcourts alike, and laid the foundations of the subsequent prose of all Europe. His speeches, of which fifty-eight out of over a hundred survive, reflect all the stresses and strains of the crumbling republic, in which for three decades he lived and worked at the center of events. They also reveal Cicero the man, and so, even more remarkably, do his eight hundred unique letters, written to Atticus and other friends.

The personage who emerges is humorous and warmhearted, extravagant, as unable as the next man to see how to make a city-state govern an empire, overrespectful to the nobility to which he did not belong, and intensely eager to tell everyone of his success in stifling Catiline's second-rate coup —an excusable form of self-praise because, being a "new man," he enjoyed no built-in backing of his own. Moreover, Cicero, despite his occasional political successes, did not have the right temperament to be a first-class Roman politician. For one thing, he always took too rosy a view of his own

Wall painting from villa at Oplontis (Torre Annunziata) near Pompeii. First century B.C.

position and influence. And, worse still, he possessed a fatal lawyerlike ability to see both sides of every question and lacked the ruthless decisiveness that Roman public life required. Yet on two or three occasions in his lifetime, by an excruciating effort, he screwed up his courage to abandon vacillation and stand up and be counted against tyranny, and the last of these stands cost him his life.

Cicero, despite all his own faults and the faults of his age, had accepted the Greek idea, now current among Roman jurists and other thinkers, of a natural law *(ius naturale)*, which was a corollary of the admission of noncitizens to Rome's legal system *(ius gentium)* and which ought to be observed by all mankind. That is to say, he was convinced that right is right and wrong is wrong objectively, and that no pronouncements or laws can make them otherwise. And what was most wrong of all, he believed, was for one person to tyrannize others. Following up the precepts of the Stoic philosophy founded two and a half centuries earlier, he accepted its injunction that men and women should treat one another generously and honestly. They must do so because all human beings have their own personal value and importance. This is because, according to Stoic doctrine, all individuals share a spark of divinity that makes them akin to each other, irrespective of race or status or sex, in the universal brotherhood of humankind.

That was one of the principal elements in the *humanitas* upon which Cicero insisted, in a series of wonderfully well-written treatises on moral themes. Shunning dogma (in accordance with the views of the contemporary Athens Academy), these essays adapted Greek philosophy to Roman life and both exemplified and demanded an enlightenment of mind and character, a recognition not only of one's own unique personality but also of the personalities of others. This was the most civilized ideal, for practical purposes of living, that the world had ever seen; it has deeply influenced Western thought from his time to our own. And Cicero stressed this ideal with all the more fervent conviction because he believed that the man best equipped to teach the good life was the public speaker. As he explains in a number of analyses of that art, every orator must not only be a man of wide and liberal culture, but, if he is to do his job properly, he must also behave decently and well.

Fired by such ideas, and by the momentary acclaim that greeted his victory over the Catilinarians, Cicero adopted a political program that seemed to him to give practical expression to these doctrines. It envisaged a concept that had been discussed more than once in the previous years, a Concord of the Orders, in which the senators would be permanently allied with the knights of all Italy, municipal men like himself who had become increasingly influential in the state and had backed him strongly against the antisocial projects of Catiline. Cicero himself, however, inadvertently did more than anyone else to ruin the chances of any such concord becoming a practical possibility. When Pompey returned from his unparalleled eastern successes, Cicero promptly offended his vanity by reiterating his own achievements as savior of the country, at a moment when the other man was prepared to think of no other triumphs but his own.

Toward the First Triumvirate

Pompey was arrogant, shifty, and aloof. Yet none of the gloomy predictions of his desire to become an autocrat proved correct. Instead, as soon as he landed in Italy, he duly disbanded his troops. By so doing, he indicated clearly that despite his unquestioned desire for the greatest admiration and position that republican Rome could bestow upon him, he entertained no ambition to become a dictatorial tyrant. Moreover, as Cicero noted, Pompey was now showing a certain readiness to abandon the anticonservative faction that had given him his appointments since 70, and to side with orthodox senators instead. But at this stage he had two requests to make from them. The first was an application for land to settle his impatient veterans. This must have been foreseen and was reasonable. His second request was that all the actions he had performed in the East should be ratified as decisions of the Roman state. This was equally predictable. It could be criticized, certainly, on the grounds that he had acted largely without the customary consultations with Rome. All the same, by straining the tradition a little, his wish might have been granted in view of the gigantic gains he had brought to Rome.

Nevertheless, a series of obscure metropolitan intrigues now got under way, during which it emerged that very many leading conservatives preferred to take a short-term view and oppose his demand. They regarded his recent failure to consult the government when he was in the East as just another in a prolonged series of high-handed and illegal acts. One of their number, the former general Lucullus, added his own vindictive feelings of personal affront because Pompey had superseded and humiliated him in Asia Minor. Cato, who became tribune in 62, was another of Pompey's opponents. It was true that when Cato wanted to increase the existing free distributions of grain to keep the metropolis quiet while Catiline was still at large, he was willing enough to make use of Pompey's huge new eastern revenue for this purpose. Yet, at the same time, he also used his tribunate to block Pompey's two proposals, deploying his extraordinary powers of obstruction to the full. In the face of this pressure, the Senate continually delayed its decision about Pompey's requests; and few things contributed so greatly to the fall of the republic, which was shortly to follow, as this refusal to give him what he wanted.

Pompey the Great.

The senators also made two further ominous decisions. One of these was in relation to Crassus. After acting ambiguously towards Pompey while he was away in the East, Crassus had come to resent him greatly after his triumphant return; and now he was fully prepared to join with the Senate in blocking his two claims. Yet, in spite of this heaven-sent opportunity to enlist Crassus's support, the senators rebuffed him instead. This happened in regard to a financial matter in which he declared an interest. At the end of 61, a company of tax gatherers, who were now the most important pressure group among the knights, were claiming a rebate on the purchase price of Asian revenues they had contracted to collect, since these were proving disastrously less profitable than they had expected. They persuaded Crassus, as the most influential patron of business interests, to back their request. But Cato, not unreasonably this time, saw their appeal as an outrageous attempt to bend their perfectly clear agreement with the state —merely because it had not brought them as much profit as they had hoped. And so he persuaded the Senate to kill the proposal.

Pompey and Crassus, then, had both been snubbed. And now Caesar was snubbed as well. He had been serving as governor of Further Spain (Baetica), from which he returned to Italy in 60 to become a candidate for the consulate. But because of minor military victories won during his governorship, he had also been awarded a triumph, and he wanted to celebrate it. His right to do so, however, would have been forfeited by law if in the meanwhile he had entered the city. So he asked leave to stand for the consular elections by proxy instead of in person. Cato, however, insured that this application should be rejected. And that was not all. It was the practice at this period for the Senate to allocate to the consuls of any given year, even before their election took place and their names were known, the provinces they would be sent to govern at the conclusion of their term of office. And so now the provinces that would go to the consuls for 59 B.C. were duly allotted, and it was decided that they should not be ordinary provinces at all, but merely "the forests and cattle drifts" of Italy. This was an abnormally trivial assignment, expressly designed for one possible, or probable, contingency: that one of the consuls about to be elected would turn out to be Caesar. In other words, it was a deliberate affront directed against him personally.

The Senate had thus opposed and offended Pompey, Crassus, and Caesar —all three of them at once. Evidently its members no longer possessed the acute judgment that had won them the Mediterranean world. What happened next, therefore, seems by hindsight inevitable. The three men who had all received this treatment buried their differences with one another and joined forces against those who had insulted them. Their agreement took the form of a coalition, informal but potent, at first secret and before long publicly known, that historians describe as the First Triumvirate. Caesar asked Cicero to join this compact, but to his credit he refused. The Triumvirate was painfully different from the Concord between the Orders which he had been advocating. Far from becoming a partner in the agreement, the Senate was going to be its target and victim; it was so severely weakened that it became, for the first time, a mere political group instead of the effective government of the empire.

Later historical writers saw the event as the end of the Roman Republic, or at least as the beginning of its end. Some modern researchers have questioned this, pointing out that the triumvirs' control was not absolute, and that the traditional political activities, including more or less freely contested annual elections, still continued for another decade. Yet they continued only under the heaviest of shadows; and the oligarchy never recovered its power again.

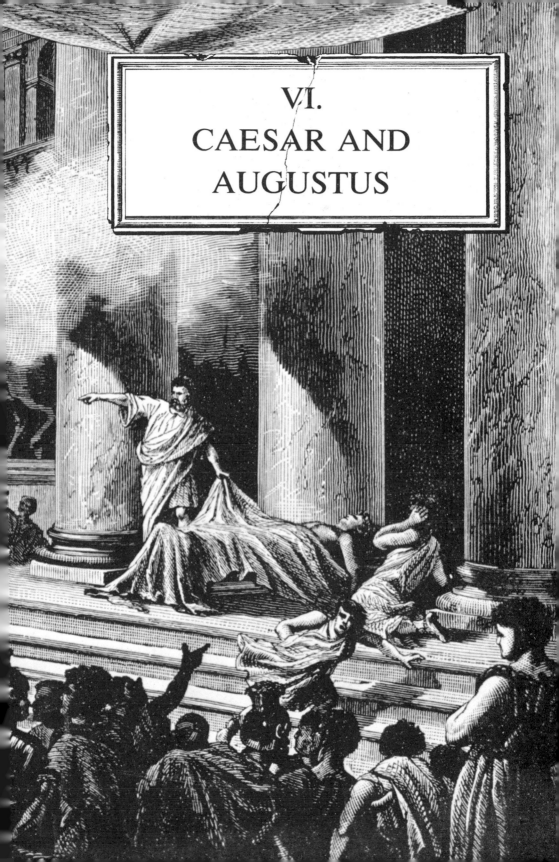

VI.
CAESAR AND AUGUSTUS

Preceding page:
Antony and the dead Caesar.

12
Caesar

The First Consulship of Caesar

When Caesar was elected to the consulship for 59 B.C., the republic was still able to exhibit faint signs of life by electing an extreme conservative, Bibulus, as his fellow consul. Nevertheless, Caesar at once pointed the way to Rome's autocratic future by pushing through a series of measures in favor of the triumvirs, Pompey, Crassus, and himself, in total disregard of the opposition.

One of his first actions as consul was to satisfy Pompey's veterans by a land bill. When his archenemy, Cato, blocked the measure in the Senate, Caesar secured its acceptance in the Assembly by forcible methods, which were held against him for the rest of his life. These methods even included the beating-up of his fellow consul. He was supported, however, by his fellow triumvirs, so that his alliance with them came to be revealed, and Pompey married his daughter Julia. Caesar then went on to insure the ratification of his new son-in-law's eastern arrangements and shared with him an enormously lucrative reward for shoring up a distressed king of Egypt. He also formed the habit of inviting Pompey to speak first in the Senate, rather than Crassus. Nevertheless, Caesar also satisfied Crassus by securing a generous financial concession for his friends the tax-collecting knights, who had been unsuccessfully demanding a rebate on their Asian contracts. And he arranged that in future the proceedings of the Senate (as well as of the Assembly) should be published openly, so that its members' freedom to conduct secret intrigues against him was severely restricted.

It was now up to the other triumvirs to help Caesar in his own political career. The governorship of Further Spain from which he was recently returned had convinced him that he possessed exceptional military talents, and these he was now eager to exploit in order to fulfill his growing ambition to become preeminent in the state. Instead, therefore, of the ridiculously unimportant province the Senate had assigned to the consuls for this year,

The family of Caesar

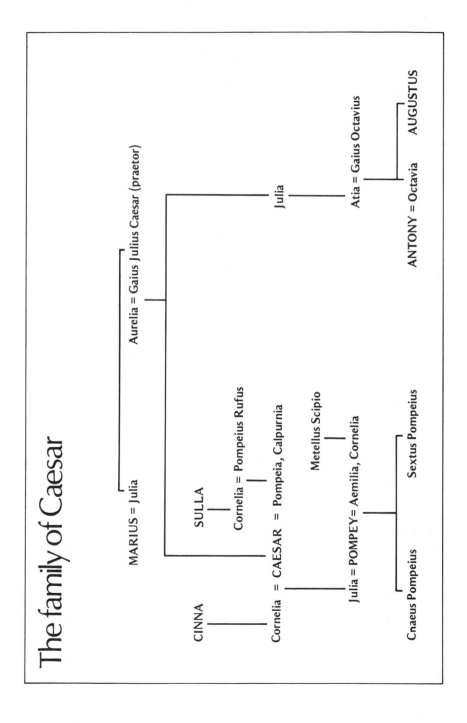

he got himself allotted an infinitely more significant province consisting of Cisalpine Gaul (north Italy) combined with Illyricum (Dalmatia). His initial purpose was apparently to lead Roman armies northeastwards, as far as the rivers Save (Sava) or Drave (Drava) in what is now Yugoslavia.

At this juncture, however, occurred the death of the governor of Transalpine or Narbonese Gaul (southern France). This was a remarkable piece of good fortune for Caesar, who saw that region as a far more promising starting-off point for military conquests and arranged for it to be added to the province already assigned to him. He knew it would be best to assume office as provincial governor as soon as his consulship was over, and to retain the job without a break for an indefinite period, since, if he became a private citizen, he would be liable to prosecution for the violent acts he had committed as consul. Before leaving Rome, however, he formed an alliance with a young politician named Clodius, a talented, eccentric radical freelance who he hoped would look after his interests in the capital, with the help of numerous inherited clients, urban gangsters, and trade corporations or guilds *(collegia),* whose mobilization and exploitation Clodius made into a fine art.

The Gallic War

In many parts of their huge unconquered tribal territories lying north of the Transalpine province, the Gauls practiced advanced agriculture, animal breeding, and working of metals. But in spite of fine cavalry, their capacity in battle was limited: once the initial charge of their horsemen and swordbearing infantry had been held up, their attacks soon degenerated into anarchic disorder. And political cohesion between the tribes and inside each of them was weak.

Between the River Seine and the Roman province lived two hundred tribes of Celtic race. The most important of them, each surrounded by a ring of lesser dependent peoples, were the Arverni (Auvergne) based on their fortress Gergovia; the Aedui, who had succeeded them as the principal allies of the Romans and had their capital at Bibracte (Mont Beuvray above Autun); and the Sequani, who were centered upon Vesontio (Besançon). While the shifting relationships among these leading tribes made it clear that Gallic unity was out of the question, their side-by-side existence at least created a certain precarious balance and, for considerable periods, a sort of peace.

This, however, was now imperiled by the Helvetii, a Celtic people of Germany who had been driven out of their homes into Switzerland and had then decided to migrate westwards, intending to traverse the whole of Gaul until they reached the Atlantic coast, where they hoped to settle. Certain

Roman leaders, however, decided that this mass migration must be stopped, since it would threaten the security of the Transalpine province. That was Caesar's ostensible reason for securing the inclusion of that province in his own command. And once his consulship had come to an end, he and the army he had got together hastened northwards.

We know a great deal about the operations that followed from his own *Gallic War*. It was the best account of warfare that had ever been written by a Roman and retained this supremacy for at least another four centuries to come. This work and his subsequent *Civil War* were entitled "Commentaries," a term that intentionally falls short of "Histories," denoting rather a commander's dispatches or memoranda, amplified by informative material and speeches (intended, as always in antiquity, to convey background rather than the actual words employed). Caesar's formidable intellect and lucid, concise Latin transform these ostensibly modest works into masterpieces. His unique inside knowledge carries extraordinary authority, though at the same time the prescribed literary form, as well as his own inclination, encouraged an egotistic approach, allowing little credit to the immense, efficient staff work behind each of his operations, or to the subordinates who conducted it and commanded his legions. Moreover, Caesar's desire to refute his political enemies at Rome leads to a good deal of distortion, not

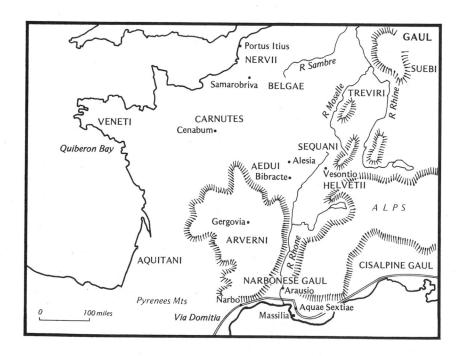

so much of the actual historical facts (which Caesar, an excellent propagandist, prefers not to falsify), but of motives, impressions, and implications.

At the outset, his numerous critics maintained that the movements of the Helvetii were no concern of Rome and that his attack on them was a piece of unprovoked aggression without precedent in the whole of Roman history. But his desire for military prestige left him unmoved by such arguments, and at Armecy beside the River Arraux he wiped out tens and perhaps hundreds of thousands of the Helvetii, while the survivors turned back into Switzerland.

Next, in the same year, he dealt with a rather more plausible menace. The Sequani, at odds with the Aedui, had imprudently invited Ariovistus, chief of one of the tribes of west Germany, to come to their aid, and in 61 B.C. he had fought the Aedui and heavily defeated them. Two years later, Ariovistus secured recognition as king and ally of the Roman people: and at the time, Caesar favored this. But soon afterwards the chief's territorial ambitions began to cause widespread alarm among the Gauls, who appealed to Rome; whereupon Caesar, scenting the prospect of another and more dramatic military campaign, reversed his favorable attitude to Ariovistus and declared that the Gallic appeal must be accepted. At first he was somewhat worried by political disloyalty among some of his own junior officers; but before long he stamped this out. Then, on the plain of Alsace, he engaged the Germans and put them to flight. Ariovistus escaped but died soon afterwards, and Caesar's friends declared him the triumphant successor of his relative Marius as destroyer of menacing western barbarians.

North of the Seine were the numerous and warlike Belgae, Germans by origin, intermarried with Celts. At first they had been content to see the Helvetii and Ariovistus defeated. But when Caesar established his winter quarters on Gallic territory, the Belgae grew deeply suspicious of his intentions and began to mobilize their war potential of three hundred thousand men. Thereupon Caesar raised two new legions in Cisalpine Gaul, bringing his total up to eight, and prepared to tackle the combined Belgic force. It soon became clear, however, that this had fallen apart, owing to the failure or virtual nonexistence of supply services; and in the end only the most powerful of these tribes, the Nervii, were still able to keep an army in the field. They possessed unusually good infantry, but in 57 Caesar annihilated them on the River Sambre, after a desperately hazardous battle. As a result of only two seasons of military operations, Gaul already looked incapable of offering any further resistance.

In Rome, Pompey proposed a thanksgiving of unprecedented duration to celebrate these victories of his fellow triumvir Caesar. Even the republican Cicero felt able to second the proposal. But he did so out of gratitude not to Caesar but to Pompey, for Cicero had been in trouble. The executions during his consulship had not been forgotten, especially by Clodius, who also nursed a strong personal grudge against him. As tribune Clodius, dominating the streets and guilds of Rome with his gangs, succeeded in driving Cicero into exile (58). But in the next year he went too far. For one thing, he introduced an unlimited distribution of grain to the population of Rome, entirely without payment, a measure that heavily outbid Cato's earlier measure of the same kind and seemed to many people excessively radical. And then he showed signs of turning against Pompey, who suspected instigation from Crassus and, looking around angrily for new allies, recalled Cicero from his banishment.

He came back jubilantly and hoped that the triumvirate was breaking apart. But disappointment awaited him. In 56 the three leaders met together at Luca (Lucca)—a place which was just inside Cisalpine Gaul (part of Caesar's command), and which was chosen for the meeting because Caesar did not want to leave his province and face prosecution. At their conference the triumvirs came to a complete agreement once again and decided how to fulfil their future ambitions. Pompey and Crassus were to become consuls together for the second time in 55. Then Crassus, who was envious of his colleagues' military triumphs, would take up a command against Parthia, an Iranian feudal empire beyond the Euphrates, which had broken away from the Seleucids in the third century B.C. and was the only substantial foreign power confronting Rome anywhere in the world. Pompey was awarded the rich provinces of Spain for five years and, by a concession anticipating the future arrangements of Roman emperors, was allowed to govern them *in absentia* through subordinates, while he himself remained at Rome and virtually controlled its administration. Caesar's provincial command was likewise prolonged for a further five years, so that he could extend his new conquests in Transalpine Gaul.

However, it at once became apparent that this country was not yet fully conquered after all. For the Veneti of western Brittany, a people with a powerful fleet, were in rebellion. In the previous year, they had duly surrendered to one of Caesar's officers, a son of Crassus. But then they learned with anger that Caesar was planning an invasion of Britain, which would seriously upset their control of cross-channel trade. As a protest, they placed Caesar's requisitioning officers under arrest. But he sent a fleet against them, and they were crushed in a battle in Quiberon Bay (56). Expeditions dispatched to Normandy and Aquitania (southwestern Gaul) were equally successful, and then early in the next year, Caesar threw back a German migration from the east, as he had already done three years before, but with even greater slaughter.

He had prepared for his attack on these Germans by a treacherous breach

Silver *denarius* issued in Spain depicting Pompey the Great
(CN. MAGNVS IMP*erator*) after his death.

of faith that caused Cato at Rome to remonstrate, though his motives were political rather than humanitarian. In any case his objections were not widely shared. Moreover, Caesar at this juncture greatly impressed metropolitan opinion because he built a bridge over the Rhine and led a force across it for a brief stay on the other side, where no Roman commander or troops had ever set foot before. The bridge was a display of his army's superb engineering, but it was also a demonstration that there were no bounds to the frontiers of Rome and his own ambitions.

This last purpose was once again in his mind when, as the Veneti had foreseen, he launched his first expedition to Britain. A subsidiary motive was his desire to lay hands on the considerable, if somewhat exaggerated, wealth of the country, particularly in metals. And he also wanted to harry certain local Belgic rulers on the island—men descended from migrants from northern Gaul who had formed important tribal groupings in Britain and had supported their continental kinsmen against Caesar. But his main purpose was to eclipse Pompey as a leader of armies to hitherto unknown lands.

Pompey, not to be outdone, later objected that the English Channel was merely an insignificant mud flat. But Caesar had reason to disagree. When, after embarking from Portus Itius (Boulogne or Wissant), he had landed near Walmer or Deal on the southeast coast of England and had put two

British helmet of bronze, probably of first century B.C.

legions ashore, many of his eighty ships were heavily damaged on the beach by high tides that he had not foreseen. The ambush that this encouraged the British to attempt was duly beaten off. However, the entire Roman force sailed back to Gaul only eighteen days after its arrival.

The British tribal leaders had agreed to provide hostages. But very few of them were handed over or dispatched, and nothing else had been achieved either. So in the following year, Caesar, after cowing the recalcitrant Belgic Treviri on the Moselle, led a second and larger expedition to Britain. This time he took five legions and two thousand cavalry on eight hundred ships—by far the largest fleet the Channel had ever seen and larger than any it was to see again until 1944. Embarking at the same point as before, he landed a little farther north, near Sandwich, and at once marched into the hinterland. But history repeated itself, for a storm in the night destroyed forty of his ships and disabled most of the rest. So he had to return to the coast to organize repairs, reinforcements, and protective measures.

Meanwhile the British tribes, dropping their habitual feuds for the moment, had appointed King Cassivellaunus of the Catuvellauni (Hertfordshire) as commander in chief of their united forces. But Caesar, beating off guerrillas as he went, forced his way across the Thames—the British tribes in his rear failing to provide a diversion—and stormed the king's capital at Wheathampstead, near St. Albans. Then, after a stay of three months on the island, he and his army were transported back to Gaul.

Meanwhile, Cassivellaunus had formally surrendered, given hostages, and promised tribute, and when Caesar told Rome that such remote and exotic peoples had submitted, it made impressive propaganda. But he also hoped that he had established a network of client and semiclient states beyond the imperial frontiers, as Pompey had done in the East. Time showed, however, that this had not been achieved, and as for direct control, Rome did not succeed in annexing any portion whatever of Britain for nearly a hundred years to come.

When Caesar returned to the mainland, he planned to split up his army at a number of separate winter quarters in different regions of Gaul, for it had now become even clearer than before that the conquest of the country was far from complete.

The first trouble that occurred was among the Carnutes, a tribe in the wooded interior around Cenabum (Orléans). Their territory was of particular importance because it contained the principal meeting place of the Druids, religious leaders who dominated civil and legal and educational affairs throughout Gaul. Among the Belgae, too, in the northern part of the country, outbreaks of rebellion indicated the dismaying possibility that detachments of Caesar's army might be isolated and cut to pieces; one tribe revolted, another massacred a garrison of one and a half legions, and a further garrison under Cicero's brother was only narrowly saved from a hostile horde at Samarobriva (Amiens). And it was in that town that Caesar decided to spend the next winter, instead of moving into Cisalpine Gaul as had been his custom at the end of each previous campaigning season. Then in 53, at Samarobriva and elsewhere in the north, he summoned three conferences of Gallic chieftains in an endeavor to stamp out disaffection.

Nevertheless, in the following year the Gauls rose in general revolt. They conferred the supreme command on the only talented leader they produced in these wars, Vercingetorix of the tribe of the Arverni in central Gaul. That winter Caesar had returned to the Cisalpine part of his command. But now, on hearing the news of the rebellion, he hastened back across the Alps with unexpected speed; and Vercingetorix decided that the only way to stop him was by a scorched-earth policy of destroying every Gallic settlement that might provide the Romans with supplies. Caesar directed his attack against

Gallic coin showing Vercingetorix of the Arverni,
who led the revolt against Julius Caesar in 52 B.C.

the chief fortress of the Arverni, Gergovia. But there he received his first
serious setback of the war and was compelled to break off the siege, while
the other principal tribe of the region, the Aedui, was encouraged by his
discomfiture to join the insurrection. Caesar had sent his deputy Labienus
to the north, but now he summoned him back. Together, they besieged
Vercingetorix who, by an unwise decision following a defeat, had retired
behind the walls of the fortress of Alesia (Alise Sainte Reine). Huge reinforcements came to relieve him, and for four days Caesar's army had to
resist an attack from both directions. But then the Gallic relief forces were
routed, and although there were still resisters to mop up—a process accompanied by grim atrocities—the Great Revolt was at an end.

The Gauls had, on the whole, failed to unite with any effectiveness. And
the losses they had suffered were appalling: at least a third of all their men
of military age were killed, and another third sold into slavery. And now
their large territory, reduced to subject status, was assessed for Roman
tribute, at first as a series of client states dependent on the old Transalpine
province in the south, and subsequently as three separate new provinces. By
the annexation of this land which forms a bridge between the Inner and the
Outer Seas, the whole concept and character of the Roman Empire had
been transformed. It was no longer a purely Mediterranean dominion any
more, since a vast conglomeration of territories in continental and northern
Europe had now been opened up to Romanization.

Caesar had shown himself to be one of the supreme military commanders
of all time. But was he a highly original general, or one who perfected a
machine he had inherited from earlier commanders? The truth lies some-

Monument of the Julii at Glanum (Saint Rémy in S. France).
Second half of first century B.C.

Relief of Barbarian prisoner on triumphal arch at
Carpentorate (Carpentras). Probably of Augustan date.

where between the two views. He learned from others all that could be learned about the workings of the Roman army, but he also left his own stamp on every part of the machine. His powers of endurance were phenomenal. A first-class horseman, he also thought nothing of covering a hundred miles a day in a light carriage on terrible roads—while all the time dictating official letters or literary works to relays of secretaries. But his outstanding personal qualities as a commander were speed, timing, and adaptability to rapidly changing circumstances. His generalship was breathtakingly quick in mind as well as in movement—far too quick for his enemies.

Sometimes this brilliant rapidity produced alarming mistakes and perils. But he became used to extricating himself from such hazards and achieving total victory by the narrowest of margins. His "Commentaries" pay tribute to the luck for which he was famous. But a commander has to harness the lucky odds in his favor, and that is what Caesar almost invariably achieved. He attracted unbounded admiration from his legions, whom he often addressed with great eloquence—for he was second only to Cicero as an orator. And he linked them to himself still more firmly by doubling their pay.

In Rome, however, during the last four years of his Gallic campaigning, the political situation imposed by the triumvirate had gradually fallen to pieces. As always, Caesar was keeping the closest possible eye on the city through his numerous and effective agents and by a massive correspondence passing between Rome and Gaul more rapidly, sometimes, than letters do today. But the news that reached him from the capital became increasingly disquieting, since, although Pompey remained nearby, incessant disorders, largely fomented by Clodius, virtually reduced its public life to chaos. Moreover, Julia, Caesar's daughter and Pompey's wife, died in 54, so that the links between the two leaders were seriously weakened. And then the triumvirate ceased to exist because its third member, Crassus, in his attempt to overcome the Parthians, met with total disaster. At the town of Carrhae in Mesopotamia (Haran in southeastern Turkey), his army was totally defeated by a highly trained force of ten thousand Parthian horse archers; and when he went to negotiate with their commanders, they put him to death (53). This meant that Pompey and Caesar, with their rival aims and ambitions, now stood alone in direct confrontation.

Early in the following year, Clodius was murdered, and in the resulting emergency Pompey assumed his third consulship, holding the office for some months without a colleague. Some detected in him a taste for permanent one-man rule; but there is no real evidence that this is what Pompey had in mind. In order to retain his friendship Caesar suggested new marriage ties between their families. But Pompey now took a significant deci-

Silver tetradrachm of Orodes I of Parthia, whose general Surenas
killed Crassus at Carrhae in 53 B.C. Fortune is shown
offering the seated king a palm branch.

sion by rejecting Caesar's proposed bargain and marrying Cornelia, daughter of the highly aristocratic Metellus Scipio, whom he elevated to become his fellow consul. Conservatives such as Metellus were willing enough to form an association with Pompey, at least until Caesar was got rid of, though they hoped to put him in his place later on. And he in his turn, as this new marriage alliance revealed, was no longer averse to them either. That is to say, he was moving away from Caesar, of whom he was increasingly frightened and jealous, though he still could not bring himself to alienate him completely.

As for Caesar's aims, it remained essential to his career, and perhaps even to his survival, that his present governorship should not be followed by a period without office, during which he could be subjected to prosecutions. According to the existing law the earliest year for which he could aim at a second consulship was 48, so he had somehow to retain his command right up until then. In consequence, he expressed the desire to become a candidate for that consulship, when the time came, *in absentia.* Pompey obligingly agreed to this—while at the same time arranging for his own absentee governorship of Spain to be extended for another five years. But very soon afterwards, he allowed himself to be pushed by his advisers into less friendly measures towards Caesar; and these culminated in a decision that the appointment of a new provincial commander to replace him should be allowed to come up for discussion in the Senate in March 50 B.C.

But Caesar had the backing of a young tribune, Curio, who persistently vetoed demands that any such successor should be appointed. And then Curio himself produced an alternative suggestion: that Caesar should, indeed, resign from his post, but that Pompey should simultaneously resign from his absentee Spanish governorship. This idea seemed attractive to numerous senators, but a small group of diehards insured its rejection. Near the end of the year, however, the proposal came up for a second time, and Curio induced the Senate to agree to it by a very large majority, whereupon the diehard faction vetoed it once again. The deadlock was complete, and on the following day one of the consuls, an ultraconservative, called on Pompey to take up the command of all the forces of the republic. Pompey accepted the commission, "unless a better way can be found," and took over two legions that had been about to depart for Syria.

Negotiations continued; but when a message from Caesar arrived in Rome, the young tribune Antony (Marcus Antonius), who had succeeded Curio as his representative, could scarcely induce the senators to allow it to be read. They proceeded instead to pass their emergency decree with Caesar as its target, and Antony and a colleague hastily left Rome for the north. Then on the night of January 10, 49 B.C. Caesar crossed the small river Rubicon, which formed the border between Cisalpine Gaul and eastern Italy. When he moved across this bridge, taking a single legion with him, he was breaking Rome's law of treason which forbade a governor to lead his troops outside his province—a law that Sulla had formulated precisely with the aim of curbing such acts against the government.

And so, as Caesar himself declared, the die was cast, and the crossing of this little stream was one of the formal turning points in Roman history. It meant that the nation was plunged into an empire-wide civil war for which neither side was ready. Yet, in a sense, the real turning point had come a decade earlier, when the republic was already to a large extent superseded by the autocratic triumvirate. During the intervening years, its inevitable disintegration had accelerated; and now it had entered a catastrophic, terminal phase.

Catullus and Lucretius

But the fifties B.C. had not all been war and politics. For example, this was also the time when two of the world's outstanding poets completed much or most of their work. The twenty-three hundred surviving lines of Catullus (b. ca. 84–d. 54 B.C.) were found inscribed on a manuscript discovered at Verona. This had been his native city, for he, like other writers of Latin poetry at this time, was a product of Cisalpine Gaul. For their formal inspiration, these men went back to the poets of Alexandria whose learned, individualistic, sentimental tendencies had dominated Greek literature during the previous two centuries. Yet the new, Latin Alexandrian movement differed considerably from its Greek predecessor in purpose. The function of the latter had been to revive a tired culture by injecting novel and topical elements; whereas Roman poetry, despite certain achievements in the past, was still raw and unrefined when these influences overtook it, preparing the way for the technical perfection of Catullus.

Yet although this formal mastery is fully displayed in his jewel-like miniature epics, it was not by these longer poems that he influenced the world of the future, but by his shorter pieces. Some of these give expression to a heartbroken and heartbreaking intensity—inspired by his love for the hopelessly unfaithful "Lesbia," who was really called Clodia and may have been a fashionable, immoral sister of the politician Clodius. Casting himself free of the impersonal objectivity of the Greeks, the poet feels an irresistible excitement, which he compels his readers to share; and the virtuosity and precision of his language heighten the forcefulness of its impact. Catullus is the product of agonizing tension between a powerful mind and tormented emotions. He responds to the demands of love with an unprecedented seriousness, veering between ecstasy and desperation; and both are communicated with a total intimacy designed for an elite circle of close, like-minded friends. Thus, although his verses fully reflect the lively, dangerous, immoral, and precarious social scene of his day, the service of the community is no part of his aim and the service of its leaders even less: Caesar and Pompey he mentions briefly and contemptuously as irrelevancies, introducing them only because of his fastidious distaste for the upstarts who gained power as their supporters.

His older contemporary Lucretius (b. ca. 94–d. 55 B.C.) does not mention these great men by name at all. It was an extraordinary age that could produce two such totally different poets. Lucretius was an adherent of the philosophy of the Athenian Epicurus (b. 341–d. 270 B.C.), who had sought to prove that the universe was completely material, consisting of nothing but atoms and the space in which they move. The Epicureans were an austere, unpretentious, and unambitious sect who had gained a certain amount of support in Italy, and now had adherents in Rome. But Lucretius, with startling incongruity, transformed the philosopher's undistinguished Greek prose into a burningly impassioned Latin poem on the nature of the universe, *About Reality,* or *How Things Are (De Rerum Natura)*—the only philosophical poem of antiquity that has come down to us in its complete form.

It offers a flashing profusion of visual images, for this poet was a vivid panoramic painter of words. The scientific doctrine he presents is of no more than historical interest today, as a link between Greek and modern atomists. Yet its presentation displays Lucretius as the most original, adventurous, imaginative, and dedicated thinker of his day, and perhaps the most formidable intellectual ever to write in the Latin tongue. His interpretation of the universe in a wholly materialistic fashion prompted him to declare, like Epicurus but with a great deal more vigor, that fear of the gods, and above all fear of death, is completely unwarranted and pointless. Yet even if the world is merely a chance pileup of atoms streaming in a meaningless void, they do not move, Lucretius feels, in a totally predetermined fashion, but on the contrary show independence of movement and sometimes swerve unpredictably—which means, he concludes, that individual persons are not slaves to fate but remain free agents; and his picture of the triumphs of the human brain and will, which have created civilization, is one of the supreme expositions of what men and women are capable of achieving. Our purpose in life, Lucretius and his master declare, should be happiness. This assertion has damned the Epicureans in the eyes of posterity on the grounds that they are advocating sensuous pleasures—a mistaken conclusion since, like other philosophies of the day, they equated happiness with something altogether different, namely, freedom from disturbances *(ataraxia),* only procurable by the acquisition of the right kind of knowledge.

Caesar and Pompey, the poet must clearly have thought, did not possess this kind of knowledge at all, and it was therefore predictable that he should not refer to them. But he expresses, in forthright terms, the poorest possible view of all the politicians whose rat race was dragging the Roman Republic down to its final extinction:

> Men lost,
> Confused, in hectic search for the right road,
> The strife of wits, the wars for precedence,
> The everlasting struggle, night and day,
> To win towards heights of wealth and power.

The Civil War

After crossing the Rubicon, Caesar moved forward rapidly into the center of Italy. He divided his small force into two columns, one of which he himself led to Ariminum (Rimini), where he was joined by the friendly tribunes from Rome, Curio and Antony; and then both his columns pressed on, and one town after another opened its gates to them.

His enemies included most of the senior senators and indeed, theoretically, the greater part of the empire; and this made them too confident. They were also too jealous of Pompey and would not allow him the powers a commander needed; and they had totally underestimated Caesar's capacity to complete a rapid invasion of Italy. His troops were highly experienced after all the battles of the Gallic war, whereas Pompey's veterans, on the other hand, had become less efficient during twelve years of peace, and his best legions were in Spain, unable to give him any help. So, in the face of

Caesar's advance, he retreated southwards through the Italian peninsula, while his uneasy allies, the consuls, fled from Rome, departing in such haste that they even failed to take the reserve treasury with them.

At Corfinium, however, east of Rome, the wealthy nobleman Ahenobarbus, disregarding Pompey's order to retreat and join up with him, endeavored to make a stand against Caesar, whom he detested. But he was soon compelled to surrender, whereupon Caesar allowed him and the fifty senators and knights who were with him to go free. It was a novel and striking display of clemency to Roman citizens, very different from his earlier treatment of Gauls and Germans. Then in March, only sixty-five days after the campaign had begun, his enemies evacuated Italy altogether; the consuls set out across the Adriatic, followed by Pompey himself who skillfully evaded attempts to blockade him in Brundisium harbor. He was probably right not to persist in forlorn efforts to fight Caesar in Italy and justified also in making for the eastern provinces, for his favorite strategy was always to fight from carefully prepared positions of superior strength, and in the East he had huge resources to draw upon, which even outweighed his military power in Spain. Cicero, however, thought his decision to leave Italy was wrong. But all the same, after an inconclusive personal interview with Caesar and prolonged waverings, he decided that Pompey's side was the

lesser of the two evils and obeyed his injunction to join him at Thessalonica (Salonica) in Macedonia.

Caesar could not pursue his opponents yet, for the command of the sea was in their hands and threatened the grain supply of Italy. So Curio, acting on his behalf, seized the wheat-producing island of Sicily, though he was then defeated and killed in north Africa. Meanwhile, Caesar himself, after convening Senate and Assembly meetings at Rome, set off by land to attack Spain, the chief remaining Pompeian stronghold in western Europe; and once there, he cornered and overwhelmed the enemy forces near Ilerda (Lérida).

Meanwhile, in southern Gaul, the Greek city-state of Massilia, which had entrusted its defenses to Ahenobarbus after his release, was forced to surrender to Caesar, who allowed the place to remain autonomous but, in fact, brought its long career of independent statehood to an end. He was still there when he learned that a mutiny was threatening among four of his legions at Placentia (Piacenza) in Cisalpine Gaul—a painful incident omitted from his *Civil War.* One of the troubles was that the soldiers deplored his policy of clemency, since it deprived them of their loot. After quelling the mutiny by an oration, he paid his second visit of the year to the capital, where he assumed for a brief period his first tenure of the post of dictator, which Sulla had revived thirty-two years earlier. This enabled him, during an eleven days' stay in the capital, to fulfil his long-standing ambition of arranging to become consul in the following year. And his brief dictatorship also gave him a chance to make a start with some of his gravest administrative problems.

Then, finally, he moved against his opponents in the Balkans, eluding a flotilla intended to stop him; and after a nerve-racking delay of three months, Antony managed to reach him from Italy with reinforcements. Caesar endeavored to blockade Pompey's key base Dyrrhachium (Durrës in Albania), but the attempt was a disastrous failure, and he recoiled inland into the Thessalian plain. There, in the largest battle ever fought between Romans, his superior generalship won the day near Pharsalus (48). Pompey himself escaped, first by land and then by sea, and after abortive attempts to land at Aegean ports, decided to proceed to Egypt; he chose it because the government of the boy-king Ptolemy XIII had backed him against Caesar in the civil war. But as Pompey landed on the Egyptian coast, he was struck down and assassinated, for the Egyptian politicians intended to be on the winning side.

They also wanted to leave Caesar no excuse for staying in Egypt, for he was known to be on his way, in hot pursuit of Pompey, and very soon afterwards he arrived. His intention was to extort an enormous sum from this wealthy and still ostensibly independent country. But the official reason for the visit was to arbitrate between the monarch and his half-sister Cleopatra VII who had been driven into exile. When, however, Cleopatra, a highly intelligent twenty-one-year-old charmer, secretly came to see him in Alexandria, Caesar, over thirty years her senior, took her into the palace and lived with her as her lover. Thereupon he found himself perilously besieged by the royal army, which favored the king. It was not until March of the following year that the arrival of a relief force enabled him to bring his Egyptian enemies to battle south of the delta of the Nile. Ptolemy XIII was defeated and killed, and Caesar confirmed Cleopatra as queen of Egypt and a client of Rome and of himself. Then, after a five-day campaign against the son of Rome's old enemy Mithridates VI, in Pontus, culminating in total victory at Zela (Zile), Caesar at last returned to Italy and the capital.

He had been away for a long time, much too long. Antony, his deputy at Rome, had not been able to stop some of his fellow nobles from getting out of hand; and Caesar also had a second threat of mutiny to deal with. He averted it only just in time, for Pompey's death had not meant the death of his cause, and his sons Cnaeus and Sextus, supported by many prominent Romans in north Africa and Spain, were now ready for battle. At the height of winter Caesar crossed over to north Africa, and after a campaign involving many hardships fought a totally successful battle on the isthmus at Thapsus (Ras Dimas). The enemy commander Metellus Scipio, Pompey's father-in-law, killed himself, followed shortly afterwards by Cato, whose suicide at Utica provided the republicans with a martyr and a saint.

After a magnificent triumph in Rome, Caesar left the city again before the year was over and made at once for southern Spain. There, in the following spring, he won a grim and horrifying soldier's battle at an unidentified place named Munda. Labienus, who after serving as his deputy throughout the Gallic campaigns had joined the other side in the civil wars, fell in the holocaust, and Pompey's son Cnaeus was caught and killed soon afterwards. His brother Sextus got away and lived on to plague Caesar's successors; but as far as Caesar was concerned, the gigantic and immeasurably costly convulsion of the civil war was over.

Henceforward he employed the title *Imperator* as a special, personal appellation, not with the meaning of its later derivative "emperor," but to show that he was the military commander who totally surpassed all others.

The Dictatorship of Caesar

During the brief intervals between these campaigns and then, when they were over, in the single year of life that still remained to him, Caesar began to show that he was a genius, not only as a commander, but, as an administrator as well.

The first need, as always in these times, was to reward his ex-soldiers, whose loyalty, in spite of near-mutinies, had gained him his victory. So Caesar, who now possessed enormous wealth, settled these retired legionaries in thousands. In the first place he established colonies for them in Italy. But there, if he was to pursue his much-heralded policy of clemency, he could procure only a limited amount of land. So he also initiated at least forty such foundations in the provinces. Among these new colonies were settlements at Corinth and Carthage, both rising again out of their destruction just a hundred years earlier, and both destined to become impressive cities once more, Corinth as the capital of Roman Greece and Carthage as its counterpart in Africa and the largest city of all the western provinces.

The colonies of Caesar included veterans who could always be called out again for military service, so that these towns became important bastions of imperial defense—and of potential support for Caesar's regime. But the settlements were not intended for veterans alone. The most original feature of his foundations was the inclusion of civilians as well—including eighty thousand of the capital's penniless unemployed. As well as helping to break down old barriers between Romans and provincials, this meant that Caesar, like no one else before him, had seriously begun to tackle the obstinate problem of the impoverished workless population of the city.

Having founded his colonies, Caesar laid down for them a standard system of local government on Roman lines. The colonies in the East, of which besides Corinth there were relatively few, remained isolated outposts of Romanism in areas that remained predominantly Greek. But more than three-quarters of the new foundations were in the West, and throughout these regions they acted, during the centuries to come, as potent instruments of Romanization. Caesar also gave citizenship liberally on an individual basis—for example, to men who practiced medicine at Rome.

But the greatest of his achievements, though lacking in melodramatic glamour, was probably his long and patient handling of the problem of debt. This had been an intractable difficulty, time and time again, for more than four centuries. But it had never been so painful and hazardous as it was now. Owing to the disturbances of the past fifty years, many Romans had fallen more grievously into debt than ever, and in spite of sporadic attempts at mitigation over the years, the harsh laws that were still in force cast many of these debtors into total destitution. Caesar, who had been heavily in debt himself, knew very well how things stood; he had seen how the Catilinarian conspiracy was largely supported by desperate debtors, and then he himself had been obliged to grapple with such problems on behalf of the provincials when he was governor in Further Spain.

Yet would-be reformers in this field, as his knowledge of Roman history could warn him, had always found themselves caught in a dilemma. Something had to be done for the victims of the system, whether their misfortunes were their own fault or not. On the other hand, as Cicero was always saying, anything approaching a general cancellation of debts would destroy private property—and thereby usher in chaos.

At the beginning of the civil war the debt crisis had entered a new and even graver phase because of a shortage of currency. Much coin had been hoarded against better times, and most of what remained was gone to pay the armies. This meant that whereas men were being urgently requested by their creditors to repay what they had borrowed—and were eager enough to do so, since interest rates had risen from four percent to nearly twelve—they could not find the money and had to raise it by selling everything they possessed, at the wretched prices that were all they could get in the prevailing emergency. So Caesar, in 49, started upon a long, patient series of attempts to deal with this harrowing situation. First, the hoarding of coin was forbidden—a regulation, admittedly, that could scarcely be enforced, though it did put more cash into circulation. Secondly, creditors were compelled by a new measure to accept any land or other property offered them in repayment of their loans and to accept it at prewar prices assessed by special commissioners. Of course, they complained bitterly, whereas the debtors, on the other hand, felt that Caesar could have done a great deal more to help them. However, the fact that both sides were dissatisfied suggests that his proposals were not unreasonable. Yet they caused severe tension at Rome, and he himself was by now at Alexandria, unable to deal with it. Taking advantage, therefore, of his prolonged absence, a trouble-making praetor advocated a moratorium on all repayments of debt and payments of interest; and then another politician, a tribune, made the classic revolutionary proposal that all debts should be completely canceled. However the praetor came to a violent end, and the tribune's proposals were halted at the instance of Antony, Caesar's deputy in Italy, by police measures costing eight hundred lives.

On his return, Caesar, far from pleased, was forced to conclude that his earlier measures, like those of so many previous reformers, had not gone far enough to satisfy the debtors' violent grievances. He therefore decided to cancel all interest due since the beginning of the civil war—insofar as it had not yet been paid, whereas the equivalents of payments that had already been made were to be deducted from future capital repayments. These measures, we are told, wiped out one-quarter of all debts at a single blow.

Once again, a serious loss had been inflicted on creditors. Yet they were obliged to admit that they would never have seen the rest of the money anyway—and that Caesar was not the destroyer of private property his enemies had made him out to be. Indeed, it was a significant feature of the civil war that the most able financiers, unlike senior senators, had mostly chosen to take his side. After his new regulations came into force, financial confidence began to come back, and once more money was freely lent and borrowed. In this field, Caesar had achieved more than any previous Roman statesman; he had broken the back of the republic's most unmanageable problem.

That was hard, laborious, unspectacular work, but Caesar also had all the appetite of great potentates for splendid spectacles to distract the people from their hardships. Moreover, huge portions of the wealth he accumulated in his victorious wars were spent not only on celebrating triumphs but also on erecting magnificent buildings. A great new hall for public business, the Basilica Julia, was under construction in the Roman Forum; and close by another Forum named after Caesar himself began to take shape. Its colonnaded precinct flanked a shrine of Venus the Mother (Genetrix), since it was from this goddess, through the mythical Aeneas, that the Julian family claimed to be descended.

The Forum of Julius Caesar and Temple of Venus Genetrix at Rome.

He placed a statue of Venus in the temple and beside it a gilt bronze statue of Queen Cleopatra VII was also installed. She could see it for herself, because in 46 she arrived in the city, with her surviving thirteen-year-old half-brother (with whom she officially shared the throne) and her infant son Caesarion whose paternity she ascribed, perhaps rightly, to Caesar. The ostensible purpose of her visit was to confirm her father's treaty of alliance and friendship with Egypt's patron Rome. And thereafter, while she stayed on at the capital for the rest of Caesar's life, it is possible to identify certain of his actions that show the influence of herself and her country. For one thing, his plan to establish magnificent public libraries at Rome was based on the world-famous library of the Ptolemies attached to the museum at Alexandria. Secondly, his ambitious, though uncomplete, projects to dig a canal through the Pomptine (Pontine) marshes, south of Rome, and another through the Isthmus of Corinth in Greece, must have owed a great deal to Egypt, which was the home of these skills. Furthermore, Caesar's revision of the gravely dislocated Roman calendar, a reform that with minor adjustments has survived until the present day, was directed by an Alexandrian astronomer.

Besides, Cleopatra, to whose Ptolemaic mind the Roman nobleman's ideal of free speech and action seemed absurd and undesirable, may have helped to prompt a trend towards autocratic impatience which people were noticing in the supreme *imperator*. It was true that in his administrative activities he could not, and did not, act alone but needed the assistance of the Senate. But it was a Senate modeled according to his own wishes and intentions. Raising its membership from six hundred to nine hundred, he enrolled the men who had helped him to gain power—bankers, industrialists, and army officers—and this influx permanently transformed the Senate's character. He was also able to include in its ranks an unprecedentedly large number of men who had held state offices. This was because he had increased the number of state posts in order to meet the greater needs of the expanded Roman world—and their holders automatically became members of the Senate. They, like the other new senators, were men who were loyal to himself, since, although the annual elections to consulships and other offices still continued, the successful candidates were almost invariably the people he wanted.

The point was emphasized by the depiction of his own head on the national currency, the first portraits of any living man or woman ever to appear on a Roman coin. And Caesar's rising personality cult was stressed still further by the large number of his portrait busts that were made and distributed around Italy and the provinces. This marked an important stage in the development of one of Rome's outstanding art forms. It was an art that had first developed among the Greeks of recent centuries who were interested in personality and literary biography. Like biographers, the Greek sculptors had increasingly desired to stress the unique, private, pattern of the personage they were depicting, and when he was a ruler, it was their function to show him to the world as a great man but also as a distinctive individual.

And then the Romans, in their turn, very often employing Greeks or Orientals to do the job, but relying also on native Etruscan and other Italian sculptural traditions, showed themselves extremely receptive to these same aims, which coincided with their own interest in national and family history and moral character. From the third century B.C. onwards, the sculptural portrayals of individuals had received increasing attention in the city; and after 100, Roman portraiture began to become a major art. Portraits also started to appear on the national coinage of the period, which was issued by a committee of three young mint officials of leading families elected each year. Imitating bronze or marble busts or statues, now lost, the designers of these coins first selected early or legendary Roman heroes for portrayal in imaginative fashion; and then with greater boldness and a closer approach to realism, the recently dead, including Sulla. But it marked a decisive step forward when heads of the living Caesar appeared on his coins, in January or February 44 B.C.

They imitated sculptural portraits—some of which still survive today. It was Caesar himself who gave these sculptors their first really important opportunity. His fine sensitive features brought out the best in them—and skillful artists could even capture the piercing gaze of his dark eyes. Their task was vitally important because his great position in the state demanded an interpretation of his personality in all its aspects. In this way, then, was launched the great series of portraits of the rulers of the empire, which are among its principal artistic gifts to Europe.

The few examples of his surviving busts that can be dated to his lifetime cunningly blend realism with grandeur—for Caesar was as grand as any king. Yet he had no intention of reviving the ancient Roman kingship in his own family, since it was traditionally equated with tyranny. Instead, the constitutional status he chose for himself was the dictatorship, like Sulla before him. From 49 onwards, Caesar was reappointed to this post a number of times, and in 46, by an innovation, for as long as ten years. But then, in February 44 B.C., he was appointed dictator for the rest of his life—PERPETVO, as his coins unequivocally assert. This was an exceedingly grave step to have taken. The conversion of what had originally been intended as an emergency, short-term office into a permanent autocracy meant that the other nobles, however many consulships and other offices

Bust of Julius Caesar.

they might be permitted to hold, would never again be able to get their hands on the real controls and profits of public life.

But their resentment, evidently, did not weigh with Caesar, who was forming plans that he considered to be of immeasurably greater significance. Above all, he wanted to leave the intrigues of the capital and get back among his admiring, incomparable army. He was consumed by a desire for further military glory, and it had to come soon since he was fifty-six and suffered from precarious health, being susceptible, apparently, to epileptic attacks. But there was still time for him to rival Alexander the Great—and in the same part of the world that Alexander himself had invaded, since Crassus's defeat and death at the hands of the Parthians nine years earlier urgently needed to be avenged. However, a considerable Roman force was first detached to eastern Europe in order to cow the powerful kingdom of Dacia, whose rulers had recently extended their sway from the national homeland in Transylvania (Rumania) as far as the Black Sea. The role of these legions was preparatory; once Caesar had suppressed the Parthians and perhaps extended his conquests like Alexander into the remotest regions of the Orient, it was believed that he intended to wheel back through southern Russia and continental Europe, completing the annexation of Dacia and further vast territories on the way.

But the East was Caesar's first objective, and its provinces witnessed the marshaling of the great Roman army to await his arrival. He was to leave the city on March 18, 44 B.C. When this became known, the news brought the growing hostility of the nobles to a head. It was distasteful enough to be governed by a perpetual dictator on the spot, but the prospect of government by his aides or secretaries in his absence was nothing less than intoler-

Silver *denarius* of Julius Caesar
as perpetual dictator (DICT. PERPETVO), 44 B.C.

able, for it was they who were going to represent him and enforce his orders during his prolonged forthcoming absence abroad; and the two chief secretaries, Oppius and Balbus, were not even senators.

There had been suggestions of conspiracies against his life before. But now planning began in earnest. Its chief instigator was Cassius, a proud man who had come over to Caesar in the civil war but did not feel he had been sufficiently rewarded. And Cassius won over another personage who had likewise changed sides, his less dynamic and more philosophically minded brother-in-law Marcus Brutus, who although a special protégé of Caesar was obsessed by the glory of his own legendary forebears as liberators of the republic. Another leading conspirator was Brutus's distant relation Decimus Brutus Albinus, who had been one of Caesar's principal commanders in the Gallic war and was designated by the dictator for a consulship in the future. With these and others to lead them, the various small separate groups of malcontents coalesced into a single body of sixty determined plotters.

Caesar was perfectly well aware that many noblemen detested him. But a mixture of fatalism and contemptuous pride caused him to ignore the evident threat. Since he had restored the Roman world to prosperity and peace, and since, if he ceased to be at the helm, these benefits would disappear, he professed himself unable to believe that anyone could seriously want him out of the way. Indeed, so little was he concerned with the evident danger to his life that he even disbanded his personal bodyguard of Spaniards and refused to agree to suggestions that he ought to reengage them.

Then, three days before he was due to depart for the east, the Senate gathered for a meeting in Pompey's theater; and there the conspirators surrounded him and stabbed him to death. Not long before, all senators had

Silver *denarius* of Brutus issued in the east (43-42 B.C.),
commemorating Caesar's murder on the Ides of March (EID. MAR.)
by daggers and Cap of Liberty. The moneyer is L. Plaetorius Cestianus.

sworn an oath of allegiance to the father of their country, as Caesar had now come to be called; they were clients bound to protect their patron, just as a son is obliged to protect his own father. But at the moment of supreme reckoning they rushed out of the building, and Caesar lay where he had fallen.

For all his immeasurable abilities as a general and administrator, he had failed, and would probably have continued to fail, to rescue Rome from its major dilemma. It was this: the republic, obviously, had become impotent, and because this was so, there was no practical alternative to one-man rule. Yet one-man rule was just what the nobles, although themselves incapable of ruling any more, categorically refused to accept; and so they put Caesar to death. It seemed an insoluble problem. Yet there now came another sort of man altogether, who performed the seemingly impossible task of finding a solution after all; he was the nineteen-year-old Octavian, grand-nephew of Julius Caesar who had adopted him in his will as his son.

13
Augustus

The Second Triumvirate

After Caesar's murder, his right-hand man Antony, consul in 44 B.C., used a variety of methods, including the falsification of the dead man's papers, to gain control of events; and he took steps at the same time to arouse the people against the assassins, Brutus and Cassius, who before long retreated to the east. Yet for all the growing power and popularity of Antony, who in spite of a taste for riotous living was a politician and general of considerable gifts, Cicero, true to his distaste for autocrats large and small, attacked him fiercely in a series of brilliant speeches, the *Philippics*. And with Cicero's encouragement the young Octavian, exploiting his testamentary adoption by his murdered great-uncle Caesar, gradually emerged as a rival to Antony and gained the support of the Senate.

In April 43 a senatorial coalition including Octavian defeated Antony at Mutina (Modena) in Cisalpine Gaul and compelled him to withdraw into the Transalpine (Narbonese) province. There, however, he was joined by a number of commanders, including Lepidus (son of the consul of 78 B.C.), a henchman of Caesar who had succeeded him in the chief priesthood of the state. In November, Octavian, smarting from an unwise snub by the Senate, became reconciled with Antony and Lepidus at a conference in Bononia (Bologna), and the three men were granted a five-year autocratic appointment with the task of reconstituting the government—the Second Triumvirate which, unlike the first, was a formal creation of the state. The institutions of the republic, from the consulships downwards, still continued to exist. But the power lay with the triumvirs, and this was ratified by law.

After a holocaust of their political enemies, in which three hundred senators and two thousand knights were proscribed and hounded to death, Antony and Octavian crossed the Adriatic and won two battles at Philippi in Macedonia against Brutus and Cassius, both of whom committed suicide

ITALY

CISALPINE GAUL

Verona

Cremona
Placentia
Mantua
Campi Raudii

Pistoria R Rubicon

Luca

Ariminum

Arretium

Asisium

R Tiber

Tibur Corfinium
Rome Sulmo
Ostia
Aquinum
Arpinum
Pontine Marshes
Capua
Puteoli Pompeii
Brundusium
Capreae
Mt Vesuvius

SICILY

0   100 miles

(42 B.C.). Antony was the main victor, though Octavian's prestige was
enhanced by the recognition of Julius Caesar as a divinity of the Roman
state, since this made his adoptive child the son of a god. Antony assumed
control of the eastern provinces and Octavian took over most of the West;
but in these regions he encountered serious opposition, first from Pompey's
second son Sextus, who was conducting piratical attacks from Sicily, and
then from a brother of Antony in Italy itself. Antony and Octavian, however, came to a fresh agreement, confirming the division of the empire
between them (40 B.C.)

But their relations with one another showed increasing signs of strain.
This was partly because offense and suspicion were caused in the west by
Antony's liaison with the queen of Egypt, Cleopatra VII. In recent years,
Rome had become familiar with feminine power. During the last decades
of the republic, women lived in complete freedom. They owned wealth in

their own names and looked after it themselves. And this liberty was reflected in their social and domestic arrangements; for instance, they now reclined at dinner like the men. Clodius's sister Clodia had been a famous beauty who lived hard and fast. And Roman women exerted greatly increased political influence, too. After Caesar's death, Brutus's mother held a conference to decide what her son and his friends should do, and Brutus also received exhortations from his masterful wife. But the most strong-willed of all was Antony's wife Fulvia, who without consulting her husband had joined his brother in rebelling against Octavian. However, she died, and in 40 Antony married Octavian's sister, Octavia, and in these circumstances his simultaneous association with Cleopatra, a descendant of formidable queens who had more ambitious ideas than any Roman matron, was unacceptable not only to Octavian, whose family was insulted, but also to conservative Roman opinion in general. Caesar's affair with Cleopatra had passed muster because it was he who remained in control. But people suspected that the more easy-going Antony, by whom she had two boys and a girl, was under her thumb—and Octavian spread the word that this was so.

In 37 a second partial reconciliation between the two men provided for a five-year renewal of the triumvirate. But the understanding proved short-lived, since henceforward Antony, abandoning Octavia, lived openly with Cleopatra, who built up under his overlordship an extensive imperial system of her own including many client states. Soon afterwards, however, the balance of Roman power began to change in Antony's disfavor. An expedition he launched against the Parthians, in the hope of annexing Armenia, proved unsuccessful, though he rectified the defeat later. Octavian's fleet, on the other hand, under his former schoolmate Agrippa, who although unpopular with the nobles was a commander of genius, totally defeated Sextus Pompeius's fleet off Cape Naulochus (Venetico) in Sicily (36). At this point, too, the third triumvir Lepidus, seeking to contest Octavian's western

Silver tetradrachm of Antony and Cleopatra VII of Egypt, 34-33 B.C.

supremacy by force, failed to command the support of his own legions and was disarmed and forced into retirement. He was allowed, however, to retain his chief priesthood until his death in 12 B.C.

Octavian's deliberate rivalry with Antony for the eventual mastership of the Roman world was becoming increasingly apparent, and in 33 the two leaders exchanged propaganda attacks. As this barrage continued with unprecedented virulence into the following year, Antony formally divorced Octavia, whose brother thereupon retaliated by publishing what purported to be Antony's will containing damaging evidence, probably forged, of the ascendancy exercised over him by the foreign queen Cleopatra. Each leader induced the populations under his control to swear allegiance to his cause and his person, like the oaths sworn by clients to their patrons (32). The oath sworn by the Italians on this occasion to Octavian *(coniuratio Italiae)* became a famous precedent for the emperors of the future. But it scarcely availed to conceal grave dissatisfaction aroused by his exactions throughout the Italian peninsula.

Having raised as much money as he could, Octavian declared war—not indeed against his compatriot Antony, but against Cleopatra. With her as his companion—and she provided a substantial proportion of his ships and supplies—Antony had brought up his navy and army to guard strongholds along the coast of western Greece. But at the beginning of 31 B.C., while it was still mid-winter, Agrippa succeeded in sailing from Italy across the Ionian Sea and capturing decisive strongpoints along the Greek coast, and, after Octavian had also arrived, Antony was finally cornered in the Gulf of Ambracia (Arta). At the battle of Actium, just outside the gulf, he tried to extricate his ships in the hope of continuing the fight elsewhere. But although Cleopatra, and then Antony himself, succeeded in breaking out, only a quarter of their fleet was able to follow them.

Both fled to Egypt. When the country fell to Octavian (30 B.C.), they committed suicide at Alexandria. Their conqueror declared the country a Roman possession, thus eliminating the last survivor of the three Greek monarchies that had succeeded to the heritage of Alexander; and he made it a unique sort of province, under his own direct control. His seizure of Cleopatra's treasure made him wealthier than the Roman state itself. Above all, it enabled him to pay off his veterans, for whom in due course he founded no fewer than seventy-five colonies, mostly in the West.

The battle of Actium had not been a very spectacular engagement in itself since the strategic issue had already been settled elsewhere. Nevertheless it was hailed by subsequent writers as one of the most decisive battles ever fought because it established Octavian's position as master of the entire Greco-Roman world. It also meant that this empire would be dominated, for a very long time to come, by the West, and not the East. By the "East,"

Reconstruction of bridge at Augusta Praetoria (Aosta), where Augustus founded a veteran colony to protect the passage of the Alps (3 B.C.).

we should understand in this context not the sinister Orient which Octavian's propagandists equated with Antony's dominions, but Rome's eastern provinces and client states in which the ruling classes were Greek. Actium firmly kept this Greek half of the empire in second place. If Antony had won, there might well have been some sort of partnership between Romans and Greeks under his overall rule. Instead, the future political leadership of the empire lay with Italy and Rome, as Virgil a few years later unequivocally pronounced while paying tactful tribute at the same time to Greek cultural supremacy. It was not until another three hundred years had passed that the Greeks started to get some of their own back, after the capital had been shifted to Constantinople and Greek began to replace Latin as the official language of the Byzantine Empire.

The Principate of Augustus

From now on, by a long and gradual series of tentative, patient measures, Octavian established the Roman principate, a system of government that, while not dispensing with republican forms, ultimately depended on himself as the first man of the state *(princeps)* and enabled him to maintain in all essentials absolute control over its affairs.

He gradually reduced his sixty legions to the relatively small figure of twenty-eight, that is to say, to about one hundred and fifty thousand men, which was all he felt he could pay for or recruit. In 28 B.C. he and Agrippa conducted a census of the population for enlistment and taxation purposes, the first of three censuses held during his reign. The soldiers of Augustus's legions in the West were mostly Italians and therefore Roman citizens, but in the East they included many provincials, granted the franchise unofficially on enlistment. These legionaries were supplemented by about the same number of auxiliaries, drawn exclusively from the provinces; and there were already the beginnings of a policy by which they were rewarded by Roman citizenship on their discharge. This was all part of a quietly liberal policy of enfranchisement, sponsored by Augustus. In an empire containing between seventy and one hundred million inhabitants, he raised the total number of Roman citizens, men and women, from about five million to more than six, including an increase of citizens in the provinces from about one million to nearly two.

Remembering that Caesar had been murdered because of his recourse to naked power, he understood that the nobles would tolerate his autocracy only if he concealed it behind acceptable republican traditions. For the first eight years after his victory at Actium, the constitutional basis of his power remained a continuous succession of consulships. But in the middle of this period, in 27 B.C., he pronounced "the transfer of the state to the free

Silver coin *(denarius)* of Augustus (28 B.C.) commemorating the annexation of Egypt.

Diploma of Hadrian conferring Roman citizenship on auxiliary soldier on retirement.

disposal of the Senate and people," thereby earning the misleading, though outwardly plausible, reputation of the restorer of the *res publica,* or ancestral system. At the same time he was granted, for ten years, an area of government comprising not only Egypt, which was his personal domain, but also Gaul (with the Rhine commands of Upper and Lower Germany), Spain, and Syria, the three territories containing the greater part of the Roman army. He ruled this huge collection of "imperial" provinces through governors who were his own subordinates *(legati).* Pompey, likewise in absentia, had governed Spain in similar fashion. The principal remaining provinces remained "public," administered by nominees of the Senate (proconsuls) in the old customary fashion, though with improved efficiency and honesty—since governors of all types, proconsuls and *legati* alike, and the procurators who governed minor provinces, were now salaried officials under close supervision from Rome.*

Octavian, however, believed—and this belief was nearly always justified —that the supreme prestige *(auctoritas)* to which his public offices and achievements, and his sonship of the god Julius, entitled him, were sufficient safeguards against any defiance by governors or commanders. Besides, he was always able, directly or indirectly, to control their appointments, just as he was able, when he considered it desirable, to bring unobtrusive influence to bear on elections to the consulships and other state posts. These offices continued to exist in ostensibly republican fashion; and, in order to calm the ferocious in-fightings between families, groups, and factions which still for a time remained a feature of public life, he contrived that the occupants of the posts should comprise an appropriate blend of nobles and Italian "new men," including in both categories those who had supported him in the civil war.

Such were the members of Augustus's new Senate, which he reduced in numbers from Caesar's nine hundred to the earlier figure of six hundred. He was elected its president and overshadowed it by his grandeur. Yet he did not diminish the Senate's functions but actually enlarged them, so that it possessed, for example, its own high court of justice, alongside another new "imperial" court presided over by himself. The Senate's strength was no longer political but administrative; the achievement of the new order was to take politics out of administration for the first time in Roman history. This was only one of the many acts of transformation that Augustus performed, veiling them always under the guise of traditionalism.

Four days after the new political arrangements were announced in 27 B.C., the ruler's name "Caesar" was supplemented by the novel designation "Augustus." It was a word that carried venerable religious overtones, being linked with the verb "increase" *(augere)* which was also the root of *auctoritas* and probably of *augurium,* the practice of divination, which lay deep in Roman tradition. The adoption of this term "Augustus" to define his new status as the leader of the nation indicated his superiority over the rest of humankind and yet avoided dictatorial or divine appellations that would cause conservatives offense. It is true that, like other leaders before him, Augustus did not refuse divine status in the provinces, although, officially at least, his worship there was conducted in conjunction with the goddess

---

*The governor of Judaea, however, was still called *praefectus;* and so was the man in charge of the major but peculiar new province of Egypt.

Statue of a Roman nobleman carrying the busts of his ancestors. Early first century A.D. (the head, though ancient, does not belong to the statue).

Silver coin of Claudius (A.D. 41-54) at Ephesus depicting the temple of Rome (left) and Augustus (right), where they were worshipped by the provincial Council of Asia (COM*mune* ASI*ae*).

Silver coin *(denarius)* of Augustus as father of his country *(pater patriae)* and chief priest *(pontifex maximus)* (left, right).

Rome. It was an imperial cult that served as an instrument for encouraging loyalty and was subsequently adopted by the local communities of Italy itself. Yet at the same time, the ruler also showed his patriotic reverence for the ancient Roman religion not only, as we have seen, by adopting a name reminiscent of augury, but also by reviving many ancient ceremonials and repairing numerous temples that had fallen into decay during the prolonged civil wars. He also became chief priest, though meticulously postponing his assumption of this office until the death of its incumbent Lepidus (12 B.C.).

Military operations continued in numerous areas, and the eastern frontier was pushed a large distance forward by the annexation of a huge area of central Asia Minor under the name of Galatia (25 B.C.). At the other end of the empire, however, Mauretania (Morocco and west Algeria) reverted from provincial status to that of a client kingdom, for such dependent monarchies were still relied upon to play a large part in frontier defense.

Augustus himself visited Gaul and directed part of a campaign in Spain until his health gave out. In 23 B.C., he fell ill again and was thought to be on the point of death. Believing, amid rumors of plots, that the constitutional position was still unsatisfactory, he terminated his series of consulships—which were unpopular with the nobles because they took jobs away from themselves. But he retained his own provinces. Moreover, in order that he should not be without ultimate sanctions in the senatorial provinces as well, he was granted a power *(imperium maius)* that raised him above their proconsuls. But this somewhat novel power, separated altogether from office and its day-to-day preoccupations, was intended for only sparing employment, particularly in crises or on personal visits, though it could also be tactfully exercised on other occasions as well.

Another exploitation of this fruitful idea of authority without office was his permanent assumption of the powers of a tribune of the people (*tribunicia potestas,* 23 B.C.). Earlier he had accepted certain privileges of the tribunes. The fuller tribunician power he now assumed gave him the right to convene the Senate, but above all, it enveloped him in a popular aura because of the traditional role of the tribunes as defenders of the oppressed, and he endowed it with special significance by using it to date the years of his principate. It was the sort of reputation that Augustus needed, because, in spite of legal reforms improving the lot of the poorer classes, he tended to back the established order as the keystone of his political system and wanted to counteract the impression that this was all he cared about.

Agrippa, too, was granted superiority over the proconsuls, presumably to make sure that these provinces would remain under safe control in case one of the ruler's recurrent illnesses proved fatal. The next to die, however, was not Augustus himself but his young nephew Marcellus (23 B.C.), who had been married to his daughter Julia and seemed destined for further special favors. After his death, Julia became the wife of Agrippa, who continued to travel and fight as the deputy of the *princeps* and even shared his tribunician power (18 B.C.). And meanwhile Augustus, too, undertook a fresh round of extensive journeys. Important reorganizations were set afoot wherever he went. Moreover, immense popular satisfaction was caused in 20 B.C. by an agreement with the Parthians, who not only returned the legionary standards taken from Crassus thirty-three years earlier, but also recognized (though only briefly) Rome's protectorate over Armenia.

Then, in 19 B.C. there was some adjustment of Augustus's constitutional powers to allow him to exercise them more freely in Italy, though still in not too open or direct a fashion. And the following two years witnessed social legislation vigorously seeking to encourage morality and marriage and bring the family as an institution under public protection. These endeavors were immortalized by Virgil and Horace; but they did not enjoy the resounding success of his measures in other fields.

We think of Augustus as the inaugurator of an imperial line, the first emperor. Yet the conglomeration of powers that added up to his position as *princeps* was something that could not, constitutionally speaking, be handed on to any other single person after his death. Nevertheless, there was obviously speculation that this was what must eventually happen—as there had already been—while Marcellus was still alive. Since his death, Agrippa must have seemed, even more than before, a likely candidate for this succession and his powers continued to be renewed together with his master's. But the nobles would never have accepted this "new man"; and Augustus appeared to be indicating his own, alternative views regarding likely eventual successors when he adopted, as his own children, Gaius and Lucius, the sons of Agrippa and Julia. Yet they were only three years and one year old respectively, and Augustus, as time went on, hedged his bets in two ways: first by favoring the career not of one of them but of both, and secondly by giving important military employment to his grown stepsons, Tiberius and Nero Drusus, the sons of his wife Livia by a previous marriage to a member of the Claudian clan. Marching across the Alps, they occupied large parts of what are now Switzerland, Austria, and Bavaria, annexing these territories as the provinces of Noricum and Raetia (16–15 B.C.). By such operations and others the empire was extended northwards and eastwards from the Alps to its historic, long-lasting frontier along the Danube.

It was probably during this period that an executive committee *(consilium)* of the Senate was established in order to help Augustus to draft senatorial business. His vast burden of work was also gradually lightened by the expansion of his own staff to include, at the higher level, a number of knights. Although this personal staff was still relatively small, its development announced the beginnings of a civil service, which had never existed during the republic but was destined to become a vital feature of the imperial system. Gradually, too, and by patient trial and error, Augustus reformed the administrative structures of Rome and Italy and the entire empire. Once again, knights played a prominent part, serving not only as the chairmen and members of important commissions at home, but also as his financial agents (procurators) in every province, and as governors of small provinces and even of one extremely important and special one, Egypt.

In 12 B.C. Agrippa died—many hostile nobles absenting themselves from his funeral—and Augustus, while still furthering the careers of the dead

The family of Augustus

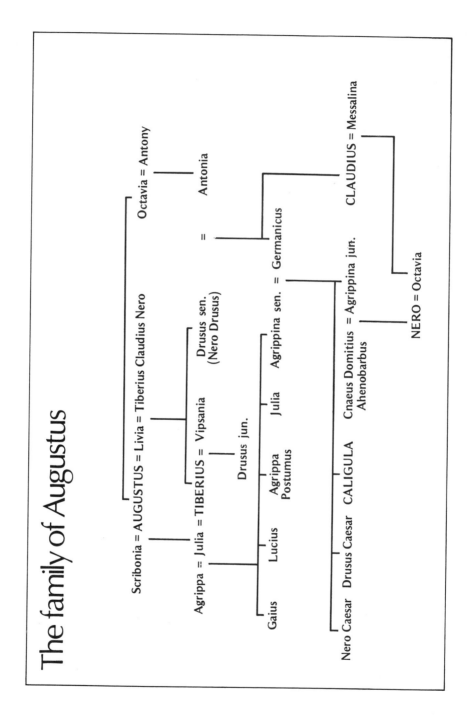

man's children, compelled his widow Julia to marry Tiberius, against the wishes of both of them. During the next three years Tiberius returned to military life, moving northwards the limits of the province of Illyricum (Yugoslavia) and creating a new middle Danubian province of Pannonia (Austria and Hungary; later in the reign, the frontier was extended to the river mouth, providing yet another province, Moesia. At the same time his brother Nero Drusus crossed the Rhine and invaded Germany as far as the Elbe. This was the first step towards the annexation of the country, for it was Augustus's ambition to replace the Rhine by the Elbe as the empire's frontier, thus creating a much shorter boundary line within which huge numbers of the previously free, warlike Germans were to be safely included and absorbed.

Tiberius, who replaced Nero Drusus in Germany on the latter's death (9 B.C.), was elevated three years later to a share in his stepfather's tribunician power. But shortly afterwards, at his own wish, he threw up all his laborious responsibilities and withdrew into retirement on the island of Rhodes. This dramatic step was ascribed to jealousy of his stepson Gaius, who was introduced to public life amid great publicity in the following year; and so was his brother Lucius three years later. But only a very short time afterwards, by an extraordinary chance, both of these young men were dead (A.D. 4, 2). Augustus might have preferred, as hitherto, to keep several potential heirs simultaneously in play, but he now had to realize that this could no longer be done. He may have harbored certain doubts about the personality of Tiberius. But, if so, they had to be forgotten, for now there was no other possible successor. So Augustus adopted him as his son, with powers that, in everything except prestige, made the two men equal.

Tiberius's next task was to fill a large gap in the middle of the proposed new Elbe-Danube line by taking over Bohemia, at that time the nucleus of an unprecedentedly well organized German empire. In A.D. 6, a two-pronged Roman invasion of Bohemian territory was already under way. But then, suddenly, news came that the recently annexed regions of Illyricum and Pannonia had broken into desperate rebellion, which took three years to suppress. And the reconquest of the area had only just been completed when disaster struck across the Rhine as well; a talented German, Arminius, a chieftain of the Cherusci and a Roman citizen, led his people against the unwary Roman commander in the area, Varus, and killed him and destroyed his three legions in the Teutoburg Forest near Detmold. The result was that the annexation both of west Germany and of Bohemia had to be postponed indefinitely—and, as it turned out, forevermore—with incalculable results for the future of Europe, since these millions of Germans remained outside the Roman world. Whether the annexation might have been practicable before, when Augustus had twenty-eight legions, remains an open question. But with only twenty-five, it was out of the question.

Moreover, even with twenty-eight legions, he had never attempted to supplement the frontier army by the maintenance of a central strategic reserve that might have made it possible to deal with this sort of emergency. That was partly because a reserve army of such a kind, if stationed for example in north Italy, might be turned by some ambitious general against himself. Such a contingency was never far from Augustus's mind, or from any later emperor's mind either. He sought to provide against attacks on his own person by creating a permanent bodyguard. Earlier Roman commanders had maintained personal guards, and Augustus developed these precedents by the creation of a standing Praetorian Guard of nine cohorts, which he stationed partly in Rome and partly in other towns of Italy. He also established a city police at Rome consisting of three cohorts *(cohortes urbanae)* under a newly appointed prefect of the city. A watch or fire brigade *(vigiles)* was also instituted; from A.D. 6 it consisted of seven thousand freedmen.

Yet meanwhile he was still finding difficulty in recruiting sufficient men for his legionary force, reduced in size though it was. Nor did he find it easy to pay their salaries or, on retirement, their rewards. These consisted initially of the traditional land allotments, largely in his Roman colonies, and later, when land began to be exhausted, they had to be paid out in money instead. In A.D. 6, therefore, he founded a new military treasury, the *aerarium militare,* which was to defray legionaries' retirement pensions from the proceeds of indirect taxes. This was only one of a number of administrative innovations that the aging and tiring ruler introduced during the last decade of his life, with the help and perhaps the guiding initiative of Tiberius.

In A.D. 13 Augustus deposited his will at the House of the Vestals at Rome. It included a summary of the military and financial resources of the empire, and an ingenious political testament, the Acts *(Res Gestae)* of the Divine Augustus, known also as the Monumentum Ancyranum because its best-preserved copy is on the walls of the temple of Rome and Augustus at Ancyra (Ankara), capital of his new province of Galatia. Then, in the following year, he died, and Tiberius became emperor.

After many earlier successes, Augustus's policy of military expansion had ground to a halt in his last years, and he himself left Tiberius the advice not to continue it. By his reorganization, on the other hand, of the entire machinery of civilian government, he had proved himself one of the most gifted administrators the world has ever seen and the most influential single figure in the entire history of Rome. The gigantic work of reform that he carried out in every branch of Italian and provincial life not only trans-

Gravestone of the centurion Marcus Caelius, who fell in Arminius's ambush of Varus in the Teutoburg Forest in A.D. 9.

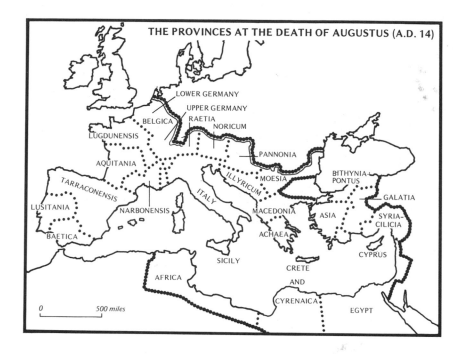

THE PROVINCES AT THE DEATH OF AUGUSTUS (A.D. 14)

LOWER GERMANY
UPPER GERMANY
BELGICA   RAETIA
NORICUM
LUGDUNENSIS
PANNONIA
AQUITANIA
BITHYNIA-
PONTUS
ILLYRICUM   MOESIA
TARRACONENSIS
ITALY
GALATIA
LUSITANIA   NARBONENSIS   MACEDONIA
ASIA   SYRIA-
CILICIA
BAETICA   ACHAEA
CYPRUS
SICILY   CRETE
AFRICA   AND
CYRENAICA
EGYPT

0   500 miles

formed the decaying republic into a new regime with many centuries of existence ahead of it, but also created a durable efficient Roman peace. It was this Pax Romana or Pax Augusta that insured the survival and eventual transmission of the classical heritage, Greek and Roman alike, and made possible the diffusion of Christianity, of which the founder, Jesus, was born during this reign.

The dilemma Caesar's career had posed—its demonstration that whereas the empire needed one-man rule, the nobles would tolerate no such thing —had been miraculously solved by Augustus. He had two things on his side: the Roman people's utter weariness of civil war, and his own subtle mastery of publicity in a wide variety of forms. Although, therefore, in every respect that mattered he was scarcely less an autocrat than Caesar had been, he contrived to cloak his absolutism in guises that looked old-fashioned enough to pass muster. True, the humble majority of the population of the empire, who were concerned only with keeping life together, had no time to care about such clever nuances, yet even they were able to appreciate the diminished risks of sudden death. But the people who positively approved of his republican facade included the nobles, or at least a substantial proportion of their number—despite occasional plots, when they reflected on their loss of political power—and above all others he gained and retained the loyalty of the knights and the middle class, whom this new regime notably benefited and enriched.

Many of the satisfied beneficiaries were not Roman but Italian, for Augustus felt and encouraged a new patriotic feeling for Italy, echoed by Virgil's insistence on the country's identity, which he helped to make as vivid as Rome's. This ideal was very different from the Greco-Roman concepts of Antony and Cleopatra. Augustus's narrower view was based on his own small-town Italian origins; and these origins were partly responsible also for his puritanical social policy and his antiquarian attachment to the ancient religion.

He summed up this whole pro-Italian, pro-Roman trend of his policy by the title that he chose to have conferred upon himself in 2 B.C. It was *pater patriae,* father of his country; Caesar had experimented with the designation, and Augustus adopted it as the climax of all his endeavors and the final expression of his regime. His proclaimed fatherhood of all Romans and Italians went back to the most ancient roots of the community, in which the *pater familias* had been the revered key figure. Moreover, by equally

The beginning of the Latin text of the *Res Gestae* of Augustus inscribed on the walls of the Temple of Rome and Augustus at Ancyra (Ankara) in Galatia (the *Monumentum Ancyranum*).

antique custom the patrons of clients were often described as their fathers;
and in this sense Augustus, by accepting the title of father of his country,
was following up the oath that all Italians had sworn to him in 32 B.C., and
asserting that all Roman citizens, without exception, were his clients and
that he was their patron—thus extending this traditional institution, in his
own interests and person, to the whole people of Italy and to the colonies
of Roman citizens in the provinces as well. And by implication he was
extending his patronage even more widely still, by suggesting that the whole
empire, non-Roman and Roman alike, constituted his clients, and so did the
dependent kingdoms beyond. His sympathies, that is to say, were not so
narrowly Italian that he took no thought for his other subjects and allies.
Indeed, as befitted the author of a number of literary works (now all lost),
his chauvinism was modified by a well-informed admiration of Greek culture that Virgil and the other literary personages of the time entirely shared.
The conventional view of his character, in ancient times, differentiated
between his cruelty in his youthful years and his mildness when he was
older. But there was not so much need or occasion for cruelty in his later
career as there had been earlier on; and when, even towards the end of his
days, harsh measures were needed (for example, in the suppression of
alleged conspiracies), he often remained ready enough to apply them. But
nothing short of this degree of political toughness could ever have produced
such vast results.

His domestic life, too, though simple and homespun, was conducted on
ruthless lines. It is true that, although unfaithful to his wife Livia, he
remained devoted to her. Yet when his daughter Julia and granddaughter
of the same name moved in immoral smart circles suspected of subversion,
he exiled them one after another, without compunction, and his third
grandson, too, suffered banishment and perhaps violent death as well. And
as for his male relatives who acted as his principal helpers, he was loyal to
them but drove them as fiercely hard as he drove himself. He needed them
because the burden was so heavy, and he especially needed the exceptional
talents of Agrippa and Tiberius in the military sphere because, unlike most
famous Romans before him, he himself was not a particularly effective
general or admiral and could even be regarded as a coward. Be that as it
may, his physical condition was subject to a large number of recurrent
weaknesses and disabilities. They were intensified by a well-developed strain
of hypochondria; but his ill health was very real as well, and when he was
young, it was only his indomitable will that enabled him to survive—a
strange preliminary to such a uniquely active career, lasting until the age
of seventy-six.

Augustus was short of stature, but his fine countenance with its calm and
mild expression proved a godsend to the best sculptors of the time, Greeks

and Hellenized easterners who devoted to his features a remarkable series of sympathetic, moving interpretations. These portrayals, displaying a discreet blend of idealism and realism, were reduplicated throughout the empire in thousands of busts, statues, and portraits on coins. Less successful perhaps, though some think otherwise, is the majestic but somewhat stiff Altar of Peace (Ara Pacis), consecrated in 13 and dedicated in 9 B.C. Its reliefs depict scenes from the patriotic Roman mythology and a religious procession in which the leading figures of the state take a dignified part.

Augustus was also the greatest of all adorners of Rome. Something of the monumental, classic grandeur of his buildings can still be seen today in the Theater of Marcellus and the remains of the massive Augustan Forum. Flanked by huge colonnades and side apses, the new precinct culminated in the Temple of Mars the Avenger—the avenger of his adoptive father, the god Caesar, who had himself started this precedent of constructing new Forums. Outside Rome, too, there were innumerable arches, trophies, and other memorials of the Augustan age. And from his wife Livia's mansion on the outskirts of Rome, at Prima Porta, comes a reminder that not all the art of the period was formal and grandiose. One of the rooms is adorned with wall paintings that create the illusion of an enchanted garden; beyond a trellis are orchards and flower beds in which birds and insects perch among the foliage.

The Economic Basis

This elegance, and the whole way of living for which it stood, was the product of a new solidity in the finances of the empire. The relationship of the central state treasury, the public *aerarium,* to the treasuries of the provinces is still imperfectly understood. Augustus, it is true, proudly recorded his own gifts to the state. But the state's profits from running the rich, peaceful, senatorial provinces must somehow have been pumped in the reverse direction, so as to pay for the imperial frontier provinces which required heavy expenditure.

The principal direct taxes paid by the population of the empire, other than Rome and Italy which enjoyed exemption, were two in number, a levy on all occupiers of land *(tributum soli)* from which came the far greater part of the revenue, and a poll tax *(tributum capitis)* collected in Egypt, Syria, and certain other areas. These taxes were based on the results of censuses, which Augustus organized throughout the provinces. The statistics thus gathered made it possible to fix the sums the state required, so that Augustus, pursuing further a tendency initiated by Caesar, was able to eliminate private tax farmers from the direct taxation system altogether. Indirect taxes, however—the only dues to which Roman citizens were liable—were

Head of Augustus from Aricia near Rome (above left).

Head of Augustus from Pergamum (above).

Augustus (left).

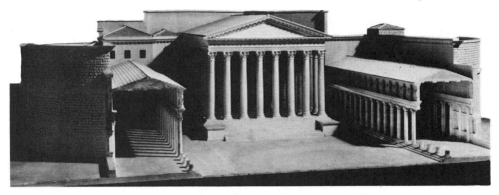

Reconstruction of Forum of Augustus and Temple of Mars Ultor (the Avenger) at Rome. Inaugurated 2 B.C.

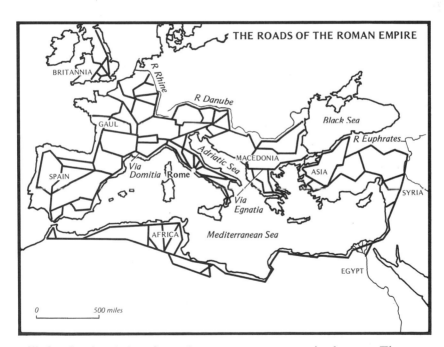

still, for the time being, farmed out to contractors as in the past. The most important of these indirect levies were customs dues. But their rates, at two or two and one half percent, were low enough not to hamper commerce.

Its free operation was insured by a system of fleets which, for the first time, were organized to police the Mediterranean, so that maritime interchanges gained in speed and security alike. The principal naval bases were on the west and east coasts of Italy at Misenum and Ravenna. But the most important means of communication and organization was provided by the comprehensive network of roads extending throughout Italy and the provinces. By the second century A.D. there were more than fifty thousand miles of first-class roads in the empire and over two hundred thousand miles of lesser roads; and Augustus himself had played an enormous part in extending these ramifications. The roads were systematically and resourcefully distributed, designed, constructed, and drained, with careful adaptation to local materials and conditions. They were made to span rivers by the creation of soaring powerful bridges; and they penetrated mountains by tunnels that aroused admiration for centuries.

Already in the later republic, despite all the disturbances of that period, the great increases in individual wealth had stimulated interregional trade, and now, in the favorable circumstances created by Augustus—it became solidly established as a significant economic factor: the normal rate of interest fell to four to six percent, the lowest level of ancient times—Italy still took the lead in commercial activity. A fine building at Pompeii, constructed for the guild or corporation of the fullers, shows how efficiently the men engaged in such businesses organized themselves. New industries for woolen goods sprang up in other Italian cities as well, while metalworking at Rome and Capua flourished, and glassblowing became a prosperous activity in Campania and north Italy alike. For the most part, relatively small-scale enterprises were prevalent. But the pottery of Arretium (Arezzo) was an exception, since these products, their red glazing a trade secret, were widely exported outside the peninsula.

Painting of light Roman warships, probably Liburnians, from the Temple of Isis, Pompeii.

The road between Antioch and Beroea (Aleppo).

And Italy in return bought a large range of provincial wares, including slaves, grain, metals, marble, linen, papyrus, furs, and ivory. The provinces, too, displayed a greatly increased commercial activity, which is illustrated, for example, by the impressive porticoed Augustan marketplace at Lepcis Magna in north Africa. This trade was stimulated by intensified mining operations, increasingly under imperial control. And it was also encouraged by an impressive reform of the currency that retained the former gold and silver but introduced a new token coinage in two attractive metals, yellow brass and red copper. This coinage was primarily intended, as always, for the needs of the army and the state. But trade benefited too, and coins of Augustus in all metals are found abundantly throughout the western provinces. Many bronze coinages of individual cities were also sanctioned, for example in Spain at the outset of the imperial epoch and for a much longer period in the eastern provinces, where they circulated alongside the imperial gold and silver for three hundred years.

The currency in the precious metals is also found in considerable quantities outside the empire. There was a picturesquely varied influx of goods from beyond its borders. For example, silk came from China to be woven and dyed in Syria and combined with a linen warp on the island of Cos; and large numbers of *denarii* found at Coimbatore in southern India had been brought there to pay for pepper. But these luxury imports from abroad were much less important than exchanges within the empire itself.

Nevertheless, neither at this nor at any later period of antiquity did trading ever become the economic basis of the Roman world, for it could never achieve really large dimensions as long as the manufacturers showed so little interest in productive expansion or the technological advances required to achieve it. Instead, they were mostly content with the simple satisfaction of their own material needs; and the continued employment of numerous slaves made it unnecessary to save labor. Moreover, there was never a real mass market to provide an incentive to large-scale endeavors, and capitalism was still embryonic, so that no clear distinction was made between capital and labor costs.

Besides, there were severe practical problems. Fuel was scarce; and transportation, while risky and erratic by sea, was extremely slow and expensive on land—it did not pay, for example, to cart grain for more than fifty miles. For all these reasons the entire commerce and industry of all the empire together probably never amounted to more than ten percent of its total revenue. All the rest came from agriculture, principally wheat, with barley second. Here too, however, the prohibitively heavy cost of land transport hampered development. Methods of cultivation, too, did not advance very much further; and there was no planned reinvestment of agricultural profits. Once again, there was more interest in mere acquisition than in better production. For example, long-term loans to encourage improvements in output were nonexistent; and state intervention to help agriculture remained limited.

Nevertheless, the need to provide such support had to figure to a certain extent in the calculations of emperors. This was because, to prevent unrest, they considered it one of their most essential duties (as certain late republican politicians had already felt before them) to provide the people of Rome with sufficient grain at cheap prices. Most of this was imported, especially from north Africa (Tunisia), which had replaced Sicily as the granary of the capital, and an increasing amount began to come from Egypt as well. However, the great increase in the production of cereals in those and other countries did little to improve the depressed situation of their cultivators. The slaves remained slaves; and the huge "free" agricultural population of the empire likewise did not benefit markedly from the Augustan peace. The burden of the land tax, from which the state derived most of its funds, fell mainly upon their shoulders. And even if it might be something of a relief that the government no longer employed intermediaries to collect it, this tax was not progressive in its operation—that is to say, it fell with equal percentual weight on large and small incomes, thus hitting the poor much more heavily than the rich. And additional unfairness was caused by the failure of this form of taxation to take account of different qualities of soil and of the fluctuations in annual yields.

So the great bulk of the "free" population of the Roman world, comprising the inhabitants of the villages and rural areas, remained extremely poor, living at bare subsistence level. They were also, politically, almost nonpersons. The political structure of the empire was still founded on its city-states, no longer wholly independent like those of earlier Greece but still, subject to ultimate dependence on Rome, enjoying varying degrees of local autonomy. Each city was allowed to control rural territories of its own, not so large as the increasingly enormous lands that belonged to the emperors, but nevertheless very often of substantial size; and they paid for their own amenities by exploiting such possessions. Yet the inhabitants of these rural zones lacked the privileges enjoyed by the citizens of the towns that ruled over them.

For those citizens, the Pax Augusta was a splendid thing. It meant the triumph of the bourgeoisie—the businessmen and traders and all the people who had a share in the city-state system everywhere and participated in its profits. This whole section of the population had, in effect, taken over the power previously wielded by the old political upper class. And, in Italy especially, Augustus also paid particular attention to the very large, indeed numerically preponderant, class of freedmen—ex-slaves and their children. By allowing them, in many cases, to intermarry with full citizens (18 B.C.) and by calling upon them to provide priests for the growing local imperial cult, he found them a place in the social and civic system. And they gained for themselves a considerable share in the universal middle-class well-being —with the hope of even higher things, for not long after Augustus's time they were becoming state secretaries, and Petronius's *Satyricon* tells how they could make enormous fortunes. Such tycoons, it is true, were exceptional; but many other freedmen, too, fared better than they had ever fared before.

And so, not indeed from the humble farm laborers, but from a considerably wider section of the population than had ever flourished in the previous history of Rome—or for that matter of any other country either—Augustus deserved the compliment that was paid to him in the last days of his life. As the ship on which he was traveling sailed beside the busy Campanian port of Puteoli, it passed a merchant vessel that had just arrived from Alexandria. Thereupon its crew and passengers, wearing white robes and garlands, burned incense and offered a salute to the father of their country, crying out that it was to him that they owed their lives, freedom, and prosperity.

Augustan Literature

Alongside Agrippa, the most important of Augustus's advisers, especially in the earlier part of the reign, had been the Etruscan Maecenas (d. 8 B.C.). Through him, the ruler was able to win the goodwill of some of the greatest and most influential writers the world has ever known, and this approbation they freely expressed, even though all of them displayed a strong vein of independence as well.

Virgil was born in 70 B.C. near Mantua in north Italy, of a family that seems to have been partly of Etruscan origin. Later, he moved to the region of Neapolis (Naples), where his father, expropriated by the Second Triumvirate (41 B.C.), came to join him. Virgil first astonished literary circles in Rome by the novelty of his *Eclogues (Bucolics)* (45–37 B.C.). These ten short poems transmuted into a melodious, evocative Latin the pastoral themes introduced to the Greek literature of Alexandria more than two centuries earlier. This is a timeless, unreal Greek countryside, blended with Italian elements, and designed for sophisticated townsmen; an idyllic rusticity that conflicts in the poet's heart with the need to come to terms with imperial Rome. The fourth poem in the collection, written in a euphoric moment of reconciliation between Antony and Octavian (40 B.C.), reflects the widespread belief that a savior was about to appear and rescue the world from its prolonged miseries. He remains unnamed, but elsewhere in the *Eclogues* the task of salvation is attributed specifically to Octavian, the future Augustus.

The four longer *Georgics* that followed (36–29 B.C.), dedicated to Maecenas, celebrated in verse of a new flexible subtlety the beauties and labors and rewards of the rustic life, and the glorious antiquarian, legendary past of the rich Italian countryside. The *Georgics* are the supreme literary expression of that emotional love for Roman Italy which was a feature of the times, and became the center point of Augustus's policy and peace: the peace for which he is praised from the heart in these profoundly evocative poems.

Next Virgil turned to heroic epic, in the tradition that went back to Homer. But the sensitive subtleties of his *Aeneid* are very far removed from Homer's balladlike extroversion. And so is the hitherto unimaginable rhythmical elaboration and sonorous majesty of this poetry, extracting from the Latin language its ultimate, complex potentialities of emotion and sound and artifice. The Trojan Aeneas, escaping from the Greek sack of Troy, is destined for many wanderings and adventures. In north Africa, he encounters the mythical Queen Dido of Carthage, and the sadness of their doomed romance owes less to the Homeric epic than to the much more recent Greek poetry of Alexandria, magically transformed. Finally Aeneas reaches Italy.

As he lands on its shores, he is taken down by the Sibyl into the underworld, a scene in which the poet discloses his deepest reflections upon the nature of the universe. Then, after a visit to the place that was later to become Rome, Aeneas is compelled to join battle with the peoples of Italy. The wars end in peace, he marries a Latin bride, and Rome's foundation will follow —for this is what the poem is really about.

Its theme is largely war—the *Aeneid* is an *Odyssey* followed by an *Iliad,* this warlike section being indebted to the national, epic tradition of Naevius and Ennius, who had first adapted the Homeric genre to Latin poetry. War leads to peace, and it is the Augustan peace of which Virgil is thinking. His age, following upon the prolonged nightmare epoch of civil strife, was one of those times in the history of the world when order looked even more important than liberty, and Augustus's feat in bringing peace seemed to Virgil the greatest of all possible national gifts—and most of his contemporaries agreed with him. Yet Aeneas in the poem wins his war, and becomes a true exemplar of the virtues, only after he has suffered bitterly: and among his most poignant ordeals is his parting from Dido, enforced by Jupiter and destiny.

Dido is, in one sense, a symbol of Rome's most perilous enemy of the past, her kingdom of Carthage; and those who listened to the poet reciting the *Aeneid* must have thought of that other hostile queen of living memory, Cleopatra. And yet, although Dido's efforts to detain Aeneas are against the divine will, she is portrayed with heart-wringing sympathy—it is almost as if Virgil's sorrow at her tragedy has for the moment got the better of his knowledge that Aeneas acts rightly, indeed inevitably, in leaving her. And the same thing appears to happen again when the poet begins to describe Turnus, the tough leader of Aeneas's Italian foes. For Turnus, too, is plainly fighting against what is fated to happen, and yet he, too, is allotted almost more than his share of nobility.

Despite, therefore, the radiant future that will lie ahead for Rome after Aeneas has prevailed, Virgil was telling us that wars turn to dust and ashes and weariness. In the end, he reckoned military conquest lower than the conquest by human beings of their own souls and hearts. He was a man deeply divided within himself. The benefits Augustus had brought to a war-torn world inspired him with deep gratitude. Yet he also knew better than anyone else that such triumphs, like all the Roman triumphs that had ever been, are built on pain.

In 19 B.C. he was in Greece, where Augustus, who happened also to be there, persuaded him to sail back home in his company. But Virgil fell ill, and after returning across the Adriatic to Brundisium he died. The *Aeneid* was not quite completed, and before leaving Italy, he had made his literary executor promise to burn it in the event of his death. Perhaps he felt that

Manuscript of Virgil's *Aeneid* (fourth century A.D.),
showing Aeneas received by King Latinus.

the two conflicting ideals that tear the poem apart were too much for its
unity. But when he was dead, Augustus gave orders that his wish should
be disregarded, and he had the *Aeneid* published just as it was.

The second of the outstanding Augustan poets, Horace, was born in 65
B.C. at Venusia in Apulia, in southeast Italy. His father, who probably came
of the hillman stock of Italy's central highlands, had been a slave and
subsequently an auctioneer's assistant; he could afford to send his son to a
famous school at Rome, from which he moved on to the empire's most
favored center of higher education, the Academy of Athens. At the battle
of Philippi (42 B.C.) Horace served as an officer on the side of Brutus and
Cassius, but after their defeat he returned to Italy. There his family farm,
like Virgil's, had been confiscated by the victorious triumvirs; but he obtained a job at Rome and got to know Maecenas.

His *Satires* (35 and 30 B.C.) reject careerism and advocate wisdom attained through serenity, in the manner of a Greek philosopher. But they vary in theme, and so does another of his poetic collections of this time, the *Epodes* (ca. 30 B.C.), which sometimes assails social abuses with a bitterness that is more than just a literary convention. Then, after Maecenas had given him a farm in the Sabine hills, Horace published his famous *Odes* (23 and 13 B.C.), treating of love, wine, nature, friends, moderation, and state affairs. While representing himself, in these short poems, as the heir to the Greek lyricists, he displayed a sensitive, economical mastery of words that is wholly Latin and his own. And meanwhile he was also composing his *Epistles* (ca. 20–15 B.C.), which were more profound and mature versions of the *Satires* and incorporated some of the most influential literary criticism the classical world ever produced. The man who emerged from these later works is kindly, tolerant, humane, and mild, but by no means lacking in strength, which reveals itself in a spirit of astringent, detached realism; and Horace is a gentle but persistent mocker not only of others, but also of himself.

Augustus, against whom he had formerly fought at Philippi, became his friend, through Maecenas. Indeed, later he became virtually the court poet, for in 17 B.C., two years after Virgil's death, he was asked to compose the *Carmen Saeculare,* a hymn designed for the antique Secular Games, which Augustus had revived to purge the state of the evils and crimes of the past and provide a solemn, religious sanction for his regime and its moral reforms.

Nevertheless, when the ruler offered him the post of his private secretary, he declined; and the praises of the new order throughout his poems are interwoven with tactful but firm assertions of his own personal independence. Horace was as ambivalent, in his own way, as Virgil. Like him, he welcomed Augustus's attempts to revive the old Roman virtues and traditions; and above all, he felt immense gratitude for his termination of the civil wars. Indeed, after the prolonged convulsions of the recent past, this achievement seemed so great to Horace that he had no eye for whatever hardness the new regime might possess. All the same, he always remained his own master and kept the core of his quiet but distinct personality intact.

Another member of Maecenas's circle was Propertius of Asisium (Assisi) in Umbria, who was junior to Virgil and Horace by about fifteen and ten years respectively. Like them, he had been impoverished by the civil wars and had Augustus to thank for the revival of his fortunes. Unlike them, however, he devoted his poetical genius and mythological learning, during the greater part of his career, to a theme that had nothing to do with the new regime—the passion of love. On this subject, despite the usual claims to be Romanizing the Greeks, he wrote elegies of a new, obsessive subjectivity, spanning the shifting and obscure border of what is classic and what is romantic. Only in his last writings did he turn to poems of public significance, giving expression to the blend of myth and patriotic antiquarianism that had so profoundly inspired Virgil.

This, again, was the inspiration of Livy of Patavium (b. ca. 59 B.C.–d. A.D. 17) throughout his entire life. His *History of Rome* from the earliest times is an unparalleled achievement that took forty years to complete. It consisted of one hundred and forty-two "Books" (nearly one hundred and seven of them are lost), which would have filled some twenty or thirty modern volumes. Writing in fluent, lush prose and making loftily imaginative, uncritical use of a wide variety of sources, he offers highly colored evocations of the foundation and early epic age of Rome and provides many rousing narratives, including a superb account of Hannibal's invasion. Rome, as the chosen object and instrument of providential destiny, receives its supreme glorification from Livy; and so does the Roman character, for it is to Livy more than any other writer that we owe our idea of what this was, or rather of what he and his compatriots wanted and believed it to have been in the past. Rome's traditional heroes and their actions, as he so vividly depicted them, were handed down to later Europe as revelations of what the human spirit can achieve. And the most favored of these heroes was Augustus, restorer of peace and of the republican moral standards still greatly respected in the cities of Livy's own Italian northland. It was in this traditional spirit that the ruler himself placed statues of all the victorious Roman generals of ancient times in his resplendent new Forum; and to the historian, whom he thus translated into sculpture, he was a friend.

Yet at the same time Livy, like Virgil and Horace, still retains a considerable degree of detachment from the Augustan order. He always felt deep sympathy with humble individuals caught up in the great warlike crises. And when he dealt with the later years of the republic, we learn from surviving abridgments that he expressed doubts whether Caesar's career had been beneficial, and favored Caesar's enemy Pompey by glossing over his youthful brutalities, so that Augustus, the adoptive son of the deified dictator, half jokingly called him a "Pompeian." Besides, there are other strange omissions from these summaries as well. For example, despite his general approval of Augustus's endeavors to revive the old morality, we find no appreciation of the specific reforms that the ruler had already begun to set in motion very shortly after Actium.

On the contrary, Livy, in the introduction to his whole work, shows notable caution about the feasibility of any real return to the glorious past. "Our defects are unendurable to us," he declares, "and so are their cures." At first sight this looks surprisingly unfriendly towards Augustus's aspirations. However, such lack of interest in current changes combined with nostalgia for the good old times was not as anti-Augustan as might be thought, since it harmonized with Augustus's own claim that he was not, formally speaking, an innovating autocrat at all, but the restorer of ancient republican ways and customs. Livy was therefore free to pursue his romantic idealization of the Rome that had vanished forever.

The poet Ovid of Sulmo (Sulmona in the Abruzzi) (b. 43 B.C.–d. A.D. 17) was the only one of these writers whose aloofness veered over into catastrophe. Although only some twenty years younger than Livy, he belonged to a very different generation, no longer brought up amid civil war and, although able enough to turn out a patriotic poem, no longer much concerned with Augustan nationalism or morality. Ovid's elegiac couplets look at men and especially women with a not unfriendly or an altogether untender gaze, although the humor to which his observations move him sometimes seems cold-blooded or even clinical. Yet this astringency does not strike a chill because of his incomparable genius for vivid description and narrative, which has been one of the greatest influences Rome has exerted upon the culture of the Western world. This gift as teller of stories finds its fullest expression in the *Metamorphoses,* a vast Arabian Nights of every sort of myth, folk tale, anecdote, written in a lighter version of Virgil's epic meter.

In spite of occasional references to Augustus's glories in these poems, the sort of poetry Ovid was writing did not much appeal to the *princeps;* and so in A.D. 8 the blow fell, and the poet was exiled to far-distant Tomi (Constanța in Rumania). He himself describes the charges that had led to this disastrous result as "a poem and a mistake." The poem to which he refers was perhaps *The Art of Love,* far too immoral for the tastes of Augustus, who disapproved of the smart metropolitan society in which such things were cynically talked and laughed about; Ovid's self-indulgent individualism clashed sharply with Augustus's conception of his age. The "mistake" may have had something to do with the banishment for adultery of Augustus's granddaughter Julia, her lover being executed at the same time for alleged plotting. Perhaps Ovid, the emperor suspected, had known more than he should—and ought not to have remained silent about it.

He was never recalled from Tomi; and nine years later he died, having occupied his time in writing further, much sadder elegies in which he obliquely contrasts the spiritual authority of poetry with the supreme temporal power that had punished him. He is part of the reverse side of the Augustan society: the member of the ruling class who rejected the values the ruler decreed, the poet who was not serious or public-spirited enough to live in this bracing climate of the new Rome, and survive.

VII.
THE IMPERIAL
PEACE

Preceding page:
Goddess Cybele on processional carriage drawn by two lions.

14

The Inheritors of Empire

The Successors of Augustus

Tiberius (A.D. 14–37),* whose unfair depiction is the most brilliant achievement of the historian Tacitus, was a proud member of the ancient Claudian clan who had a splendid record of military and administrative achievement. But he was also grim, caustic, and suspicious and lacked Augustus's talent for public relations. In particular, despite his strongly emphasized desire that the Senate should play its part in imperial decision making, he found it difficult to get on with senators, both individually and *en masse*.

During the first years of his reign, he employed as his principal generals his nephew Germanicus—whom Augustus had required him to adopt as his son—and his own son Drusus the Younger. Both were immediately engaged in the suppression of legionary mutinies that had broken out after his succession in Germany and Pannonia (northern Yugoslavia) respectively. Subsequently, Germanicus fought three massive but unproductive campaigns against the Germans beyond the Rhine frontier, momentarily repeating the earlier Roman advance as far as the Elbe (A.D. 14–16). Then he was transferred to a major appointment in the East. This terminated in his death (19), which caused widespread sorrow. Four years later Drusus the Younger also died, so that Tiberius had already lost his two principal heirs; there were suspicions that both of them had been murdered, but probably they died natural deaths.

Meanwhile a strong personal position was built up by Sejanus, prefect of the praetorian guard. In 23, this astute Etruscan concentrated the guardsmen, previously dispersed around a number of Italian towns, within a single new barracks at Rome itself. The government displayed continual fear of real or imagined conspiracies, which existing treason laws were employed

---

*Dates indicated for emperors and popes are those of their reigns.

277

to suppress, amid complaints about the vagueness of the laws and their perilous potentialities as weapons of tyranny. Sejanus took the lead in initiating such accusations and became more powerful still after Tiberius, in 26, retired from Rome to the Campanian island of Capreae (Capri), never to set foot in the city for the rest of his life. Sejanus also encouraged the emperor to detect seditious intentions in Germanicus's evidently indiscreet widow Agrippina, the daughter of Agrippa. She and her two elder sons (the heirs apparent) were arrested in A.D. 29–30 and put to death or forced to commit suicide during the following years, leaving a young third son Gaius Caesar as the probable successor to the throne. He was known as Caligula —"Little Boots"—because of the miniature military uniform he had worn as a child.

Meanwhile Sejanus, with some difficulty, induced the emperor to promise him a marriage connection; and although as praetorian prefect he had previously been a knight and not a senator, he gained the consulship in 31 as the colleague of Tiberius himself. But his downfall promptly followed. It appears probable that he was plotting against Caligula, whose succession would mean an end of his ascendancy. At any rate that was the information that came to Tiberius's ears; and so he secretly transferred the praetorian command to his own confidant Macro, who arranged for Sejanus to be

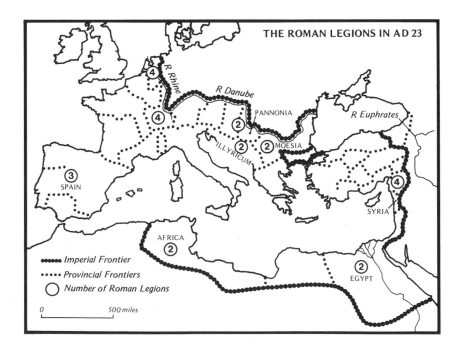

THE ROMAN LEGIONS IN AD 23

•••••• Imperial Frontier
••••• Provincial Frontiers
◯ Number of Roman Legions

0   500 miles

The north wall of the Praetorian Camp, constructed by Sejanus in A.D. 23. The upper part belongs to the city wall of Aurelian.

arrested in Rome during a meeting of the Senate. This was done, and its members immediately ordered his execution, which was carried out and followed by many other deaths among his political friends.

The empire as a whole was still governed well, though on the somewhat static lines imposed by the conscious employment of Augustus as a model; and the provinces scarcely felt these metropolitan tremors. Yet the career of Sejanus had been instructive. It had displayed the need all emperors were bound to feel for a helper they could trust; and it had underlined the extreme peril they ran in trusting such a deputy too much and delegating too much power to him. The crisis had also underlined the equivocal position of the army and particularly of the praetorian guard, which was intended to protect the ruler but might instead be employed by its prefect to offer a lethal threat to himself or his relations. As it happened, however, the guard did nothing to help or avenge Sejanus, and under Macro's direction it remained loyal to the emperor.

Among Tiberius's entourage at Capreae was Caligula; and when in A.D. 37, at the age of seventy-nine, the emperor died, it was he who became the next emperor. The transition was arranged by the officers of the praetorian guard, who thus launched their career as emperor makers. Their commander, Macro, however, did not long survive, nor did the late ruler's grandson, who had been left a share of his personal estate, thus incurring Caligula's animosity.

Caligula was the first emperor to show aversion to the long hours of laborious duty needed to keep matters under control, preferring instead to delegate work to the Greek or Hellenized ex-slaves who were his secretaries, so that he himself could concentrate on a round of amusements instead. The turning point of his reign came in A.D. 39 when he formed a powerful dislike for the Senate, an attitude that became strongly accentuated when one of their number, the commander in Upper Germany on the Rhine, was detected in a plot. Caligula himself marched north to organize its suppression, which was accompanied by executions and banishments in high places.

Irremediably frightened by this narrow escape, Caligula abandoned proposed expeditions against the still unconquered "free" Germans across the Rhine, and against the British, and returned to Rome (A.D. 40). There he gave expression to far-reaching ideas for the conversion of the tactful Augustan principate into a thorough-going autocratic system on the lines of the absolute monarchies of Greece. Although honors were showered on him with extravagant lack of restraint, conspiracies and rumors of conspiracies continued to abound, and security precautions around his person were sharply intensified. Before long, however, the praetorian high command decided that he was a bad risk, and early in the following year a group of its officers murdered him, together with his wife and infant daughter.

After his death, his fifty-one-year-old uncle Claudius was hailed emperor by the guardsmen. Handicapped by infirmity—he was probably spastic— he had devoted his time to scholarly pursuits, obtaining no preferment until belated consulship four years previously, But now, because he was the brother of the much-loved Germanicus and the only surviving adult male of the Julian and Claudian clans, the senior praetorian officers who killed Caligula had insured that he should ascend to the throne in the dead man's place. The Senate, however, which had discussed a possible restoration of the republic after Caligula's murder, included many members unwilling to accept Claudius, and in the year following his accession, they supported a rebellion planned by the governor of Upper Illyricum (Dalmatia). This terrified Claudius just as a similar seditious move had upset Caligula, and the suppression of the plot was followed by another fierce tightening of precautions and by further measures against senators of dubious loyalty—measures that in turn led to a fresh crop of real or suspected conspiracies, followed by a renewed wave of treason trials.

At the same time, however, the government of Claudius was impressively active in provincial and foreign affairs. Just a century after the reconnaissances of Julius Caesar on the island of Britain, the southern and central regions of England were now occupied, in what was perhaps the best

The Fosse Way, frontier of Claudius's British province, at its intersection with Watling Street at Venonae (High Cross).

planned of all Roman conquests, and their annexation as the province of Britannia immediately followed. Claudius himself came to the country in A.D. 43 for the decisive capture of Camulodunum (Colchester), which became the capital of the new province. Mauretania and Thrace were also taken away from client rule and added to the empire; and colonies were established in the frontier zones and elsewhere. Moreover, there was a conscious and perceptible liberalization of policies concerning enfranchisements, admissions to the Senate, and appointments to offices of state, for which Gauls, in particular, were now encouraged to apply. The emperor also displayed considerable ability for long-term projects. For example, the grain supply of the city was organized on a permanent basis, and the port of Ostia underwent reconstruction to facilitate this traffic.

Claudius himself devoted unremitting absorption to the judicial duties which were one of the most important functions of an emperor. His predecessor's employment of Greek freedmen as advisers and imperial secretaries was continued and extended, and this was a period when certain of these men, especially Narcissus and Pallas, rose to great power. However, Claudius still kept such officials, for the time being, under his firm personal control and employed a senator, Lucius Vitellius, as his principal counsellor. For a number of years, too, his young wife, Messalina, who had borne him a daughter Octavia and a son Britannicus, remained more interested in indulging herself than in exerting power. In 48, however, she was charged, perhaps rightly, with conniving in an attempt by one of her lovers to seize the throne or supplant Claudius by Britannicus; and both she and her lover were put to death.

Bronze coin of Cunobelinus (Shakespeare's Cymbeline)
at his capital Camulodunum (Colchester). After his death, Claudius
invaded England (A.D. 43).

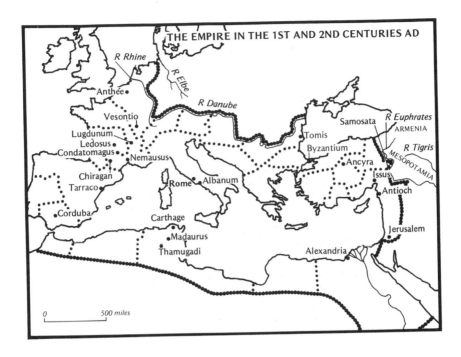

The initiative in suppressing out this conspiracy had been taken by Narcissus. But his moment of power ended abruptly in the next year when Claudius married again, selecting his niece Agrippina the Younger, who had not been Narcissus's preferred candidate. For the rest of his reign the aging emperor, overworked, worried about plots, and weakened by infirmity and drink, increasingly lost his command of what was going on. The government was in the hands of Agrippina and of Pallas—who had supported her marriage to Claudius—and of another of her protégés, the new praetorian prefect Burrus, who came from southern Gaul. Stamping out her opponents, Agrippina arranged in A.D. 50 that her own thirteen-year-old boy, by a former marriage to a nobleman, should be adopted by Claudius as his son, taking the name of Nero: so that it was evident that he, rather than Britannicus who was four years younger, would eventually succeed to the throne.

And then Claudius suddenly died (54). It is believed, probably with good reason, that Agrippina had fed him poisoned mushrooms. With the help of the praetorian commander and of his tutor, the leading writer Seneca, Nero succeeded peacefully to the imperial throne. In view of his youth, it was Agrippina herself who became the effective ruler of the empire. Her preeminence, however, was brief, since already in the following year it was rapidly becoming eroded, and Nero had started to assume his imperial duties. Yet when certain liberal ideas he initially proposed, relating to tax reforms and the prohibition of gladiatorial combats, proved impracticable, he lost interest in public affairs, and felt that chariot racing, music, drama, and sex were more rewarding activities. In consequence, the empire was largely governed by the harmonious, efficient partnership of Seneca and Burrus, backed by their senatorial supporters. At the same time, important military operations against the Parthians took place under the empire's leading general, Corbulo (58–60), and then in Britain the ferocious revolt of Queen Boudicca (Boadicea) of the Iceni (East Anglia) in 60 was put down.

Meanwhile Nero, fearing that his mother, discontented with her retirement, might encourage a conspiracy, had enticed her to the Campanian coast, where he caused her to be assassinated (59). Seneca and Burrus may or may not have been involved in her death, but from now on they found it increasingly difficult to keep the emperor in order. In 62 Burrus died, and Seneca, believing it impossible to carry on without his help, went into voluntary retirement.

The emperor's chief counsellor was now Tigellinus, a seedy figure whom he had made joint prefect of the praetorian guard; in this capacity he presided over a revival of the treason law, under which a number of prominent nobles, as in earlier reigns, were executed on suspicions of conspiracy. Nero, long since estranged from his young wife Octavia, divorced her and put her to death, marrying a famous beauty Poppaea—formerly his friend Otho's wife—who before long bore him a short-lived daughter (63). In the next year Rome was ravaged by a savagely destructive fire for which the government penalized the small Christian movement as scapegoats. Suspicions that Nero himself had been responsible for the fire were probably unwarranted. But they gained strength when work was at once started on his new palace, the Golden House, designed to extend with its parklands over a wide area of the city and situated partly on the sites of houses that had been gutted by the fire.

Furthermore, in 65 the emperor's reputation deteriorated further when he carried out a long-cherished ambition by appearing in his first public performance on the stage. Senators were profoundly shocked, and soon afterwards the first of a series of plots, or alleged plots, against his life was detected and betrayed. One of its casualties was Seneca; and another was Tigellinus's colleague as praetorian prefect, in whose place was appointed a personage as sinister as Tigellinus himself, a certain Nymphidius Sabinus, who claimed to be Caligula's illegitimate son. In the following year a new security drive wiped out a group of senators of philosophical republican inclinations, and leading military commanders, too, were compelled to kill themselves. They included Corbulo, who had become a national hero after victories and negotiations that brought peace to the Armenian frontier for half a century to come. But Nero was afraid of such outstanding commanders, and when a major revolt broke out in the turbulent minor province of Judaea, he deliberately assigned its suppression to a man credited with only moderate talents and ambitions, Vespasian.

Meanwhile, the emperor himself was conducting an extended artistic and dramatic tour of Greece. It culminated in his ostensible liberation of the country. This phil-Hellene gesture, echoing an earlier liberation more than two and a half centuries earlier, did not, of course, restore political liberty to the Greeks, but it brought them a welcome exemption from Roman taxes. However, during Nero's prolonged absence from the capital, his position became seriously undermined since provincial governors and army commanders, feeling that their lives were in danger, felt tempted to rebel. Soon after he had finally returned to Rome, Vindex, the governor of Gallia Lugdunensis (central Gaul), broke into open revolt (68). His insurrection, however, was defeated by his colleague from Upper Germany in a battle at Vesontio (Besançon), and he did not survive. But then Galba, governor of Nearer Spain, whose bad relations with Nero's local agents had prompted him to make secret contacts with Vindex, was hailed emperor by the soldiers of the single legion he commanded, and this was confirmed by the Senate at Rome. Nero found himself abandoned even by the praetorian guard, and in June he committed suicide.

The Year of the Four Emperors

Galba, who was about seventy-one years of age, came of a family of resplendent nobility and wealth. Although he now assumed the titles "Caesar" and "Augustus" which had been borne by emperors of the Julian and the Claudian clans, he was not in any way related to them; and the fact that he was the first ruler to come from outside that imperial house is his principal significance.

When he learned that Nero was dead, he marched slowly on Rome, where in his absence an incipient coup by the praetorian prefect, Nymphidius Sabinus, was easily stamped out. But when the new emperor arrived outside the city in October, he caused a bad impression by killing a number of marines who had come to meet him, and his meanness over money, combined with an unwelcome choice of advisers, rapidly undermined his security. The bad news traveled, and on New Year's Day, A.D. 69, the army in Upper Germany overthrew his statues and called on the Senate and Roman people to choose a successor. But on the following day, the Lower German forces saluted an emperor on their own account, their governor

Vitellius, son of Claudius's chief adviser and the grandson of a knight in the service of Augustus; and the garrison in Upper Germany then accepted their choice.

On hearing what had happened on New Year's Day, Galba decided that, lacking a son of his own, he must adopt an heir from outside his family to offer hope of continuity. This was an important precedent for future emperors, but of no avail to himself because the selection he made, a young man of the same highly aristocratic background as himself, proved immediately disastrous, for it earned the fatal displeasure of Otho. Aged thirty-seven at this time, he had been a close friend of Nero until Nero had annexed his wife Poppaea and sent him out to be governor of Lusitania (Portugal); and in that capacity, Otho had been the principal supporter of Galba's revolt, so that, although himself an Etruscan whose Roman nobility was of comparatively recent origin, he now expected the succession to the imperial throne for himself and felt deeply disappointed that another man had been preferred to him. On January 15, therefore, in singularly brutal circumstances, he had Galba put to death, thus earning notoriety as the first emperor to arrange his predecessor's murder. And Galba's heir and advisers were slaughtered on the same day.

Once these horrors were over, however, Otho's government displayed signs of moderation. Egypt, north Africa, and the legions of the Danube and Euphrates declared in his favor. Nevertheless, he must already have known, when he seized power, that Vitellius had likewise been hailed as emperor in Germany. And now Vitellius's legionaries, under his generals Valens and Caecina, moved rapidly southwards in the direction of Rome. In early March, they were already across the Alps; and they had reached the banks of the Po before Otho's advance guard was ready to hold them up. Otho himself left Rome later in the same month, and although reinforcements from the Danubian legions were expected to join him at any moment, he decided that the enemy must be engaged before they arrived. He himself would remain back in reserve, while the action was fought by his generals. However, in the ensuing engagement near Cremona, known as the First Battle of Bedriacum, his commanders were resoundingly defeated. The praetorian guard wanted to fight on in his cause; but he refused to permit them to do so. and committed suicide. It was April 16, and he had reigned for three months.

The Senate immediately recognized Vitellius as emperor, and he followed his generals down towards Rome. Though a man of only average ability, he was more than just the preposterous glutton of tradition since he had certain ideas of his own. For example, it was only with reluctance that he adopted the traditional titles "Caesar" and "Augustus," which had been used by Galba and Otho but seemed to him too reminiscent of the defunct

Relief of Roman soldier on the base of the Column of Nero at Moguntiacum (Mainz) in upper Germany, A.D. 66.

Julio-Claudians. Instead, he preferred to emphasize the consulship, to be held permanently, as the basis of his position; and he relied on being able to found a dynasty since unlike so many of his predecessors he had a young son of his own. He also endeavored to strengthen his position by disbanding Otho's praetorian guard in favor of a larger body composed of his own legionaries. However, on arrival in the capital, he learned that the eastern legions had transferred their allegiance to Vespasian, the governor of rebellious Judaea; and the Danube armies did the same, thus for the first time assuming their historic emperor-making role of the future. So another phase of this prolonged and complex civil war inevitably lay ahead.

The plan Vespasian adopted was that he himself should remain in Alexandria, where he could cut off the supply of grain to Rome, while his principal supporter Mucianus, governor of Syria, was to set out on the long march to the west. But meanwhile a Danubian legionary commander named Primus, who had joined Vespasian's cause, made a sudden dash for Italy, apparently without awaiting orders from his new chief. Vitellius planned to hold the line of the River Po against him, but his former generals, Valens and Caecina, were both unavailable to command his troops since Valens was ill and Caecina had deserted. In late October, therefore, the almost leaderless Vitellian army, superior in numbers but tired after a forced march of thirty miles, was overwhelmed by Primus in the Second Battle of Bedriacum; and as the victors advanced on the capital, Vitellius's remaining forces melted away. Yet he still had active supporters inside Rome itself, and Vespasian's brother Sabinus, who happened to be prefect of the city, had to barricade himself against them on the Capitoline Hill. But this proved of no avail, since as Primus's troops forced their way within the walls, the position of Sabinus was stormed by the Vitellians, and he was captured, killed, and thrown into the Tiber. And Vitellius himself, who had gone into hiding, was discovered by the invading army and lynched.

Vespasian and His Sons

The Senate promptly declared Vespasian his successor, and a week or two afterwards his main force arrived in the city under the command of Mucianus, who put an end to the ambitions of Primus by superseding him. Reducing the praetorian guard to its earlier and smaller dimensions, Mucianus directed the government in the name of Vespasian until the new emperor himself reached the city some ten months later.

Soon afterwards, his relative Cerialis put down a serious Gallo-German nationalist revolt against Roman rule that had broken out on either side of the Rhine, under Civilis, a Batavian, and Classicus of the tribe of the

Treviri. Further to the south, Vespasian annexed the Upper Rhine–Upper Danube reentrant, in order to make the empire's defense line better and shorter. And meanwhile, the new emperor's elder son Titus had almost completed the suppression of the First Jewish Revolt by capturing the rebels' capital, Jerusalem (70). In the following year Vespasian and Titus celebrated a magnificent joint triumph.

With the help of Mucianus (until his death some five years later), Vespasian now addressed himself to the reconstruction of the empire and its defenses, gravely damaged by the civil wars. He was a man of less distinguished origins than his predecessors, being the son of a Sabine tax collector of knightly rank. Moreover, he himself had correspondingly plain tastes and was proud of them. He was a man who, although in basic matters autocratic enough, was easy to get on with and accessible. Yet he worked without stopping; and he decided things by prosaic common-sense methods that made him one of the most effective of all the emperors. It was no mere coincidence that his three immediate forerunners had survived for only a few months each, after which they all perished violently, whereas his own reign lasted for ten years, at the end of which he died a natural death. Although none of the three others had been lacking in ability, he was a far better ruler than any of them.

Of necessity, his financial policy, after the vast expenditures of the civil wars, had to be stringent: tax rates were drastically increased and new sources of revenue invented. Yet Vespasian succeeded in raising funds to strengthen the eastern frontier which was now, after the wars of the previous decade, more heavily garrisoned than before—and he also showed himself a pioneer in the educational field by endowing new professorships. His provincial policy, too, was liberal since he furthered the Romanization of Spain as Claudius had Romanized Gaul; Vespasian wanted to avail himself of administrative capacity wherever it could be found. And, with this once more in mind, once again following in the footsteps of Claudius, he revived the ancient censorship (73–74), utilizing the office not only to purge the Senate of men who had sided against him but also to augment it by many new members, provincials as well as Italians.

His fellow censor was his son Titus, whom, although no one had ever made such use of a member of his family before, he also employed as his praetorian prefect. Vespasian rightly disregarded rumors that the young man cherished designs against him, and when, like all rulers as they grew older, he deteriorated in energy and health, he was able with Titus's help to carry on effectively. Moreover, as the first emperor to have a son of his own blood whose maturity and distinction already fitted him to succeed to the throne, he openly declared his intention of founding a new dynasty with Titus as his heir.

Painting by Ducros (1748-1810) of the Arch of Titus, erected by his brother
Domitian to commemorate his suppression of the Jewish Revolt.

Brass *sestertius* of Vespasian (A.D. 76) showing the Temple of Jupiter, Juno, and Minerva on the Capitol, restored after its destruction in the Civil Wars of 69.

Yet there now followed a period in which his political opponents, mainly old-fashioned aristocratic republicans who justified their ideas from Greek philosophy, expressed a good deal of hostility to the new dynastic program; and Titus rigorously put down a conspiracy in which Vitellius's former general Caecina was involved. This was early in A.D. 79, which proved to be the last year of Vespasion's life. During the summer, near his Sabine birthplace, he succumbed to a stomach chill and died.

Titus's tenure on the throne (79–81) was so short that it is impossible to say whether his charm, for which he was famous, would have carried him through a longer period of rule or not. For the second time, he sent away his mistress, the Jewish princess Berenice, whose liaison with him cannot have been popular in senatorial circles. In the provinces, attention was principally concentrated on Britain, where Agricola, governor from 77, consolidated the Forth-Clyde line and advanced tentatively as far as the River Tay. At the capital, Titus made himself popular by lavish expenditure. Yet at the very outset of his reign, Italy had been struck by disaster when an eruption of Vesuvius, dormant since before the beginning of history, had buried Pompeii, Herculaneum, Stabiae (Castellamare di Stabia), Oplontis (Torre Annunziata), and other centers, thus providing excavators from the eighteenth century onwards with the richest of all collections of evidence about the ancient world.

Titus died prematurely, at the age of only forty-two. Yet rumors that he was poisoned by his younger brother and successor Domitian were probably unjustified; though it is true that Domitian harbored a strong grudge against him, since he himself, despite stirring adventures at the end of the civil wars,

Muleteer who succumbed to fumes at Pompeii during the eruption of Vesuvius in A.D. 79. Liquid plaster was pumped into the cavity left by the decomposition of the body.

had been given far fewer opportunities of distinguishing himself in subsequent years.

When Domitian now became emperor in his turn, he showed little sympathy with the old republican forms in which most earlier rulers had clothed their autocracy, but instead followed a meticulously thought-out policy of systematic absolutism. As time went on, and particularly after his adoption of the unprecedented title "perpetual censor" (84–85), this tendency caused consternation among the senators. As a counterblast, the emperor realized he must achieve popularity with the army—for which he was eager in any case, since he was ambitious to become a conqueror of foreign lands.

Conquest in Britain, however, did not appeal to him, and Agricola's plans to annex part of the Scottish highlands were dropped. But success was achieved in southwestern Germany, where the frontier line, pushed forward by his father, was advanced once again (83). Domitian's principal objective, however, was the kingdom of Dacia (Rumania), whose king Decebalus had almost restored it to the power its monarchs had boasted more than a century earlier. Sent to bring him to order, Domitian's generals suffered a couple of severe defeats. Then, finally, the military situation was restored. Yet Decebalus survived—because of what happened next.

In 89, within the borders of the empire, the seditious pattern of the previous dynasty now began to repeat itself, and the Roman commander in Upper Germany rose in rebellion. Domitian swooped down and mercilessly crushed the revolt. But his suspicions of the senators, already considerable, were greatly increased by this traumatic event. Under treason procedures revived for the purpose, a substantial number of leading Romans were executed. They included, as on earlier occasions, men of republican philosophical inclinations; but as Domitian, always a nervously irritable man, became increasingly afraid of retaliation, terror began to spread among the rest of the senatorial class. The legionaries, it is true, continued to support him strongly. But among those alienated and frightened were the commanders of the praetorian guard. And they, without the knowledge of their own soldiers, joined his wife Domitia, daughter of the eminent general Corbulo, in a conspiracy that struck the emperor down in A.D. 96.

Trajan, Hadrian, Antoninus

The sixty-six-year-old lawyer and former consul, Nerva, who was declared his successor on the very same day, must have been privy to the plot. But it caused such great anger in the army, and especially among the rank and file of the praetorian guard, that after a short interlude he was humiliatingly compelled, in the following year, to hand over Domitian's assassins and allow them to be executed. Immediately afterwards, to save his throne and his life, he adopted a son and heir from outside his own family. Nerva was acting like Galba before him, but his choice was a great deal more successful. It fell on Trajan, aged forty-four, the governor of Upper Germany; his adoption inaugurated a period of over sixty years in which successions to the throne were determined by adoption rather than by birth. In subsequent cases, however, it was usually reinforced by matrimonial ties —and would never have happened at all if the rulers had had sons of their own.

Trajan's father was descended from Roman settlers in Further Spain and his mother was a Spaniard; he was the first of the emperors to come from a province, and his origin was symptomatic of the rise of the provincial element within the ruling class. The way to the highest office was now becoming open to all educated men, regardless of race and nationality; at present, westerners such as Gauls and Spaniards were still advancing much more rapidly than north Africans and easterners—though their turn would come later.

Attractive and affable, Trajan possessed the rare qualification of popularity among Senate and army alike. His governmental policies were progres-

Trajan (A.D. 98-117).

Brass *sestertius* of Trajan, "the best ruler" (OPTIMO PRINCIPI),
celebrating his endowment for poor children (ALIM*enta* ITAL*iae*).

sive. In Italy, one of his achievements was the foundation of the *alimenta,*
a system of financial provision for poor children. He also lightened the
burden of taxation in the provinces; and a series of letters preserved by Pliny
the Younger, his governor of Bithynia in Asia Minor, displays his humane
care for the welfare of the provincials—combined with a suspicious preoccupation with internal security and a paternalistic tendency to interfere in
the affairs of the ostensibly self-governing cities when their finances, as
frequently happened, were unsound.

An ever-increasing program of impressive public works was also carried
out on Trajan's orders. The spiral reliefs on his column at Rome indicate
the source of the vast expenditure on such projects: they were paid for by
the wealth of conquered Dacia. Domitian had been obliged to leave the
country unsubdued. The forces with which Trajan invaded it were even
more formidable. He enlarged the Roman army to thirty legions, each of
which, moreover, was increased in size; and the auxiliaries who fought
alongside them were supplemented by new kinds of native troops *(numeri),*
which comprised national units from un-Romanized tribes, equipped with
their own arms and cuirassed horsemen. With this great army, the emperor
overran Dacia in two large-scale wars (101–106). Its capital Sarmizegethusa
(Gradistea Muncelului) was captured and destroyed, and Decebalus was
driven to suicide. His kingdom became a Roman province, and gigantic
sums of gold and silver were seized and brought to Rome, the last really
large profits its treasury ever derived from a war. But the end of the Dacian
campaign meant that there was a new, long frontier to protect; and from
now on the numerical superiority of frontier troops shifted permanently
from the Rhine to the Danube and Dacian garrisons.

But there were also the eastern borders of the empire to be considered; and Trajan had decided that the peace concluded half a century
earlier with Parthia must be brought to an end because it had not pro-

Reliefs from Column of Trajan, Rome: heads of Dacian and Roman soldiers
(above and right).

vided a satisfactory imperial boundary. But when Armenia, the traditional bone of contention between the two states, fell to him with ease
(114), he decided to go onwards and annex the whole of Mesopotamia as
well, with infinite prospects of conquests ahead that might make him
the first authentic successor of Alexander the Great. Parallel Roman
forces simultaneously descended the Tigris and Euphrates, the Parthian
winter capital Ctesiphon was taken, and the end of the following year
saw Trajan at the Persian Gulf. Never before had a Roman commander
marched so far, and it would never happen again.

However, it was a transient success. Far behind the advancing Roman
army, in one eastern province after another, the Jews of the Dispersion
broke into savage revolts, encouraged by their numerous coreligionists in
Parthian territory temporarily occupied by the Romans. And meanwhile,
the Parthians themselves rallied their forces and attacked Trajan's extended

lines of communication. He suppressed the rebellions where he could and even uniquely proclaimed the conversion of the kingdom of Parthia into a Roman client state. But this was little more than an empty gesture; and almost immediately he turned back towards home. Either he decided that it had all been in vain—in which case it must have been the hardest decision of his life—or he hopefully believed that he could leave the scene because the arrangements he had recently made would endure, though he can scarcely have been laboring under such a massive delusion. But there is a third possibility also, for perhaps, whatever the military forecasts, his weakened health had made him unable to carry on. He was ill, suffering from high blood pressure, followed, it would appear, by a paralytic stroke in A.D. 116—though it may be that his illness was in part the psychological outcome of failure. At all events, in the following year, in the southeastern corner of Asia Minor, he died.

Brass *sestertius* of Trajan (ca. A.D. III) depicting his bridge
over the Danube built by Apollodorus of Damascus.

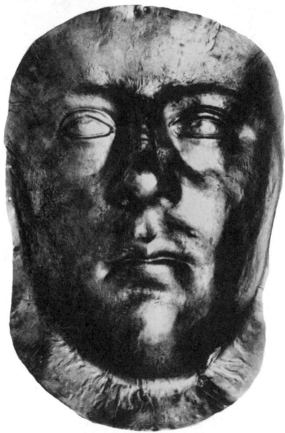

Gold death-mask of a client-king of the Cimmerian Bosphorus,
which supplied grain for Roman armies
on the Danube and in the east.

One of the brass *sestertii* of Hadrian celebrating his restoration of provinces: here his native country Spain.

Hadrian, found in Judaea where he crushed
the Second Jewish Revolt (A.D. 132-35).

Gem-portrait of Antoninus Pius (A.D. 138-61).

Trajan's talent for civil government, the popular aggressiveness of his military policies, and his agreeable, accessible personality had earned him the title of the Best Ruler *(Optimus Princeps)* Yet whereas his Dacian campaigns had brought in a great deal of money, the vastly ambitious Parthian campaigns that followed cost enormous sums with little or no compensating political or military advantages. True, these displays of might may have helped his successors to keep the peace. Yet, by and large, Trajan remains a classic example of a good man carried away by the exciting Roman tradition that conquest was glorious.

His successor Hadrian, a distant relative from the same part of Spain, had accompanied him to Rome at the outset of his reign and then served him in many important posts, enjoying his special favor. On Trajan's deathbed, it was given out that the emperor had adopted him as his heir, but this, though possible, remains uncertain.

In any event, Hadrian now assumed the imperial powers. Without delay, he decided—as his predecessor may well have decided already—that the newly occupied eastern territories were untenable, and so, unwilling for adventures when he needed to consolidate his own power, he abandoned all that was left of Trajan's temporary conquests and withdrew the Roman frontiers to the Euphrates again, much to the dissatisfaction of militarist senators. Then he set out for Rome and subsequently for the lower Danube frontier where there was trouble. While he was away from the capital, however, four of the most eminent senators, all former consuls, found themselves accused—with how much justification is uncertain—of plotting against his life and were put to death, probably by the independent initiative of his praetorian prefect (118). This treatment of the four ex-consuls permanently damaged his relations with the Senate. Moreover, although he was assiduous in his attentions to that body, it became clear that he did not estimate class and rank very highly.

The remarkable feature of Hadrian's twenty-one-year-long principate was the fact that he spent more than half of it outside Italy, traveling widely throughout the provinces of the empire. His motives for all these journeys were varied. One was pure curiosity; he was the most fanatical of all the many Roman sightseers. But in addition, as the designs selected for his coinage confirm, he had formed a novel conception of what the imperial territories meant. He saw them no longer as a collection of conquered provinces, but as a commonwealth in which each individual province and nation possessed its own proud identity. Yet probably the foremost aim of his travels was to keep the army, in which he maintained an expert interest, in a state of skilled readiness; and he made efforts to improve the living conditions of the soldiers, deprecating the harshness of previous rulers. One of the first fruits of this active military policy, following upon a minor reverse on the British frontier, was the best preserved of all the fortifications of the empire, Hadrian's Wall from Tyne to Solway, manned by fifteen thousand auxiliaries watching over the bare brown hills that rolled away to the still unconquered north.

Fighting in the empire was infrequent. But there was one serious war towards the end of his life, a Jewish rising—not of the Dispersion this time, as in the previous reign, but in the homeland of Palestine itself. Hadrian's establishment of a Roman colony and temple at Jerusalem, now renamed Aelia Capitolina after the emperor's family name Aelius, caused great anger among the Jews, and under a talented leader, Bar Kosiba, they launched the ferocious and bloodily suppressed Second Jewish Revolt (132–35). Hadrian, a keen Hellenist—and himself a talented writer and musician—felt no sympathy with a race that could not, like every other people in the empire, be content with the dominant Greco-Roman civilization and its ideas.

Reconstructed section of Hadrian's Wall at Vindolanda (Chesterholm).

Following up the governmental policies of Trajan, Hadrian aimed, like him, at enlightened centralization—and he pursued it with particular skill. His was a remarkably many-sided personality, full of bold ideas yet at the same time devoted to administrative efficiency and deeply concerned with justice and the law. Yet he continued to be dogged by the unhappy relations with the senators which had marred his early years. Then, in 136, a dangerous plot, perhaps genuine, resulted in further executions, whereupon Hadrian, who had no son and was sick, decided that he must proceed rapidly with the adoption of an heir. His first choice, who took the name of Aelius after him, died almost at once and was replaced by the fifty-one-year-old Antoninus who soon afterwards, on Hadrian's death, succeeded peacefully to the throne (138).

Antoninus, like his two predecessors, was of western provincial origin, his father being a man of consular descent from Nemausus (Nîmes) in southern Gaul. His reign was aptly summed up by the conferment of the title Pius, indicating devotion to his duty, the gods, his country, and his adoptive father. He also achieved a careful balance in his relations with the Senate, showing deference to its prestige while quietly continuing to centralize the administrative machinery and taking steps to cut down unnecessary public expenditure. In Britain, he advanced the frontier and constructed a new Antonine wall from the Forth to the Clyde (141), though subsequently there were outbreaks of raiding within the province. The southern frontiers, too, suffered from occasional unrest and rebellion. Nevertheless, the greater part of the empire enjoyed peace during the twenty-three years of his reign.

15

Imperial Society

Imperial Art and Architecture

The sculptural portraiture of private persons, men, women, and children, flourished throughout the imperial period.*

But above all it is the emperors of the age and their relations who are depicted in a series of extraordinarily skillful portrait busts, designed to acquaint the peoples of the empire with the personalities their rulers wished to present to them. Augustus had been shown in many guises, but under Claudius a new problem arose, for his knobbly countenance seemed to defy accurate representation. Some sculptors compromised, other idealized. When his stepson Nero succeeded to the throne, they had to think once again how to depict the rapidly increasing grossness of the imperial features; and they achieved remarkable success. Far from minimizing or evading the idiosyncracy of Nero's appearance, they cleverly cherished his peculiarities, and even endowed them with a certain impressiveness, by infusing just that touch of elevation that made the emperor seem, if still a fat lout, at least a lout of slightly superhuman dimensions.

The men who designed the heads on the coins, too, performed triumphs that earned the admiration of the Renaissance, their contrasted interpretations of Nero and the bleak Galba proving particularly noteworthy. Under Vespasian, portrait sculptors and coin engravers had to rise to a new challenge—an emperor who belonged to an unpretentious social class and wanted to show it. Some artists, it is true, tried to iron out his rugged, whimsical features into something more orthodox. But others depicted them exactly as they were, or even added a touch of amusing caricature. Trajan is shown as an impressive soldier or as a responsible and thoughtful administrator. But the most interesting of the male portraits of the epoch

---

*And Egypt maintained a superb tradition of portrait painting on the panels inserted in mummy cases.

Ceiling of villa at Oplontis (Torre Annunziata) near Pompeii.

comes from the principate of Hadrian. He was partly homosexual (as Trajan also had been), and the posthumous heads of the boy Antinous, who was loved by Hadrian and died young, show a dreamy gaze suggesting the tragedy of that early doom.

Sad, meditative little children of the imperial house are likewise portrayed with keen psychological sympathy, and the women of successive dynasties, too, were made known to the public through the same sculptural medium. The ladies of Vespasian's house evidently did not share their emperor's desire to reflect his middle-class origins, for they are elegant and frequently change their elaborate hairstyles. The portraits of this age aim at a new, smooth, fluent surface texture, enhanced by the subtle use of flesh and hair tints, of which only traces survive today. The sculptors are fond of deep incisions, appropriate to the strong sun and shadow in which their busts and statues originally stood.

The same vigorous interplay of light and shade appears on a relief upon the inner face of the Arch of Titus of Rome, depicting soldiers carrying the spoils taken from the Jerusalem Temple in A.D. 70; the artist creates the illusion that the procession is viewed through an open frame, silhouetted against the sky. But the outstanding example of this relief sculpture is the continuous series of spiral designs on the Column of Trajan. Towering over the massive new Forum designed by his great architect Apollodorus of Damascus, the reliefs, more than a hundred in number, offer a bird's-eye view of numerous events in the emperor's Dacian wars. This panorama includes no fewer than twenty-five hundred human figures, and a wide variety of incidents is selected for illustration—battles and sieges, the capture of prisoners of war, visits by envoys, marches and journeys, buildings

Relief from Column of Trajan, Rome: Dacians attack Roman camp.

and fortifications, and above all, events relating to the emperor himself, the addresses he delivered and the sacrifices he made to the gods, and the deeds he performed that illuminated his solicitude and clemency.

Among other great arts of the early empire was the painting of walls; and as a recently discovered example has reminded us, of ceilings as well. The bulk of the pictures that have come down to us are of an earlier date than the great reliefs that have just been mentioned. They appeared (together with elegant stucco decoration) in town houses at Pompeii and Herculaneum and in country villas that adjoined those cities at Stabiae (Castellamare di Stabia), Oplontis (Torre Annunziata), and elsewhere. The eruption of Vesuvius that overwhelmed the region in A.D. 79 preserved a great many of these paintings; most of those that survive belong to the period immediately preceding the eruption, since much redecoration, displaying a new brilliance and richness in color, had taken place as a result of earthquake damage in 62. Figure paintings, often derived from lost Greek originals, were greatly in favor; very often they were devoted to the mythological and theatrical themes dear to Nero. Moreover, as in his own Golden House at Rome, an earlier taste for architectural vistas was now revived, displaying a new baroque, scenic illusionism that experimented with effects of spatial recession drawing their inspiration from stage designs.

There are also paintings of romantic landscapes, and fantastic Nile scenes, studies of still life, and portraits. On some walls the overall pictorial design includes painted panels as center points, but it would have seemed wrong to the architects and artists who planned these houses to spoil their organic structure and decor by affixing detachable panel pictures like modern canvases to the walls. Similarly, the floors were meant to be seen without carpets or mats and instead were covered with vivid mosaics, in large patterns or small, sometimes, like the paintings, reproducing Greek masterpieces of the past. This was one of the most enjoyable and picturesque of Roman arts; when transferred to walls, vaults, niches, apses, and ceilings, a process that had already tentatively begun, it led the way to the mosaic decoration that was to line the interiors of Byzantine churches.

These paintings and mosaics adorned large terraced villas opening out upon the sea and town houses which still retained their traditional grouping around the atrium, though by this time the architectural designs showed increasing variety and elaboration. Sometimes, however, these houses of the rich, for example at Herculaneum, had begun to be divided up by partitions in order to serve a somewhat less prosperous social class. There were also other forms of housing for the middle class and poor, and on this subject recent researches at Pompeii have yielded a good deal of information,

Stucco relief of athlete from Villa di San Marco,
Stabiae (Castellamare di Stabia).

Mosaic showing the first wine drinkers,
from New Paphos, Cyprus, fourth century A.D. (above).

Mosaic at Emporiae (Ampurias) in Spain (opposite).

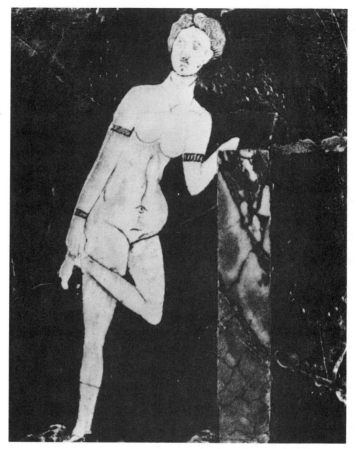

Inlaid polychrome marble of Venus doing up her sandal: from Pompeii.

revealing domestic arrangements of considerable variety and a general standard of living (not only for the richest elite) never achieved again until the
nineteenth century. Quite a lot can also be learned about the humble accommodation of slaves in both the town houses and the rural dwellings *(villae
rusticae),* which often combined private suites for the use of their rich and
mainly absentee proprietors with elaborate farms worked by their agents,
tenants, and servants.

In another respect, too, Pompeii is a uniquely informative source of
evidence for the lives of its ordinary citizens. At the moment when the
eruption buried the town (as, no doubt, at all other times as well), the walls
of buildings were covered by many thousands of graffiti that have survived
and display extraordinary variety. Very often, there are references to the

annual civic elections—which were still hotly contested in these smaller towns, unlike Rome—and one such election was imminent at the time when the eruption took place. The graffiti also have much to say about current theatrical and gladiatorial events. Moreover, like their counterparts today, they recorded many curious aspects of the loves and erotic fantasies of a great number of individuals.

The lives of the inhabitants of Pompeii are also illustrated by the surviving remains of about twenty inns and one hundred and twenty bars. At the ancient colony of Ostia, on the other hand, which was the port of Rome, only two inns and fourteen bars have come to light, since the people of this place apparently preferred to drink in the social clubs of their trade corporations *(collegia).* The community was rapidly expanding to keep pace with a massive development of port facilities. Claudius, who was eager to direct the skills of his architects and engineers away from showpieces to practical projects, gave the town a new harbor connected by canals with the Tiber; and temples, baths, warehouses, and granaries were constructed. Then, subsequently, Trajan added a landlocked hexagonal inner basin, and Ostia came to handle the largest volume of goods of any ancient Mediterranean city apart from Alexandria.

In these prosperous years, the population of this great business center grew rapidly to a total of approximately one hundred thousand. This expansion dictated a revolution in housing for the not particularly wealthy, in the

Warehouses *(horrea)* at Ostia beside the Tiber.

course of which the Pompeii-type dwelling of earlier days was largely replaced by tall apartment blocks that accommodated greater numbers of people. Made of brick, which was no longer concealed as in the past by stone or stucco facings, these large buildings were strongly constructed and relied for their architectural effect on the spacing and scale of their windows, which had panes of selenite, mica, or glass and were framed by small external balconies. The interiors of the apartments, adorned with good mosaics and wall paintings, often contained seven rooms or more and sometimes as many as twelve. These blocks did not normally possess a private water supply of their own, but, as at Pompeii, public cisterns fed from the aqueduct were liberally distributed around the public places of the town.

In very few other cities of the empire has substantial housing been excavated, but the Ostian type was no doubt more characteristic than the Pompeian; it was the empire's most important contribution to urban living. And at Rome itself, too, increasing signs of the same sort of apartment blocks have lately come to light, in addition to many other types of residential accommodation. It is true that, up to the second century A.D., we still have complaints of rickety, ill-constructed, highrise tenements in the capital. Some of the worst abuses, however, had been eliminated by Nero, who made efforts to impose a more spacious plan and scale.

He was given this opportunity by the Great Fire of Rome (A.D. 64) which he was unfairly accused of having started himself to make room for his Golden House *(Domus Aurea),* for this and its parklands took over nearly four hundred acres of what had formerly been the most thickly inhabited zone of the city—the largest piece of land that any European monarch has ever carved out of his capital to make a residence for himself. The Golden House, like palaces erected by Greek monarchs of earlier days, was not a single unified structure but consisted of a number of separate pavilions set among elegantly designed formal landscapes. The central porticoed building contained an octagonal hall that can still be seen today, though it is now beneath the ground. It was lit from a round hole in the center of the cupola and made unprecedentedly enterprising use of the brick-faced concrete that had been Rome's greatest architectural discovery.

Nero's successors abandoned the Golden House; but Domitian ordered the construction of a new imperial residence on the Palatine. In addition to the private quarters of the emperor, it included state apartments, consisting of two groups of imposing halls separated from one another by a colonnade. Domitian also built a magnificent villa looking down onto the Alban Lake, complete with theater and amphitheater. It has not survived;

but much can still be seen of a later and considerably more elaborate country palace erected by Hadrian near Tibur (Tivoli). Extending for a mile across the slopes beneath the city, this complex virtually forms a whole town in itself. The architect exploits the gently undulating site by ringing every change on the theme of curve and countercurve; and his impressive mastery of concrete achieves all manner of ingenious, romantic effects, with nostalgic reminiscences of the Greece the emperor loved. This Villa of Hadrian, wrote Mortimer Wheeler, "stripped and shattered though it be, remains the most fantastic material creation of the Roman genius: of a particular Roman genius, which had travelled far and experienced much, and had learnt to temper affairs with sentiment, sentiment with reason."

And another building that owes its design to Hadrian was Rome's Pantheon. His reconstruction of Agrippa's original temple is the best preserved today of all the edifices that the ancient Romans ever built; it is among the most admirable of all their achievements. The huge colonnaded portico leads into a rotunda one hundred and forty-two feet high and wide. Its concrete interior wall contains vaulted niches and recesses which show that by now the Romans had pretty full trust in their mastery of this material so that they could boldly lighten it by inserting such cavities; and the dome that they superimposed on these walls, surpassing Nero's Golden House, proved durable enough even to survive the removal of its gilded bronze tiles in the seventh century A.D.

From its circular central opening, a smoothly and regularly diffused stream of light descends into the rotunda. The great space is tranquil and sublime. But unlike an earth-bound Greek temple, it dwarfs men and women by its hugeness. This cavernous grandeur warns humans that they are in the presence of all the gods—for that is what "Pantheon" means, and its niches were probably intended for statues of the old planetary divinities. And in this astrologically minded age, the central opening of the dome represented the sun, while the starlike rosettes on its curved internal surface reflected the majestic rhythm of the heavenly bodies.

Such was one of the greatest among the innumerable shrines devoted to the religious needs of the Roman population. But ample provision was also made for their pleasures. There were enormous bathing establishments, of which something will be said in describing a later epoch, when the constructions of such buildings reached its climax. And there were also theaters everywhere. But there was also another sort of entertainment altogether, provided by the Flavian Amphitheater. Begun by Vespasian and completed by Titus, it was designed for gladiatorial combats and the slaughter of wild animals, and it could also be flooded to stage imitation sea fights. Known much later as the Colosseum, after the colossal statue of Nero that had

The interior of Hadrian's Pantheon after G. P. Panini (1691-1765).

stood nearby, this amphitheater, the earliest in the city to be built completely of stone, remains, for all its horrific purpose, one of the most marvelous buildings in the world.

These elliptical amphitheaters were like two semicircular theaters placed back to back. The curving exteriors of Greek theaters had normally displayed two stories of arcades, and Rome had a theater with three. But in its final form the Colosseum was extended up to four of these stories, of which the topmost was walled and windowed, but the three lowest consisted of open arches in continuous arcades. Classical columns are to be seen, engaged in these great rows of arches, but they are there only to provide ornamentation and scale. The essential constructional units are the massive concrete-covered piers that support the arches. The Colosseum displayed, with unique majesty, the genius of Roman architects for dramatic effects and exerted a vast influence upon the buildings of later Europe.

It provided seats for about forty-five thousand spectators and standing room for five thousand more. The emperor's platform was at the center of one of the long sides, facing the sections reserved for state officials and the holders of the games. There were also places for foreign envoys, imperial ladies, Vestal Virgins, and priests. The entertainments provided in these arenas remained extraordinarily popular, and rulers found it advisable to arrange and finance such displays on a munificent scale and to listen patiently to the popular demonstrations and protests and demands that the audiences of pampered Rome, by tradition, seized the opportunity to stage on these occasions. As for the gladiators, their legal and moral status was utterly degraded, but many graffiti bear witness to the admiration and excitement that they nonetheless provoked in the hearts of the public, especially women.

The pattern of the Colosseum was reduplicated throughout the Roman world in other amphitheaters of widely varying dimensions. And indeed, it was these first and second centuries A.D., when the Pax Romana gained such remarkable strength, that provided by far the greater part of the immense material remains not only of amphitheaters but also of very many other kinds of buildings that are still to be seen in Rome and its provinces.

Economic and Social Imbalance

The cities of these regions, abounding in prosperous, public-spirited benefactors competing with one another in their lavish contributions to municipal amenities, were entering upon the climactic period of their development, destined in some areas never to be equaled again in later times. The consequent orgy of urban construction produced many spectacular achievements,

The Temple of Bacchus-Dionysus (?) at Heliopolis
(Baalbek in Lebanon), ca. A.D. 150.

among which Thamugadi (Timgad) and other cities in north Africa may perhaps be singled out because they have never been built over in later ages and therefore survived on a monumental scale.

Such cities often originated from military camps but rapidly outstripped these origins and displayed striking advances in industry and commerce. In these fields of activity, the provinces had truly come into their own and had begun to eclipse Rome itself. For example, the glass and bronze wares of Italian Capua were superseded by products made in Gaul; and the most important pottery industry was similarly displaced, first to Condatomagus (La Graufesenque) in the south of Gaul (ca. A.D. 20) and then to Ledosus (Lezoux in the Auvergne). Next, in the second century A.D., the main output of pottery was from the Rhineland, which became before long the principal industrial area of Europe. For the first time in history, this region had caught up with the industrial production of the eastern Mediterranean; while the Danube area, too, along the whole of its length, was developing an east-west commercial axis of great importance for the future. Nor was this kind of expansion a European phenomenon only, since in Asia as well, and in Syria where the towns stretched almost uninterruptedly throughout

Mosaic of two gladiators from Curium, Cyprus. Fourth century A.D.

Relief of gladiator from Ephesus (Selçuk).

a single vast urbanized zone, the export trades in textiles and other materials continued to flourish and multiply.

Yet the fundamental facts of Roman trading remained the same as before and were subject to the same limitations; it was still, on the whole, a hand-to-mouth affair with no solid capitalistic infrastructure or foundation. And, above all, the basis of the imperial economy was still not commerce but agriculture. In this sphere, at first sight, there were certain encouraging signs. For example, many fruit trees were brought as far as the shores of the Rhine, Danube, and Atlantic, and planted; and olives were introduced into the steppe lands of southern Tunisia and southeast Spain, which became the principal centers of the empire's production of oil. Spain also produced and sent abroad a great deal of wine: the Monte Testaccio on the outskirts of Rome is a mound consisting of fragments of forty million jars that had once been full of cheap wine imported from Spanish vineyards.

The rich farmer-landowners possessed and lived in huge residential and agricultural complexes. Among many hundreds of such "rustic villas" may be named Cheragan (on the Garonne, in Gaul), covering forty acres and housing four or five hundred dependents; and Anthée (near Philippeville in Belgium), which included a large residence and twenty other buildings within a thirty-acre walled enclosure; and Chedworth in Britain, which was another luxurious administrative center for a substantial group of farms. The owners of such palaces were very wealthy men, although on the whole this was an age not so much of a few millionaires as of a great many affluent bourgeois.

Nevertheless, in spite of all this development, the basic facts of the agricultural economy were still much as they had been in earlier years. For one thing, the placid rhythm of the Antonine world still depended, though perhaps to a slightly lesser extent, upon slaves; and they were still wholly

The amphitheatre at Capua (S. Maria Capua Vetere).
Mid-first century A.D., remodeled by Hadrian.

Large bronze coin of Tiberius (A.D. 14-37) at a veteran colony (Carthage?) in north Africa. Altar-precinct, inscribed PACE AVG*usta* PERP*etua,* "in the perpetual Augustan peace."

excluded from the area of political and social privilege. But excluded also —and this too was no novelty—were the "free" agricultural workers who formed an even larger proportion of the population. It was not the depressed rural poor of the countryside but the prosperous people of the cities who felt loyalty to the imperial regime in gratitude for services rendered.

In the eighteenth century, the historian Edward Gibbon believed that the

Public lavatory at the Hadrianic Baths at Lepcis Magna.

Antonine age witnessed greater happiness and prosperity than the world had seen before. And he may even have been right, because prosperity had never been very widespread, any more than it is now. True, it was not very widespread in the time Gibbon was writing about either, for it did not extend to the poor cultivators of the land who comprised most of the Roman world's inhabitants. Nevertheless, the limited circle of those enjoying favorable conditions had been considerably enlarged. And to that extent, there was some justification in the praises that the second century Asian orator Aelius Aristides, anticipating Gibbon, lavished on the imperial system of the day, eulogizing the lush amenities and secure, universal communications that were owed to the Antonine peace.

Even if the poor did not secure many of these material blessings, at least Roman law as it entered, under the initiative of Hadrian, upon the first and most creative and philosophical period of its Golden Age, was now doing a good deal to protect them from the worst illegalities of exploitation. For example, the treatment of slaves (despite their exclusion from privilege) was controlled by an increasing number of legal safeguards—devised out of a combination of humaneness with a self-interest that saw advantages in their well-being. And the free poor, too, unprosperous though they remained, likewise benefited from current legal reforms.

These tendencies were apparent in the activity of Hadrian's north African jurist Salvius Julianus. Famous for his concise formulations, Salvius collected and revised the successive edicts that praetors had for centuries been accustomed to pronounce at the outset of their year of office. This meant that, from now on, the edicts could be recognized as permanently valid; and his publication of them diffused among the subject populations of the empire a far clearer understanding of the legal safeguards to which they were entitled than had hitherto existed.

The same trend was manifest in the work of one of Salvius's pupils and employees, Gaius. His renowned *Institutes,* the only classical legal work to have come down to us in substantially its original form, includes suggestions that their author was especially interested in provincial legislation and had discussed it previously in writings that have not survived. That is to say, the study of the law was now displaying a new and much more attentive interest in people who were not Roman citizens; the legal barriers between privileged citizens and all the rest, for centuries a fundamental feature of Roman life, were becoming eroded.

And yet, despite all these measures, *equality* had come no nearer than it had been before. All that had happened was that these old civic differences between Roman citizens and the rest were being replaced by another distinction altogether. This perpetuated the division of the community (other

Above: Thamugadi (Timgad) in north Africa, founded by Trajan in A.D. 100 for legionary veterans.

Left: Temple at Sufetula (Sbeitla in Tunisia). Mid-second century A.D.

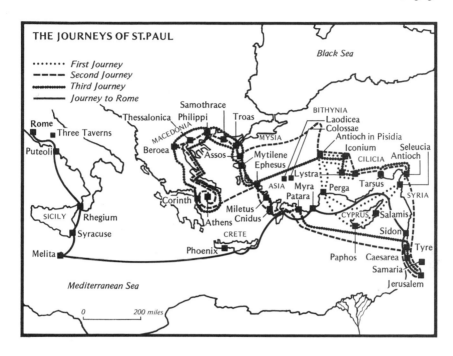

THE JOURNEYS OF ST. PAUL

· · · · · · · First Journey
‒ ‒ ‒ ‒ Second Journey
▬▬▬▬ Third Journey
———— Journey to Rome

Black Sea

Samothrace
BITHYNIA
Thessalonica Philippi Troas Laodicea
Rome Colossae
Three Taverns MACEDONIA MYSIA Antioch in Pisidia
Puteoli Beroea Iconium Seleucia
Antioch
Assos Mytilene CILICIA
Ephesus
Lystra Tarsus
ASIA Myra Perga
Corinth Patara SYRIA
Miletus
SICILY Rhegium Athens Cnidus CYPRUS Salamis
Syracuse CRETE Sidon
Phoenix Tyre
Melita Paphos Caesarea
Samaria
Mediterranean Sea Jerusalem

0   200 miles

than slaves) into two main groups to which the law gave entirely separate treatment. The superior class *(honestiores)* included senators, knights, land-owners, soldiers, civil servants, and town counsellors. Everyone else belonged to the lower category *(humiliores)*, who possessed inferior legal rights and incurred heavier penalties in the courts, including many punishments that only noncitizens had suffered before. Roman law, despite all its concern for equity, had always favored the upper echelon of society, from which its own practitioners originated; and now, from the time of Trajan or Hadrian onwards, such preferential treatment became crystallized in legal forms. This greater explicitness was ominous, for beneath the tranquil surface of second-century life, it confirmed the depressed status of the underprivileged and thus deepened the basic rift that in the following centuries would help bring the empire down.

So inequalities were perpetuated; and this seems paradoxical, seeing that the Roman lawyers were at the same time producing measures displaying a new considerate solicitude. But the inequalities derived from a social system that unchangeably presupposed them, whereas the solicitude stemmed to a considerable extent from that Stoic philosophy to which Cicero had owed much of his moral inspiration in an earlier epoch.

From Seneca to Apuleius

In the imperial age the most eloquent exponent of this system was Nero's minister Seneca (b. ca. 4 B.C.–d. A.D. 65), son of a rhetorician from Corduba (Córdoba) in Further Spain. In contrast to earlier Roman tragic drama, of which almost all is lost, we have nine tragedies attributed to Seneca. These plays, to which Shakespeare and other European dramatists owe a very great debt, breathe the enlightened tolerance and humanity of Stoicism, including its sympathy for slaves. And more explicitly still, this same spirit pervades Seneca's literary letters and ethical treatises, which the Renaissance came to value for the moral guidance they provided.

He also set the tone for a new phase of Roman literature by his use of scintillating verbal tricks and vivid pointed epigrams to which the lapidary Latin language so readily lends itself. This same sparkling, oratorical, "Silver Latin" style, combined with a similar Stoic viewpoint, was adopted by Seneca's nephew Lucan in his poem the *Civil War* or *Pharsalia.* Its subject was the struggle between Pompey and Caesar*; but it displayed a philosophical viewpoint, gradually veering towards antimonarchism, that increasingly broke up his friendship with the reigning emperor Nero. Despite its many purple patches and digressions, this mordant, powerful poem won great fame in the Middle Ages and earned its author a place as one of Dante's four Lords of Highest Song.

Nero's fatal displeasure eventually fell on both Seneca and Lucan; and it descended also on his "arbiter" of court fashions, Petronius, who wrote a lively, scandalous picaresque novel known to us as the *Satyricon,* that is to say, *saturikon libri,* tales of lascivious behavior—for here Senecan moralizing takes a rest. The preceding centuries had produced many sorts of Greek fiction, including fake biographies, fantastic travel stories, romantic novelettes, satirical efforts in mixed prose and verse, and pornographic sketches. Petronius gathers all these threads together in a highly entertaining Latin narrative of three disreputable but elaborately educated young homosexuals on the move around the Greek towns of south Italy; and their journey is also intended as a mocking comment on the contemporary Roman social scene.

This work, of which a large portion, but by no means all, survives, includes poems and prose discussions that give the author his opportunity to offer criticism of currently fashionable writings. And, in addition, Petronius includes oblique, humorous echoes of earlier literary works. Thus the antihero's renunciation of women for boys is intended as a burlesque of middle-brow, heterosexual, Greek love romances, and descriptions of the

---

*For the battle of Pharsalus, see p. 231.

Painted shop sign of cloth merchant and felt maker Marcus Vecilius
Verecundus, Pompeii.

Relief of men towing boatload of wine on the River Durance. From Cabrières
d'Aygues; second century A.D.

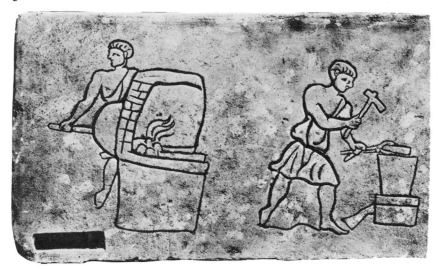

Graffito of iron works from Catacomb of Domitilla, Rome.

wrath of the phallic god Priapus are a parody of the wraths of the Homeric gods. The *Satyricon* also contains set pieces or short stories, of which the longest and most famous is the *Dinner of Trimalchio,* a self-made vulgar industrialist of slave origin living in Campania, who emerges as the most entertaining comic figure of all ancient literature. His banquet and reminiscences, as well as the coarse, colloquial remarks of his friends, guests, and hangers-on, reflect needle-sharp observation and keen sensual gusto—and incidentally, they provide unique historical material. Although fiction did not qualify as a separate branch of literature in ancient classifications of the subject, it was the most vigorous and creative literary form of the time; and many centuries later, too, in the mixed beginnings of the modern European novel, admiring recollections of Petronius were still to play a great and varied part.

In the generation that followed him, the most original talent was that of Martial (b. ca. A.D. 40–d. ca. 104), the outstanding epigrammatist of the ancient world. Although Spanish, Martial caught the authentic Italian note of riotous, mordant satire and has imprinted his definition of this term on subsequent European letters. His witty, humane, obscene little poems cast a vivid light upon the social picture of his day.

Juvenal, born in about A.D. 50 at Aquinum (Aquino) in southern Latium, strikes a grander and also harsher note; and his sixteen long poems reveal him to be one of the supreme masters of the Latin tongue and the foremost of all Roman satirists, who did more even than Martial to establish satire as a tradition of the Western world. Juvenal had started life as a rather unsuccessful rhetorician; and neither forgetting nor forgiving the relative poverty from which he partially emerged—only partially, for he never obtained adequate recognition—he flays the evils of the contemporary Roman scene with ironical, savagely pessimistic invective. This is ostensibly directed against personages belonging to the past; yet its ferocity is really aimed at the present as well. Although Juvenal wrote during the time of Trajan, in a Rome much more relaxed than it had been under the hated Domitian, the empire still seemed to him a sick, maladjusted organism, overflowing with deplorable men and vicious women.

Letter on papyrus from Theen to his father complaining that he had not taken him with him to Alexandria, ca. A.D. 200.

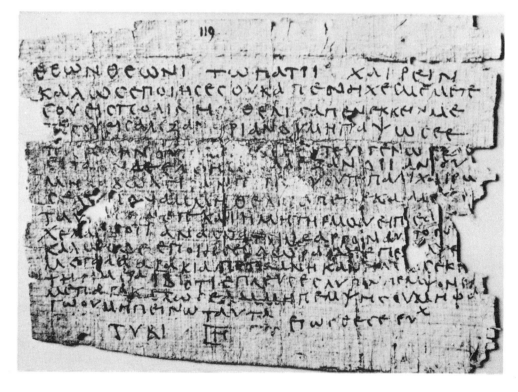

An equally damaging view of Roman society, once again despite the current Trajanic improvements, was implicit in the work of Tacitus (b. ca. A.D. 55– d. ca. 116?), the greatest of Roman historians. Perhaps the son of a tax collector in one of the provinces of Gaul, he became a well-known advocate; though, as he explained in his *Dialogue on Orators*, times of imperial peace do not encourage forensic pleading to flourish as it had under the republic, and in consequence he moved over to a political and administrative career. But the hazards he and other Romans had undergone under Domitian continued, even after that emperor's death, to prey on many minds; for example, Tacitus criticized him posthumously in a biographical essay in praise of his own father-in-law Agricola, who, according to the historian, had received insufficient imperial appreciation for his governorship of Britain. Germany, too, was the subject of a special moralizing study of great ethnological interest, the *Germania,* providing a reminder that Tacitus never commits the error of regarding Rome, or even its empire, as the only existing world.

Then he turned to his supreme achievement, the narration of Rome's history from the death of Augustus to the death of Domitian (A.D. 14–96). This survey is divided into the *Histories* and the *Annals.* Of the former work, dealing with the last twenty-eight of those years, only the first part, describing the convulsed Year of the Four Emperors, is still extant. But the greater part of the subsequently published *Annals,* dealing with the earlier period from Tiberius to Nero, has survived. Tacitus draws upon studies by earlier historians, now lost, but transforms them by the massive power of his own personality; and these haunting, penetrating, moralistic analyses of the men holding such monstrous power in their hands comprise our earliest and only extensive account of the imperial phenomenon. Tacitus was unique for the meticulous care with which he collected and sought to verify and evaluate his facts, far exceeding in this respect the fascinating biographers who were his contemporaries, Suetonius and Plutarch, writing in Latin and Greek respectively. His claim to impartiality, however, cannot be accepted, since his hatred of Domitian, for example, overflows into unfair bias against an emperor he saw as Domitian's forerunner, Tiberius. Incisive, abrupt, tortured, and unfailingly stimulating, Tacitus's literary style is also frequently poetical in its vocabulary and construction, echoing tragic drama (which he had at one time attempted to write) in its awareness of the implacability or malevolence of destiny and in its stress upon the more sinister aspects of the imperial regime.

Nevertheless, these gloomy implications sometimes clash strangely with the more favorable facts that Tacitus was far too good a historian to suppress. Thus he was able, for example, to weigh up objectively the credit and debit side of Roman rule as it appeared to the peoples of the empire.

And the relative advantages of absolute monarchy and the old republican system are presented with equal objectivity—so that, in later Europe, not only revolutionaries felt able to claim his support for their cause, but autocrats as well. If Tacitus felt in his romantically republican heart that one-man rule was wrong, his powerful intellect also told him that Rome could not avoid it.

In consequence, his heroes are often men like Agricola, who quietly got on with their jobs under even the most deplorable of emperors—and this, indeed, was what Tacitus had done himself, and so also, before his accession to the throne, had Trajan, in whose reign the historian was writing. Yet, in spite of this conclusion reached on rational grounds, Tacitus's spirit was moved by observing how men and women, even in times of tyranny and terror, still find themselves able to rise to remarkable heights of heroism; people like the ex-slavewoman Epicharis, who, when cruelly tortured, still refused to betray her fellow conspirators against Nero.

Under the Antonines, a very different sort of commentary on the life of the empire was provided by the Greek author Lucian of Samosata (Samsat in southeast Turkey), who wrote a series of adroit and sometimes amusing essays ridiculing such targets as religious charlatans, overpretentious philosophers, and travelers who told exaggerated tales.

His capacity for story telling was shared in full measure by a contemporary Latin writer of unique gifts, Apuleius. Born in about 123 at Madaurus (Mdaourouch in Algeria), he became one of the leading lecturers in popular philosophy (sophists) who were peculiarly characteristic of this century, gaining such renown that they could address even emperors with confidence and arrogance. Apuleius was the archmanipulator of an unfamiliar sort of Latin prose; artfully combining the florid with the archaic, for which there was a current vogue, it creates a sort of language that is on the way to the Middle Ages. Moreover, he was also a lawyer, and his *Apologia*—one of the few Latin speeches, other than Cicero's, that have come down to us—is a startlingly extravagant defense against charges that he was a magician, which in Saint Augustine's view was precisely the right name for him.

The same fantastic, luscious style, incorporating a wealth of Roman and Greek literary echoes, reappears in Apuleius's *Metamorphoses* or *Golden Ass,* the only Latin novel that has survived in its entirety. Adapting, perhaps, a simpler Greek work but creating something entirely original in the process, the writer tells of a certain Lucius, who is accidentally turned into a donkey and undergoes many other fantastic experiences. The numerous stories this long narrative incorporates include the worldwide Cinderella folk tale of the fairy bridegroom, which Apuleius combines with the Greek myth of Cupid and Psyche; and his account of their weird, romantic adventures attracted endless admiration and allegorical interpretation in the literatures of later antiquity and of medieval and Renaissance Europe as well.

The Mystery Religions

When Apuleius describes, with all the wealth of his exuberant imagination, how his hero is initiated into the mysteries of the Egyptian goddess whose merciful hand raises up and saves the fallen souls *(psychai)* of human beings, he seems to be recording a profoundly felt experience of his own. And this is based on an ecstatic empathy with the Mystery faiths and Savior cults that marked, in a sense, the transition between decaying state paganism and rising Christianity. It was true that the gods and goddesses of the old national religion of Rome still provided a great stimulus to patriotism and for this purpose were exported to the provinces, where they were deliberately identified with the local, native divinities of each region. Yet they were too sterile to fill the spiritual vacuum during these first centuries of our era when men and women became increasingly preoccupied with the urgent needs of their own souls for something that would satisfy them; and the enormously widespread acceptance of astrological doctrines, maintaining that everything was irremediably fixed by the stars, was another factor that caused many to turn their panic-stricken attention to other and more comforting sorts of faith instead.

What they turned to, above all, was a passionate belief in certain saviors who would endow their chosen devotees with a life of blessedness after they were dead. There was a new, rather hopeless humility abroad, a sinking of the heart, and instinct of isolation and defeat; since no reliance could be placed in this world—and this was an age when scientific studies were in total retreat—ever-increasing numbers of peoples throughout the Roman empire pinned their hopes on the next world instead, longing for an individual victory over evil and death in a happy hereafter. It was to these yearnings that the pagan Savior cults responded with their thrilling, dramatic, sometimes orgiastic ceremonials, their solemn rituals of progressive initiation *(mysterion),* and their holy books claiming unique revelation and knowledge. The strength of these religions was that they were all things to all people; and they were among the most vigorously lively features of contemporary Roman society and thought.

These Mystery Savior faiths went back to the elaborate secret rituals of Demeter in early Greece and to the disturbing, frenzied worship of Dionysus, the liberator of mankind, which was celebrated in the *Bacchants* of Euripides. Among the kingdoms of Alexander the Great's heirs this Dionysiac cult, as a setting for Mysteries, became particularly widespread, and its subsequent arrival in Italy, where the god was known as Bacchus, had alarmed the Senate into a repressive reaction (186 B.C.). But then this religion became accepted among the Romans and attained enormous popularity. The ecstatic element tended to be toned down into mere hedonism, the afterlife being often depicted as just a jolly party with facilities for alcoholic and sexual gratification.

More profound excitement, however, was inspired by the Mystery cult of Cybele, the ancient, divine earth-mother of Asia Minor. Admitted to Roman cult in 204 B.C. and later celebrated in an extraordinary poem of Catullus, the worship of Cybele, accompanied by stirring ritual dramas, raised hopes of immortality to a fever heat of excitement, as the resurrection of her youthful consort Attis, god of all that annually grows and dies, was enacted amid scenes of resplendent pageantry.

Innumerable people throughout the Roman Empire believed passionately in Cybele. But even more, like Apuleius, believed in the Egyptian Isis. Accompanying her in the liturgical drama was the god of the underworld, Osiris, who stood like Attis for the birth and death of the year; and the annual Finding of Osiris was the occasion for unrestrained jubilation and excitement. As the worship of Isis turned into a cosmopolitan Mystery religion, her major festivals provided ceremonies equaling or even exceeding those of Cybele in their theatrical, emotional appeals to ear and eye. Her penitents roamed the streets of the cities intoning hymns, or competed with one another in acts of piety and self-mortification, or contemplated the magnificent images of the goddess and meditated upon her countenance. All barriers of caste and race were thrown down and distinctions of sex as well, for among these worshippers were great numbers of women. To them the worship of Isis, like many of the successful beliefs of the world, made a direct and specific and powerful appeal—this Goddess of Ten Thousand Names was their own glory and gave them equal power with men.

From the first century B.C., when senators' suspicions of Egyptian ideas failed to keep the cult of Isis out of Rome, right on until the final decline of paganism many hundreds of years later, her faith remained the most widespread of all the religions of the Roman empire, the only Savior cult that had a real chance of becoming universal.

16

The Jews, Jesus, and Paul

The Jews

The religion, however, that in the end turned out to defeat all the others originated not in Egypt or Asia Minor, the homeland of the cults of Isis and Cybele, but in that other historic center of religious movements, Palestine.

Nearly a thousand years before the birth of Jesus, this little country had controlled a great empire under King David and his son Solomon. After them, however, it had split into two kingdoms, a northern (Israel) and a southern state (Judah), which later fell to successive imperial powers, Assyria (721 B.C.) and Babylonia (597–586 B.C.) respectively. Subsequently the Persians had taken over the whole territory, and then it came under the Ptolemaic and Seleucid monarchies in turn. Finally, in the second century B.C. the Jewish nationalist movement of the Hasmonaeans (Maccabees) had broken away from the Seleucids and succeeded in reestablishing national independence.

In total contrast to the Greeks and Romans, the Jews adhered to a strict monotheism, venerating their ancient holy books with an all-engrossing, literal-minded reverence that declared that every past and present and future happening was a fulfillment of divine prophecy. They believed that their Laws had been handed to Moses on Mount Sinai by God himself, who "gave him the two tablets of the Tokens, tablets of stone written with the finger of God." These tablets, forming a Covenant that was the supreme cornerstone of the Jewish conception of history, were held to have been inscribed with the first five books of the scriptures, the Torah (Pentateuch in Greek), which is often translated "Law" but originally meant instruction by divine revelation. Next in importance to the Torah, in what Christians later named the Old Testament, came the prophets. These glorious figures were credited with deeds and utterances inspired by the Torah and forecast and prefigured by what had been said in it. The Psalms, too, traditionally

Bronze coin of Augustus (posthumous) at Nicopolis in Epirus (*Sebastou Ktisma,* i.e., his foundation to celebrate Actium) with figure of Isis described as *Myrionymos,* Lady of Ten Thousand Names.

though erroneously attributed to King David, were invested with similar authority.

And then in the second century B.C., under the Hasmonaean dynasty, arose the most determined, serious, and progressive element in the Jewish spiritual leadership of the day, the Pharisees or "Separated." They opposed the Hasmonaean monarchs because the latter, in their view, were wrong to combine kingship with the antique high priesthood in their own persons. Yet the Pharisees were not political activists but favored submission to the divine will even if this meant endurance of worldly oppression. Although they held that individuals would eventually rise bodily from the dead, they discounted the possibility, which some other Jews were now envisaging, of a violent, simultaneous, universal resurrection that would bring all life on earth to an apocalyptic end. Nor were the Pharisaic thinkers fundamentalist or fanatical, but on the contrary, while duly stressing the applicability of the Law to all human problems and insisting as much as anybody on the distinctively religious character of Jewish life, they were also eager to adapt their faith to modern needs, for example, by accepting oral interpretations as an integral part of the written canon.

Though the Pharisees' movement remained lay and unofficial, it served as a focus for national Jewish hopes and aspirations. And, in poverty-stricken Palestine, the leading members of the movement, though they themselves mostly were of middle-class origin, often championed the cause of ordinary people and the oppressed; though other Pharisees displayed a tendency to puritanical formalism that earned them charges of complacency. Their strength lay in the synagogues, which existed in every Jewish town. At these focal points of spiritual life, the popular religious universities of the day, the Torah was carefully studied and expounded, and fervent prayers were offered for the revival of the nation.

The Pharisees' agents and assistants were the doctors of the Law or "scribes" (Sopherim). Qualified jurists with pupils, it was they who decided what details of conduct were required to give practical effect to the Torah. Unpaid laymen, and not men of wealth, they gradually became the country's most influential section, in place of the old landed aristocracy. But that aristocracy, too, was still strong. It consisted mainly of a group known as the Sadducees; they followed an unspiritual policy directed towards the survival of the established order and the avoidance of rebellion; and it was they who controlled the ancient, revered Temple at Jerusalem, which after desecration by the Seleucid occupying power had been rededicated by the Hasmonaeans. Moreover, it was from the Sadducee ranks that the high priest was periodically appointed and the hereditary priests under him who organized the Temple's manifold activities.

In the first century B.C. the Hasmonaeans were maintained on the throne by Pompey as his clients; but later they succumbed to Antony, who replaced them by a monarch from Idumaea in the south of the country, a man bearing the name of Herod (37 B.C.). As a protégé of Antony and thereafter for a quarter of a century a dependent of Augustus, Herod expanded Judaea and made it one of the most prosperous of Rome's client kingdoms. To distinguish him from later Herods, he became known as the Elder or the Great. He was a deeply suspicious man and struck down a number of individuals, including his closest relatives, for fear of possible sedition. Yet under his rule the rest of his subjects were able to flourish—including the greatest of all Pharisee thinkers, Hillel and Shammai.

Jesus

Herod died in 4 B.C., and Jesus had probably been born slightly earlier; the date A.D.I to which his birth came to be attributed was based on a miscalculation by a sixth-century monk.

Almost all our information about Jesus is contained in the four Gospels (to which the other, noncanonical, Gospels do not add very much). Their writers are known as the evangelists, from the Greek word *euangelion,* "Good News"; and they were identified from the earliest times as his apostles Matthew and John, and Saint Paul's companions, Mark and Luke. Yet these, despite recent efforts to argue to the contrary, can scarcely have been the real authors of these writings. Who those authors were cannot now be determined. Nor do we know where the Gospels were written, or when; probably they reached their final form between thirty-five and sixty years after Jesus's death. But the main difficulty these works present, from the historian's point of view, arises from their intention to edify, to spread belief in the divinity of Jesus; that is to say, they were not designed *primarily* as historical evidence. In attempting, therefore, to extract historical information from what they record, a distinction must be made between those passages that bear the stamp of the early Christian church and those that seem to go back to Jesus himself. And, contrary to pessimistic estimates, the main lines of his career and thinking and teaching can to some considerable extent be reconstructed.

When Jesus was still a boy, the core of Palestine was directly annexed by the Romans as the province of Judaea (A.D. 6), governed not by a senator but by a knight, who in this territory was known as its prefect. Under his general supervision Rome allowed the Jews a measure of internal self-government under a Council (Sanhedrin) directed by the high priest. Adjoining this Judaean province, to its north and east respectively, were the

territories of Galilee and Peraea. These continued to form the princedom of one of Herod the Great's sons, Herod Antipas (4 B.C.–A.D.39), who ruled, as his father had ruled before him, by the grace of Rome.

On the desert fringes of Judaea and Peraea, in about A.D.28–29, a mysterious Jewish preacher, John the Baptist, attracted widespread attention by proclaiming to his coreligionists (not to Gentiles) the imminence of the Kingdom, or rather "kingship," of God. This was not a new idea; despite the scepticism of Pharisees, many Jews had long believed that their earthly miseries would one day end when the divine rule would be achieved upon earth and the Lord would usher in universal perfection. They had also emphasized the need for repentance, and so did John, stressing that it must be a total change of heart. When this came to pass, he declared, the sins of Jewish men and women would be forgiven. And he set a seal on the process by performing baptisms in the River Jordan—a new development of the periodical ritual ablutions familiar in ancient Palestine, converted by the Baptist into a once-and-for-all event that radically and permanently transfigured the spiritual nature of its recipients.

One of those who received John's baptism was Jesus—an unquestionably historical happening since the early church would have dearly liked to omit it (seeing that Jesus was supposedly sinless) but could not because of its authenticity. He had probably been born not at Bethlehem in Judaea—a fiction inserted to fulfill an old Testament prophecy—but at Nazareth (or possibly some other small place) in the northern land of Galilee. This was a country of fairly recent conversion to Judaism that produced numerous devout sages, though it was looked down on by Jerusalem as bucolic in its way of life and incorrect in matters of religion. Jesus's mother was Mary, who was married to Joseph.

Soon after John had baptized Jesus, Herod Antipas placed him under arrest as a potential revolutionary, for sedition was rife, especially in these border areas. Thereupon Jesus returned to Galilee and began his mission. It contained, at least initially, the same ingredients as the Baptist's, but with one remarkable amendment. Jesus, while continuing to proclaim the Kingdom of God, no longer preached, like the Baptist and other Jews before him, that this was imminent, but that *it had already begun to arrive*—by his own agency, on the direct order of God. This conviction was the key to Jesus's entire career. It dominated all his thoughts and actions and every item of his ethical and social teaching. For example, his many parables—brilliant narratives of imaginary happenings in daily life, endowed with an underlying spiritual significance—derived from and depended upon this single-minded idea.

The same is true of his alleged miracles. These—healings or exorcisms on the one hand and conquests of nature (such as walking upon water) on the other—were "signs" in the traditional Jewish sense that they not only prefigured salvation but also at the same time actually helped to bring about what they prefigured. And in certain passages of the Gospels it is implied not so much that these miracles "actually happened" as that their primary significance was symbolic; they were descriptive gestures or enacted parables, once again relating to the inauguration of the Kingdom of God. His healings in particular (some of which must surely have been authentic) were directly and explicitly linked by Jesus to the forgiveness of sins—conferred by himself and the product of repentance—that was the accompaniment of this dawning Kingdom.

The Jews, however, regarded the forgiveness of sins as belonging to the One God alone. What they had thought when the Baptist proclaimed this doctrine in connection with his own baptisms is scarcely known. But when Jesus proclaimed it, once again, as his own personal prerogative, they were shocked because he seemed to be usurping the divine authority and thus infringing upon their cherished monotheism.

Yet Jesus continued to admit that the completion, the full realization, of the Kingdom of God upon earth had not yet taken place; like many other Jewish thinkers he believed that it would take place almost immediately. His entire program of teachings and preachings was based on these two assumptions: the familiar belief that the Kingdom would be brought into full and final effect on the earth almost at once, and the more startling conviction that he himself, by God's will, was beginning to bring it into effect already, there and then. This second assertion placed everything in a new light. Repentance now meant not only a complete change of heart but a change of heart that specifically accepted Jesus's message about himself.

Later on, the evangelists, and especially Luke, laid special stress on Jesus's compassion. And no doubt he had a deeply compassionate character. But the actions and gestures revealing this quality were, once more, motivated by his total concentration on the Kingdom of God as a haven into which every Jew had the possibility of entering. As for Gentiles, the Kingdom of God was not a concept that would have had any meaning for them, and it does not appear from the Gospels that Jesus, any more than the Baptist, directed his preaching towards them at all, apart from a few isolated individuals who happened to come his way. But owing to his belief that all Jews, indiscriminately, could be admitted to this Kingdom, he paid particular attention to the Jewish poor because they were "poor in spirit"; that is to say, lacking material strengths of their own, they depended on God's help and were therefore especially accessible to his invitation to enroll in the Kingdom. Sinners, too, received a welcome from him because they too, once they repented, would obtain admission—all the more readily since they lacked the complacency of the consciously virtuous. And forgive your enemy, he amazingly said, and turn the other cheek, because what can possibly be the point of petty worldly enmities in the face of this great, overriding opportunity for all Jews to enroll in the Kingdom together? He said the words, "Suffer little children to come unto me," not for any compassionate or sentimental reason, but because their simple, unspoiled directness provided just the approach needed for the ready acceptance of Jesus's message. And he welcomed women around him, too, because it was absurd to suppose that the Kingdom was open only to one of the two sexes. In this respect he differed from the Jewish teachers of the time, the scribes, who were not surrounded by women in this way. Nor did the scribes go outside the synagogues in each town, as he did, in order to preach to a much wider Jewish public.

As a teacher, Jesus was brilliant but unorthodox. He was also, like John the Baptist before him, seen by many of his listeners as heir to the ancient, extinct succession of prophets. And some hailed him as the Messiah or anointed one (Greek *Christos*). This was, according to Jewish tradition, the personage who would eventually come to rescue oppressed Israel, and who, according to more recent theories, would receive the aid of superhuman hosts in performing this task. To harmonise with this warlike view of his function as the liberator of Israel, he was credited with descent (variously described) from the royal house of David. And Jesus was also ascribed a mysterious and variously applied designation, "The Man" or Son of Man. At certain times in the past, in keeping with a Jewish tendency towards corporate and communal concepts, this term had been used to denote all Israel, or the remnant of Israel that would be saved, though it may latterly have acquired a more specific reference to a future single individual who would perform this salvation. Some also regarded Jesus as Son of God. All Israelites were in a sense Sons of God, though the term had tended to be applied to great secular and spiritual leaders. But Jesus, whose mother was Mary the wife of Joseph, was believed to have no father but God himself.

But how, in the light of these contemporary ways of thinking, did Jesus see himself? This has been greatly disputed. But it seems probable that he felt that none of these designations—except perhaps the suitably ambiguous "Son of Man"—sufficed to describe his mission, which he believed to be unique. In holding this belief, he followed other Galilean sages before him who had likewise claimed an exceptional, personal intimacy with God. And so did the devotees of Qumran, a semimonastic settlement near the Dead Sea, whose scrolls, discovered in nearby caves during the past thirty years, have thrown much light on the contemporary, varied Jewish scene: they reveal, for example, the veneration of a Teacher of Righteousness, who had once lived on the earth and would, it was believed, come to live on it again.

We have no evidence that Jesus saw himself in just this light, but, like the Teacher of Righteousness whom the dedicated inmates of Qumran revered, he believed that he enjoyed an altogether peculiar relationship with God.

This, like his claim to forgive sins, brought him into collision with the most active Jewish religious group, the Pharisees, and with their associates the scribes. In the face of this opposition, his mission in Galilee, in which he was assisted by his twelve principal disciples (apostles), ended in failure —as he himself openly admitted. And as his support dwindled, the local prince, Herod Antipas, saw a chance to get rid of this preacher, who was not only inconvenient, but also potentially subversive because his insistence on the dawning actuality of direct rule by God himself implied a disloyal attitude to earthly monarchies. Antipas, by this time, had executed the Baptist. And at this juncture, now that Jesus's mission was manifestly unsuccessful, it was probably Antipas once again who compelled him to leave Galilee.

At all events that is what Jesus did; and in about A.D. 30, or perhaps 33, he proceeded by gradual stages to Jerusalem. He was making his way deliberately to the center of the Jewish establishment. Yet he knew these leaders would not accept him; and he must, therefore, have foreseen his death—a prospect he seems (though this is not universally agreed) to have clothed in the thoughts of the Suffering Servant eloquently depicted by the prophet Isaiah, while likewise recalling the stories of the martyrs who at different times had died for Israel. Jesus, like other Jews, believed many of his experiences fulfilled the predictions and prefigurations of the Torah, prophets, and psalms, and purposefully directed every action to this end; thus his entry into Jerusalem was carefully arranged, in keeping with a prophetic text, to show that his kingship was not of this world. And next, once again in deliberate fulfillment of a scriptural passage, he directly challenged the most politically powerful Jewish group, the Sadducees, by entering their domain, the precincts of the Temple, and driving out the traders who did their business there.

In consequence, with the connivance of one of his twelve apostles, Judas Iscariot—who was probably, like others, disappointed by Jesus's refusal of an earthly role—the Sadducees placed him under arrest. He was charged with threatening to destroy the Temple (an unlikely accusation) and was also accused of claiming to be the Messiah and Son of God and King of the Jews—to which he gave no clear answer, since neither an affirmative nor a negative reply would have offered an adequate explanation to such an unsympathetic audience. He was then handed over to the provincial prefect Pilate (Pontius Pilatus). Pilate was reluctant to judge the case since he had experienced great trouble with Jewish disputes on earlier occasions. But finally he agreed to give judgment and convicted Jesus of sedition against the Roman imperial throne on the grounds that he refused to deny that he was King of the Jews. And so Pilate gave orders for his crucifixion.

Three days after Jesus's death on the cross, his followers believed that they saw him resurrected upon the earth and that he then ascended to heaven. And thus had begun the process by which the failure of his lifetime was converted into triumph after his death—one of the few revolutions in the world's history that has lasted.

Paul

But Jesus's posthumous triumph took a long time to become manifest. That it took place at all was due to the extraordinary accident, or act of providence, that made a man of towering gifts into one of the disciples of the crucified Jesus. He was Paul, a Jew of quite different origins from his new master, for whereas Jesus came from Galilee, an appendage of the homeland, Paul belonged to the Dispersion (Diaspora), comprising the communities of Jews in countries other than Palestine. The first Dispersion had taken place in the early sixth century B.C. after Jerusalem and its Temple had been destroyed by the Babylonians, who took many thousands of Jews away into foreign captivity. Some, later, were repatriated by the Persians who succeeded to the Babylonian Empire, but the Dispersion continued to increase in numbers, particularly when the Ptolemies introduced many Jews into their new city of Alexandria and then again when the Seleucids, who took their place as rulers of Palestine, settled many families in Asia Minor and subsequently drove many more out of Judaea by persecution. By the time of Paul, the Jews of the Dispersion were to be numbered in millions, comprising a sizable minority in many or most of the principal cities of the eastern Roman provinces.

Paul himself came from the self-governing Greek city of Tarsus in Cilicia (southeastern Asia Minor). He claimed descent from the Jewish tribe of Benjamin and belonged to a family of strict Pharisees. It seems probable that he spent his youth at his native town, learning his father's craft of weaving goat's hair into tents, carpets, and shoes. Tarsus was a center of advanced Hellenic culture, so that Paul was familiar with Greek and wrote in that language. The Jews in Greek cities like Tarsus were accorded a quasi-autonomous community status by the Roman authorities. But Paul's family enjoyed a more unusual distinction as well. They were among that section of the local population, never numerous in such towns, that had been granted Roman citizenship. Perhaps it was Paul's father who had acquired this franchise, either as a reward for services to Rome or because he had been a slave and was subsequently freed. At all events, although he gave his son the Jewish name of Saul, this was replaced, on occasion, by a Latin equivalent, Paulus—probably chosen because of its resemblance to his original name. Thus the young man possessed the remarkable triple qualification of belonging to the Jewish, Greek, and Roman civilizations all at the same time; no one else in ancient history spans, as he does, all those three different worlds.

But above all, he was a Jew, and a very active one; indeed he may well have been a member of an ultrapious group active in the Dispersion. At all events, soon after the crucifixion, he began to object strongly to Jesus's disciples and the Messianic claims they were putting forward on his behalf. In accordance with the coercive powers that the Romans delegated to their Councils at Jerusalem and elsewhere, the Jewish authorities were pursuing fierce sanctions against these dissidents. And in enforcing these sanctions, Paul tells us that he, himself, played an active part; perhaps he received his instructions from the local Council at Tarsus or Antioch and set out from one of these cities on his punitive missions.

In any case it was on one such disciplinary journey, perhaps in about A.D.36, that he made for Damascus, an important "free" city of Syria that contained a Jewish community of considerable size. It was the devotees of Jesus among their number whom Paul had been commissioned by his Jewish chiefs to bring to order. But instead—he later declared—while he was on his way to Damascus, a mighty light flashed upon him and blinded him and felled him to the ground; and at the same time he heard a voice. Psychologists describe such experiences under the name of photism, a sensation of light or color accompanying some other species of sensation and especially a sound. The sound Paul believed that he heard was the voice of Jesus ordering him to enter Damascus where he would learn of a new task to perform. When he recovered, therefore, from his blindness, he went on into the city, where Jewish converts to Jesus's doctrines told him to go and preach to the Jews the glorious message (Gospel) that Jesus himself had been preaching to them a short while ago. And he gladly accepted this message since his experience outside the gates of Damascus had utterly changed his attitude to the followers of Jesus, so that, instead of being their remorseless persecutor, he now believed, no less fanatically, that they were right after all.

For what followed we have a remarkable source, the letters of Paul himself, written in Greek. The earliest of these documents perhaps dates back to about A.D.50, only twenty years at most after the crucifixion of Jesus; so it antedates the first of the Gospels by at least sixteen and probably twenty years and constitutes by far the earliest Christian literature. Paul's vigorous, violent personality emerges from these epistles with stunning force; he was a strange addition indeed to the humble and uneducated adherents of the infant church. Despite his powerful intellect, he often wrote paradoxically and ambiguously—his letters were dashed off to meet the current needs of the moment, so that even the one with the greatest claims to a measure of comprehensiveness, the *Epistle to the Romans,* was not by any means intended as a systematic corpus of his views.

Furthermore, the letters were not primarily written with historical aims in mind. And yet they convey a great deal of invaluable information. Facts can also be derived from the *Acts of the Apostles.* But this work, from the historian's point of view, is considerably less reliable. It was written much later, under a strong shadow cast by the events of the intervening period, and the first half of its contents consists largely of miracles of which the historian can take no cognizance. Nevertheless, the rest of the book contains a good deal of by no means unreliable historical material.

The letters and the *Acts,* therefore, taken together, make it possible to give a fairly accurate idea of Paul's career and teaching. It becomes clear that, during the period immediately subsequent to his conversion, the embryonic Jewish movement that had accepted the Messiahship of Jesus was still based upon Jerusalem, the center of the Jewish faith and the place where Jesus had died. At first it was Peter, Jesus's close personal associate, who headed this Jewish Christian community and the fairly extensive missionary movement that it began to direct towards its fellow Jews in Judaea and neighboring lands. But in due course James the Just, the brother of Jesus, took Peter's place. After Paul had been converted, there was, for a time, no split between himself and this group, and he worked as its missionary to its fellow Jews, first in Arabia (southern Jordan) and later for ten years in Syria and Cilicia.

Then in about 45, with his friend Barnabas, he set out on the first of those far more widespread journeys of his, which so notably exploited the improved communications of the Pax Romana for the benefit of Christianity. This first great journey, lasting several years, took him not only to Syria but also to Cyprus and Asia Minor as well. The intention of Paul and Barnabas was to speak in synagogues to their fellow Jews. Yet matters did not turn out that way. For one thing the Jews were against Paul, since they objected to what they regarded as his deification of Jesus and the rejection of monotheism that this seemed to imply; and they carried their hatred of his teaching even to the lengths of physical violence. Furthermore, a strong disagreement arose between Paul and his own Jewish Christian mother church—a disagreement that before long caused the division of the Christian community into two virtually separate parts—one Jewish, and the other consisting of Gentiles, to whom Paul, rejected by the Jews, increasingly addressed his teaching. In particular, the Gentiles who accepted the new faith proved unwilling to undergo circumcision and the dietary restrictions required of Jews; and whereas Paul saw no possibility of enforcing such practices upon them, the Jewish Christians deplored this permissive attitude. Nevertheless, he set out with a series of different companions on two further huge journeys during which he addressed himself once again ever increasingly to the Gentiles, who did not make such injurious objections. These travels covered a period of about eight years, including one and a half years spent at Corinth, in Greece, and three at Ephesus (Selçuk) on the west coast of Asia Minor.

On returning to Jerusalem in about A.D.58, Paul was subjected to accusations of blasphemy by the angry Jews, and the Roman authorities arrested him to save his life. While still detaining him at their provincial capital Caesarea Maritima (Sdot Yam), two successive Roman governors deferred a decision on these charges, anxious to evade the obscure but inflammable questions at issue. However, when Paul, as a Roman citizen, requested that his case should be transferred to the court of the emperor Nero at Rome, his appeal was granted; and after an eventful journey, including shipwreck at Melita (Malta), he spent two years in the city, first under informal house arrest and then in prison. Finally, following a trial or trials, instigated this time not by the Jews but apparently by his other enemies the Jewish Christians, he was condemned to death and executed, either in 64 when the Christian community at Rome was persecuted as scapegoats for the city's Great Fire, which had destroyed the city, or possibly a year or two later.

There was something wrong with Paul, what he called his "thorn in the flesh"—either a physical ailment or more probably a sexual problem, since although, like Jesus, he adopted the un-Jewish practice of enlisting women to help him in his ministry, he wrote somewhat sourly about sex. But the characteristic of Paul that most greatly struck the imagination of those who came after him was his fabulous perseverance and endurance. Wherever he went, he urgently argued, remonstrated, appealed in support of the new sort of Judaism that he believed to have been made necessary and inevitable by Jesus's crucifixion. Oscillating strangely between modesty and self-confidence, he was unimpressive in presence and manner; but he hectoringly repeated over and over again his demands for utter obedience.

It was obedience to a novel cause. The reason why Paul became converted was that he found he could no longer accept the normal Jewish view that the Torah was the answer to all the problems of life. Criticizing this whole code far more sharply than Jesus—who had merely stated that he came not to destroy the Law but to complete it—Paul denounced its provisions as over burdened with legalism and unrealistic in its demands for perfection. Like other Jews, Paul held that the Fall of Adam had plunged the whole world into evil ways. But unlike them, as he looked around at its ills and above all at the miseries of the Jewish people in their homeland, he felt that the Torah had, for centuries, failed to end these tribulations and was still

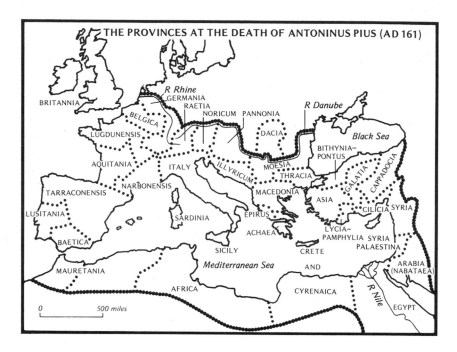

THE PROVINCES AT THE DEATH OF ANTONINUS PIUS (AD 161)

failing to end them now; so it could not possibly be the answer he was looking for.

That being so, mere oral explications to its doctrines, such as the Pharisees were prepared to offer, did not seem enough; instead, a total change was needed, something that would turn the whole of this abominable history into complete and abrupt reverse. And in his desperate perplexity, although he had never known Jesus himself, Paul seized on the astonishing, moving tales of his Crucifixion and Resurrection and Ascension and decided that these reported events possessed exactly the saving power of reversal that he was looking for. That was not, obviously, the same as Jesus had preached, since when Jesus was preaching these events had not yet happened. Moreover, in strange contrast to the later Gospels, Paul is almost totally uninterested in any and every supposed occurrence in Jesus's life before the Last Supper. It was his death only, and what followed after his death, that Paul declared to be redemptive (by God's Grace, besides which he held all human initiatives to be negligible). He was very well aware that Jews and Greeks alike would find it singularly hard to understand that these happenings *have anything to do with us.* Yet that is what he believed, and what he devoted his life and eloquence to explaining to the outside world. In comparison with the central, overwhelming significance of the redemp-

tive power of Jesus's death and what followed it, the whole Jewish code, in
fact all knowledge in any ordinary sense of the word, seemed to him useless
and pointless.

Yet many Jews and Jewish Christians alike considered that this rejection
of the Law was nothing better than an open invitation to license, and they
therefore refused to join him in throwing the Torah overboard. In consequence, both communities turned against him; and his career seemed to
have ended in total failure. His churches for Gentile converts did not
prosper, or even in many cases continue to exist. Instead, such Christian
communities as survived in the Dispersion preferred to follow the Jewish
Christian church, based on the very code he had spurned. His reputation
at the time of his death was at its lowest ebb.

But then the course of events was remarkably changed by the First Jewish
Revolt (A.D.66–73). The province of Judaea had never been a credit to
Rome. Elsewhere in the empire, Roman government, if sometimes un-
imaginative, had generally been relatively successful, or at least peaceable.
In Judaea, on the other hand, successive provincial governors, men lacking
senatorial rank and supported only by a small garrison of non-Jewish
auxiliaries, had been obliged to grapple with an almost continuous and
ever-worsening series of internal crises, embittered by mutual incomprehen-
sion of each other's religious attitudes. As a result, an underground terrorist
movement developed, or rather several distinct movements; and finally the
imprudent actions of one of the governors triggered off open revolt. With
all the resources of the Roman Empire against them, the rebels had no
chance of success. Besides, they chose the worst possible moment for themselves, when Rome had just made a durable peace with its eastern enemy
Parthia. For a time, it is true, the Jewish insurgents were given a lucky
reprieve by the prolonged Roman civil wars after Nero's death. But the end
was bound to come, and the obliteration of Jerusalem and its Temple by
Vespasian's son Titus in 70 marked the end of the nation's life in Israel for
more than two thousand years.

When the Jews, because of this rebellion, fell into total disgrace with the
Roman occupying power, the Christians in their midst urgently needed to
convince the Romans that they themselves lacked any taint of Judaism. But
in this respect the split in their ranks proved damaging. The Jewish Christians, despite all their efforts to prevent this, became discredited in Roman
eyes along with the Jews; and so they dwindled gradually into a scattering
of insignificant sects, which failed to survive into the modern world. The
Gentile Christians, on the other hand, escaped this Roman stigma and lived
on to become the dominant force and theme of the Christianity of the
future. Within the first two decades following the revolt, it was they who
produced all four Gospels: books that preach a sharp dissociation from the

Jews and present the Jewish Christians, too, as exemplified by Jesus's apostles, in a very unfavourable light.

And so, because of this strange reversal of circumstances, Paul's Gentile mission had prevailed after all. True, much of his own teaching still seemed too daring and provocative, and the *Acts of the Apostles* which deals with his career says remarkably little, indeed virtually nothing, about the content of his message. Yet because his ministry had been directed to the Gentiles he had to be rehabilitated. The *Acts,* therefore, chooses to praise him, not for his embarrassing views, but on the safer grounds that he was an indefatigable missionary; and "the greatest example of endurance" was what he remained.

Moreover, later on, at a time when to talk of Jesus Christ and simultaneously practice Judaism had been declared wholly impossible, feelings moved still further in Paul's favor. Indeed, there was an attempt by Marcion, in the second century A.D., to raise him to a startling, overriding eminence. But this proved unacceptable, and it was the cautious, sober interpretation of his career that prevailed; he could be praised as an intrepid missionary, but his awkward radical thoughts must be damped down. Yet often, in later years, the reverberations of the true Paul have been heard through this deliberate softening and muffling, and they have sometimes been explosively loud. By extending Christianity to the Gentiles, it was he who had made it into a world religion. And since then he has been the greatest single source of all its successive spiritual revivals. Whenever the faith has been in danger of flagging, the memory of the man who first spread it far and wide has been revived time after time to give it new life.

The Redeemer on the Throne. Mosaic from Basilica di S. Apollinare Nuovo, Ravenna. Sixth Century A.D.

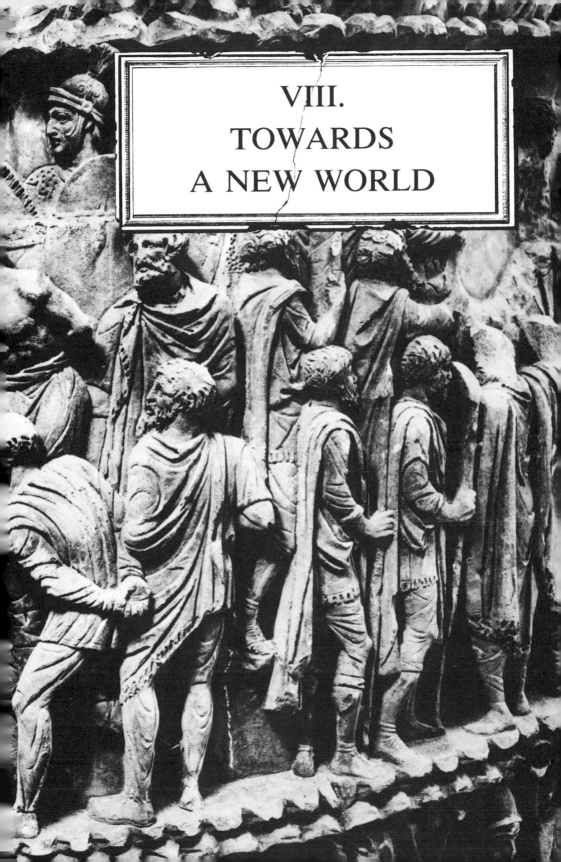

VIII.
TOWARDS
A NEW WORLD

17

Collapse and Recovery

Marcus Aurelius and His Son

When Antoninus Pius died in 161, he bequeathed the empire to Marcus Aurelius, his adopted son and the husband of his daughter. But Marcus Aurelius promptly appointed a co-emperor, Verus, who had likewise been an adoptive son of Antoninus but had not hitherto enjoyed the same degree of preferment. This regime of an imperial pair, which lasted until Verus's death in 169, was an important innovation that would be seen again during the centuries to come. However, the two emperors were unequal in stature. Marcus Aurelius, whose inmost thoughts have come down to us in his *Meditations,* was both phenomenally hard-working and a man of the highest ideals. Verus, on the other hand, though attractive, was a lightweight. Nevertheless, when a crisis arose in the East because of Parthian encroachments on Armenia, it was he who was sent to deal with the situation, and in 163–66 his generals reoccupied Armenia and annexed Mesopotamia.

But at about the time when these campaigns were coming to an end, an event in another part of the imperial frontier lands heralded the permanent transformation of the world scene. German and other tribesmen, "barbarians" as the Romans called them, began to pour across the upper and middle and lower reaches of the Danube in a wide series of formidable, collusive thrusts. In the preceding years, during a long period of relative stability, many of the Germans had outgrown their relatively simple agricultural techniques and became determined, if they could, to abandon their marshy forest clearings for the richer territories that lay within the Roman borders. The fighting that now resulted was more serious than anything of the kind that had been seen before, and it continued to engage the personal attention of Marcus Aurelius for the remaining fourteen years of his life. Breaking through into the provinces of central and eastern Europe, the land-hungry Germans even crossed the Alps into Italy itself, where they destroyed cities

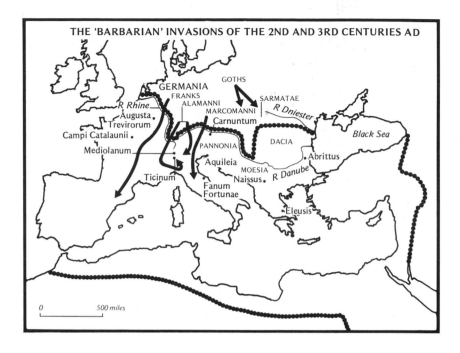

THE 'BARBARIAN' INVASIONS OF THE 2ND AND 3RD CENTURIES AD

and laid siege to the Adriatic port of Aquileia. Almost simultaneously, another German tribe penetrated most of the Balkan peninsula, plundering Eleusis very close to Athens.

The Roman armies, though incapacitated by an epidemic brought back from the East—perhaps the novel scourge of smallpox—gradually and painfully regained control of the military situation. It faced Marcus Aurelius with a financial emergency of almost desperate dimensions. Yet, while pressing ahead with border defense, he also formed two further ideas for dealing with this unprecedented German pressure. One was to admit large numbers of tribesmen into the empire as settlers and potential auxiliary soldiers. This had been done before, for example by Augustus and Nero; and Marcus Aurelius now adopted the policy on a much more systematic scale. In various parts of Italy and the northern frontier provinces, these German settlers were assigned to Roman proprietors or the leaseholders of imperial domains and legally tied to their new plots of land. The emperors who organized such arrangements have often been accused of barbarizing the provinces. But these settlements can also be regarded as a counterblast to racial prejudices, though not a sufficiently decisive one; and at least they supplied the Roman world with cultivators and soldiers whose services it needed.

Marcus Aurelius's second solution involved the annexation of Marcomannia (Bohemia) and a further province of Sarmatia to its east, providing the empire with frontier defenses that were shorter in length and depended on mountains instead of the Danube. But like Augustus before him, who had first formed this intention of annexing Bohemia, Marcus Aurelius never succeeded in carrying out his plan. It was put off, first because of a serious rebellion by his principal eastern general (175), and then because he himself died. After his death, the proposed annexations were abandoned. It is unlikely that they would have been a success, for the easier frontier would scarcely have compensated for the difficulty and expense of recruiting enough troops to garrison such huge and warlike territories. Probably the empire had already expanded to the farthest limits that were practically possible.

Because Marcus Aurelius had a son of his own, Commodus, he elevated him to be his heir, thus abandoning the principle of adoption from outside the family that had been pursued by his four immediate predecessors. Since, however, Commodus's excessive addiction to emotional religions and gladiatorial sports made him one of the most eccentric of Rome's emperors, his father has been blamed for this reversion to the hereditary doctrine. Yet, unlike the four rulers before him, Marcus Aurelius could not have found a generally acceptable candidate outside his own house, so that any adoption would have provoked rival candidatures and civil wars. And they at least were avoided since, when he died, the transition to Commodus's rule was managed peacefully.

Thereafter, however, the first batch of authentic or rumored conspiracies against the new emperor came almost at once. They made him extremely hostile towards the Senate. But since, while eagerly developing his own personality cult, he showed no desire to govern the empire himself, the effective power remained in the hands of successive praetorian prefects. Finally one of them, Laetus, the first north African to hold this post, became

Brass *sestertius* of the young Commodus distributing largess, A.D. 172-73.

Bust of African. Later second century A.D.

convinced that Commodus's growing megalomania and antisenatorial feeling had become too hazardous and decided that he must die, and commissioned a professional athlete to murder him.

The Dynasty of Severus

The city prefect Pertinax was elevated to the throne, but when his martinet discipline and financial meanness quickly angered the guardsmen, Laetus withdrew his support and allowed him to be killed after a three-month
reign. The situation recalled what had happened after the termination of
Rome's first imperial dynasty, when Galba had likewise acquired a reputa-

tion for stringency and failed to establish himself. And from now on the analogy developed further, during the long period of civil war that ensued. The chaotic events of these months served to emphasize, once again, the insuperable flaw in the arrangements governing Rome's imperial successions, a flaw that was to become increasingly disastrous in the years to come.

The successor to Pertinax, a rich senator Didius Julianus, set an unedifying precedent by purchasing the throne at an auction held by the praetorians; soon afterwards, however, he terminated the emperor-making career of their prefect, Laetus, by putting him to death. But from the provinces news came, almost immediately, that two governors had been declared emperor by their legions. They were Severus, a forty-eight-year-old north African, proclaimed at Carnuntum (Petronell) on the Danube in Upper Pannonia, and Niger whose troops saluted him in Syria. Obeying a command from Severus, the Senate put Didius Julianus to death after a reign of nine weeks. Then Severus marched south and entered Rome. But before dealing with his eastern rival Niger, he felt it necessary to conciliate the most influential of the western provincial governors, his fellow African Albinus in Britain. So he gave Albinus the title of Caesar, which was the equivalent of pronouncing him heir to the throne, although Severus had two sons of his own, Caracalla and Geta, aged five and four respectively. Then he set out for the east and overwhelmed Niger at Issus, at the point where Asia Minor and Syria meet (194). Encouraged by that success, he felt strong enough to declare his own elder son Caracalla his heir after all, thus breaking openly with Albinus, whom he defeated and killed in 197 in a fierce battle at Lugdunum (Lyon).

Although the civil wars were so reminiscent of the strife of 68–69, they had lasted much longer and proved far more damaging to the empire. The numerous casualties included twenty-nine members of the Senate; and Severus still remained suspicious of the senators who survived and excluded them from his administrative posts, which he filled with knights of purely military training.

Since the Parthians had given aid to his enemy Niger and had made inroads into Roman territory, it was against them that Severus next turned (197–99). He captured their winter capital Ctesiphon and reasserted Rome's claim to Mesopotamia, but he did not attempt to repeat Trajan's short-lived advance to the Persian Gulf. Nevertheless, Parthia was dealt an unprecedentedly severe blow, which proved to have weakened it permanently—as Rome would later have reason to regret.

On his accession, Severus had replaced the praetorian guard by his own Danubian soldiers and doubled its size. And at the same time he had substantially increased the city police as well. Now, moreover, on returning

Bronze head of Septimius Severus.

from the East, he stationed a new legion just outside the capital, at Albanum (Albano Laziale). This set a novel precedent, for hitherto no legions at all had been stationed in Italy by any previous emperor; and Severus's move has sometimes been interpreted as an African's deliberate indication that Italian supremacy over the provinces was coming to an end. And this was, indeed, gradually happening. However Severus's primary motive in stationing this unit in Italy was probably not political but military. It was based on his recognition that the imperial army needed a central reserve capable of being sent wherever it was needed—a reserve that Augustus had neglected to provide for.

He had fixed the number of Roman legions at twenty-eight, later reduced by losses to twenty-five. Trajan had maintained thirty legions, and Severus now raised this total to thirty-three, including a larger proportion of provincials than hitherto. Severus also increased the native soldiery that had been employed since the previous century, relying especially on mounted archers from Osrhoene (Mesopotamia) and Palmyra (Syria), who were available for dispatch around the empire wherever the need arose. Severus elevated the army to these unprecedented dimensions because he knew that a big and permanent change had taken place; ever since the frontier crisis of Marcus Aurelius, imperial defense had become a far graver problem than ever before.

Besides, another purpose of the enlarged army, in Italy as elsewhere, was to minimize the ever-present possibility of sedition. And with this purpose once again in mind, he took a number of steps to make the officers of the legions a privileged class and tie them firmly to his own person. In due course, many former soldiers of his new guard were promoted to officer status, which in consequence assumed a more democratic appearance. And the other ranks of the army, too, were considerably better paid and rewarded than hitherto. This was a development that, as we shall see, caused lasting hardship to the taxpayers and in the end, throughout many areas of the Roman world, virtually wiped out the middle class of society. Yet it was both logical and inevitable if the empire was to face up to its new military problems.

Three years later, Severus took his new army into action, setting out with his wife and two sons for Britain, where tribal attacks had caused the Antonine Wall to be abandoned, and had breached Hadrian's Wall. The large-scale invasions of Caledonia (Scotland) that he now proceeded to undertake yielded, as usual in this area, no permanent results, but Hadrian's Wall was rebuilt and restored as an effective frontier. Soon afterwards, however, at Eboracum (York), the emperor died (211). He was reported to have given a last piece of advice to his sons: "Be on good terms with one another, be generous to the soldiers, and don't care about anyone else!" Whether that is authentic or not, he had launched the empire on a new path by giving overall priority to the requirements of a greatly expanded army.

Severus was an extremely purposeful man, determined to exercise rigorous control of all that went on. It is therefore surprising to find that he became as thoroughly dependent on his praetorian prefect as any ruler before him; no doubt the personal burden of empire was so enormous that even the most strong-minded ruler found he needed a confidant. And so the prefect Plautianus, a fellow townsman of Severus, gained an extraordinary and almost autocratic authority (197). But as he did so, the emperor's Syrian wife Julia Domna, an able woman surrounded by a personal court of learned scholars and writers, became his enemy. And Caracalla, too, unhappily married to Plautianus's daughter, came to hate his father-in-law and in the end brought about his downfall and death (208).

Julia Domna, wife of Septimius Severus.

Severus left the empire jointly to his two sons. It was a mistaken arrangement since they hated one another; and Caracalla, a temperamental and
violent young man, almost at once had Geta murdered. Then, in 213, he set
out for Germany, where he defeated some of its tribes and bought off others
with a subsidy, winning considerable popularity among his troops. Next he
set off for the East, identifying himself with Alexander the Great whose
conquests he was eager to rival. Although an attack on Armenia failed, he
pushed forward the frontier of Mesopotamia and invaded Media, to its
north. But near Carrhae (Haran) he succumbed to an assassin (217). This
was his Mauretanian praetorian prefect Macrinus, who was alarmed that
Caracalla might be intending to put him to death.

Macrinus's principal claim to fame is that he was the first Roman emperor who had not been a member of the Senate, but was only a knight. His
reign was brief and undistinguished. His conclusion of the Parthian war on
not very favorable terms, followed by retrenchments in military pay, made
the army look back longingly to the reign of his predecessor; and Severus's
Syrian sister-in-law, Julia Maesa, was able to organize a rebellion in which

The family of Septimius Severus

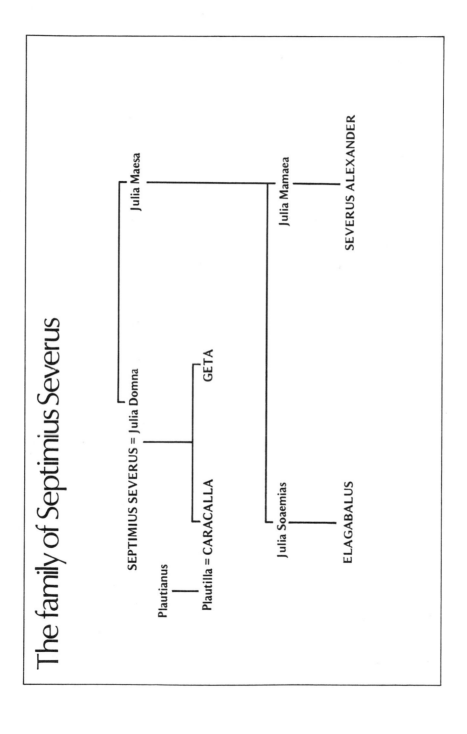

Plautianus

Plautilla = CARACALLA

SEPTIMIUS SEVERUS = Julia Domna

GETA

Julia Maesa

Julia Soaemias

ELAGABALUS

Julia Mamaea

SEVERUS ALEXANDER

Macrinus was defeated and lost his life. The new emperor was her fourteen-year-old grandson, known as Elagabalus after El-Gabal, the sun god of their home town Emesa (Homs), of whom he was the hereditary priest.

When he and his grandmother and mother reached Rome, the young monarch, a promiscuous sexual invert, devoted himself entirely to the worship of his oriental divinity; and his neglect to adapt its cult to the religious institutions of Rome deeply alienated the senatorial class. Alarmed for her own and her family's future, Maesa switched her allegiance to another of her grandchildren, Severus Alexander, the fourteen-year-old son of her daughter Julia Mamaea; and the two women, by an opportune bribe, induced the praetorians to murder Elagabalus and his mother. Maesa died shortly afterwards, but this unprecedented phase of personal feminine rule went on, since throughout the reign of her son that was now to follow, it was Mamaea who ruled the empire. The later tradition that Alexander's reign witnessed a revival of senatorial influence was largely fictitious.

In its later years, Mamaea's government became preoccupied by simultaneous threats on both major frontiers. In 231 she and her son left Rome for the East to repel an invasion of Mesopotamia by the Persians (Sassanians), who had overthrown the Parthian kingdom and replaced it by their own much superior power.* After heavy losses on both sides, the Romans temporarily recovered their Mesopotamian province. But then Alexander and Mamaea had to return to the west to deal with a perilous German menace on the Rhine. They attempted to buy off the German aggressors, but this proved unpopular with their own officers and cost them their lives (235).

The Disintegration of the Empire

The officer who emerged from the mutiny as emperor, the giant Danubian peasant Maximinus I, might have dealt effectively with Rome's external foes, but the severity with which he treated his own subjects led to his death in 238. In that single year, the empire saw the coinage of no fewer than seven Caesars. The survivor among them, Gordianus III, was a youth of thirteen whose praetorian prefect governed the empire effectively until the deaths of both of them on an eastern expedition. Then came a renewal of the series of soldier emperors. Their first batch, however, seemed unable to measure up to the formidable accumulation of threats within and outside the imperial borders alike. Philip the Arabian (244–49) sought to distract attention by celebrating the thousandth anniversary of Rome. But Decius (249–51), who came from the same region as Maximinus, overthrew him and then himself fell to German (Gothic) invaders. His successor

*See below, p. 367.

Gallus (251–53) had to deal not only with similar onslaughts but also with an unfamiliar and prolonged pestilence, perhaps bubonic plague. Finally, as economic disasters proliferated, Valerian (253–60) was captured by the Persians. His son, co-ruler, and successor Gallienus (253–68) found himself confronted with internal and external problems of every kind.

The main internal difficulty, throughout the whole of this period, was the proliferation of military usurpers. Between A.D. 218 and 268 about fifty usurpers assumed the imperial title, either at the capital or in some other part of the empire; and out of the twenty-seven "regular" emperors of the third century (insofar as they can be distinguished from usurpers), seventeen were killed at the hands of their own people—all but one of them by the troops—and two of the others were forced to commit suicide. Therein lay one of Rome's most grievous and costly problems. The old custom by which its rulers were appointed by the Senate had become a threadbare farce. In reality, with a few unimportant exceptions, they were placed on the throne by one or other of the armies, after which the Senate was ostensibly asked for its approval—but, in reality, merely received the information. Since local recruitment was now prevalent, the armies on many occasions were stronger in parochial *esprit de corps* than in patriotism. But above all their motive for changing emperors was greed; they felt eager for the lavish gifts that their protégés were always compelled to distribute. In consequence, the soldiers acclaimed new imperators with ludicrous or tragic frequency; and the previous incumbent was nearly always killed.

This totally unstable situation at the top created paralysis in the empire's defenses, not to speak of its finances. There were constant, costly civil wars. Time after time, a frontier operation against a foreign foe had to be called

Base silver *denarius* of Decius (A.D. 249-51)
depicting the two Danubian provinces of Pannonia.

Man and two women in Pannonian costume.
From Intercisa (Dunapentele) on the Danube.

off because the monarch of the time was obliged to turn back to face a rival
Roman army. Sometimes the commanders who found themselves successively elevated to the throne would have lost their lives to their own troops
if they had not consented. But much more often, they were willing; the lure
of the purple was too great—however briefly it was likely to be worn.

After asserting his claims, a new emperor almost always tried to have a
successor available, to give the illusion of dynastic stability. There were two
traditional ways in which he could attempt this. One way was to bring
forward and promote his own son or another close relation, so that when
he himself died there might be a smooth takeover inside the family. The

armies, in theory, liked a dynastic succession of this kind because it insured the continuity of their pay, although their attachment to any proposed dynasty wore off rapidly if the ruler proved parsimonious or ineffective in the field. The senators, on the other hand, generally preferred a second method of securing the succession, according to which the ruler, after consulting with themselves, adopted a suitable heir from outside his own house. This procedure had worked well in the second century A.D. But during the anarchic years that ensued, there was scarcely an opportunity to give it a try. The fact was that any and every doctrine about how to arrange for a peaceful succession, whether by heredity or adoption, remained theoretical and irrelevant, since all such efforts almost invariably failed.

The Danubian armies were by far the largest in the empire, and during the recurrent civil wars of this epoch it was their candidate, more often than not, who gained the throne. Maximinus I, though stationed elsewhere at the time of his succession, was a Danubian ex-ranker put

Gravestone of Yorkhai, son of Ogga, and his daughter Balja, from Palmyra. Later second century A.D.

forward by a unit from his homeland. Decius, too, was born in the same country, of an Italian family. Neither maintained his power for long; the more successful emperors from the Danube region were still to come. But already it was producing most of the best officers in the army and the best soldiers as well. And when not engaged in promoting the imperial claims of one of their countrymen, they were more patriotic than troops from elsewhere. Their hearts were filled with the frontiersman's proud and emotional confidence that their protection of their own homes was protecting Italy and Rome as well.

In reversal of the situation of early imperial times, the Rhine armies had now become smaller than those of the Danube. That meant that they felt neglected by Rome in favor of the Danubian legions; and this official attitude, they felt, unfairly impeded them in carrying out their defensive tasks, which were terribly severe in the face of German invasions. That was why, in a time of grave crisis, they put forward Postumus (259–68) as an emperor of their own. He set up independent consuls and Senate at Augusta Trevirorum (Trier) on the Moselle; not only Gaul, but Britain and Spain rallied to his cause, and for fourteen years, under himself and his successors, western Europe was a large separatist state, confronting Rome in a cold war that broke at intervals into open hostilities.

The eastern garrisons, too, second only to those of the Danube in size and strength, were equally ready to put forward rulers of their own choice. Elagabalus (218–22), the grandnephew of a Syrian empress, was a nominee of that country's soldiery. And thereafter a number of emperors and would-be emperors continued to be proclaimed by these eastern armies, including Philip (244–49), the son of an Arabian chief.

But the most vigorous, durable, and menacing of the oriental dissidents came from the oasis city of Palmyra (Tadmor), upon the borders between Syria and Mesopotamia. Annexed by Rome in the early first century A.D., Palmyra possessed a good water supply and was located at an important desert crossroads; and from the time of Severus onwards, its excellent mounted archers played a strong part in frontier defense. Moreover, when Parthia succumbed to the more dangerous Persians, Palmyra became even more important, indeed indispensable, as a bastion of the empire. Indeed, in the reign of Gallienus, its chieftain Odenathus was made the semi-independent commander of Rome's entire defensive system in the East. But when he fell to assassins (266–67), his gifted and learned widow Zenobia declared her total independence and expanded the dominions she already held in Syria and Mesopotamia by annexing Egypt and the greater part of Asia Minor as well. Then she declared herself Augusta, empress of Rome, and her son was hailed as Augustus (ca. 270).

The dismemberment of the empire, from which both Zenobia and Post-

Fort at Qasr-al-Hêr, near Palmyra. Second century A.D.

umus had torn enormous territories, could scarcely go further. Moreover, it came at a time when Rome's external enemies had never been stronger and more menacing.

The threats from beyond both the eastern and northern frontiers, already productive of anxiety, had begun to increase with appalling sharpness some forty and fifty years earlier and were still getting graver and graver.

The massive changes in the East have already been briefly mentioned. Way back in the previous century, the situation had first begun to look easier, since Rome's enemies, the Parthians, were gradually declining in strength. This was partly because of their recurring warfare against the Romans; and the invasion of Severus, in particular, weakened their hold over their feudal dependencies. One of these was Persis (Fars) in the deep south of Iranian chauvinism; and in 223–26 its prince Ardashir (Artaxerxes) of the Sassanian dynasty, ruler of a large area extending from the Persian Gulf to Isfahan, invaded Parthia and overthrew the last of its monarchs. His own Sassanian dynasty that replaced it ruled from Ctesiphon in Babylonia, but the religious capital was now at a holy city near Persepolis

Bronze coin of Zenobia, Queen of Palmyra
(A.D. 269-71), issued at Alexandria in Egypt
which she conquered before her defeat by
Aurelian.

Gold stater of Ardashir (Artaxerxes) I (d. A.D. 241),
who founded the Sassanian dynasty of Persia.

on Persian territory, the residence of the glorious monarchs of his race eight centuries earlier.

The Sassanians combined pride in this ancient tradition with a willingness to take over Parthian institutions. But the new state was far more formidable and centralized than Parthia. It was also intensely nationalistic, claiming the right to all the Roman Empire's eastern territories in the name of its own ancestral inheritance. This aggressiveness, backed by an efficiently centralized administration, enormously worsened the strategic situation of Rome, confronting it with a military threat that equaled the gravest German menaces from the north. The Persian army, reinforcing the traditional mail-clad Parthian horsemen by recruitment from newly created nobles, was the most up-to-date attacking force of the age. And the Romans failed to reduce this new foe to manageable proportions or bring it to a workable agreement. Their eastern military operations, hitherto something of an imperialistic luxury, now became a direly urgent and hugely expensive necessity.

After initial fierce but indecisive fighting in the frontier regions, Shapur (Sapor) I (Ca. 234–70) adopted, at his coronation, the provocative title of "King of Kings of Iran and non-Iran." He was the most dangerous single enemy the Roman emperors had ever had to confront. Every year, he raided deep into their provinces; and during the first two decades of his reign he launched three major invasions. Mesopotamia and Armenia were overrun, and Antioch, the capital of Syria, was temporarily lost to Rome as well. Then, in the last of these campaigns in 260, the Roman emperor Valerian himself fell into Shapur's hands near the Mesopotamian town of Edessa (now Urfa in southeast Turkey). This event, the most inglorious in all Roman history, continued to be emphasized over and over again in Persian propaganda; and Valerian remained a captive for the rest of his life. His son Gallienus did not succeed in rescuing him, or did not try. The only consolation for Rome was that when its eastern commander Odenathus, the prince of Palmyra, made overtures to Shapur I, the Persian decided to reject them. This decision and Shapur's savage treatment of the Roman provinces he overran were imprudences that, by a narrow margin, eventually saved these territories for Rome.

During these same disastrous years the Romans' position on the Rhine and Danube boundaries, too, deteriorated gravely. For years, it is true, there had been fighting on either side of the two rivers. But new German peoples appeared, who were far more dangerous than any that had ever been seen there before. They were the Goths. Leaving their Scandinavian homes before the beginning of our era, they had come to the lower Vistula, and

Silver drachm of the Persian (Sassanian) King Sapor (Shapur) I (A.D. 241-72), who captured the Roman emperor Valerian.

then during the second century A.D. various pressures forced them onwards in a southwesterly direction, until finally they established themselves near the mouth of the Danube. During their migrations they had acquired some culture and political cohesion, and although remaining weak in army tactics and siegecraft, they absorbed a number of Roman military techniques.

In the 230s—at the very time when the eastern frontier, too, was the scene of perilous new threats—these Goths began to surge across the lower Danube, and the Romans tried to appease them with a subsidy. In the following decade, however, this ceased to be paid any longer; perhaps no money could be found to pay it with. But the cessation infuriated the Goths who, encouraged by rebellions within the empire, crossed the river again and penetrated far into the Balkans (248). The commander of the Danubian armies, Decius, defeated this invasion with such success that his troops declared him emperor in the following year. But his attempt to reinforce the Danube defenses proved inadequate, for in their monarch Kniva the Goths had a leader capable of grandiose strategies, threatening Rome almost as perilously as Shapur at the opposite extremity of the empire; and Kniva's supreme triumph came in the marshes at Abrittus (near Razgrad, west of Varna), where he defeated and slew the emperor Decius himself.

These two menacing foes at either end of the empire, the Germans and Persians, took collusive advantage of each other's attacks on the forces of Rome, which were consequently faced with prolonged, gigantically costly warfare on two fronts that made all previous border operations look trivial in comparison. While Persians overran the Orient, and rebellions and epidemics (perhaps bubonic plague) paralyzed Roman defense, the Goths, joined by other peoples, ravaged the Balkans and even drove deep into the central plateau of Asia Minor, as far as the central plateau (253). Moreover, they took to the sea as well, obtaining ships from the Greek coastal cities and swooping on major Black Sea ports, with disastrous effects on the empire's grain supplies. And meanwhile other German tribes, too, joined the onslaught along the entire length of the European river frontiers. Among them was the powerful confederacy of the Franks, who broke right through the Rhine defenses, overran Gaul and Spain, and extended their raids as far as north Africa.

Since one man could not face both ways at once, the imperial armies, in such regions as remained to them, were now divided between two commands, anticipating the later division between the eastern and western empires. Valerian took the East and Gallienus the West, and after Valerian's capture by the Persians Gallienus fought on. In the last year of his life (268), utilizing the Heruli—recent arrivals in the Black Sea area— as their sailors, the Goths mustered unparalleled numbers of warriors and ships at the mouth of the River Dniester; and Greece and Asia Minor were

Bronze head of Claudius II Gothicus
(A.D. 268-70) from Aquileia.

ravaged yet again. The invaders, laden with plunder, began to return northwards by the Balkan land route; and the Roman Empire had reached the
lowest depths of disarray.

The Military Recovery

But in fact an extraordinary recovery was about to begin. It was preceded
by Gallienus's reorganization of the army. He had completed the separation
of the officer corps from the senatorial career—thus making the military
system more professional. And, above all, he had set up a new, mobile
strategic force, based on cavalry, that had now for the first time become an

element of primary importance in the previously infantry-dominated imperial army. The headquarters of the new formation was at Mediolanum
(Milan), which was now virtually the advance capital of the empire. This
troop concentration in Italy was an important extension of the ideas of
Severus, who had located a legion on Italian soil. It was also a step that was
to have far-reaching effects in later times, both militarily since it at last
created a powerful reserve, and politically because it encouraged a growing
tendency to stop seeing Rome as the world center. Yet such a force, for all
its strategic benefits, was at the same time a grave security risk, as was
confirmed when its very first commander tried to make himself emperor,
and then its second, the future emperor Aurelian, led a successful plot that
put Gallienus to death.

Yet Gallienus's new army, at the very end of his life, had won a major
military triumph against his foreign foes. As the Goths returned northwards
through the Balkans, he succeeded in cutting them off, winning the bloodiest battle of the century at Naïssus (Niš in Yugoslavia), in which fifty
thousand enemy soldiers met their deaths (268). And soon afterwards, when
a group of west German tribes, the Alamanni, struck into Italy itself, his
Danubian successor Claudius II (268–70) crushed them beside Lake Bena-
cus (Garda) and then defeated the Goths in further battles, which rightly
earned him the title of Gothicus. Then he was struck down by the continuing epidemic and died; but the expulsion of the Goths was completed by
an emperor who was an even more brilliant commander, Aurelian, known
as "hand on hilt" *(manu ad ferrum)*. Meanwhile other Germans, too, were
continuing to pour through the Brenner Pass; but Aurelian engaged these
as well and overwhelmed them in two battles in northern Italy, at Fanum
Fortunae (Fano) and near the fortress of Ticinum (Pavia).

Gold coin *(aureus)* of Aurelian (A.D. 270-75) at Siscia
(Sisak in Yugoslavia) commemorating the reestablishment
of imperial unity (CONCORDIA AVG*usti*)

Then Aurelian turned on Queen Zenobia of Palmyra. Asia Minor and Egypt were recaptured and brought back under Roman rule; and he twice defeated her principal general in Syria (271). Palmyra itself fell to him, and then revolted, and then fell again, and the queen walked in golden chains at Aurelian's triumph. And with her walked Tetricus, the last monarch of Postumus's splinter state in the West. Following upon the suppression of Zenobia, Aurelian had immediately moved right across the empire to Gaul and defeated the rebel army on the Catalaunian Plains (near Châlons-sur-Marne), after Tetricus himself had deserted his own soldiers and joined him (224).

Yet Aurelian was still conscious that many perils existed; and he built a new defensive wall around Rome, enclosing all the regions that had been added to the city since the last wall had been built six hundred years earlier. Moreover, he decided that the defenses beyond the lower Danube, heavily infiltrated by barbarians, were no longer tenable, and in consequence Dacia a province since the time of Trajan, was abandoned, and the frontier brought back to the river, which provided a shorter and stronger boundary. And then another Danubian warrior Probus (276–82) repelled a massive three-pronged German attack on Gaul and drove other Germans (Vandals) out of the Balkans. Next, his former praetorian prefect Carus (282–83), who succeeded him as emperor, struck north against further hordes of Germans and then moved east against the Persians, and even temporarily occupied their capital Ctesiphon.

The entire military picture, inside and outside the empire alike, had been transformed out of all recognition within the space of only fifteen years. It was the most extraordinary warlike achievement, or cumulation of varied, simultaneous achievements, in the whole of Roman history. Rome had seemed in a state of such advanced disintegration that recovery could scarcely be imagined. Yet by the exceptional talents of successive Danubian generals, commanding troops as good as any that Rome ever produced, the seemingly impossible had come to pass, and the empire was restored.

The Collapse of the Economy

Yet the restoration had taken place against a background of fierce economic dislocation; this made it even more remarkable, but it also meant that an enormous human price was paid. At the beginning of the century, Severus and Caracalla had decided that the civilian population must sacrifice every comfort and amenity to insure the loyalty of the army. And this policy had not been changed.

Moreover, the prevailing hardships were intensified by a collapse of the imperial currency. The ancients expected currency in the precious metals

Gold medallion of Gallienus (A.D. 253-68) presented to a senior officer "because he had remained loyal" (OB FIDEM RESERVATAM).

to contain the quantities of fine metal that corresponded to the values attached officially to each denomination; the public refused to tolerate gold and silver coins of token weight. But the Roman government, pressed for funds, could not refrain from lightening the weights of these pieces, and, above all, they adulterated the silver. This had been done for a long time, but in the third century A.D. the process became so blatant that people would no longer accept the base money with which the market was flooded. In consequence, inflation reached, even by modern standards, preposterous heights: between the years 258 and 275, despite an attempt by Aurelian to stabilize the coinage, prices in many or most parts of the empire rose by nearly one thousand percent. The result, for a population also tormented by unprecedented wars and epidemics, was misery.

But what was most serious for the imperial government was that this inflation, which they themselves had inadvertently caused, meant that the wages of soldiers, as of other state employees, were practically wiped out. So successive emperors, in order to protect their very existence, had to employ special methods to augment these perilously diminished pay packets. Among these methods was the distribution of donatives—special money gifts (originally war spoils), either handed out by emperors at the beginnings of their reigns or on other joyful occasions, or left (and known to be left) in their wills. It had long been customary to supplement army pay by such bonuses; and after the transient predecessors of Severus had been killed because they failed to hand over the donatives they had promised, the third century A.D. witnessed sharp increases in the size and frequency of these awards. Moreover, they consisted, at least on imperial accessions, not of the contemporary coins of debased silver, but of pieces of pure gold. To quell a mutiny after the death of Gallienus, we learn that the soldiers were given twenty of these gold coins each; larger pieces, the imposing gold medallions of the time, were presented to senior officers.

But the huge sums required to pay these donatives had to be obtained by increases in taxation. The land tax and poll tax, the direct contributions that provincials normally had to pay, were not the best ways of obtaining such revenue. These taxes fell unfairly, because nonprogressively, upon an agricultural economy like Rome's, and in bad times there was a strict limit to what could be raised by such means. So instead, the emperors, starting apparently with Caracalla, demanded an extraordinary income tax known as crown money *(aurum coronarium)*, originating from a republican custom of levying gold crowns for triumphs, although now the crowns were commuted into cash. Yet the raising of all this money, from whatever source, was of little avail because the rapid rise in prices meant that the sums needed for the army were far beyond what any monetary taxes could provide. Accordingly, the Roman government, from the Severan period onwards, also proceeded to raise revenue by other means. First of all they confiscated personal property whenever they had a chance. And, secondly, they raised supplementary taxes not in cash but in kind, that is to say, by levying supplies of foodstuffs and other goods *(annona militaris)*. This had been done before, in national emergencies, but now the practice was organized on a far more systematic scale. And, once collected, the proceeds of these levies in kind were recycled to the troops in the form of free distributions of rations, clothing, and the materials needed to make

Relief from funeral monument at Noviomagus (Neumagen), showing four Gauls or Germans paying taxes or rents. Early third century A.D.

arms and equipment. As the quality of money deteriorated, these distributions rapidly became the principal means of remunerating the troops.

During the previous century, rations and uniforms and arms had been issued to soldiers against deductions from pay, but as the system of payments in kind gained in momentum, it became customary to exempt them from such deductions. As for the civilian populations, who were compelled to hand over these supplies, at first they were paid for what they provided, and as late as the 230s such cash transactions are still recorded. But by that time the money the authorities offered in compensation fell far below the inflated prices the suppliers could have secured for themselves on the free market. Moreover, it was now becoming increasingly rare for the government to offer contributors any payment at all; and by the middle of the third century forced deliveries for the army, without recompense, had become prevalent and normal.

Moreover, for some time before that—apparently from the days of Severus—each province had also been required to hand over food directly to the troops stationed within its borders. Landowners extracted the required products from their tenants, and the leading officials of the cities were ordered to see that their citizens contributed what was demanded. Worst of all perhaps was the unforeseeable irregularity of such claims, which fell like thunderbolts upon the population. We have inscriptions recording grievous local discontents and desperate appeals for relief.

It may seem strange, at first sight, that so vast an empire could not maintain an army of between a quarter and half a million strong without resorting to these assessments reminiscent of a prehistoric nonmonetary economy. But now that money had become so much less useful, the army could only be supplied at all by these more primitive methods. In the technologically backward Roman world, food, clothing, weapons, and armor were expensive to produce and transport. Yet the soldiers had to have them in huge quantities, and they could have them only if the subjects of the empire contributed the materials. Besides, not only the army but the imperial civil service, too, had to be paid for, and the inhabitants of Rome as well, who, even if the city had lost some of its political power, were allowed to retain a subsidized status as privileged parasites.

It was in against this grim economic background that the great Danubian soldier-emperors succeeded so amazingly in restoring Rome's military equilibrium on both sides of the frontiers. But the strain on the civilian population, outside the capital at least, was appalling and seemed almost impossible to endure.

18

The Climax of
the Pagan Empire

The Stoicism of Marcus Aurelius

Yet it would be a complete mistake to regard this tumultuous epoch merely as a time of military and economic vicissitudes. On the contrary, it was also an age of extraordinary intellectual and spiritual achievement—in several respects the culmination of the pagan world.

The keynote had been set at the outset of the period by the emperor Marcus Aurelius. He was one of those rulers, rare in human history, whose practical achievements have been eclipsed and outlived by what he wrote. His dramatically intimate disclosures of his deepest thoughts, entitled by editors "his writings to himself" and later known as the *Meditations,* are the most famous book ever written by a monarch. Their language is Greek, and they are framed in literary form, but they were meant to be private notes and intentions, and their author did not intend this highly personal master-piece of self-scrutiny and self-admonition to be published.

Marcus Aurelius's doctrine was an austere one and provided no comfort —except that of putting its tenets into practice. Men and women must just strive onwards, he declares, and continue their laborious efforts as best they can, with patient, long-suffering endurance; they must turn inwards and be strong, and draw on their own inner lives and resources, and thus renew themselves and find the courage to get on with their daily existences; and his was almost unendurably burdensome. Life is desperately short and transient, says Marcus Aurelius, a temporary visit to an alien land. And all we have the power to do, as long as it lasts, is to act as responsibly and unselfishly and kindly as we can to those who are our fellow travelers on this transitory enterprise. Much of this is the old Stoicism, but none of its previous devotees, even Seneca or a more recent exponent, the eloquent, lame, ex-slave Epictetus (b. ca. 55–d. 135) from Asia Minor, had ever communicated the urgency and hardness of self-reliant moral and social effort in phrases that strike home so poignantly. True, Marcus Aurelius is a fatalist; much, he believes, is predestined and cannot be altered. Yet, all the same, much else *can* be altered and improved by the efforts of our own will—which we must summon up the discipline to use as it should be used. As the Stoics had always said, we have a share of the divine spark so that it is only natural and right for us to see each other as kinsfolk—as brothers and sisters who should treat each other decently, members of a single cosmopolis of which the Roman Empire, for all its imperfections, seemed to its ruler the most complete earthly expression.

Marcus Aurelius sought to reinforce these ideals with a rigorously ascetic attitude typical of the age that was now beginning. Nowhere can one find more relentless attacks on the "twitchings of appetite" that were all that the pleasures of eye, ear, food, and sex appeared to him to amount to. Moreover, as one hard year succeeded another, his spirit was tortured by ever more serious doubts about his own personal adequacy. All he could do was struggle on, fighting off moods of depression and battling against a sensitive distaste for disagreeable people and sights that made him more human than any other antique Stoic. Left far behind are the bright classical incentives to material achievement, the sunny sense of unlimited power. But in terms of humanly decent principles, translated scrupulously into a consistent way of living, Marcus Aurelius's creed was the culmination of ancient paganism and of Rome.

A Great Age of Lawyers

He had also done much to carry onwards the Golden Age of Roman Law ushered in earlier in the century by Hadrian. Marcus Aurelius's legal adviser, Quintus Cervidius Scaevola, was a popular consultant jurist who left extensive written works behind him. This practice of writing everything down was a fairly new practice among jurists, based on Greek rather than Roman custom. A high proportion of the lawyers of the day were easterners, and although Cervidius himself probably was not, many of the cases he describes come from provinces of the eastern empire.

Cervidius was also the teacher of the emperor Severus. In his reign this legal Golden Age developed a second phase that, although perhaps less abundantly creative than its predecessor, produced one of the most far-reaching of Rome's contributions to posterity, comprising the working out and writing down of existing principles over the entire field. The products of this vast enterprise offer extraordinary insights into the secrets of how the imperial machine worked. Moreover, Severus, following occasional earlier precedents, chose the greatest jurists of the day—some of the greatest of all time—as his praetorian prefects who were also entrusted with vital

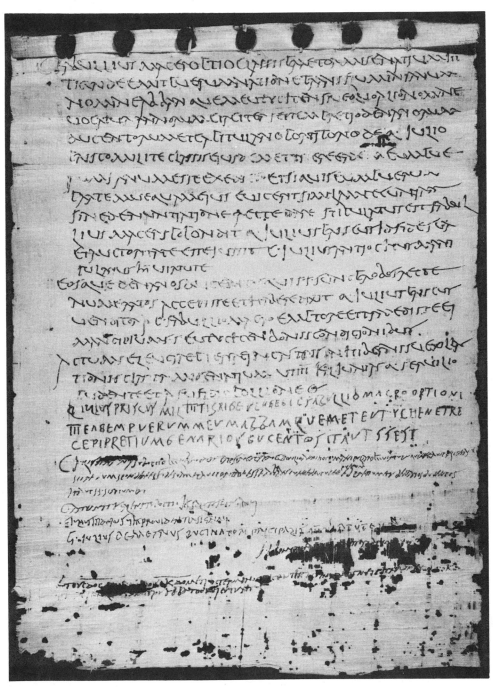

Papyrus recording the purchase of the seven-year old slave boy Abba or
Eutyches by Gaius Fabullius Macer of the navy, A.D. 166.

judicial functions, including both direct and appeal jurisdiction; and, in addition, they exercised a general control over the imperial finances.

One of them, Papinian, who was perhaps from Syria or north Africa, became praetorian prefect from A.D. 203 until 212, is the most famous name in all Roman jurisprudence. He never wrote a comprehensive treatise but compiled extensive collections and summaries of legal decisions. Independent, not averse to changing his mind, master of terse and exact Latin, he produced solutions which are original and closely reasoned and which give the fullest weight to considerations of equity and humaneness. And then Ulpian, who came from Tyre in Phoenicia, was joint prefect from 222 to 223. His massive works, destined to cover the whole range of the law, are businesslike and unaffected and superlatively clear; he displays an easy, reliable mastery of all this gigantic, complicated material. And another praetorian prefect of the time was Paulus. His writings, the most voluminous of all, include the *Opinions (Sententiae)*. The work that has come down to us under this name may be an anthology taken from a number of his books; and it also contains later interpolations. But Paulus, as far as we can judge, while falling short of Ulpian's lucid precision, excelled him in breadth, independence, and powers of penetrating argument.

Reconstruction of Baths of Caracalla (in foreground).

Reconstruction of Baths of Caracalla (interior).

When, three centuries later, Justinian's jurists summed up the achievements of Roman law, more than half the contents of this *Digest* came, directly or indirectly, from these three writers—Papinian, Ulpian, and Paulus.

The distinction between the legal treatment of one social class and another, the *honestiores* and *humiliores,* still continued and may even have been intensified. Yet in many other respects, paradoxically enough, these jurists displayed enlightened attitudes. Thus, while striving to maintain the fundamental institutions of Roman law—the family, private property, and sanctity of contracts—they also modified these concepts in a philanthropic and democratic direction, corresponding with a new sensitiveness for suffering, of which this age saw so much. Thus Ulpian proclaimed that all human beings are born free—so that slavery is unnatural. And there was an acceleration of already existing tendencies to protect the poor, weak, and defenseless.

However, this trend was not exclusively, or even primarily, humanitarian, but was directed towards the elimination of all possible causes of discontent or disloyalty that might prevent the maximum exploitation of all classes to serve the state and pay its enormous taxes. Indeed, this fiscal aim was expressly claimed by Caracalla when he published the most famous legal measure of antiquity, known as the *Constitutio Antoniniana* (212–13). With the exception (despite Ulpian) of slaves, it bestowed upon virtually the entire population of the empire the status of Roman citizens, which had hitherto been restricted to Italians and an elite minority of provincials. But the purpose of this measure was, in fact, to increase the numbers of those who had to pay the indirect dues on inheritance and slave emancipation— these being taxes that fell upon citizens of Rome. And the elevation of almost every free person to citizen rank was not, in fact, a very sensational development. The differentiation between citizens and noncitizens had become increasingly blurred for a century past, as the lawyers had recognized by their substitution of the altogether different distinction between the two main social classes. So the enactment of Caracalla, although dramatic in its finality, was not so much an epoch-making event in itself as a step in a gradual and already well-advanced process of standardization.

Standardization, once again, and a more concrete approach to genuine equality were apparent in a great spread of secondary education during this same third century A.D.

New Buildings and Portraits

And the same approach is illustrated by the amenities provided for the people of Rome, notably the stupendous baths that were inaugurated by Severus but bear the name of his son Caracalla who completed them. There were finally eleven such public baths in the pampered capital and smaller replicas and variants in almost every town of the empire. They displayed much ingenious multiplicity of function, being designed not only for luxurious bathing at various temperatures, but also for all the diverse social activities of an elaborate community center in which many people, belonging to a wide spectrum of social and economic classes, spent a substantial part of each day.

All the features that had appeared in thermal establishments of the earlier empire were to be seen on a massive scale in the Baths of Caracalla, enriched by every sort of novel elaboration. Surrounded by an enclosure containing gardens, open-air gymnasiums, and art collections, the main building was provided with vast unseen services of heating, water supply, and drainage, designed to deal with the needs of sixteen hundred bathers. The bathing accommodation included a circular domed hot room; and the central feature of the whole complex was a great cross-vaulted central hall or concourse containing a swimming pool. This hall, measuring one hundred and eighty-five by seventy-nine feet, is so large that men and women almost vanish inside its immensity; for all its services to human comfort, this is the architecture not of humanism but of a new age in which the individual is one of a mass. A new age, too, is heralded by the architectural style, since the load of the intersecting vaults, with their increased span and assurance, is carried not on a row of independent columns but on only four enormous piers dividing the hall into three bays—vaults and piers alike being constructed of the concrete that made these enormous, lightly soaring buildings possible.

Nor was third-century architecture the only art to display a strong move away from the traditional classicism; marked changes were apparent in portrait sculpture as well. This had long been one of Rome's outstanding achievements, and in these difficult times its practitioners rose to heights of originality and psychological skill they had never attained before.

Contrary to what is often believed, these developments started as early as the reign of Marcus Aurelius. His best-known busts, it is true, are as emptily classicizing as any of the less inspired products of the immediately preceding age of Antoninus. But a few of Marcus Aurelius's surviving heads are startlingly different and give us an almost violent impression of what the author of the harrowing *Meditations* was really like. And, by the same token, the reliefs on the Column of Aurelius at Rome show a different world from the Column of Trajan: a world in which wars are no longer military parades and triumphs, but, as Virgil had known long ago, scenes of horror and tragedy.

Under Commodus and Caracalla the portrait sculptors of the emperors take a rest from the seriousness of Marcus Aurelius's philosophy, instead providing richly baroque interpretations of these outrageous autocrats. But then, in the years of turbulence and desolation that followed, the artists returned to their search for the inner man and woman, with astonishing results. The clue to these triumphs is their departure from faithfulness to nature. Now that the classical world is on its way out, strict adherence to physical accuracy is subordinated to more intangible, nonnaturalistic processes of introspection. As in earlier times, it was the portraiture of the emperors themselves that directed the most original trends and attracted the finest talent, since the propaganda of these rulers demanded that their features, after suitable interpretation, should be made known to the world. But in the mid-third century the emperors were of a new type, tough soldiers, rugged and careworn. And it is evident that each successive ruler was very willing for his subjects to see him laden and afflicted with these cares and anxieties, which were endured on their behalf and enhanced by his artists almost to the point of dramatic caricature.

So these men provide a startling series of portraits, particularly during the ruinous years A.D. 235–68. Their faces are made to reflect, quite deliberately, the almost unbearable strain to which their vigilance to stave off disaster was subjecting them. The Danubian giant Maximinus I, for example, hated by the senators but a victorious commander of armies, is presented by his sculptor with imposing vividness; his close-cropped hair and beard, sketched with light, rapid, pointillist chisel strokes, reflect the illusionistic techniques of painting. The personality of Philip the Arabian, too, is revealed in a highly charged impressionistic study of his mobile, suspicious features and flickering brows. There is also a violently asymmetrical, nervously glaring Decius—the subject also of distinguished coin portraits—and the forehead of his successor Gallus is grotesquely furrowed.

A slight stiffening of features, a certain hardening of anatomy, and the simplifying of volume have begun to remodel and distort these faces into inorganic forms that correspond not to the human shape but to deeper movements within the soul and the universe. Some portraits emit an aura of intense feeling, almost as though they are representing the tormented visage of a medieval mystic. And tremendous play was made with the eyes, their irises and upward rolling pupils deeply incised with the sculptor's drill: they were seen as the mirrors of the soul, reflecting its inmost light—the doors by which the viewer could pass straight into the mind of the man or woman who is portrayed. This was an age in which the torments of practical

Gold bust of Marcus Aurelius from the
veteran colony of Aventicum (Avenches).

life were counterbalanced by an intense concentration on spirituality.

We are reminded of the greatest of these pagan spiritual revivals when we see the portrait busts of Gallienus, for they display a temporary regression from the military austerity of his predecessors, displaying him in the guise of a Hellenic philosopher. He was the friend and patron of Plotinus, the greatest philosopher the Roman Empire ever produced.

Plotinus, Mithras, and Mani

Born in A.D. 205, perhaps at Lycopolis in Upper Egypt, Plotinus studied philosophy for eleven years at Alexandria, and after joining an imperial expedition against the Persians settled in Rome as a teacher, remaining there, in touch with the cultivated court of Gallienus, until he eventually retired to Campania, where soon afterwards he died (ca. 269–70). His instruction took the form of seminars and discussions that he recorded in a series of essays written in Greek. They were primarily intended for the

Relief of beheading of German prisoners on Column of
Marcus Aurelius, ca. A.D. 180-93.

guidance of his students, one of whom, Porphyry of Tyre, collected and published them in six books known as the *Enneads,* from *ennea,* "nine," because this was the number of treatises in each book.

Plotinus saw the living universe as a complex, ordered structure that continuously and perpetually descends in an unbroken succession of stages from its transcendent First Principle. This principle, the single immaterial source of all existence and all values, pours itself out in an eternal downward rush of generation that brings into being all the different levels of the world as we know it, in a majestic, spontaneous surge of living forms. Yet this downward radiation has a reverse counterpart as well, for in the eternal dance of the universe there is always an upward impetus also, an upsurging towards identification and unification with the First Principle, the One.

The One, as Plotinus conceived it, is beyond thought or definition or language—the negation of number and movement and space and time. And yet in another sense, it is the very opposite of negation, for it is superabundant reality and goodness, absolute and pure. Plotinus's One has been said to be nearer than any other Greco-Roman philosopher's concept to the God of the Christians. Yet there is no great resemblance, all the same. This One is not, like the Christian God, a power that intervenes in earthly things since, although their creator, it remains wholly external to them and outside all the orders of being, "light above light." And its creative activity leaves it unchanged, just as the sun, too, engenders its own encircling illumination while staying undiminished itself.

Yet, remote though the One is, this incessant generation of which it is the agent insures that every level of the cosmos is intimately linked with every other. Above all, the structure of the One is repeated in the structure of human beings, and they all contain within themselves the potentiality of union with the One: their life, like the life of all the universe, is an upward yearning urge, an impulse to climb back to the summit and reunite themselves with the One. The whole philosophy of Plotinus seeks to animate our dulled sense of the supernatural and bring us back to our true nature and source.

The intermediaries in this contact between the One and the human body are Mind and, below it, Soul. Universal Mind is the timeless thought force and Soul the direction that emanates from it, but once again they are not only the divine working organisms of the universe as a whole but also present within each and every individual person. Lowly and degraded though our mortal bodies are—since Plotinus shared the increasingly widespread distaste for the corporeal that we have seen in Marcus Aurelius— the souls and minds of every man and woman provide steps by which they can rise to the heights.

Indeed, by so doing they can, though only on the rarest occasions, catch

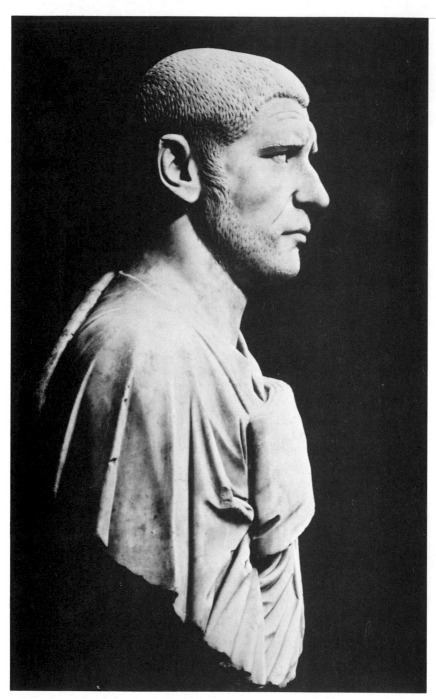

Philip the Arabian (A.D. 244-49).

Egyptian mummy-portrait, later second century A.D. Mummy portraits
of this sort were common in Egypt during this period.

Head of a Roman, ca. A.D. 240-50.

a supreme glimpse of the One itself and even reunite with it. They can achieve this by looking within themselves. Many earlier philosophers had spoken in praise of such contemplation. But it was Plotinus above all who saw it as the dynamic device for thinking away the limitations of body and space and time into nothingness, until we merge with the supreme reality itself. And he was confident that he himself had more than once, by harsh discipline, experienced this mystic union in which his personality became truly awakened to what it was.

He is the Western world's pioneer of those who have believed they can achieve such ineffable joyous reunion by intellectual discipline alone, without the need for religion or drugs. Many maintain today that such experiences do not, as he believed, genuinely apprehend something that lies outside, but are entirely inward happenings. Yet in any event Plotinus possessed the urgent, troubled need and power to communicate to others this "blessed fullness" and to endow it with a luminous, enchanting splendor that made all the political and economic disturbances of the day fade away into irrelevance.

Such, then, was one answer to the widespread, painful crisis of human identity throughout the vast and increasingly regimented and tormented Roman world. In this successful search for intimacy in a bottomless universe Plotinus presents paganism, during this final century of its prolonged supremacy, at its noblest. But he offers no likelihood that it could maintain itself, as Christianity was about to do, as a faith for all classes since his words were manifestly directed to an intellectual and spiritual elite.

Yet there was also another pagan belief, during this same epoch, that much more nearly competed with Christ for the control of the Western world. This was the cult of the Sun, which was revered by millions of the inhabitants of the Roman Empire; and its religion for a time even became the state worship. From the remotest periods of antiquity onwards, people had concluded from their observation of nature that they must greet the Sun's orb as a beneficent divinity; and their conviction was confirmed afresh each day as the god rose again. In due course, he played a part in many writings of the Greeks. He was identified with Apollo; Plato hailed him as the author of all light and life; and from the time of Alexander the Great and his successors the faith in his potency had spread throughout the Mediterranean world. Moreover, there was an ever-increasing tendency to explain the other traditional deities in terms of the Sun, in all but monotheistic fashion.

To Rome, the divinity of the Sun came very early on; and then, centuries afterwards, in the superb dome of Hadrian's Pantheon, the central opening, surrounded by starlike rosettes, represented the solar orb. Moreover, the cult of this deity offered flattering analogies to the imperial regime and its resplendent, sunlike leaders. Under Severus, whose wife Julia Domna came from Syria where reverence for the Sun was especially strong, its worship almost took command of the whole state religion. There was a brief interlude when their grandnephew Elagabalus (A.D. 218–22), to the alarm of conventional Romans, tried to bestow supremacy upon his own local Syrian version of Sun worship, which was accompanied by bizarre, outlandish trappings. But his failure did not delay the continued rise of solar beliefs in more acceptable forms, and the light-filled imagery of Plotinus reveals how deeply such ideas pervaded current thought. Before long, the emperor Aurelian established a massive temple of the Unconquerable Sun as the central and focal point of the entire religous system of the state (274). The birthday of the god was to be on December 25, and this, transformed into Christmas Day, was one of the heritages that Christianity owed to his cult.

For a time, at a critical juncture, the symbiosis of the two faiths was very close. Constantine the Great, in the years preceding his Christianization of the empire, and even later while this process was actually under way, concentrated all the resources of a vast bronze coinage upon the single design of the Sun god, accompanied by the inscription *To the Sun, the Unconquerable Companion* (SOLI INVICTO COMITI) (ca. 309). At this juncture, the Sun cult could well have become the religion of the Mediterranean area for an indefinite period ahead. But it did not do so, in the end, because such a divinity was too impersonal, too lacking in urgent human appeal. Devotees of the Sun themselves felt that this excessive remoteness failed to satisfy their needs, and a branch of the cult came into being in order to respond to such yearnings. It was the worship of an ancient Iranian deity, Mithras, who was god of the Morning Light, and from the first century A.D. onwards he was identified with the Sun himself. But unlike solar cult the ritual of Mithras always retained its private character. State approbation, it is true, was not lacking, but in marked contrast to the Sun's innumerable appearances on the official coinage, Mithras never appeared on the coins at all. Mithraism was not a court religion and had no public ceremonies or professional priestly class. It was personal—supplying the intimate element that the Sun faith lacked.

And its popularity increased at great speed, especially at the great cosmopolitan ports and trading centers of the West, where the worshippers at such shrines included numerous merchants. But it was above all the army, and particularly its officers, who accepted and diffused these beliefs. The Mithras of legend was a hero figure, unconquerable like the Sun himself, a superman for critical times—and he was also an ethical, austere model of conduct and the patron of truthful dealings and obligations, excellently suited to an age of rising asceticism, whose good faith, purity, and continence his worshipers must seek to emulate. Moreover, all the excitement inherent in initiations of an elect, which played such a prominent part in contemporary religion, was offered by the melodramatic form and staging of his rites.

The worship of Mithras, then, possessed ideas, moral urgency, and intimate emotional force. And its baptisms and sacrifices and communal meals offered resemblances to the rituals and sacraments of the Christians. Yet it was Christianity, instead, that won the day. The "biography" that was Mithras's holy book was unconvincing. Above all, it failed to persuade its readers that he had ever really appeared on this earth to provide help for human beings. Sculptors, it is true, displayed him as compassionate, yet his religion still was lacking in the tenderness and sympathy that alone could solace the poor for their misfortunes. Besides, Mithraism had no place for women; and it is they, as the cults of Isis and Cybele and Jesus made clear, who provided the largest numerical support for successful faiths.

Mithras, attending the Iranian Sun god in eternal opposition to his evil enemy, linked solar theology with the other outstanding pagan movement of the time, that of the Dualists, who believed in the conflict between good and evil powers contending with each other for the control of the universe. This belief goes back to very ancient times; to millions of people it has appeared the only possible explanation of what they see in the world with their own eyes. Evil manifestly exists. But how can this be so, if a benevolent and all-powerful God or gods created and controls the world? It seems a glaring contradiction; and many have therefore felt convinced that there must be *two* opposing forces, a good and an evil power, locked in a struggle that has so far, very manifestly, by no means come to an end.

The Athenian dramatists had been racked by the problem, and so were their philosophical compatriots. Then Persian ideas seeped into Greek and Roman lands, explaining the origin of evil in terms of the dualistic struggle. An enormous, fantastic variety of dualistic beliefs gradually arose, but through them all ran the conviction that the world, created by the evil power, has to be condemned and thrown off, and that men and women escape the imprisoning vileness of the body by purging what is nonspiritual within themselves. Since human souls are fragments of the vast luminous divine light beyond the sky, every person contains a spiritual element, too. But the spirit is incarcerated in the body, awaiting its freedom. And to teach how such liberation was to be achieved was the business of the Dualists, known as Gnostics from *gnosis,* "knowledge." This was the secret enlightenment they were able to impart to their initiates, who thus gained special privileges in this world but above all won that salvation in the world to come, which was the aim of all the leading religions of the day.

The culminating period of this Dualist movement started in about A.D. 240 when a young Persian named Mani began to preach, addressing great crowds at the national capital Ctesiphon and the large Greek city of Seleucia which lay on the opposite bank of the Tigris. A contemporary of Plotinus, Mani taught for thirty years, displaying lofty spiritual and artistic gifts and wide learning. His fundamental principle was this clash between good and evil, Light and Darkness. In the remote past of the universe, he declared, the Dark had encroached on the Light, and we are still suffering from that invasion, since Primal Man failed to repel it, and his failure and fall were what created our flawed world. Yet as life still pursues its dirty path, pronounced Mani, there is hope, for the dirt and Darkness is slowly being blotted out by Light; and once this process is completed a Savior will return (whom he identified with Jesus Christ, though this was not a Christian religion), and all will be Light once again. But meanwhile the human body, as other philosophers had reiterated, remains an encumbrance. The cosmic conflict could only be won by ascetic self-denial on the part of every human being, in hope of sloughing off this loathsome world.

Mani was an organizer of genius, and his aim was to found a religious community of his Manichaeans that would embrace the entire earth. In the end, he proved too radical for the Persians, whose kings, bowing to vigorous exponents of the traditional national religion, put him to death (ca. 274–77). Yet by then their empire was filled with his doctrine; and before another century was gone, it had permeated huge regions of the Roman world as well.

But the Roman government hated these Manichaeans for political reasons because it regarded their Persian origin as deeply suspect and potentially seditious; and so they suffered repression. And later, too, when the Christians made their bid to become the national religion of Rome, Manichaeanism found itself unable to stand up to them either. It was too passive and pacifist to offer really effective rivalry, and too ascetic and antisocial to form a powerful, cohesive church. Besides, the theological solution of the Manichaeans, for all its attractive features, ultimately failed to carry the day. Their story was epitomized in the career of Saint Augustine. As a young man he became one of them, because he was unable to accept the idea that God, who must be good, could ever have created evil. But after nine years he abandoned this Manichaean allegiance because he concluded that their division of the deity into two halves was hateful and shocking— and, in consequence, impossible to believe after all.

19

The Supreme State and Church

The New State of Diocletian

While these last manifestations of paganism were reaching their climax, the Roman Empire had become a very different place.

The first of the two great agents of change was a Dalmatian of humble origin, Diocletian. After rising to become commander of the imperial bodyguard, he successfully asserted his claim to the throne (284) and two years later appointed an old Danubian comrade Maximian as joint Augustus. Then, after some years of urgent frontier fighting, he converted this dual regime into a system based on four rulers instead, the tetrarchy. This he did by nominating two further Danubians as secondary emperors or Caesars: Galerius from Serdica (Sofia), who was to preside over parts of the East under his own ultimate control; and Constantius I from Naïssus (Niš), who was to rule over western areas under Maximian. The tetrarchs had four separate capitals, all endowed with magnificent buildings. For himself, Diocletian selected Nicomedia (Izmit) on the Sea of Marmara, a choice reflecting the increasing strategic importance of the Bosphorus Strait, while Galerius resided at Thessalonica (Salonica) in Macedonia. In the West, although the Senate remained at Rome, Maximian's court was at Mediolanum (Milan), and Constantius had his headquarters at Treviri —the former Augusta Trevirorum, now Trier, located at a crossing of the Moselle commanding the natural lines of communication between northern Gaul and the Rhineland. The great basilica and baths and city gate (Porta Nigra) of Treviri are still to be seen.

There had been partitions of the empire before, but this arrangement was more elaborate and thoroughgoing and was intended to be permanent. It was designed to fulfill military needs and to insure, in due course, an orderly series of collegiate imperial successions. Nevertheless, although the tetrarchy multiplied authority, it did not officially split it; the empire was still

an undivided unit. Legislation was in the name of all four men; the law of
one Augustus was the law of the other, and both Caesars were obliged to
obey them both.

Constantius and Diocletian put down rebellions in Britain (ca. 287–96)
and Egypt (293–94 and 297–98) respectively, and from 302 they campaigned
successfully across the Rhine and the Danube. And Diocletian and Galerius
also fought the Persians; they were defeated at first, but then Galerius
eventually won a victory of a completeness granted to few others in Roman
history, which he celebrated by the erection of an arch at Thessalonica. In

Silver head of Persian (Sassanian) king at about
the time of the war with Diocletian and Galerius.

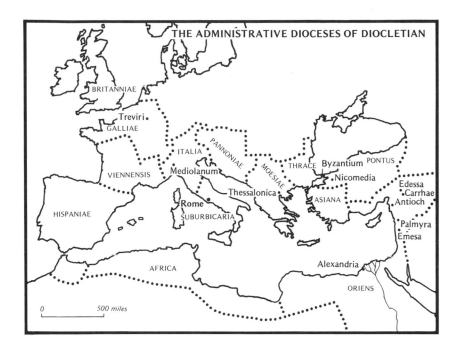

THE ADMINISTRATIVE DIOCESES OF DIOCLETIAN

305 Diocletian, whose health had become precarious, took the unprecedented step of abdicating from the throne and induced the reluctant Maximian to do the same. They retired into private life at Salonae (Split, in
Yugoslavia) and in Lucania (southwest Italy) respectively, and Constantius
I and Galerius became Augusti in their places.

Diocletian had left a remarkable heritage, for he was the greatest imperial
organizer since Augustus. One of his reforms was to raise the number of
provinces from fifty to a hundred; since their areas were now relatively
small, it was hoped that provincial governors would have little opportunity
to revolt—especially as their posts were now completely separated from
military commands. A further innovation was the grouping of the provinces
into thirteen major units or dioceses. These dioceses, which in some cases
pointed the way to national groupings of the future, were administered by
governors general, and they in turn depended on the four praetorian prefects (one attached to each ruler), who had now shed their military duties
and concentrated exclusively on the civil administration.

Another of Diocletian's tasks, undertaken with the help of his fellow
tetrarchs, was to overhaul the entire structure of the Roman army. Pursuing
his predecessors' interest in mobile formations, he created a new mounted
guard that consisted mainly of Germans. This guard, known as the *scholae*

palatinae after a portico in the palace where they awaited the imperial orders, was incorporated into one of the two major branches into which the entire army was now divided. This was the mobile field force; divided into four formations, one for each ruler, these *comitatenses* ("soldiers of the retinue") included a certain proportion of infantry, but cavalry was their particular strength. The second major division of Diocletian's army was the frontier force, stationed along the much strengthened border fortifications; in consequence these troops were later known as *limitanei* or *riparienses,* ("men of the frontier" or "men of the river banks"). This frontier army was recruited by systematic annual conscription among Roman citizens. But extensive use was also made of the warlike tastes and various specialist skills of barbarian tribesmen. These recruits included numerous Germans, as well as men from the highlands of Asia Minor. Diocletian also expanded the hitherto somewhat insignificant fleet.

The total military strength of the empire was now half a million or more, a good deal larger even than the expanded army of Severus a century earlier. These massive dimensions made it all the more necessary that the taxes needed to pay the soldiers should be duly gathered in. Throughout the previous half century, these exactions had caused the peoples of the empire immeasurable hardship. Diocletian did not, could not, lessen the burden. On the contrary, he increased it to the very utmost that manpower and food production and transport could bear. But at least he tried to insure that the levies were distributed fairly.

In particular, he issued an edict fixing maximum prices for all goods and transport costs, and maximum wages for all workers throughout the empire (301). It seemed to Diocletian that in order to bring in the taxes, and in order to fulfill another aim too, the reduction of the dishonesty of army contractors, a degree of confidence and stability had to be restored; and this could be done only by establishing stationary price levels. His edict on this subject, the most valuable of all ancient economic documents, was something quite new to the Roman Empire, though similar measures had occasionally been attempted in Greece. However, the tetrarchs neither owned nor controlled the means of production and consumption, and consequently they proved unable to enforce their orders. The result was that goods disappeared from the market; and so inflation resumed its inexorable course. In order to combat it, Diocletian and his colleagues had already made a determined attempt to issue a reformed, stable coinage (ca. 294), and it was in terms of this currency that the edict was framed. But he lacked the silver and gold needed to issue sufficient coins in these metals, so that the artificial relation he established between these and the token base metal issues proved untenable, and the price of commodities in terms of the latter continued to shoot up at an appalling rate.

But the emperors also made another attempt to lighten the miseries of the harassed taxpayers. What had afflicted them particularly gravely was the irregularity and suddenness of the demands that had descended upon them. To eliminate this unpredictable element, Diocletian and his colleagues placed the whole tax-collecting process on a novel, systematic, and regular basis. Henceforward, the sums and supplies required were no longer announced at varying, arbitrary intervals, but instead, a new and revised announcement was published every year. So although people might not be any better off, at least they knew where they stood. Individual Greek communities in the past had experimented with annual budgets; but this was the first time the idea had been applied on this massive empire-wide scale. The preparations of the budget were placed in the hands of the four praetorian prefects, who thus, in addition to their duties as supervisors of the governors general of the dioceses, retained the position of the principal finance ministers of the empire which their predecessors had occupied during the previous century.

The taxation system for which they now became responsible was still based overwhelmingly on agriculture, as in the past. But an effort was made to mitigate the unfairness of the old system in which variations between harvests and qualities of soil had been ignored. A new method of assessment was now worked out, according to which agricultural land was divided into units of measurement deliberately calculated to take varying crops and qualities and regions into account; and it was on this basis that the periodic censuses of empire were henceforward to be conducted.

However, this new arrangement was not as effective as it might have been, because of the many imponderables and complexities involved; and it also had a sinister side effect, for the scheme greatly advanced a process of which there had already been signs earlier, the compulsion of the populace to stay at work, on a hereditary basis, in the places where they were registered. Under Diocletian and his successors this principle was broadened to insure that the tenants of large estates did not escape such compulsions; and besides, it was also extended outside the agricultural field to include members of guilds or corporations, and government employees of every kind.

In order, then, to maintain the imperial defenses, a totalitarian state had been devised—theoretically almost as thoroughgoing as the police system advocated by Plato, though there was no practical likelihood that every coercion and prohibition thought out by the emperors and their jurists could ever be brought into effect.

All these measures of coercion were directed towards a more efficient mobilization of resources against internal rivals and foreign foes. Imperial publicity does not refer to the former peril directly since there was a tacit propaganda assumption that the Roman army could not be anything but loyal. But there was continual, increasing emphasis on the tetrarchs' role as triumphant defenders against their numerous external enemies. From now on, imperial coin propaganda concentrates remorselessly on this first and most imperative demand that the Roman people had to make of its rulers—victorious leadership and prowess. These personages, who alone stood between themselves and catastrophes even worse than those they were already undergoing, understandably seemed larger than other human beings. And this aggrandizement was reflected in imperial ceremonial that developed into a formidable pattern far removed from the early principate and closer in spirit to the contemporary Persian rival and foe.

Thus the mighty palace-fortress at Salonae (Split), to which Diocletian withdrew after his abdication, centered upon a grandiose Hall of Audience. Beneath the arch that surmounted its facade the retired, revered emperor made his public appearances as if framed by the vault of heaven; and as he paused, bejeweled and haloed, before entering and taking his throne in the shrinelike hall, and momentarily stopped again as he left, the assembled multitude accorded him homage as if he were the image of divinity itself.

Such, it was now felt, must be the treatment accorded to the men who represented the ancient, renowned, and now revived Roman state; and through them it was the state itself that was glorified. The most Roman and patriotic of all cults was the worship of Roma herself; and Diocletian, son

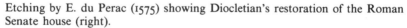

Etching by E. du Perac (1575) showing Diocletian's restoration of the Roman Senate house (right).

Gold medallion of Diocletian at his capital Nicomedia (ca. A.D. 294).
"To Jupiter the Preserver" (IOVI CONSERVATORI).

of the loyal Balkan provinces, gave even more massive and widespread publicity to this concept than any other ruler before him. When he reorganized the imperial coinage, he and his fellow rulers expressed this idea on the token pieces, made of bronze with a light coating of silver, that circulated throughout the empire. The slogan they chose for reduplication on all these millions of coins celebrated the Genius of the Roman People (GENIVS POPVLI ROMANI)—an antique idea personifying that particular principle, virile yet coming from a source beyond human eyes, which enabled the life of Rome and Romans to continue from generation to generation.

This principle seemed, above all, to be embodied in the emperors themselves. To describe them officially as gods, in these spiritually minded times, did not always seem suitable and decorous—and, besides, the multitude of past deified princes had downgraded this sort of symbolism. But there was also long precedent for describing the rulers instead as companions of a god; and it was in pursuance of this formula that Diocletian and Maximian pronounced Jupiter and Hercules to be their special personal companions and the patrons of their respective houses. The divinities they thus selected were above all else patriotic in their appeal; and in this monotheistic epoch that allowed most of the Olympians to fade into an amorphous amalgam, national propaganda concentrated its efforts upon deities, such as Jupiter and Hercules, who fulfilled the time-honored roles of protectors of the Roman leaders and their people.

The Growth of Christianity

This revival of paganism, on an even more emphatically national basis than before, was accompanied by violent persecutions of the faith that had become its principal competitor—Christianity. Moreover, as earlier, these official attacks corresponded with the wishes of a considerable section of the public. As the pagan cults were increasingly identified with patriotism, popular hatred of the supposedly unpatriotic Christians attained new and formidable dimensions.

Since the composition of the Gospels two hundred years earlier, the Christian community, though still only a small minority of the total population, had grown steadily. By A.D. 200, it had gained a sense of permanent identity by establishing the components of the New Testament, a canonical scripture that had eliminated a host of deviant writings and was refreshingly more manageable than the multitudinous, confusing holy books of other religions. Efforts had also been made to harmonize Christian doctrines with those of the ancient pagan philosophers, first by Justin of Neapolis in Samaria (d. 165/67), who represented the faith as summing up all that was best in antiquity, and subsequently at the Christian school of Clement of Alexandria (ca. 150–215). And then, in his compatriot and pupil Origen (d. 254–55) the church for the first time found a theologian who had thoroughly mastered Plato and other Greek thought and had received personal instruction from the head of a philosophical school—a teacher, incidentally, whom he shared with the pagan Plotinus. But at the same time, among more uncompromising Christians, there was also vigorous hostility to this whole classicizing, philosophical approach, for example, from the fierce north African Tertullian (ca. 160–228).

But while these and many other controversies flourished within the ranks of Christianity, its membership and structure were quietly expanding all the time. Origen saw the church as parallel to the empire, and it was indeed almost a state within a state. It was still, basically, an urban institution, for while its extension to rural areas in Africa and the East produced fanatical nonconformists such as Tertullian, the main strength of the Christian community lay in the lower and middle classes of the cities. And it was in the ancient city-states of Asia Minor, in particular, that the church most rapidly established vigorous nuclei, from which it could expand to other eastern territories. But Christian missionary activities had also, at a very early date, extended to the West as well, and in the third century the process accelerated. At Rome itself, for example, the numbers of Christians probably rose from about ten thousand in A.D. 200 to three or four times that total a century later.

As time went on, the local communities of the church had come under

the autocratic control of bishops. This growing importance of the episco-
pacy took power away from the local elders and, in the West, from the mass
of lay members as well. But it also made for much more efficient organization. The first of the important bishops in north Africa, Cyprian (d. 258),
whose see was Carthage, felt emboldened by this impressive system to boast
of the united, dynamic solidarity of Christians of every status and grade.
And despite all the doctrinal disputes within their ranks, his praise was
justified; for the church possessed a solidarity and a tightness of organization that were unrivaled in any contemporary religion. These qualities were
apparent in welfare measures that knew no social distinctions and displayed
a scope and range that left Jewish and Greco-Roman precedents—charities
and mutual assistance clubs—far behind. These beneficent arrangements,
with their financial basis solidly established in a bank, earned the reluctant
admiration even of pagans; and, later on, the emperor Julian the Apostate,
who hated Christianity, attributed its success to the effectiveness of its
philanthropic activities.

Yet the Christians, from an early date, had encountered opposition. The
Greek population of the East never liked them, any more than it liked the
Jews, because of their deliberate self-separation from the rest of the community, in which the followers of Jesus declared themselves to be mere stran-
gers and sojourners. As a result of this attitude, the Greeks remained largely
ignorant of their customs and in consequence made them the targets of
extraordinary accusations, including charges of obscenity and even of can-
nibalism.

Moreover, in the West, too, as Christianity gradually became better
known, the same sort of hostility towards its followers began to develop
among the inhabitants of the cities. And, before long, the same unfriendly
attitude spread to the Roman imperial administration as well. Indeed, when
the Roman government became able to distinguish the Christians from the
Jews, it liked the Jews rather better, for their religion at least was an
ancestral heritage, whereas no such excuse was available for the Christians.
Already in A.D. 64, under Nero, they were blamed for the Great Fire of
Rome. But that was a feeble charge, and in reality what was being held
against them, as Tacitus points out, was that they seemed to "hate the
human race." Nevertheless, that remained an exceptional occasion, for the
emperors were normally concerned to cool the temperature rather than heat
it; and for another century to come, they remained on the whole more
inclined to protect the Christians from the hostile public than to take the
initiative in convicting them of any crime. Trajan wrote instructions on the
subject to Pliny the Younger, governor of Bithynia. "They are not to be
hunted out," he ordered; "any who are accused and convicted should be

punished, with the proviso that if a man says he is not a Christian and makes it obvious by his actual conduct—namely by worshiping our gods—then, however suspect he may have been with regard to the past, he should gain pardon from his repentance."

Under Marcus Aurelius, however, the inhabitants of both Gaul and Asia Minor objected violently to the Christian communities in their midst, blaming the military, economic, and natural disasters of the time on their unpatriotic detachment from the common cause. Not long afterwards, Severus subjected them to the first coordinated, empire-wide sanctions, forbidding them to conduct missionary activities and imposing stringent penalties on converts. Tertullian, in retaliation, uttered open defiance against the government, declaring that no official position in the state ought to be held by any true Christian. Then there was a lull. But, before long, anti-Christian animosities began to intensify once again. In 235 Maximinus I, desiring to find scapegoats for crises and earthquakes, exiled rival Christian popes (bishops of Rome) to Sardinia and employed a new rigorousness in enforcing regulations against the sect, and particularly against its clergy. Then, as the imperial authorities became more and more desperately harassed by all their problems, the competent organization of the Christians, relatively few though they were, seemed more and more provoking, and Decius, hailed in a recently discovered inscription as "Restorer of the Cults," declared himself unable to countenance their refusal to join in communal corporate pagan observances. He therefore demanded of every Christian a single performance of the traditional religious rites; once that had been made, the local Sacrificial Commission handed out a Certificate of Sacrifice *(Libellus),* of which specimens have been found in Egypt.

The members of the church, being mainly city people, found it hard to escape notice and were dangerously vulnerable. Many, it is true, succeeded in evading the tests. But a considerable number of others, when subjected to this pressure, lapsed from their faith, at least for the time being. Others, however, who were called upon to sacrifice refused to do so and were put to death. Martyrdom had glorious Jewish precedents; and besides, Christians who underwent the ordeal felt they were imitating the sufferings of Christ himself and of Peter and Paul. Shrines of martyrs were established and revered, on the analogy of pagan heroes, and provided great encouragement to the faithful; in the words of Tertullian, "the blood of Christians is seed." And then the emperor Valerian, engulfed in an even graver military and financial situation than his predecessors, revived his anti-Christian plan and extended it to include large-scale confiscations of church property.

But his son Gallienus called a halt to this persecution, launching a policy of tolerance that lasted for forty years, during which the church established itself on an increasingly firm basis. This caused alarm to pagans such as

Plotinus's pupil Porphyry, whose work *Against the Christians* attacked them with unprecedented ferocity. And Porphyry's friends were among the instigators of the Great Persecution that now followed in A.D. 303. It was launched by Diocletian and, above all, by his Caesar Galerius, whose views on conformity were those of a military martinet. The motive of the persecutors was passionate enthusiasm for the old Roman religion and tradition and discipline, in the interests of imperial, patriotic unity. In consequence, as never before, the aim of these archregimenters was the total extirpation of Christianity. It was a struggle to the death between the one faith and the other, the old order and the new.

The first of Diocletian's edicts forbade all assemblies of Christians for purposes of worship and ordered the destruction of their churches and sacred books. Then two further edicts in the eastern provinces commanded that the clergy, unless they sacrificed to the gods of the state, should be placed under arrest. Next, a fourth proclamation extended this requirement to every member of the Christian church (304). And when, shortly afterwards, Diocletian abdicated his eastern throne in favor of Galerius, the suppression of recalcitrants was intensified still further. Bureaucracy and army joined forces to maintain these anti-Christian measures over a period of ten years, not so much in western Europe, where few casualties occurred, but throughout the eastern provinces and in Africa. And although there were apostasies once again, resistance was on the whole resolute and defiant; and perhaps three thousand martyrs died.

Constantine the Great

As soon as Diocletian had abdicated in 305, the regular, planned succession to the tetrarchy broke down in hopeless confusion, revealing that the system had no power to survive at all when no longer supported by his exceptional personality. Amid a welter of joint, competing occupants of the various palaces, Constantine I, son of the Danubian Constantius I, emerged to defeat Maxentius (the son of Maximian) in 312 at Rome's Milvian Bridge, thereby becoming sole emperor of the West; and in the following year Licinius gained unchallenged control of the East. Then in 323–24 Constantine won three great battles against Licinius and became the only ruler of the Roman world until his death in 337.

Constantine the Great was a man of impetuous and wide-ranging energy who felt utterly convinced of his duty to govern and change the world. Against a continuing background of exaction and inflation, he carried on the reforming activity of Diocletian over a very wide field, enlarging taxation and bureaucracy, tying more and more people to their jobs on a hereditary basis, and generally advancing the formidable process of regi-

Reconstruction of Milvian Bridge, Rome.

mentation in every way. Indeed, whereas Diocletian's plans had been conceived to meet a series of emergencies, Constantine's were intended for a
stable monarchy that would last for all time.

In particular, he continued to reorganize the army, which received ever-
increasing commemoration on his coins and medallions. Like Diocletian
before him, he greatly enlarged the proportion of Germans among the
troops since, after fighting successfully in their country himself, he appreciated their peculiar qualifications for tackling their own hostile compatriots across the borders. High favor, therefore, went to German generals
and other ranks as well. For example, the praetorian guard, which had
fought against Constantine on Maxentius's side, found itself abolished altogether, after an existence of nearly 350 years, and was replaced by the
largely German mounted guard *(scholae palatinae)* created by Diocletian.
Furthermore, many other Germans and Sarmatians, admitted inside the
empire as settlers, were drafted into elite cavalry and infantry units of the
new field army established by Diocletian. Thus the effectiveness of the field
corps as a central striking force and strategic reserve was substantially
increased; and it was placed under the command of a pair of newly created
officers, the Master of Horse and the Master of Foot. The frontier garrisons,
too, were rearranged and enlarged, and recruitment was enforced by severe
penalties that caused widespread terror.

With the same military needs in mind, Constantine confirmed his predecessors' conclusion that Rome was no longer a suitable capital for the
empire. An emperor who lived there was poorly placed to maintain control, at one and the same time, over the two vital imperial boundaries,
the Rhine-Danube line in the North and the Euphrates in the East.
Earlier rulers, feeling the same, had already from time to time established their residences at places more accessible to the frontier zones.
Mediolanum (Milan) was a favorite choice, and Constantine himself had
dwelt in a number of other centers, including Treviri (Trier), Arelate

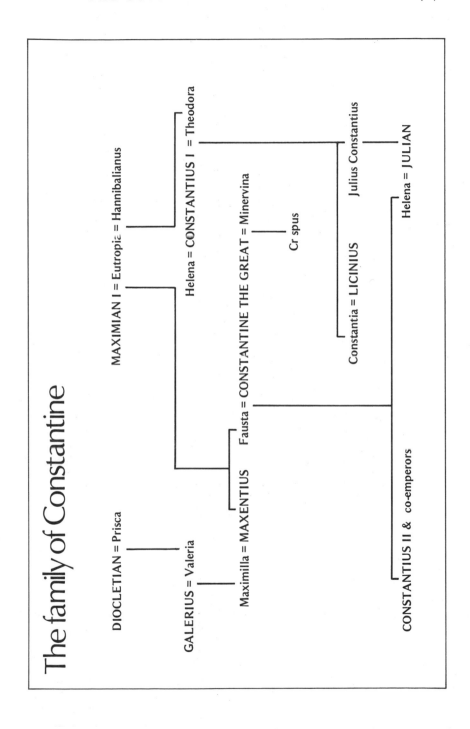

The family of Constantine

DIOCLETIAN = Prisca

GALERIUS = Valeria

Maximilla = MAXENTIUS

MAXIMIAN I = Eutropia = Hannibalianus

Fausta = CONSTANTINE THE GREAT = Minervina

Helena = CONSTANTIUS I = Theodora

Crispus

Constantia = LICINIUS   Julius Constantius

CONSTANTIUS II & co-emperors

Helena = JULIAN

(Arles), and Ticininum, (Pavia), as well as Sirmium (Sremska Mitrovica) and Serdica (Sofia) in his own native Balkans. But now he decided that the ideal site for simultaneous supervision of the Danube and Euphrates defenses was the city of Byzantium on the strategic Bosphorus Strait; and there he founded Constantinople, on the site where Istanbul is today (324–30).

Like Rome which formed its model, the new city was given a Forum and a Senate of its own, and its people received free distributions from the grain fleet that had served the ancient capital. It was true that Rome lost none of its privileges, and at first Constantinople and its senators ranked only second. Nevertheless, Constantine intended to make his new foundation the future metropolis of the empire; and this revolutionary decision set the

The Arch of Constantine.

Silvered bronze coin of Constantine the Great at
his new city Constantinopolis (CONST.), formerly Byzantium.
XP (Christos) on standard: "the National Hope" (SPES PVBLICA).

scene for the Middle Ages—and for the eventual supersession of Latin by
Greek as the official language of the state.

Constantine also carried through a second and even more far-reaching
and fateful revolution. This was the conversion of the empire from paganism to Christianity. The persecutions initiated by Diocletian and Galerius
had not achieved their aim; and as they ran their course, it became clear
that the pagan community regarded the whole campaign as exaggerated,
disliking the Christians rather less than they disliked the tyrannical government. And so Galerius, during his terminal illness, had issued, in conjunction with Constantine and Licinius, the Edict of Serdica granting freedom
of worship to all members of the Christian faith (311). In other words, this
was the first time that they were granted a measure of legal recognition,
although it was delayed in the East for two years because Galerius's successor Maximus II Daia (defeated by Licinius) refused to concur.

Meanwhile, in the West, Constantine's victory at the Milvian Bridge (312)
was won, as he later asserted, under the auspices of the Cross, and in the
following year he and Licinius, who had meanwhile defeated Maximinus,
echoed Galerius's pronouncement of tolerance towards the Christians in the
Edict of Mediolanum (Milan). Constantine always felt a strong, impulsive
need for a divine companion and sponsor. For a time the Sun god, whose
worship was ancestral in his family, had been his choice. But although this
deity continued to be depicted on the coins until 318–19, Constantine had
already disclosed, at the time of the Edict of Mediolanum, his own personal
adherence to Christianity; and the One Supreme Power, to whom the
literature and inscriptions of the time made numerous vague allusions, was
identified, more and more explicitly, with Jesus.

And so Constantine, speaking of "the most lawful and most holy" religion of Christ, initiated over a period of years a series of measures openly favoring its adherents. Christian priests, other than those of dissident sects, were exempted from municipal obligations, and imperial funds were sent to subsidize churches in the provinces. At Rome, the bishop, or pope, was lodged in the Lateran palace, and the church borrowed imposing features from the court ceremonial and was granted its own jurisdiction. Church and state were to be run in double harness. However, as the emperor became increasingly conscious of his own sacred mission, the successive councils of Arelate (Arles) (314) and Nicaea (Iznik) (325) showed that it was he who was the master. At Nicaea, he attended the council meetings himself, and in the intervals between the sessions he went down among the bishops and joked with them in bad Greek.

And yet, at the time when Constantine raised the Christian community to these lofty heights, its position throughout the empire had been relatively insignificant; the church had lacked political and social and economic power alike. Its elevation, therefore, to become the ruling section of the empire was one of the most surprising phenomena in Roman history. The emperor's motives have been endlessly analyzed and discussed. But it appears that he and his advisers experienced a growing conviction that, however uninfluential the Christians might be at present, the course of events was working, or could be made to work, in their favor—since they alone possessed the universal aims and efficient, coherent organization that, in the long run, could unite the various conflicting peoples and classes of the empire in a single, all-embracing harmony which was "Catholic," that is to say, universal. It was in this belief that he launched his ecumenical missionary drive and, as time went on, became increasingly intolerant of other faiths.

So Constantine's Christianization of the empire, though it still bears the appearance of a strangely bold and unexpected step, was based on far-reaching statesmanlike calculations. Nevertheless it would be mistaken to regard Constantine's personal conversion as coldly calculating and nothing else. On the contrary, he was a profoundly religious and emotional man. But why did he choose the Christian religion—and not, for example, the Sun worship to which he had been earlier devoted? The reason was that he felt a powerful need for a personal savior; and in this the cult of the Sun was deficient. Mithraism, it is true, attempted to fill the gap. But its key figure lacked one indispensable feature. Mithras, like other pagan saviors, was never thought to have actually appeared on earth and taken part in the history of humankind. But Jesus was believed to have done just this and to have intervened to save all men and women, in the most dramatic and moving way possible. That made him by far the most satisfying savior of all; and it explains why Christianity won the struggle over the minds and hearts of Constantine and his subjects. The paintings in the catacombs, and reliefs and other works of art of the period, demonstrate the point clearly —for it is in his role as Savior and as worker of the miracles that brought and symbolized salvation that they chose to portray him.

Bronze coin of Philip the Arabian (A.D. 244-49) of Apamea (Dinar) in Phyrgia, depicting Noah's Ark, which some believed to have come to land nearby.

Jewish sarcophagus from Vigna Rondanini Catacomb with Menorah (seven-branched candlestick).

But it may still, perhaps, be wondered why the religion that succeeded paganism as the dominant faith of the Western world was Christianity and not Judaism. Judaism, too, had such a great deal to offer, and it had recovered very effectively from the consequences of the Second Revolt (A.D. 132–53), attaining great solidity once again in the third century A.D. And besides, the two faiths, parent and offspring, possessed so much in common. They both, unlike the pagan cults, offered a philosophy as well as a cult; and more than ninety percent of Christian ethics had already appeared in the Jewish scriptures. Moreover, the social and philanthropic services of the two religions were once again comparable, though the centralized arrangements of Christian bishoprics were more efficient than the local efforts of individual Jewish communities and presbyteries. The Christians also excelled in their presentation of a truly universal charity, compassion, and consolation, embracing even the sinners and the destitute. True, all these features are also found in certain areas of Jewish theology and social thinking. But they are presented more vividly in the books of the New Testament. Yet above all, it was for another reason, with which we are now familiar, that they prevailed over Constantine, and then the Roman world: because of the Christians' Savior, and his personal intervention upon the earth. This was a feature that the Jews, like the Sun worshippers and Mithraists, could not offer.

Constantine himself did not treat the Jews too badly, but the Christian rulers of the next generation regarded them with noticeably less tolerance. The Jews must be allowed to exist because Jesus had been one of them; yet their lives should be made miserable because they had killed him. And nonconformist Christians, belonging to sects that would not follow the official line, ran into trouble as well. In the words of Constantine's spokesman Eusebius, the first ecclesiastic historian, nothing was so infuriating to God as divisions in the church—they were like cutting the body of Christ into pieces.

Constantine himself was baptized at the very end of his life, after postponing this step, like many of his co-religionists, until his deathbed when he could sin no more. By that time, the Christian revolution throughout the empire was well advanced. His conversion, which had prompted it, was seen by Petrarch in the fourteenth century as the great dividing line between antiquity and the ages that lay ahead; and, indeed, he had brought a whole new world into being. Constantine himself was profoundly aware of the vastness and holiness of this task: he saw himself as the thirteenth apostle of Jesus and God's Messianic regent upon earth.

It is in this guise that he is displayed in a colossal marble head that stands in the courtyard of the Palazzo dei Conservatori on Rome's Capitoline Hill.

Constantine the Great.

Here is the man at whose court, resplendent and hieratic, men spoke in hushed tones of his "Divine Face" and "Sacred Countenance." The sculptor has conceived this countenance as a holy mask, a cult object foreshadowing the icons of the coming Byzantine Empire: an overpowering image animated with the presence of God and empowered to repel the demons lurking in every pagan idol. The head is nine feet high and weighs nine tons. It formed part of a huge seated statue, of which the wooden body and glittering robe of gilded bronze have not survived.

This vast figure, reducing ordinary individuals to nothingness beside its hugeness, stood in one of the apses of the Basilica Nova. This was a secular building, the heir to the old market basilicas—social, judicial, and commercial meeting places beside the Forum. Yet it was a basilica with a difference. Constructed mainly by Maxentius, after whom it is often named, it was

The Basilica Nova at Rome constructed by Maxentius and
Constantine the Great.

altered by Constantine who changed the principal orientation from the long
to the short axis. The Basilica Nova was based on the bold idea of isolating
the central cross-vaulted hall familiar in Roman baths and converting it into
an independent structure. It consisted of only three bays, separated by huge
internal piers, after the fashion of the bath halls of Caracalla and Diocletian.
The lofty nave and aisles, lit by huge half-circular windows anticipating the
Romanesque cathedrals of the future, were no longer roofed by flat ceilings
like the old market basilicas, but surmounted, like the halls of the baths,
by great curving, intersecting barrel vaults. The Basilica Nova, of which
three lofty spans remain today, represented the climax of Rome's greatest
architectural achievement: its discovery how to exploit the significance of
interior space.

But the future lay with another sort of basilica, not secular but ecclesiastical. Constantine's religious transformation stimulated the greatest architects of the day to serve the requirements of the new national faith; and these magnificent successors of the humble house-churches of the past were their major creations. Like the Basilica Nova, they were rectangular and longitudinal. But, in contrast to that building, they contained side aisles separated from the loftier nave, not by a few massive piers carrying rounded arches, but by long rows of columns supporting flat architraves. And flat, too, was the ceiling that surmounted this central nave, since cross vaults like those of the Basilica Nova would have distracted the essential concentration of Christian churches on drawing the eye towards the East. The great

Bronze medallion with heads of St. Peter and St. Paul.
Later third century (?) A.D.

colonnades created a single irresistible tide of nave and aisles flowing onwards towards the cross on the canopied altar, and to the apse that rose skywards beyond, enshrining the throne of the bishop, the representative of God. This culminating point of the Christian basilica was glimpsed from afar by those who entered the building from the west and saw the rays of the rising sun pouring through the windows of the apse upon the celebrant who stood facing his congregation. In the rest of the building there was holy penumbra, in which gilt mosaics and bejeweled objects lavishly glistened.

Little can be seen of Constantine's basilica churches today, since they were demolished by later generations in favor of the monuments they themselves were eager to erect upon the same sacred sites. Yet his grandiose basilicas, in their day, added up to the greatest architectural accomplishment of any single man in Roman history. At his new foundation of Constantinople, he founded the Church of the Holy Wisdom (Santa Sophia), later replaced by Justinian's even mightier building. At Rome too, which retained enormous spiritual importance as the burial place of the martyred Peter and Paul, there was the Basilica of St. Peter (ca. 333–37), lit by sixteen great windows and flanked by massive transepts. And, before St. Peter's, Constantine had already built, alongside the Lateran palace which was the residence of the popes, the church that was called after himself, the Basilica Constantiniana, which later bore the name of St. John Lateran instead and became the cathedral of the city.

Beside it was erected a centralized octagonal baptistery, which became the prototype of many others and has survived today. And Constantine built much larger centralized churches as well, which, like his basilicas, represented a major architectural revolution—and, like them again, have suffered the fate of total disappearance. They included the cross-shaped Holy Apostles at Constantinople and the palace church of the Golden Octagon at Antioch, dedicated to Harmony—the divine power that creates unity within the empire, the Christian community, and the universe. In Palestine, too, there were great Constantinian buildings. The Holy Sepulchre at Jerusalem combined both the longitudinal and centralized formulas, since it was a rectangular basilica built to enclose a circular martyr's shrine.

The Successors of Constantine

Constantine was determined to achieve hereditary succession to his throne, but his endeavors to arrange this were less successful than anything else he attempted. In 326, on reports of a plot, he ordered the execution of his wife and his eldest son by an earlier marriage. Then he groomed for the succession the three boys who remained to him, together with the two sons

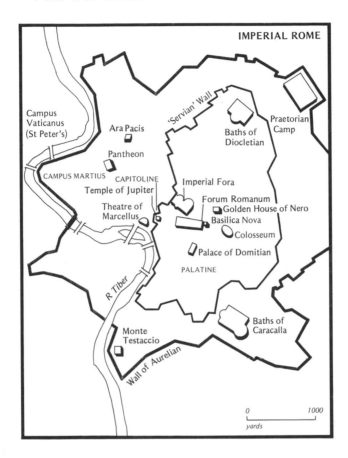

IMPERIAL ROME

Campus Vaticanus (St Peter's)

Ara Pacis

Pantheon

CAMPUS MARTIUS   CAPITOLINE

Temple of Jupiter

Theatre of Marcellus

'Servian' Wall

Baths of Diocletian

Praetorian Camp

Imperial Fora

Forum Romanum

Golden House of Nero

Basilica Nova

Colosseum

Palace of Domitian

PALATINE

R Tiber

Monte Testaccio

Baths of Caracalla

Wall of Aurelian

0   1000

yards

of a half brother. Within thirteen years after his death, however, all these five had been eliminated, except one, who was Constantius II.

While prodigious monetary inflation and taxation continued within the empire, Constantius fought against Persia and then turned to the West to put down usurpers. Meanwhile he was converting Constantine's establishment of Christianity into a lasting reality. He himself, however, belonged to the Arian sect, regarding Christ, being the Son, as younger than God and inferior. Under Athanasius, bishop of Alexandria, five times exiled, this sect was overtaken by Catholicism and Constantius's attempts to grapple with the theological disputes that were splitting the state apart bore no fruit. He appointed his cousin Constantius Gallus to be his Caesar and presumptive heir, residing at Antioch; but in 354, on suspicions of disloyalty, he recalled Gallus and put him to death. Then he appointed a new Caesar, the dead man's half brother Julian, who won an important series of campaigns against the Germans and restored the Rhine frontier. Thereupon his troops proclaimed him emperor, and conflict with Constantius II was inevitable; but before the clash came, the emperor died (361), and Julian succeeded in his place.

He had reacted strongly against his Christian background and is known as the Apostate because he abandoned the faith altogether. He noted that his Constantinian relatives, steeped in crime, had failed to practice what they preached, and he spoke for the financially depressed gentry of the ancient Greek towns of Asia Minor, who felt a distaste for the glaring affluence of the court and despised its intellectual confusions as uncultured. Instead, Julian in his youth had derived from men of learning, including his tutor and a well-known philosopher of the day, a passion for classical literature and the deities of the pagans; and these admirations emerge strongly from his surviving speeches, essays, and letters, in which he manipulates the Greek language of his day with confidence and skill.

When he came to the throne, he openly professed adherence to the beliefs of the pagans and reinstituted their cults, endowing them with substantial grants in aid and an organization intended to compete with the Christians. He also proclaimed general toleration of all religions. However, not only was the Christian church deprived of its financial privileges, but in the religious disorders that followed its members were penalized more severely than the pagans. A particularly controversial measure forbade them to teach in the schools. To strike a further blow against their faith, Julian offered encouragement to the Jews, whose lot had become worse under the Christian regime; and he even planned to allow the reconstruction of the Temple at Jerusalem, destroyed nearly three centuries earlier. Another

Silvered bronze coin of Julian the Apostate (A.D. 361-63) at Sirmium (Sremska Mitrovica in Yugoslavia). The bull symbolizes leadership: "The Safety of the State" (SECVRITAS REIPVBLICAE).

reason for this move may have been a desire to protect the rear of his army from Palestinian revolts during forthcoming eastern campaigns. But owing to the absence of any real enthusiasm on the part of either Julian or the rabbis, who were content with their teaching centers in the synagogues, this plan to elevate the Jews at the expense of Christianity came to nothing.

And the same, indeed, was true of the whole of his angry anti-Christian campaign. He believed he possessed a divine mission to heal a sick society. But his character, a curious blend of opportunism and preciosity, was alien from any diplomatic compromise; and he was too deeply imbued with classical traditions to reach out and understand the common man of his day. His Canute-like attempt to roll back the Christian tide was too anachronistic to prevail.

In other directions he succeeded better, for he was a hard-working and conscientious administrator. He did what he could to revive the declining fortunes of the city-states in the eastern part of the empire—the communities from which much of his political support was derived. He temporarily cured the raging monetary inflation by placing an extensive gold coinage in circulation. And above all, he made a courageous attempt to cut down the ever-growing and all-encroaching imperial bureaucracy.

But his major ambition was to deal drastically with the Persians, who had become menacing once again during his predecessor's reign. After elaborate preparations, Julian marched eastwards, in one of the most determined invasions of Persian territory for centuries, and won a victory (365). But his column was constantly harassed by the enemy, and in one of these skirmishes in the Zagros foothills, he received a wound from which he died. His successor, a Danubian officer named Jovian (363–64), reversed both his principal policies, negotiating an unpopular peace with the Persians and restoring Christianity—of which he was a pious adherent—as the religion of the empire.

IX. THE TRANSFORMATION OF EUROPE

Preceding page:
View of Ancient Rome by Samuel Palmer.

20

The Fall of
the Western Empire

Valentinian I and Theodosius I

In A.D. 364 the army acclaimed Valentinian I, another Danubian, as emperor; and he was the last impressive ruler the western empire had. Valentinian was tall and vigorous, with fair hair and gray blue eyes, and although his opponents sneered at him as a man of barbarous origins, he had received a thorough education. Although jealous, cruel, and easily angered and frightened, and often at sea in his judgment of civilian officials, he was a fine soldier and an energetic organizer. He disliked the Roman aristocracy and felt an unusually strong sense of duty towards the poor. More unusual still, he tolerated differences of religious opinion.

Concluding that in the interests of national defense there should be a second emperor beside himself, Valentinian gave the East to his brother Valens, who took up his residence at Constantinople. He himself kept the West, ruling at Mediolanum though the Senate still remained at Rome. His treasury was impoverished by the division since revenue from the richer eastern provinces ceased to flow in. Nevertheless, at his death eleven years later he left the western empire stronger than ever; no one could have believed that it would shortly be entering upon the final phase of its long life.

Valentinian achieved this excellent result by dealing vigilantly with a host of successive emergencies. First, the Germans had burst across the Rhine, seizing the fortress of Moguntiacum (Mainz). But the emperor defeated them three times and then marched up the Neckar valley and won a major victory in the Black Forest. Remaining in the north for seven years, he constructed a complex new system of defenses and weakened his enemies by deliberately stirring up dissensions between one tribal group and another Meanwhile, numerous Germans continued to be admitted as settlers within the western frontiers. In 374–75 Valentinian repelled and avenged another great incursion of Germans across the middle and upper Danube.

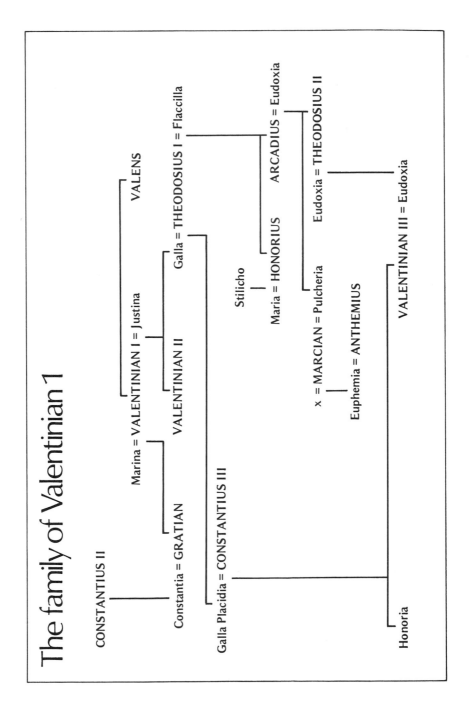

The family of Valentinian 1

Silver dish *(missorium)* showing Valentinian I with his army.

Not long afterwards, however, while listening to the insolent words of German envoys, he burst a blood vessel and died, leaving his throne to his sixteen-year-old son Gratian.

Three years later the other, eastern, Roman empire suffered a setback of unprecedented gravity. Beyond its borders, two great German states had taken shape, the Ostrogoths ("bright Goths") in the Ukraine, and the Visigoths ("wise Goths") based upon what is now Rumanian territory. But a non-German people living further away, the Huns, had burst through into the lands of these two peoples in about A.D. 370. The Ostrogothic state crumbled before the onslaught of their formidable cavalry, and two hundred thousand Visigoths, too, were driven by the Hunnish invaders across the Danube into the eastern Roman empire, where its authorities permitted

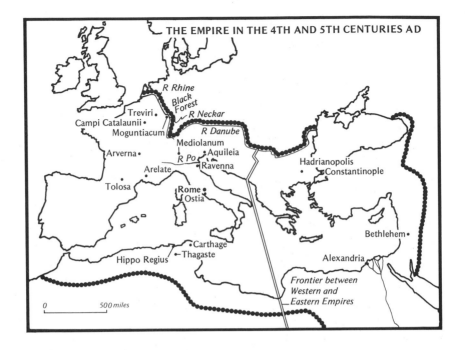

THE EMPIRE IN THE 4TH AND 5TH CENTURIES AD

R Rhine
Black Forest
Treviri
Campi Catalaunii
Moguntiacum
R Neckar
R Danube
Arverna
Mediolanum
R Po
Aquileia
Arelate
Ravenna
Tolosa
Rome
Ostia
Hadrianopolis
Constantinople
Bethlehem
Carthage
Thagaste
Hippo Regius
Alexandria
Frontier between Western and Eastern Empires
0   500 miles

them to settle. Incensed, however, by their unjust treatment at the hands of these functionaries, the Visigothic chieftain Fritigern broke into revolt and ravaged the Balkans, while other northerners forced their way across the Danube in their wake (376). Valens marched rapidly from Asia to deal with the crisis and passed to the attack at Hadrianopolis (Edirne, Adrianople) in Thrace. But the Visigothic cavalry drove off the horsemen of the Romans, and the imperial infantry fell almost to a man. Valens himself perished; and his corpse disappeared without a trace.

His nephew Gratian, emperor in the West, had failed to reach the scene in time to help him. And now he appointed, to succeed Valens at Constantinople, a new colleague Theodosius I, the thirty-two-year-old son of a Spanish landowner and general. For the next decade Theodosius ruled the eastern empire and added to it by inducing his western counterparts to cede the greater part of the Balkan peninsula. Then, putting down two usurpers in the West, he momentarily reunited the two imperial thrones before his death in 395. Theodosius was blond and elegant and eager to please, but greedy, extravagant, and unreliable, veering from brutal judicial sentences to quick pardons, and from frenzied activity to idleness. He became known as "the Great" because of his insistence on rigorous Christian orthodoxy.

This was one of the main features of his reign; the other was the acceptance, despite the disaster at Hadrianopolis, of a mass of Visigoth settlers within the imperial borders (382). There they could live under their own rulers but must supply soldiers and agricultural workers for the Romans—the first of a series of German nations on which this allied, "federate" status was conferred.

The Frontiers Broken

After Theodosius's death the empire was once again divided, and this time the division became permanent. The East went to his eighteen-year-old-son Arcadius (395–408), and the western throne at Mediolanum to his younger son, Honorius, aged eleven (395–423). Both boys, as they grew older, turned out to be unintelligent and incompetent, and the task of ruling the two empires fell to their regents. The effective ruler of the West was Stilicho, half Roman and half German, who was married to Honorius's cousin. Although he was a general of unusual brilliance and vigor, Stilicho's career, which might have saved the West for a time, was darkened by two clouds. The first was his hostility to the eastern empire, where he arranged that his counterpart as the guardian of its young emperor, Rufinus, should be assassinated. The second flaw in Stilicho's reputation was his unwillingness to deal firmly enough with the Visigoths' new ruler Alaric, a chieftain whose ability won him special and quasi-royal prestige. Alaric had shown his aggressive intentions by a series of invasions deep into Italy itself (401–3) —events that induced the timid Honorius to move his capital from Mediolanum to the Adriatic coastal town of Ravenna, which was protected by marshes from the land side and provided an escape route by sea. Yet Stilicho, instead of resolutely proceeding against Alaric, preferred to keep him sound and strong as a counterpoise to the eastern Roman state. And indeed in 405, after destroying an Ostrogothic invasion under Radagaisus at Faesulae (Fiesole), Stilicho developed plans for military action against the eastern government.

But on December 31 of the following year his designs were interrupted by the gravest and most fateful of all the German invasions of the West. On that day a mixed army of men from a number of different tribal groups—Vandals, Suevi, Alans, Burgundians—crossed the ice on the frozen Rhine and, sweeping aside half-hearted resistance, plundered Moguntiacum (Mainz) and Treviri (Trier) and many other border towns. Next the invaders fanned out into Gaul beyond, continuing to ravage wherever they went and marching on throughout the entire country as far as the Pyrenees. With only a few exceptions, of which Tolosa (Toulouse) was one, the Gallic cities did not put up a fight. It

Stilicho (d. A.D. 408) on ivory diptych.

proved a decisive breakthrough because the Rhine barrier could never again be repaired.

Stilicho did nothing effective to block the invaders, at first because he was still preoccupied with his plans for invading the East, and then because the shock waves of the German onslaught threw up several usurpers in the Roman armies that were supposed to repel them. One of these men crossed over to the continent from Britain, which henceforward, denuded of troops, passed gradually into the hands of Saxon immigrants who had been allowed to settle in the country. Stilicho was under heavy pressure from the Visigoths, whose leader Alaric insisted that he should be given four thousand pounds of gold from the western imperial treasury. Stilicho compelled his reluctant Senate to agree, but soon afterwards found himself accused of plotting in collusion with Alaric to place his own son on the throne. Although this may not have been true, a mutiny was fomented against him at Ticinum and his supporters were massacred. He himself went to the emperor at Ravenna; but Honorius had him put to death (408). For half a century to come, no German was to follow in his footsteps as commander in chief in the West. But, meanwhile, as the immediate sequel of his death, the Roman troops began to slaughter the families of their federate German fellow soldiers, who, in consequence, went over to the Visigoths.

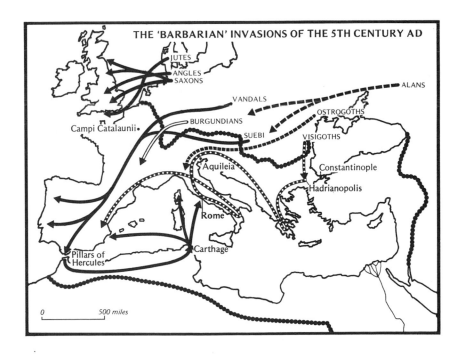

THE 'BARBARIAN' INVASIONS OF THE 5TH CENTURY AD

JUTES
ANGLES
SAXONS
VANDALS
ALANS
OSTROGOTHS
BURGUNDIANS
Campi Catalaunii
SUEBI
VISIGOTHS
Aquileia
Constantinople
Hadrianopolis
Rome
Carthage
Pillars of Hercules

0   500 miles

Gold medallion of Priscus Attalus (A.D. 409-10, 414-16), puppet of Alaric and Ataulf, at Rome which is "unconquerable and eternal" (INVICTA ROMA AETERNA).

Their leader Alaric, cut off from the helpful contacts that Stilicho had maintained with him, went on demanding money and land and, when his demands were rejected, he marched in three successive years right up to the outskirts of Rome. On the first occasion he was appeased by large payments; on the second he set up a puppet emperor, Priscus Attalus, within the walls; and when he arrived for the third time, the gates were treacherously opened to admit him. Thereupon his army moved in and occupied the city, which had not been taken by a foreign foe for nearly eight hundred years. Its capture by Alaric horrified the entire Roman world; yet although much wealth was plundered and fires were started in various areas, the number of buildings that were burned down was not very great. The Visigoths stayed in Rome for only three days.

After that, taking the emperor's half sister Placidia with him, Alaric departed and moved on towards the south of Italy, planning an invasion of north Africa. But he turned back and died, and was buried deep in the bed of an Italian river so that his body should never be found and subjected to impious treatment.

The dominant Roman military leader of the next decade was Constantius III, a long-necked, broad-headed general from Naïssus. In the year after Alaric's sack of Rome, Constantius courageously took the initiative. First, he put down no fewer than three rival claimants to the throne and established himself at the capital of one of them, Arelate, which now replaced devastated Treviri as the principal city of the western provinces. Next, in 413, Constantius granted one of the invading

German tribes, the Burgundians, the status of allies and federates and allowed them to live on the west bank of the middle reaches of the Rhine.

Meanwhile, however, the Visigoth Ataulf, brother-in-law and successor of Alaric, had moved his people out of Italy and settled them in the fertile lands of southwest Gaul. To prove his good intentions towards the empire, he married Honorius's half sister Placidia whom his predecessor had abducted from the city. But Honorius withheld his agreement to the marriage, and Constantius forced Ataulf to withdraw into Spain, where he was killed at Barcino (Barcelona) (415). Then his brother Wallia, after he returned Placidia to the Romans, was permitted to take his Visigoths back to southwestern Gaul, where they were granted federate status, with Tolosa as their capital (418). Honorius also proclaimed the delegation of his authority in Gaul to a regional administration at Arelate in which Romans and Visigoths were intended to collaborate. But the scheme never really got off the ground.

Constantius had married Placidia in the previous year—against her will, though she provided him with a son. His position was now very powerful; and early in 421, Honorius proclaimed him joint emperor of the West. However, the eastern rulers refused to recognize this unilateral appointment. This greatly angered Constantius III; but he had no opportunity to challenge them since, after a reign of only seven months, he died. Had he lived, he would have continued to provide vigorous administration. But he could never have been on good terms with Constantinople, so that it is doubtful whether his survival would have reversed the gathering process of western decline.

A quarrel now broke out between Honorius and Placidia, who sought refuge at the eastern capital, accompanied by her four-year-old son Valentinian III. But when Honorius died of dropsy in 423, an eastern army helped her to return to Italy and defeat a usurper, and the child became emperor in the West (425–55). During the first years of his titular rule, Placidia exercised autocratic control. But there was also another striking figure to be reckoned with, Aetius, a Danubian from Durostorum (Derster or Silistria in Bulgaria). As a young man he had been a hostage in the hands first of the Visigoths and then of the Huns, experiences that had given him valuable insight into these two leading foreign peoples of his time. Then, after Honorius's death, he had led a large force of Huns to try to block the return of Placidia. Subsequently, he made his peace with her government; but before long she began to find his power excessive. He took an army to north Africa, on which the Romans depended completely for their grain. At this time the country was under the semi-independent control of Boniface, a strange blend of saint and medieval knightly adventurer. Like Aetius, Boniface had at first been opposed to Placidia but had then made his peace with her, whereupon she deliberately set the two men at odds with each other. She offered her own support to Boniface. But in the ensuing hostilities he was wounded and died (432). Aetius now became the unchallenged commander in chief; and before long he began to be stronger than Placidia.

His most urgent task was to check the Vandals, a German people who had moved from Gaul into Spain and then across the strait into the vital territories of north Africa (429). Their king Gaiseric was a leader whose single-minded, far-sighted diplomacy and willpower faced the Romans with the most intractable German problem they had ever experienced. A joint army of the western and eastern empires sent against him failed dismally, and since the northern frontiers of Gaul were now breached and peasant revolts, too, had broken out within that country, the western government felt obliged to offer him peace. A treaty was drawn up, according to which the Vandals were granted federate status in Mauretania and Numidia (Morocco and western Algeria).

But this time it was a federate status that was not far removed from complete independence. And four years later, Gaiseric revealed this situation in unmistakable terms when he invaded the historic nucleus of Roman north Africa, comprising the grain lands of Tunisia and northeastern Algeria; and the ancient capital Carthage itself fell into his hands (439). It was the second city of the western Roman World; and its loss was a blow that made the dissolution of the empire lamentably apparent. At this point, the government of Ravenna felt compelled to make a revised treaty with Gaiseric. Under its terms, he retained the regions he had lately seized, while ostensibly giving Mauretania and Numidia back to the western empire. But instead he broke his word and kept everything. Furthermore, he now abandoned even the pretense of federate status and instead began to rule openly over his own sovereign state, which was torn away from Roman suzerainty altogether. This was an unprecedented phenomenon; and Gaiseric was also unique among the Germans in possessing a fleet of his own, which struck terror far beyond north Africa's shores and menaced Italy itself, severing the unity of the Mediterranean for the first time in over six hundred years. Gaiseric contributed more to the collapse of the western Roman Empire than any other single man. And Aetius, although successful elsewhere in transplanting and resettling the Burgundians, was powerless to stop him.

This was also the time when the Huns, who had hitherto supplied Aetius with many of his soldiers, began to be the enemies of the Romans instead, fighting first against the eastern empire and then against the West. The Latin historian Ammianus Marcellinus saw them as deceitful, violent, greedy savages, abnormally competent as horsemen. By the early fifth century they had built up an empire of enormous dimensions, stretching all the way from the Baltic to the Danube. In 434 this entire territory was inherited by Attila and his elder brother Bleda, whom Attila soon put to death. Evil-tempered, arrogant, and tireless, this square, flat-nosed little man earned the name of "the Scourge of God," for during his nineteen-year reign he came to play almost as large a part as Gaiseric in the downfall of the Roman World.

At first, however, during the 440s, he remained on friendly terms with Aetius, concentrating his attacks on the eastern empire, which he compelled to conclude two treaties on increasingly unfavorable terms. Then, however, a new ruler at Constantinople, Marcian (450–57), refused to subsidize him any longer, and Attila finally turned against the West in order to make up this financial deficiency by looting. He was given a pretext to intervene when Honoria, the sister of Valentinian III appealed to him to rescue her from a wedding with another man whom she did not like. The Hun chose to interpret this as a proposal that he himself should become her husband, and when his demand for a dowry consisting of half the western empire was turned down, he marched on Gaul. There, on the Catalaunian Plains near Châlons-sur-Marne, he was confronted by a combined army of Aetius's Roman troops and federated Germans. The German units were partly provided by the Visigoths, and their king was one of the many who fell in the mutual slaughter that followed. Yet he fell in the moment of victory— the greatest victory of Aetius's career. It was the only battle Attila ever lost in his life; and it forced him to evacuate Gaul.

But Gaul's gain meant terror for Italy, since he and his Huns crossed the Alps in the following year, sacking Mediolanum and other leading cities. This time Aetius had no imperial army to send against him. Yet as Attila was preparing to cross one of the Po tributaries, Pope Leo I arrived on the scene from Rome; now that the city no longer contained an imperial court, its bishops, the popes, were political potentates. Pope Leo made effective use of this authority, holding a meeting with Attila beside the River Mincius (Mincio, a Po tributary) and persuading him to withdraw from Italian soil. Presumably he convinced the king that owing to famine and pestilence the Huns would not be able to feed off the land. In any case, they turned back, and Italy was free of them.

Two years later, Attila died. His empire fell apart between his quarreling sons; and before long their army faced a rebellion from their German subjects south of the Danube and suffered an overwhelming defeat. The surviving Huns retreated far to the east (455) and were never a great power again.

But by that time Aetius was dead, for Valentinian III, falsely persuaded that he was treasonable, had murdered him with his own hand (454).

Throughout two decades and more Aetius had labored to keep the destroyers of the western world in check. For a time he was almost successful, but with his assassination its terminal crisis had begun.

The Last Emperors of the West

Only six months later, two of Aetius's barbarian retainers struck down Valentinian in revenge. In spite of his personal insignificance, his death was, in its way, as decisive as the killing of Aetius. The emperor had no heir, so that his dynasty, which had exceptionally lasted for nearly a century, expired with him.

The year of his death brought immediate catastrophe. Gaiseric the Vandal, whose navy dominated the seas, landed in person at Ostia and captured the city of Rome itself. He remained for two weeks, extracting loot far beyond Alaric's briefer plundering; and on his departure he removed thousands of captives including Valentinian's widow and two daughters.

The western empire had just twenty-one more years to live. During that period, as many as nine more or less legitimate rulers could be counted. Belonging to a variety of different families, most of them could claim only the barest minimum of power; and six came to violent ends. Within the rapidly dissolving government of Ravenna, the predominant personage was now the supreme commander Ricimer. For the first time since Stilicho, a German had become the commander in chief again. Yet Ricimer's German origin was still felt to disqualify him from wearing the imperial purple itself —so instead, for he was the power behind the throne, for the next fifteen years, he set up emperor after emperor and then repeatedly unmade them as well, thus intensifying the general instability. His most able protégé was Majorian (457–61), who fought well against the Germans in Gaul and Spain but then suffered a serious naval reverse at Gaiseric's hands off Carthago Nova (Cartagena), which caused Ricimer to put him to death. The German's next candidate, Anthemius (467–72), who was supported by Constantinople as well, suffered a similar fate, followed shortly afterwards by the death of Ricimer himself.

After three more transient reigns, which witnessed the loss of a loyal remnant of Gaul to the now independent Visigoths, a new military commander, Orestes, who had been Attila's secretary, gave the Ravenna throne to his own son. The youth bore the historic names of Romulus Augustus but was generally known by the diminutive version Augustulus. But Romulus remained emperor only for the briefest of periods because a German general, Odoacer, who commanded a force of his Danubian compatriots in Italy, now proceeded to intervene. Odoacer now decided to request, within

that peninsula, the federate status and land grants that other Germans had
succeeded in acquiring in other territories of the West. When his claim was
rejected, his soldiers saluted him as their independent ruler—not as Roman
emperor, however, but as their king.

Seizing Ravenna, Odoacer declared Romulus to be deposed and dis-
missed him into pensioned retirement. This time, however, no attempt was
made to appoint a new Augustus in the West. Instead, at Odoacer's bidding,
the Roman Senate transferred the imperial insignia to Zeno, who occupied
the throne at Constantinople (474–91). Zeno demurred because the penulti-
mate, transient emperor of the West, Julius Nepos, who had been his
nominee, was still alive in Dalmatia until 480. But since the eastern empire
at this time was troubled by internal dissensions, Zeno took no action
against Odoacer, who, while politely placing the heads of Zeno (and Nepos)
on his coins, continued to rule Italy as an independent monarch, like the
kings of the Vandals and Visigoths.

In consequence, later historians fastened on this year 476 as the date at
which the long declining western empire finally fell. In recent times, there
has been a tendency to minimize the significance of this particular event
since, after all, it was only one more landmark in a long series of destructive
developments and not a very spectacular landmark at that; and, besides, the

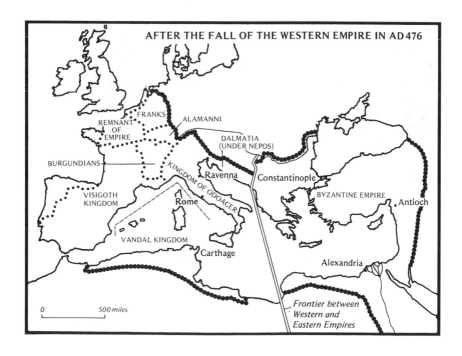

AFTER THE FALL OF THE WESTERN EMPIRE IN AD 476

system created by Odoacer in Italy was not unlike the arrangements that other German tribes had already made in Gaul and Spain. Nevertheless, this forced abdication of the last man to occupy the throne at Ravenna did have a meaning, for it signified that the last remaining country of the West, and its metropolitan territory at that, had become just another German kingdom. The western Roman empire had fallen; or it had become something else. At any rate it was no more.

21
The Fatal Disunities

The Failure of the Army

The western empire was no more because it had succumbed to its external enemies. Yet these would not have been too formidable to overcome if it had still possessed sufficient internal strength. But when the murderous blows were struck, the government could no longer muster the force to ward them off. This was because Italy and the whole Western world were hopelessly disunited within. The disunities assumed various shapes and forms. Each one of them, in itself, was damaging. In combination they made resistance to the external onslaughts impossible.

One prime cause of disunity was the failure of the rulers to control their generals. This, of course, was nothing new. It had been a defect inherent in the imperial system from the very beginning, since the Romans, for all their political skill, had never devised a workable system for insuring a peaceful transition from one ruler to the next. This defect was a standing temptation to many of their own commanders, beckoning them to make a violent bid for the immense stakes of autocratic power. Under the dynasty of Valentinian I, at least ten and possibly thirteen men from outside his house made lunges at the throne. They were all unsuccessful in the end, but all had enjoyed a considerable measure of acceptance for a time; and the struggles to put them down severely weakened the already strained resources of imperial manpower and revenue. In the words of an acute contemporary historian, Ammianus, "What fury of foreign peoples, what barbarian cruelty, can be compared with the harm done by civil wars?"

And yet, despite these troubles, Valentinian I and his kinsmen had presided over a period of comparative internal calm. At first sight, it is surprising that this should have been so, since not one of these emperors, after himself, was of sufficient caliber to carry such an enormous burden with personal distinction, and the later incumbents were almost unrelievedly dim. Yet the family remained on the throne for the record period of ninety-one years. And the measure of stability that this unbroken continuation had provided could readily be appreciated after the dynasty had gone, for chaos at once descended. However, this assumed the form, no longer of usurpations, but of a regime in which even the most ostensibly legitimate emperors were mere figureheads depending on powerful German generals. The throne passed with ludicrous rapidity from one puppet to another, and the old Roman failure to secure peaceful successions had become a major factor in the dissolution of the western empire that followed so soon afterwards in 476.

While the armies of the empire were seeking to assert themselves against one another, they were failing to perform the tasks of imperial defense that were required of them. They collapsed before foreign invaders who were, theoretically, much inferior in numbers and equipment—the sort of enemies that Rome had often encountered before and defeated. Alaric and Gaiseric may have commanded no more than a mere forty thousand and twenty thousand warriors respectively; whereas, according to the *Notitia Dignitatum,* which lists the senior officers of state and army, with their staffs, in A.D. 395, the two Roman empires between them possessed no fewer than five hundred thousand soldiers. And half of these belonged to the West, being stationed, for the most part, on or near the Rhine and Danube borders.

However, such statistics are deceptive. For one thing, as much as two-thirds of the western empire's total army consisted, not of the high-grade field force, but of the less mobile and less respected frontier troops—and it was from their ranks, moreover, that the heavy casualties in the field force had to be replenished as best they could. The result was that in terms of active, effective strength, the western Romans could scarcely mobilize bigger numbers than their foes. Stilicho, in 405, led a force of not many more than twenty thousand and even fifteen thousand was considered a substantial total for a Roman field army of the time.

This numerical weakness was largely due to the increasing failure of the imperial authorities to enforce conscription. During the earlier part of the fourth century A.D. this had been the principal source of recruitment, and Valentinian I, for example, conscripted strenuously every year. But the exempted categories were cripplingly numerous; not only slaves, as always, but also senators, bureaucrats, clergymen, and many others were entitled to opt out. Efforts to recruit the remainder of the population, therefore, had to be intensive. Even the men who worked on the emperor's vast estates found themselves called up. Yet other landlords, though required to provide recruits in proportion to the size of their estates, firmly resisted such demands, or sent only the men they were content to lose. And they had some excuse for resentment at being singled out in this way, because little attempt was made to conscript the inhabitants of the cities, who, especially if they came from Rome, were deemed useless as soldiers; so that the burden fell on the rural population, with the inevitable result that agricultural production suffered and would have suffered more still had there not been widespread evasion of the draft.

Becoming convinced, for such reasons, that ordinary measures of conscription would no longer avail, the government introduced new and stringent rules—including the insistence that if a man's father had been a soldier, he himself must become one too. This doctrine of hereditary obligation had already been put into practice earlier, with application to a wide variety of professions; and now it was directed towards the military career, insofar as the authorities had the power to assert their will, with ever-increasing sternness. As Saint Ambrose remarked, military service was no longer considered a patriotic duty, but a servitude—to be shunned. By the 440s it had become impossible to attempt any call-ups whatever except in the gravest emergencies. And a decade later we hear of no more western citizens being drafted at all.

And yet this failure occurred despite the most strenuous efforts to make army life attractive. There had been endeavors on these lines in a number of earlier reigns. Such reforms had been sharply censured by conservatives, and Valentinian I and Theodosius I, too, were charged with treating the soldiers much too indulgently—for example, when they allowed them to earn extra pay as workers on the farms. However, these inducements were varied by heavy threats, including instructions that those who sought to escape military service by amputating their thumbs should be burned alive. Yet neither the stick nor the carrot tempted men to seek the life of a soldier in such a perilous and dislocated world.

The result was, as a law of 409 reveals, that the hereditary defenders of the frontier posts just melted away. The cities were left unguarded even when invaders were almost in sight; and the encouragement of local defense groups proved effective only rarely. True, a fine general like Stilicho or Aetius could still win his battles. But on many other occasions the imperial troops were doomed to defeat before they had even caught a glimpse of a German or Hun soldier. Besides, in the frontier garrisons in particular, they were exploited by their officers, who grabbed much of their pay, and this left them unenthusiastic for battle. But this was only one small aspect of a wider phenomenon: the empire no longer inspired its soldiers to fight vigorously for its survival.

Failing, therefore, to mobilize enough satisfactory recruits, the government decided that if it could not get men, it would get money. And so, from the fourth century onwards, it accepted cash sums in lieu of manpower from those who wanted to avoid serving and from their landlords as well. It took these sums in order to pay for German soldiers to supplement and replace the elusive provincials. This in itself was not new. There had long been Germans in the Roman army; and their enrollment had been considerably increased by Diocletian and Constantine. At that time they were mostly recruited under personal contract, on an individual basis, to serve under Roman officers; and for the most part they fought well, seeing the empire not as an enemy but as an employer.

But then in 382 Theodosius I extended the process decisively and transformed it into something more novel. The German "allies" or federates whom he now enlisted were not merely individual soldiers any longer, but whole tribes, each recruited under its own chieftains, who paid their men in cash and goods received annually for the purpose from the emperor. Once introduced, this new federate participation in the army grew apace. It was widely criticized as an undermining influence, and yet, since other forms of recruitment had failed, it was probably the best remedy available. And yet it proved a failure, and its failure helped to bring the western empire down.

Social Catastrophe

One reason why it failed was the total lack of sympathy between the army and civilians. Rather than fight, the soldiers preferred to terrorize the rest of the population, who consequently loathed them.

Besides, the people resented the military for other reasons as well. Above all else, the burden of taxation they had to bear in order to keep this army in existence was appallingly heavy, so heavy that its impositions alienated

Relief of imperial official traveling with his staff.

the poor from the state forever. The laws of Theodosius I, for example, show a passionate desire to increase the extortion of revenue by every possible means. "No man," he pronounced in 383, "shall possess any property that is exempt from taxes." Harsh regimentation, for this same purpose of paying the army, had been a fact of Roman life for nearly two hundred years. But now each successive emperor continued to turn the screw a little tighter still.

Besides, the payment of these huge taxes was only one part of the contribution a citizen had to make to the state. There was also widespread requisitioning of his personal services. For example, he was compelled to supply coal and wood, and to boil lime, and to help keep public works and buildings in repair. This mobilization of compulsory labor became more stringent all the time; and violence and torture were employed to prevent evasions. Yet, at the same time, as in the military draft, there were far too many exemptions, which privileged social groups found excessively easy to obtain; and there was also a great deal of corruption, as the large number of ineffective attempts to cure this state of affairs makes glaringly clear.

It was unquestionable that, in some form or other—cash or kind or personal services or all three—huge contributions *had* to be raised, since otherwise the army and empire were not going to be able to survive. But does the historical fact that this purpose was not, in the end, achieved prove that the required amounts were too great to be raised—that their collection was a practical impossibility?

No. Probably the taxes could have been brought in, if only the system for levying them had been less inefficient. It was inefficient because it was so intolerably oppressive, leaving tax dodging as the only alternative to destitution. And it was not only oppressive but unfair, since the worst sufferers were, as always, the agricultural poor. The unfairness of the land tax, from which the state drew nine-tenths of its income, had always meant that they were hit much harder than the rich, and despite Diocletian's attempts to introduce sliding scales of crops and harvests, this situation was still substantially unchanged. Indeed, it had become worse. By 350 the sums exacted from this principal source of revenue had multiplied threefold within living memory, and after that the situation deteriorated still further. Moreover, the most important tax in kind, utilized for many years to pay government employees, had to be paid in the form of grain, so that once more it was the agricultural population that suffered. True, subsequently there was a change of method, as a result of which levies in kind were increasingly commuted to gold once again. But that was of no assistance to laborers in the fields who had no gold and were once again suffering from a galloping inflation. Moreover, they were still crippled by the general adverse conditions that had always restricted the economy of the ancient

Dog-tag fastened round the neck of a slave, promising
a reward if he ran away. Later fourth century A.D.

world—costly transportation and stagnant technology, supplemented now
by a shrinkage of cultivable land owing to encroachments by the invasions.

Slavery was not the major problem of the age. It is true that in certain
territories, such as the Middle Danube regions and Mauretania, slaves were
still numerous enough to make a substantial contribution to the labor force.
However, this did not so much increase the total number of workers available as depress the "free" poor still further, since they could not compete
with this unpaid labor and dropped out of the market altogether. Besides,
such areas with abundant slaves were somewhat exceptional. In most other
parts of the empire, at this epoch, there was no longer enough slave labor
to make any appreciable difference to the economic picture one way or the

other. Such slaves as there were sometimes helped the empire's various enemies and sometimes went around looting. But their role in the history of the period was relatively unimportant. It was on the impoverished "free" men and women of the rural countryside that the full horrors of the situation descended. They and the government were oppressed and oppressor, face to face in destructive and suicidal hostility. It was largely because of this rift that the taxes needed to support the army were not, could not be, paid in. And since that could not be done, the western empire failed to find defenders and collapsed. This was perhaps the gravest and most disastrous of all the disunities that afflicted the Roman World.

It also brought about radical changes in the structure of society. When the small farmers and agricultural laborers could no longer make both ends meet, they sought protection where they could find it. Thus whole villages formally placed themselves under the patronage of individual army officers, who, in return for the services of the villagers, were prepared to parley on

Mosaic of wounded huntsman at villa near Piazza Armerina, Sicily. Fourth century A.D.

their behalf with the imperial tax collectors. More numerous, however, were the communities that chose not officers but local landowners as their patrons. And many individual civilians did the same on their own personal account—small farmers who abandoned their homes and land in desperation and fled within the walls of the nearest great estate. This had happened before, during the troubles of the third century, but now the process repeated itself on a vast scale.

Since agricultural labor was so scarce, the landowners were content to receive these people, who defrayed their keep either by paying a cash rent, or by handing over a proportion of the crop they were allowed to grow, or by contributing the labor of their hands. Although their surrender was unconditional, at first, like the clients of the army officers, they could often rely on their new patrons to chase the tax authorities away. But later the landowners did an unholy deal with the western government, and the refugees found themselves on the tax lists once again. The emperors, that is, were glad to endeavor to prevent these tenants from moving away without their landlord's consent, so that they were wholly subjected to his control—and so were their children after them. Such men were not exactly slaves, but foreshadowed the serfs of the Middle Ages.

One of the emperors who published such restrictions was Valentinian I. He, for his part, was not prompted by any desire to grind the faces of the poor but was acting from motives of plain realism, since if there was one thing worse than being frozen into one's occupation, it was being frozen out of any job or food at all—and from that fate at least the landowners saved their refugee tenants. Moreover, in other respects, Valentinian displayed notable concern for the welfare of the poorer classes, to which he himself had belonged. In particular, he appointed functionaries described as Defenders of the People (368–70). Somewhat resembling the ombudsmen of modern countries, these officials were designed to protect the underprivileged "against the iniquities of the powerful." The praetorian prefects were ordered to nominate such a defender in every town of the western empire, and the emperor himself required to know the name of every man who received such an appointment. Unfortunately, however, his successors watered the project down, transferring the selection first to city councillors (Theodosius I)—the very men responsible for collecting the taxes—and then to committees on which the landowners were heavily represented (Honorius).

The scheme had failed. But there were still writers prepared to speak up for the oppressed. John Chrysostom, bishop (patriarch) of Constantinople (ca. 354–407), was painfully aware of the gulf between rich and poor. And above all Salvian, presbyter at Massilia (Marseille) (ca. 400–after 470), described in his work *On the Governance of God (De Gubernatione Dei)* how

God was chastising the world for its sins—a chastisement which he equated with the material oppression he saw everywhere around him. The age he lived in, like the later 1800s, was one in which poverty was regarded as blameworthy and disgraceful. Salvian fiercely rejected that stigma; and indeed he was so determinedly radical that no social class gained his favor except the destitute, whose abominable treatment by the government and the rich alike he deplored with intense forcefulness and unrelieved gloom.

The consequence of the conditions he so eloquently describes was that thousands of people despaired of making an honest living at all, and went underground to form traveling gangs of robbers and bandits. Gaul, in particular, experienced a succession of large-scale disturbances of such a kind. Indeed, such bands operated almost on the scale of a nationwide rising, in which tenants and slaves alike revolted in unison against the landlords and authorities; we learn that these Bagaudae—an old name by which they called themselves—held their own People's Courts, "where capital sentences are posted up on an oak branch or marked on a man's bones." And can you wonder that there were such terrorist gangs? asked Salvian, blaming these widespread disorders unreservedly upon the ruthlessness of the governing class.

Far back in the distant past, whole aeons away it seemed, was that not totally imaginary golden age when the various classes of the Roman state, even if never truly united because of the yawning economic differences, had at least been able to live together without seeking each other's annihilation. Now, instead, the empire had come to a time like the nineteenth century, when Disraeli made a character in his novel *Sibyl* remark: "I was told that the privileged and the people formed two nations." But in the nineteenth century the social structure managed to avoid disintegration; whereas in the fifth century it had crumbled, opening a breach through which the external enemy could batter his way in.

Yet the western empire might still have held together, brushing aside the claims of the poor, if only the rich and the government had more frequently seen eye to eye with one another. They colluded, it is true, in insuring that the tenants on the large estates should be allowed no freedom or rights. But in other respects there was very little sympathy between the imperial authorities and the upper class. In the declining Roman world this class, the topmost layer of the population, consisted of men entitled to describe themselves as senators. And even if the Senate, as such, did not count for a great deal more than it had in the earlier empire, its individual members were now more powerful than they had ever been before. Those who attended the Senate house at Rome did not see much of the emperor, whose residence was at Mediolanum and later in Ravenna. But this gave them (as it gave the popes in the same city) a certain independence of action. Constantine the Great knew the value of these senatorial dignitaries, mainly pagan though they still were; and so, while excluding them from his army, he courted their acquiescence in his policies by offering them lucrative civilian posts, and preserving and even enhancing the pompous dignity of their consulships and other sinecures.

Class consciousness and snobbery were enormous. Yet the senatorial order was not altogether closed to newcomers. Moreover, the term "senator" had come to be extended beyond those who actually sat in the Senate at Rome to several thousand additional aristocrats living outside the capital and, in many cases, outside Italy. Such men, the owners of enormous properties, may have been five times wealthier, on an average, than their forerunners of earlier imperial epochs. Their estates, to which so many displaced persons fled for shelter, were like small kingdoms in themselves, self-contained economic and social units packed with farm workers, slaves, artisans, guards, bailiffs, and hangers-on. In Gaul there was a particularly massive concentration of about a hundred powerful landowners who, with Honorius's concurrence, virtually assumed control of the country and later, with the support of the Visigoths, briefly proclaimed one of their own number as emperor (455).

The noblemen and noblewomen of the later empire were magnificent personages. But they were not particularly addicted to vicious high living —a good deal less so than their forerunners three and four centuries earlier. So the idea that the Western world collapsed because of orgies, a theory beloved by modern moralists and makers of spectacular films, must be abandoned. There had been many more orgies earlier, when the empire was had been doing well, than later when it was faring badly. More serious is the accusation that the senators of the fourth and fifth centuries stood aloof from public life. Many of them held no office of state, preferring instead to remain at home and enjoy their properties at leisure. In Rome and the provinces alike, they failed to pull their weight in state affairs. True, towards the very end of the western empire there was a change, because by then the landowners had become more powerful than the emperor himself, and some of them successfully invaded his councils. But even then many others still remained apart, living idly on their own estates and oblivious of any wider claims upon their time.

Salvian, among others, felt this profoundly and declared that the higher a man's status might be, the greater were his obligations, and the greater his guilt when, as so often, he fell short of them. By this sin of omission such a man was betraying the empire and contributing to its fall. And indeed, in spite of lip service to the romantic concept of Eternal Rome, many noblemen were not prepared to lift a finger to save the reality. On the contrary, they often actively undermined its welfare by rebuffing imperial officials, harboring deserters and brigands, and taking the law into their own hands to such an extent that they even maintained their own private prisons. Valentinian I objected to this practice with some determination; but his successors—the emperors who made an arrangement with the landowners about the tenants—virtually had to give in. And yet, even so, these upper-class personages still frequently remained hostile to the government, scoffing at the Augusti as uncultured and detesting their ministers.

In the vain hope, then, of keeping their armies in the field, the imperial authorities ruined the poor and alienated the rich. They also alienated and then very largely destroyed the solid segment of the population that came in between—the middle class. This had once been the backbone of the Greek city-states, and later on it had fulfilled the same role in the Roman Empire as well, which had likewise been a network of city-state communities. But the external invasions and internal rebellions of the third century A.D. had dealt this middle class terrible physical blows, while the accompanying monetary inflation caused their endowments to vanish altogether. And then, from the next batch of third-century emperors, who grimly pursued the enormous tasks of reconstruction, the old-fashioned ideals of this bourgeois section of the community received little sympathy. The cities of the empire, their public work programs cut to nothing or severely restricted, began to assume a thoroughly dilapidated appearance; and then in the fourth and fifth centuries, despite contrary efforts by Julian and others, their position still continued to worsen, and the old urban civilization, especially in the West, plunged into a sharp decline.

The nucleus of the middle class had been provided by the *curiales,* who comprised the members of the city councils *(curiae)* and their sons and descendants. Once, they had been munificent benefactors of their cities; but those days were gone forever. Nowadays their most important function by far was to carry out the orders they received from the central government, and above all to collect its revenues. It was the duty of the councillors, and of their offspring when their turn came, to extract from their fellow citizens the taxes in cash and kind demanded by the state and to compel them to join the army.

In other words, they had virtually become imperial agents. This meant that they had to participate in acts of oppression, and social critics such as Salvian of Massilia deeply blamed them for doing so. Yet the councillors' own personal situation, too, had become acutely difficult since they had to make up any shortfall themselves. This meant that from the third century onwards wealthy men became increasingly reluctant to serve on the city councils. It also meant that, since few new families were willing to be enlisted in such a burdensome cause, these memberships more and more often assumed a hereditary character—a situation encouraged by the imperial government, which insisted, as in so many other sections of the community, that the sons of councillors should follow in the footsteps of their fathers.

But such insistence, although reiterated with almost neurotic regularity, did not prevent these *curiales* from deserting wholesale from their posts; and indeed the entire middle class of the western empire, of which they formed such an essential part, was almost wiped out of existence. In a society that had always so largely depended on this class, its destruction left a vacuum that nothing could fill, and signified that from now onwards the population of these territories for the most part consisted of very rich and very poor. No doubt, the traditional urban civilization had always exhibited a disequilibrium since the towns were parasites upon an agrarian economy. Nevertheless, that was the system on which the ancient world had been founded, and its virtual erasure contributed substantially to the destruction and transformation of that world.

So throughout the last two centuries of the Roman West there was an ever-deepening loss of personal freedom and well-being for all except the very prosperous and powerful. The western empire had become a military camp in a perpetual state of siege, where each man was assigned a place he and his descendants must never desert. The authorities sought to impose maximum regimentation, to pay for the army and prop up the imperial structure. And yet all that they thereby achieved was to hasten the ruin of what they wanted to preserve, by destroying all the individual loyalty and initiative that alone could have achieved its preservation.

Moreover, this suicidal process was accelerated by the vast size and deteriorating quality of the civil service employed to regiment the remainder of the population. It was a self-perpetuating body because, like the town councils and so many other institutions, it became hereditary. Since the beginning of the fourth century there had been a new imperial aristocracy of service, enabling the rulers to make use of a body of helpers loyal to themselves. Before long, however, the civil servants of this new brand, who knew how greatly they were needed in order to collect the required revenue, gained confidence and betrayed an unobtrusive, but nonetheless persistent, defiance of their rulers.

Valentinian I, and some of his successors, tried to halt this trend, declaring that the civil servants owed obedience as much as any soldiers. Yet the emperors failed to prevent this rampant bureaucracy from gradually encroaching on their own imperial power and finally reducing it to almost total paralysis. It is true that some of the provincial governors and governors general, as well as some of the praetorian prefects who supervised their activities, were conscientious enough. But others, more numerous than in earlier days, were callously inhumane and corrupt—partly because the western empire was too poor to give them decent pay. The laws of the time made feverish attempts to reduce this unmanageable officialdom to order; but the very repetitiousness of such measures shows how ineffective they must have been.

These regulations are known to us because they were collected in A.D. 438 in the code of the eastern ruler Theodosius II, accepted also by his western colleague Valentinian III. This Theodosian Code contains enactments of both empires dating back a century and more. And they prove remarkably revealing. Although some are humane and enlightened, many others display an almost hysterical, repressive violence that augured badly for the survival of the weaker of the two states, the empire of the West. And, once again, these laws are monotonously repetitive—proof that they were circumvented, disobeyed, and ignored. The government was overwhelmed by the situation and powerless to improve it. And the lawyers of the period who composed such strident documents were evidently a great deal less impressive than their counterparts of earlier times. Moreover, the administration of justice, like the other operations of bureaucracy, was undermined by bribery. An anonymous fourth-century writer of *On Matters of Warfare (De Rebus Bellicis)* explaining plans for the administration and army, concludes his essay with an appeal to Valentinian I and Valens: "Put a stop to dishonest litigation!"

The rulers whose orders produced all these unproductive edicts often

Gold medallion of the eastern emperor Valens (A.D. 364-78) at Treviri (Trier): he is "triumphant over the barbarian peoples" (TRIVMFATOR GENT*ium* BARB*arum*).

lived extremely cloistered lives themselves, disastrously removed from contact with their subjects in the outside world. At the two courts of Ravenna and Constantinople, ceremonial and adulation were elaborate, and the eunuch-chamberlains who controlled admission to the imperial presence were regarded with implacable hostility, not only by the ruling class but by all others, too, who encountered their arrogance. In vain the official coinage poured out streams of rousing patriotic slogans that sank to extraordinary depths of unrealism and unpersuasiveness. There is unceasing stress on Glory, and emperors ferociously declare themselves "triumphant over the barbarian nations," when the very reverse was the case. Between the heads of the two Roman states and their subjects, there was a lamentable failure of communication.

Uncooperative Attitudes

Even so, however, the downfall of the western empire would have been delayed if only it had cooperated better with its more successful eastern counterpart. But cooperation was often poor, or nonexistent. There was an ancient, endemic, mutual dislike between the Latin-based and Greek-based halves of the Roman World, and the rulers of the two sections often seemed reluctant to come to each other's assistance and much readier to offer a stab in the back instead.

This situation was at its worst just after the death of Theodosius I had left the two regimes divided once again, and this time divided sharply and finally. The commander in chief of his son Honorius in the West, Stilicho, felt obsessive hostility towards the eastern empire, where he even had his counterpart Rufinus assassinated. Nor, as we have seen, did he act strongly enough against the Visigoth Alaric, since he always regarded the government at Constantinople as a much more dangerous enemy. When, long after his death, the West proved willing to accept an eastern nominee for its throne (Anthemius, A.D. 467–71), it was already too late. Decades of mutual ill will had sapped the strength of the western empire beyond repair, and soon afterwards it ceased to exist.

Another reason why it fell was because of a disastrous failure to assimilate the Germans in its midst or achieve a workable arrangement with their leaders. These German immigrants had constantly increased in numbers. A decisive moment came in 382 when Theodosius I allowed entire tribes to reside on imperial territory in Thrace as autonomous federate units, committed to serving in the Roman army under their own chiefs. And then again early in the fifth century, when the Visigoths and Burgundians settled in Gaul, there were once more formal partitions of land in which the local

Gold coin *(solidus)* of western emperor Anthemius (A.D. 467-72) shown with his eastern colleague Leo I who sponsored him. "The Welfare of the State" (SALVS REIPVBLICAE).

Roman proprietors handed over a third of their arable ground to the settlers; and later this proportion was doubled.

In these developments one can detect the origins of the independent European nations of the future. Yet when these Germans had first begun to establish themselves on imperial territory, they felt no ambition to become independent of Rome or spurn its institutions, desiring only to obtain a share of its benefits and, above all, cultivable soil. Even the Visigoth Alaric, who went down to history as the captor of Rome, had at first, according to the Gothic historian Jordanes, aimed at a new form of coexistence, and a single German-Roman people. And his son Ataulf (410–15) formulated the same ideal with great explicitness, stating that he had formerly wanted to establish a Gothic empire in place of the Roman state, whereas now, instead, he "aspired to the glory of restoring the fame of Rome in all its integrity and of increasing it by means of the Gothic strength."

But the Roman response to this unprecedented offer of partnership was inadequate. True, there were a few writers, inspired by pagan or Christian universalism, who paid lip service to multiracial unity. But lip service was all that it was, because even they could not restrain themselves from expressing, like so many other authors of the time, a deep repugnance for the personal characters and habits of the barbarians. Even Salvian, who bravely supported coexistence on the grounds that these noble savages were better than corrupt Roman society, commented on the nauseous smell of the Germans' bodies and clothing, and described the Goths as perfidious, the Alamanni as drunkards, the Saxons, Franks, and Heruli as wantonly brutal, and the Alans as rapacious lechers. Similarly Sidonius Apollinaris, the

highly literate bishop of Arverna (Clermont-Ferrand), while lavishly flattering successive Visigothic monarchs and observing that he and they had a
common interest in saving the empire, nevertheless objected fastidiously to
the noisy skin-clad Goths, and tattooed Herulians, and Burgundians who
stank of the rancid butter they smeared on their tow-haired skulls.

Valens's governors and military commanders subjected the immigrant
Visigoths to unconcealed, rapacious exploitation. But what was almost
worse was that the Romans generally imposed on these new, unwelcome,
and disconcerting neighbors a kind of spiritual and social apartheid. The
German immigrants seemed to them an unabsorbable lump of branded, .
subhuman outcasts; and so they set them apart, beyond a wall of contempt
and distaste. For instance, a law of 370 set a total veto on intermarriage;
and even the wearing of barbarian clothes by Romans was stringently
forbidden. This deliberate detachment, moreover, was greatly accentuated
by religious divergences, since the Arian form of Christianity, which was
adopted by the Germans, appeared to the churches of Rome and Constantinople* to deny the divinity of Jesus and was condemned as heretical.

Only Aetius, if he had lived, might have reversed the general trend, for
he knew the Germans well and handled them with tact. But he came too
late, and he was struck down, whereupon hostility to the Germans became
the rule. Some of them, in response to this treatment, behaved with apolo-
getic humility. But many more reacted by refusing to become Romanized
after all. Thus the scheme of enlisting units of Germans in the army proved
a failure and foundered; disliked and despised, they retaliated by hating the
people whose glories they had once hoped to share. True, the individual
German soldiers in *Roman* units generally remained loyal. But the federate
troops, despite good service on occasion, came to be in a condition of almost
perpetual turbulence and revolt. In 409 and 422 they acted with treasonable
disloyalty. And thereafter they got increasingly out of hand and presented
a perilous hazard.

Instead of a new unity between Romans and Germans, a deadly dishar-
mony prevailed. In recent times, a few generations ago—when racial explanations were fashionable—it was maintained that Rome fell because its
ethnic purity suffered pollution. The opposite is rather the case. Despite
intermixtures with many peoples over the course of the centuries, the tough
character of the Romans had not changed—as their continuing achievements testify. Indeed, the trouble was rather that, psychologically, they had
not changed enough; if only they had been able to adapt themselves to
getting on with the Germans, the western empire might have been preserved.

---

*For the distinction between western Catholic and eastern Orthodox, see pp. 461, 470 ff.

What happened instead was painfully displayed by the rise of Gaiseric the Vandal. Far from talking of coexistence and partnership within the empire, he raised his north African state to an uncompromising, virulently hostile independence, fiercely including both the great Roman landowners and the non-Arian clergy in his attacks. And at the same time King Euric of the Visigoths (466–484/5) was making his people in Gaul and Spain into another wholly independent nation and once again subjecting the official church to vigorous oppression. His legal code (475) rejected any kind of amalgamation between the German and Roman peoples in his kingdom, declaring them utterly separate and distinct from one another. So now segregation was the policy on both sides. The opportunity for a constructive union had been lost, and it was dramatically appropriate that the last emperor of the West was forced to abdicate in the year immediately following the publication of Euric's code.

Christians and Pagans

There were also various other causes of the downfall of the western empire, secondary and peripheral, though not altogether unimportant. One of these was the proliferation of dropouts who refused to participate in communal and public life. There were many people who found the social and economic situation intolerable and in consequence went underground and became the enemies of society. A large number of them became hermits and monks and nuns, who abandoned the company of their fellow human beings and, in the manner of modern Jesus-people or followers of gurus, divorced themselves from society, shaking the dust of the imperial system off their feet as completely as if they had never been part of it all.

The monastic movement had its beginnings in Egypt, but it was introduced to the western empire by Athanasius, bishop of Alexandria, who arrived in Rome in about 341, accompanied by two Egyptian monks. Then the popularization of the ascetic ideal in the West was carried further by St. Martin of Tours (b. ca. 330–d. 397), a Danubian who founded monasteries in Gaul. And St. Jerome, from Stridon in Dalmatia (b. ca. 348–d. 420), in addition to his immense services to Christian scholarship, wrote an account of the sort of lives led by hermits and monks, based on his own experience as creator of a monastic society at Aquileia in northeast Italy (370–73), and later at Bethlehem in Palestine. Then, early in the following century, John Cassian, founder of a monastery at Massilia (ca. 415), wrote works that induced many a nobleman to make the transition from senator to monk. By this time, however, the monastic life was no longer the end of a career but often led to a bishopric; monasticism had become respectable and was on its way to the prestige conferred upon it by St. Benedict (ca.

480–547). But in its earlier days it had attracted those who wanted to escape from the community; and at all times, granted its steadfast attempts to maintain Christianity's spiritual commitment in face of an insidious society, it deprived the state of greatly needed manpower and revenue.

On a long-term view, what proved particularly disadvantageous was the celibacy the monastic career entailed, since it, by lowering the birth rate, still further diminished the numbers of potential soldiers and taxpayers. Moreover, this urge to the celibate life, already noticeable during the previous two centuries, extended far outside the circle of monks and nuns; and preachers of the caliber of Augustine and Jerome defended it eloquently as an ideal to be aimed at by ordinary people. But it was an ideal that imposed yet another division upon a society that was profoundly divided already. The government knew what was happening and assailed the men and women who had embraced this profession of withdrawal. However, it took no forcible steps to bring them back.

Against those, on the other hand, who did not adhere to the same religion as themselves—and even to the same branch of the same religion—the authorities practiced violent coercion. This was possible because church and state were bound in a close alliance, established by Constantine the Great. The state was, at first, the controlling partner; as one of Valentinian I's bishops admitted, "the state is not in the church, but the church is in the state." Nevertheless, the imperial court having moved elsewhere, the bishops of Rome, the popes, were left free to become great men on their own account. And another bishop, not of Rome but of Mediolanum, raised the power of the hierarchy to a new peak. This was Ambrose, who occupied the see from 374 until his death in 397. Ambrose presided over a grandiose program of ecclesiastical building and rediscovery of martyrs; and he had two famous clashes with Theodosius I—from both it was the bishop who emerged victorious. After his death, the ecclesiastical initiative returned from Mediolanum to Rome, whose Popes Innocent I (401–17) and Leo I (440–61) treated with Alaric and Attila respectively, the latter with triumphant success. And in the same period mighty Roman churches were under construction.

It was Pope Leo's view that collaboration between state and Catholic church was a bargain beneficial to both, uniquely capable of binding the disunited Western world together. But not everyone agreed; and in fact the alliance turned out to have the opposite effect. This was because of the excessive, violent zeal with which the civil leaders, acting upon the requests of their spiritual partners, pressed conformity upon the pagans. By such means they transformed differences of opinion into irremediable hostilities. Valentinian I was very unusual since he stood against this policy, preferring universal toleration. But shortly after his death there was a great symbolic

Mosaic depicting St. Ambrose (d. A.D. 397).

moment in the war against paganism when his son Gratian expelled the pagan statue of Victory from the Senate house (382). After his death, there was once again keen debate on the subject; but the Christian view prevailed. And then Theodosius I passed a whole series of laws endeavoring to obliterate paganism altogether. In north Africa, however, religious riots broke out among the pagans because their temples had been closed; but this only spurred the bishops of the region to demand further and even more hostile legislation in order to "extirpate the last remnants of idolatry."

One of the ecclesiastics who took the lead in exerting this pressure on the secular power was Augustine, the outstanding churchman, intellectual, and writer of his age. Augustine was born at Thagaste (Souk-Ahras in Algeria) in 354 of a Christian mother, who converted his father. The young man received a careful education in north Africa and became professor of rhetoric at Mediolanum. After passing through a variety of religious convictions, recaptured in his passionately introspective and self-critical *Confessions,* he was ordained a priest at Hippo Regius (Annaba), where he became bishop four years later, in 395. And now he came out in favor of coercing pagans —and backsliders from Christianity to paganism as well; for Christ, he declared, like a general, must use military methods to recall deserters to his army.

The pagans were being worn down. But an attempt by one of their western sympathizers, Eugenius, to seize the throne in 392–94 gave the

The church of S. Sabina at Rome, originally founded ca. A.D. 422-32.

authorities a serious shock, and then Alaric's capture of Rome in 410 invested paganism with a new lease of life since the disaster was widely attributed to the empire's Christian regime. That was the argument that Augustine's *City of God* sought to refute; the immediate stimulus of the work was an urgent need to stem this new pagan revival. Thereafter, acts of imperial repression against the supposed peril continued well on into the 440s. These coercive measures did in the end almost succeed in their aim of extirpating paganism. Yet at first, during the crucial years of the earlier fifth century, this persecution had intensified the very disunities it was designed to eliminate; and it had thus played its part in the destruction of the western Roman Empire.

Equally divisive and destructive were the conflicts within Christianity itself. It had been Constantine's conviction that unity among all Christians was urgently necessary, not only because God and Jesus were indivisible, but also because church unity was the best way of uniting the whole empire. Yet disputes within the church continued to abound, relating to clerical celibacy, the Fall of Man, and the nature of the Holy Spirit; and the East, as always, stressed the singleness of the supreme deity, while the West emphasized the divinity of Jesus, which the Arians seemed to be decrying. It seemed, therefore, to the historian Ammianus Marcellinus, that "No wild beasts are such enemies to mankind as are most of the Christians in the deadly hatred they feel for one another." Valentinian I, it is true, remained

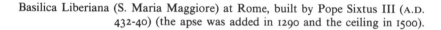

Basilica Liberiana (S. Maria Maggiore) at Rome, built by Pope Sixtus III (A.D. 432-40) (the apse was added in 1290 and the ceiling in 1500).

as tolerant to "heretics" within the Christian ranks as to pagans outside
them. But his successors displayed a very different attitude, especially
Theodosius I, who issued repeated laws and edicts against nonconformist
Christians. And Augustine, brooding on his own earlier spiritual deviations,
concluded that Christian heretics as well as pagans must be brought into
the fold by force. He quoted the scriptural text: "give opportunity to a wise
man and he will become wiser." But "opportunity" was only a euphemism
for violent suppression; and it was in the same spirit that Pope Leo I later
declared that "truth, which is simple and one, does not admit of variety."
Manichaeans and Jews, too, continued to fare much worse under the Christian emperors than under their pagan predecessors. But persecution, as
always, deepened rather than closed the rifts and made the united loyalty,
which the empire so desperately needed, even more of a will-o'-the-wisp
than ever.

Moreover, the psychological attitudes of pagans and Christians alike
were equally unhelpful to the government in its unsuccessful struggle to
insure national survival. The pagans, on the whole, relied too complacently
on the glories of the past; and the Christian theologians preached doctrines
that deprecated the importance of serving the state.

To take the pagans first, their ancient educational habits were very far
from dead. Indeed, their purveyance of the classical tradition still held the
field virtually unopposed. The Christians had no rival educational theory
or practice to offer; even Constantine himself fervently assumed the patronage of the old system without showing any desire to broaden its scope. And
so in the great universities of Rome and Mediolanum and Carthage, and
in the famous municipal schools of Gaul, the professors adhered to the
classical pattern of the Seven Liberal Arts; or rather, since four of them were
no longer much taught (Arithmetic, Geometry, Astronomy, Music), they
concentrated on the remaining three, Grammar, Rhetoric, and Dialectic.
Indeed, throughout the entire fourth century, there was a significant resurgence of these traditional subjects—though, as the middle class decayed, the
pursuit of such studies became increasingly limited to the aristocracy,
whose cultural and literary attitudes, as revealed in their refined and cli-
quish poems and letters, remained fixed in an almost uniform sterility.

These works display a romantic, nostalgic feeling for Eternal Rome—the
"Invicta Roma Aeterna" of coins and medallions. Though no longer the
governmental center of the world that had taken its name, the ancient city
was now symbolic of that world in a novel and significant manner. This was
denoted by the term "Romania," which came to signify the whole heritage
of Roman culture in the Latin West, in distinction from Gothia, Francia,
Alamannia. Emperors and officers and humbler people alike who had originated in far distant provinces and had scarcely, if ever, set foot in the city

were now thinking of themselves as "Romans" with passionate emphasis. Less than a decade after the city had fallen to Alaric, the Gallo-Roman poet Rutilius Namatianus still felt able to discern a Rome of higher reality that could never falter or fail:

> No man will ever be safe if he forgets you;
> May I praise you still when the sun is dark.
> To count up the glories of Rome is like counting
> The stars in the sky.

Rutilius was a pagan, but contemporary Christians, too, felt the impact of the classical past very strongly. It is true that they also engaged in incessant debate about the extent to which they should draw upon this pagan heritage. Augustine, for example, in spite of his immense admiration of the *Aeneid,* contrasted *your* Virgil with *our* Scriptures. Yet he also, like others, recalled that even the ancient Israelites had been permitted to "spoil the Egyptians" and take their women as concubines; and therefore, according to the same reasoning, he and his fellow Christians were entitled to abstract what they could from the pagan writers.

But the trouble about this deeply ingrained veneration of the past was that it tempted people to see every contemporary event in terms of *previous* Roman happenings. In order to ram these comparisons home, the writers call continually upon a wide range of precedents taken from the entire range of their country's glorious history. Thus when the pagan, classicizing Claudian of Alexandria, the leading poet of the age, wants to write flatteringly about his own contemporaries, he can never stop comparing them to the Scipios and Catos and Brutuses. "If we have any discernment at all," advised Macrobius in his learned symposium the *Saturnalia,* "we must always revere antiquity." And indeed, the very last western emperor of all was named both Romulus and Augustus.

Yet this propensity for looking backwards with such single-minded passion led directly to catastrophes. When, for instance, the pagan historian Ammianus writes of the recent defeat of the Romans by the Visigoths at Hadrianopolis (376), he at once compares the disaster to German invasions half a millennium earlier; his point is that such tribulations had occurred before and had been overcome—so that there is no reason why they should not be overcome once again. And later on, Rutilius Namatianus made exactly the same point. Yet the analogy was fallacious, since the German invasions five centuries previously had never offered even the slightest threat to the empire's actual survival, whereas now the degree of magnitude had altogether changed; the blow suffered by Valens at Hadrianopolis in 378 indicated a plight far more desperate than had ever existed before. But the complacent nostalgia of Roman education made it impossible to face up to such novel situations with any adequate or constructive response. "Your power is felt wherever the sun's light shines," declared Rutilius about Rome. But he was wrong, since the Roman West was approaching final collapse; countermeasures of the most determined kind were urgently required, and attitudes such as his distracted attention from this necessity.

The great Christian theologians, on the other hand, men of superior brains and character who in earlier times would have joined the public service instead of the church, were often guilty of a different but equally serious disservice to the state, namely, the active discouragement of Christians from working on its behalf, either in a peaceful or a warlike capacity. This attitude, easily justifiable from the New Testament, had been natural enough in the old days when the civil authorities were engaged in persecuting Christianity. But it is remarkable that, even after the empire had become Christian, the leaders of the church should still persist in their old conviction that Christianity was incompatible with state service. And yet that is what happened: a series of popes continued to pronounce that to work for the government was perilous to a man's soul; and St. Martin of Tours, founder of monasteries in Gaul, asked to be released from the Roman army because he was Christ's soldier and could not fight for his country. When such views took hold of the population, the power of the empire to resist its foes was weakened.

It was sapped further by Augustine. He was not, it is true, a pacifist; indeed he conceded that a literal interpretation of Christ's saying "turn the other cheek" would ruin the state. But the massive twenty-two books of his *City of God* undermined patriotism by more insidious means. In this supreme literary masterpiece of the later Roman empire, from which medieval thinkers derived a large proportion of all they knew about the ancient world, he called up all the resources of pagan philosophy and Christian doctrine alike to make a sharp distinction between the earthly city and its counterpart in heaven. Plato and Paul had told of such ideal cities before, but Augustine, writing soon after Alaric's sack of Rome, described the concept with a vividness that was altogether new. And he infused it with a distinct unhopefulness about the future of any and every terrestrial state. He had felt this before, and now it seemed to him more than ever that Christianity was the crop coming just before the icy frosts of winter—frosts that would freeze the nations of the world to death.

True, his "earthly city," which contains not only the sinners of this world but unrighteous men and women anywhere in the universe, is a wider concept than the Roman Empire. All the same, Augustine's pessimism carries gloomy implications for the future of Rome's civilization—or rather, of the *human endeavor* that was needed to maintain it. His doctrine of grace, adapted from Saint Paul, maintained that by our own unaided will, without God-given aid, human beings are incapable of achieving anything

Disc showing two young men. Fourth century A.D.

at all. It was a decisive break with the optimistic, humanistic attitudes of the classical world. And it was deeply resented by men such as Pelagius, a British or Irish theologian who, in the spirit of Cicero, laid strong counteremphasis on individual effort. Violent controversies ensued—and the Pelagians were suppressed.

Augustine had cut Rome firmly down to size. Its interests could no longer be held paramount: "Please pardon us if *our* country, up above, has to cause trouble to *yours*. . . . You would acquire still greater merit if you served a higher fatherland." And indeed, as he grew older, Augustine came more than ever to reject any identification between Christianity and empire. In terms of world politics, he did not prevail because the identification had come to stay. But his influence was widespread, and his refusal to believe in a Christian empire was a part and parcel of the West's failure to defend itself against its enemies and stave off its own collapse.

22

The Aftermath

The Successor States in the West

When Rome's rule crumbled in the west, it left the Visigoths ruling the southwest of Gaul as well as Spain, and the Burgundians in control of southeastern Gaul, while another group of German communities, the Franks, had established themselves in the north of the country. The Visigoths and Burgundians, however, whose Arian "heresy" was alien to the local Catholic populations and their bishops, were overcome in 507 by the Franks, whose pagan chief and founder of the Merovingian dynasty Clovis of Turnacum (Tournai), (ca. 482–511), had embraced the Catholic brand of Christianity with three thousand of his warriors. He was sent the emblems of a Roman consul by the eastern Roman emperor Anastasius I; yet his kingdom was not a dependency of Constantinople, but the independent nucleus of a future nation-state. Clovius and his successors extended this Frankish dominion both to the east and to the south, where Mediterranean Gaul gave them strength and culture.

Later Merovingian monarchs, however, gradually became puppets of their successive mayors of the palace, of whom one, Pepin the Short, finally deposed his overlord and founded the Carolingian dynasty (751), named after his father Charles Martel. Then a ruler of that house, Charlemagne (772–814) broke with his family's previous policy of peaceful missionary penetration, by undertaking repeated military campaigns and forcible conversions throughout the northern regions of Europe. Permanent inspectors were dispatched to the three hundred counties of his realm; and a legislative assembly was summoned twice a year. Finally, Charlemagne declared himself Roman emperor and had himself crowned at Rome by Pope Leo III (800).

In Spain Euric (466–85) and Alaric II (485–507) had fully established the power of the Visigoths; and after the collapse of the Gallic portion of their

Seal of Alaric II, King of the Visigoths (A.D. 484-507).

empire to Clovis, this Visigothic kingdom assumed a more national, Spanish character. Nevertheless, there remained a division between the Catholic south of Spain—with its Roman law and Roman, Byzantinized cities such as Hispalis (Seville)—and the new settlers, who were governed from their capital at Toletum (Toledo) and retained their own Arian religion and legal codes. However, the Visigothic regime prospered, especially under Leovigild (568–86), who annexed additional regions of the peninsula and became the first monarch in a former Roman province to strike an independent national coinage of his own. Then his successor Reccared (586–601) turned from his Arian faith to the church of Rome, thus founding Iberian Catholicism.

But Islamic power, spreading in a gigantic explosion across north Africa after the death of the prophet Mohammed (632), soon impinged forcibly on Spain. In 711 the country was invaded by the Mohammedan prince Tarik, whose successors asserted Moslem control throughout the southern part of the peninsula, relegating the Christian Spanish monarchy to its northern regions for centuries to come.

Meanwhile in Italy, after Odoacer had asserted virtual independence of Constantinople, his Ostrogothic successor Theodoric (493–526) brought unaccustomed peace and prosperity to the land. He solicitously retained the Roman civil administration, and Latin literature greatly flourished, producing such writers as Boethius and then Cassiodorus who served as bridges between the culture of the past and the medieval civilization that was dawning. Moreover, although the Ostrogothic regime was not Catholic but Arian, the Roman church continued to gain in power; and its Pope Gelasius I wrote to the eastern emperor, Anastasius I, "the world is ruled by two things, the sacred authority of the priesthood and the kingly power."

In north Africa, however, the relations of the independent Arian kingdom of the Vandals both with Catholicism and with Constantinople were subject to violent vicissitudes. But this state did not maintain itself for long, for by the middle of the sixth century, the Byzantine emperor Justinian I's general Belisarius blotted it out of existence; and then Belisarius and his successor Narses destroyed its Ostrogothic counterpart in Italy as well.

The Survival of Byzantium

The eastern empire, named Byzantine after the original name of Constantinople, remained, unlike the western, very much in existence. When the two realms had been finally separated between the offspring of Theodosius I, Arcadius and Honorius, the advisers of the former in the east had with difficulty warded off an Ostrogothic threat. During the long reign of Arcadius's son Theodosius II (408–450) that followed, power at Constantino-

Page from manuscript (eighth century) showing Cassiodorus's monastery
of Vivarium (ca. A.D. 550).

Gold medallion of Theodoric the Ostrogoth, King of Italy(A.D. 493-518),
"conqueror of the peoples" (VICTOR GENTIVM).

ple was chiefly exercised by his mother Pulcheria. Noting the sack of Rome
by Alaric, the eastern government erected new walls around its capital, and
the Huns were bought off with increasingly large sums. But Pulcheria's
Thracian husband Marcian, when he subsequently became emperor (450–
57), refused to pay Attila's subsidy, thus launching him against the West
instead. After Marcian's death, a German general gave the Byzantine
throne to another Thracian, Leo I (457–74), who saved his empire from the
German soldiery by calling in troops from Asia Minor; and their commander, his son in law Zeno, became his successor (474–91).

It was in Zeno's reign that the western empire became extinct. But the
eastern empire did not; and it nominally assumed control of the West,
though in practice Zeno refrained from interfering. But one of the chief

events of his time was a quarrel between the ecclesiastical authorities in
Rome and Constantinople, reflecting a dispute that was to rack Christendom for centuries to come and would eventually result in the permanent
division between Catholic and Orthodox. On Zeno's death his widow gave
the throne to a rich nobleman Anastasius I (491–518), who shored up a
difficult financial situation.

Then Justin I (518–27), in whose time the Slavs appeared as a major threat
in the Balkans, became the founder of a new dynasty and elevated his
nephew Justinian I to the regency and the throne (527–65). The guiding
spirit of one of the most creative epochs in human history, Justinian also
built some of the world's greatest buildings; at Constantinople his Church
of the Holy Wisdom (Santa Sophia), which replaced Constantine's basilica
of the same name, still stands, a fitting symbol of the profoundly religious
Byzantine ethos. The last emperor to speak Latin better than Greek, Justinian instigated the compilation of a Latin Corpus of Civil Law in which
a committee of sixteen men summed up and adapted the whole legal experience of Rome, condensing three million lines of earlier law books into one
hundred and fifty thousand. The reign had its fair share of troubles, including riots in the capital and one of the severest outbreaks of bubonic plague
in recorded history. Yet all the time Justinian's indefatigable administration, controlling and consulting the church, continued to adjust the imperial
system to the tasks of the future with impersonal and ruthless benevolence.
Moreover, he held his own against Persia, now reaching the height of its
power shortly before it fell to the Arabs. And Justinian also, as we have
seen, recovered Italy and north Africa, thanks to the genius of his generals
Belisarius and Narses.

These western reconquests proved impossible to maintain. Yet the eastern Roman or Byzantine empire continued to exist—for an extraordinary

Bronze coin of Justinian I (A.D. 539). On reverse, M (40) is denomination mark
(follis): NIK is mintmark (Nicomedia, Izmit).

Gold medallion of Justinian I celebrating his reconquest of North Africa from
the Vandals (A.D. 535). "The Welfare and Glory of the Romans"
(SALVS ET GLORIA ROMANORVM).

duration of time. With only a brief interval from 1204 to 1261, when its central region came under the domination of Western crusaders, it still survived until its capital fell to the Ottoman Turkish sultan Mohammed II in 1453. Many times throughout this millennial career it served as the bulwark of Western civilization against the East; and throughout almost the entire period Constantinople was by far the largest and most splendid and most learned city in Europe. Although its culture was Greek, and its superb art was a highly original blend of Roman, Greek, and oriental elements, the Byzantine emperors saw themselves as the heirs of ancient Rome and called themselves "Kings of the Romans."

But why did this eastern, Byzantine monarchy outlast its western counterpart by nearly a thousand years? Why did these two halves of the originally united empire experience such totally separate and distinct destinies? For one thing, the western realm was far more vulnerable to external attack owing to its geographical location. In Europe, it had to guard the long frontiers of the Upper and Middle Danube and the Rhine, whereas the Byzantine Empire had only the Lower Danube to cover—thus remaining relatively free to deal with menaces arising from the Asian east. Besides, if the western emperor failed to hold his river barriers, he had no second line

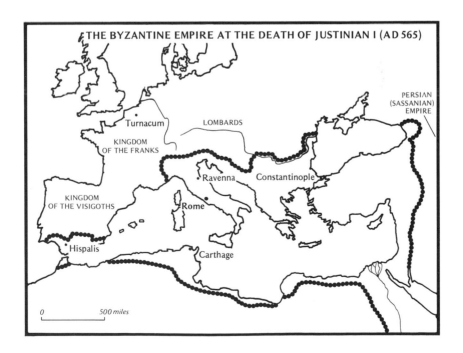

THE BYZANTINE EMPIRE AT THE DEATH OF JUSTINIAN I (A D 565)

PERSIAN (SASSANIAN) EMPIRE

Turnacum

LOMBARDS

KINGDOM OF THE FRANKS

Ravenna

Constantinople

KINGDOM OF THE VISIGOTHS

Rome

Hispalis

Carthage

0   500 miles

of defense to fall back upon, and Italy and Gaul and Spain lay wide open to the invaders; whereas to force the Bosphorus, guarded by the impregnable defenses of Constantinople, was beyond the capacity of any hostile power.

Furthermore, the eastern empire possessed a sounder social and economic structure than the western, embodying fewer glaring disunities. It did not, for example, suffer in the same way from enormously wealthy noblemen, who grudged both men and money to the government and the army. Moreover, in contrast to the West, the middle class, the traditional nucleus of ancient society, survived its vicissitudes throughout many of the dominions of Constantinople in tolerable economic conditions; and employing this class to man a professional civil service that was more effective than its western counterpart, the Byzantine authorities managed to gather in a much higher proportion of the national income than the court of Ravenna was ever able to collect. Besides, in contrast to the position today, the East was both more populous and better cultivated than the West; and its provinces had survived the ravages of the third-century invasions with greater resilience.

Furthermore, the internal political stability of the eastern empire was far more impressive. During a whole century and a half from A.D. 365, its internal peace was broken by only five usurpers (three of them in the same reign), a remarkable contrast to the proliferation of such rebels in the west. True, Constantinople had its troubles, notably savage ecclesiastical divisions. But it could weather them, owing to its inherently superior situation in other respects. That was why it was the West that fell, or had to assume new political forms, whereas the East was able to survive for another thousand years.

EPILOGUE

As far as our sources, multiple but elusive, allow us to find out what happened in the ancient Roman Empire, we have seen a rise from nothing to long ages of diverse and splendid efflorescence, and then to a massive fall or radical change. It is a story that has extended from the establishment of diminutive Tiber villages to the creation and maintenance of an enormous multiracial society, followed by its fragmentation into units foreshadowing the nations of the modern world.

With modifications, much of Rome continued to live on within these successor states; its language, government, law, church, literature, art, and habits of thinking and living were all far from dead. And of these persisting Roman elements Western civilization has remained very conscious ever since, recalling and cherishing them in one revival and renaissance after another. Yet in politics, as in art, the repetitions have never been exact, since the backgrounds can never be repeated; and that again is why, although the Roman experience unmistakably still carries lessons and warnings for today, their exact form and significance are sometimes problematical.

One thing that is clear is that we do not always want to relive the experience of the Romans; although sometimes what they did is entirely to be admired and envied, in other respects they were detestable. Most of what they achieved was based upon the use of force. The culture that has given us their unequaled masterpieces was created and maintained, in the last resort, by violent means that modern societies could not, or should not, tolerate today. We are still left, therefore, with the unanswered question of how the acute ethnic problems that still bedevil the equally large, or larger, political units of our own day can be solved without the use of such unacceptable methods. Here we should look at the second stage of the Roman process, for its forcible stages were habitually followed by phases of political settlement. At such times this people and its rulers displayed a sagacity to which no study of our own times, or for that matter any other times either, reveals an effective parallel. In other words, after conquering or absorbing

Print of the Roman Forum by Piranesi (1720-78).

a territory, the Romans generally then proceeded to administer it, if not with a great deal of social justice (as the term is understood today), at least in a remarkably pacific fashion that conferred a degree of prosperity such countries had never known before.

Another aspect of society in which the Roman experience raises thought-provoking questions—even if, once again, it does not always supply the answers—concerns the relationships between the individual and the community. In the heroic days of the Roman Republic, community spirit was enormous, and its whole tradition prevented the rise of any individuals to extraordinary importance; it was not entirely eccentric of Cato the Elder, when he was writing military history, to prefer to omit the names of Roman generals altogether. In the last days of the republic things were changing, as the rise of an admirable portrait sculpture clearly hinted. Under the imperial regime that followed, however, the opposite extreme to the republic was reached, as personality cult ran riot, focusing on the larger-than-life figures of the rulers themselves.

The modern historian demurs here, protesting that although this glaring spotlight was evidently directed upon the emperors, they did not, as individuals, exert all the effects ancient writers supposed upon the historical process, which went its own way more or less regardless of them under the influence of ineluctable social and economic factors. And there is certainly some measure of truth in that, since Suetonius's highly personal *Twelve Caesars* alone would give us a ludicrously inadequate picture of what was going on. But, equally, we must not exaggerate our reaction in the other direction, as we are inclined to do under the pressure of modern sociological thinking, not to speak of our distaste for the dictators we have seen in our own time. Indeed, it is these modern dictators themselves who warn us that it would be a mistake to react too forcibly against Suetonius and the others. Granted that Stalin, for example, in a sense reflected the current trends and tendencies around him, it would clearly be wrong to argue that those tendencies would have impelled world history along precisely the same course if he had never existed. Roman history offers the same warning in no uncertain terms. Without, for example, the very peculiar personalities and individual gifts of Augustus and Constantine, it would not have gone the same way at all.

The story of Rome, in other words, shows that individuals do count. And that does not apply only at the most exalted level either. The historian Tacitus, bemoaning the imperial autocracy, admits freely that it left room for superb courage and achievement among ordinary citizens. And Roman poetry, in spite of all the powerful ties that bound its writers to their state and society, emerges as something far more private and personal than the community-minded poetry of classical Greece.

Even though Roman history needs no updating to make it valuable and exciting, nevertheless, in our own late 1970s it is perhaps this aspect of it that most forcibly strikes the mind in the end. We in the Western world are living in times when official assessments of the desirable and practicable extent of individual freedom are sometimes being reduced and eroded with unprecedented speed and thoroughness. How do the Romans stand on this? It is true that, although their unique legal capacity contributed greatly to the democracies of the future, they scarcely even began to achieve what is regarded as democracy today, in any of the current interpretations of the term. Indeed, the lower and by far the greater part of the social pyramid comprised a vast, inarticulate majority, living scarcely above the level of bare survival, as such unfortunates had lived in all other societies ever since the beginning of time. If we are disposed to make moral judgments—and the historian should not always to refuse to do this—we may regret that this was a barrier Rome did not break. Nor, of course, has any other nation until the modern age—and even now only partially.

But, having duly taken note of that, let us consider what they *did* accomplish. Their whole immense story shows us not only what a tightly knit community can achieve by mutual cooperation, but also what possibilities for individual self-expression exist within that community. Even if the large suppressed majority still failed to benefit, Rome did attain an unprecedentedly massive measure of personal self-realization and achievement, at least among all the other and formative elements in its society: politicians, writers, artists, thinkers, architects, engineers, lawyers, and men of affairs. And it is that tradition that wins our respectful admiration and causes us to be proud that we are among its inheritors.

NOTES

PART I   ETRUSCAN ROME

Chapter 1. Rome and Etruria

Italy and Rome.   ITALY: the name is probably a Hellenized form of the Italian *Vitelia* (calf land), a name originally restricted to the southern half of the peninsula's toe. SALT ROUTE: extended inland by Via Salaria (from *sal,* "salt") from Rome to Reate (Rieti) in the Sabine country. HILLS OF ROME: originally raised by action of Ciminian and Alban volcanoes. MIDDLE AND LATE BRONZE AGE: used to be named after Terramara (*terra marna,* "rich black soil") settlements south of the Po. LATIUM: the name "Latini" was first applied to a tribal group on the Tiber north of Rome. IRON AGE: includes "Villanovans" named after a small town near Bologna. INHUMERS of Latium formed part of widespread Fossa Culture that reached its climax in seventh century B.C. PALATINE: (*Roma quadrata,* "square Rome"): two archaic cisterns and rock-cut postholes of remains on Alban Hills. ROME'S ORIGINS: it was believed that after the sack of Troy in the Trojan War (ca. 1100 B.C.), one of the Trojan leaders, Aeneas, had made his way to Italy, where he founded Alba Longa, of which Rome was a much later offshoot. Probably the Etruscans devised the Aeneas link between the Trojan saga and their own Asian origins. FOUNDATION OF ROME: 814 B.C. (Timaeus); 753 B.C. (Varro); 751 B.C. (Cato the Elder); 748-747 B.C. (Fabius Pictor); 729 B.C. (Cincius Alimentus).

The Etruscan City States.   ETRUSCANS' ORIGINS: Herodotus placed their coming more than three centuries too early, perhaps telescoping early Iron Age and Etruscan immigrants. The suddenness of the finest orientalizing tombs from ca. 700 suggests a new historical situation. (At least some influences crossed the Apennines from the north, notably to Vetulonia). ETRUSCAN LINK WITH CARTHAGE: two gold plates from Pyrgi (S. Severa) inscribed in Etruscan (ca. 500) are matched by one in Punic (Carthaginian)—or possibly Phoenician—Cypriot. GREEK AND SOUTH ITAL-IAN LINKS: Not only Ionians at Gravisca, but pottery from Cumae (mid-sixth century) at Tarquinii and Caere. METALS AT POPULONIA: the copper came from Campiglia. Later, after ca. 400 B.C., huge quantities of iron, mined on the island of Ilva (Elba), were smelted at Populonia. VOLATERRAE (Volterra) was the capital of a metal-rich zone. VOLTUMNA: the sex of the deity is uncertain.

Earliest Rome. SEPTIMONTIUM: Palatium, Velia, Fagutal, Germalus, Caelius, Oppius, Cispius, the last two being spurs of the Esquiline; eight including the low-lying Suburba, between Esquiline and Viminal. CITY BOUNDARY: *pomoerium,* a term understood to mean the strips inside and outside the wall. The Capitoline Hill was not inside the *pomoerium.* ETRUSCAN TRADE WITH ROME: seventh-century *graffiti* from Forum Boarium (Cattle Market) reflect this. By 650 Rome had close relations with Etruscanized Falerii (Civita Castellana), another frontier town 28 miles north, center of a diversified group of Faliscan towns.

Chapter 2. The Etruscan Monarchy

Etruscan Rome. GREEKS IN-CAMPANIA: first on island of Pithecusa (Latin Aenaria, now Ischia; Euboeans, ca. 775), then Neapolis (Naples, ca. 650) and Dicaearchia (Latin Puteoli, now Pozzuoli). ETRUSCAN-CAMPANIAN LEAGUE of twelve cities led by Capua: perhaps legendary. ETRUSCANS IN LATIUM: probably (though this is disputed) not conquered until after Campania, because it was so swampy. A Tarquinii inscription *(elogium)* seems to boast of the conquest of nine Latin cities; Tusculum means "Etruscan city," and Praeneste (Palestrina) tombs show a dominant Etruscan class 50 years before the Tarquins at Rome.

Early Roman Religion. ANTHROPOMORPHISM: Varro said that making statues in Greek fashion undermined people's fear of the gods.

Structure of the Earliest Roman State. LEGENDARY KING–LIST: Romulus, Numa Pompilius, Tullus Hostilius, Ancus Marcius, Tarquinius Priscus, Servius Tullius, Tarquinius Superbus. REX: also inscribed on cup now found near the Regia which *may* be ca. 530–510 B.C. Words related to *rex* are found in other Indo-European languages as well. THREE EARLIEST TRIBES: Tities, Ramnes, Luceres. SENATE: the meaning of *patres conscripti* is disputed. According to tradition there had been in earlier days still a Senate of only 100 members. POLITORIUM: 117 tombs now found, including Etruscan remains. LATIN LANGUAGE: craftsman's inscription on gold *fibula* from Praeneste (Palestrina) late seventh century; *cippus* from Roman Forum (Black Stone) late sixth century. TARQUINS: the diviner *(haruspex)* Tarnuitius Priscus is mentioned on an inscription *(elogium)* of Tarquinii. Five other Etruscan cities, including Clusium (Chiusi), were believed to have fought against Tarquinius Priscus as allies of the Latins. "Tarpeian" cliff on Capitoline Hill= "Tarquinian." Iron model of axes and *fasces* of ca. 600 found at Vetulonia. Etruscan pottery of ca. 530-520 at Rome (S. Omobono) comes from Vulci. CALENDAR OF NUMA: probably of time of Tarquins. The names Aprilis (April) and Idus (day of month) are Etruscan.

"Servius Tullius." SERVIAN TRIBES: the urban tribes (and Four Regions) are: Suburana (Sucusana), Esquilina, Collina, Palatina. The Capitoline Hill was not included in the Four Regions. COMITIA CENTURIATA: its establishment is sometimes attributed to after 450 or ca. 366 B.C. SERVIAN INFANTRY CLASSES: first three infantry of line, last two light-armed. Then came five classes of unarmed. EARLY HOPLITE SHIELD: Fabriano (near Gubbio). SENATE OF 300 MEMBERS: based on three tribes and 30 *curiae.* ALBA LONGA: from tenth century controlled line of future Via Appia. Its existence may not antedate Rome's, but its importance does. Its destruction (doubted by some) was attributed to King Tullus Hostilius. Its leading families in Rome: Julii, Tullii. OSTIA AND PONS SUBLICIUS: (from *sublicae*, "piles") legendary attributions to King Ancus Marcius. MASSILIA: founded from Ionian Phonaea (Phocaea). GREEK INFLUENCE in Latium: shown by some of the early bronze statuettes now discovered at Gabii (Castiglione). GREEK ALTAR OF HERCULES *(Ara Maxima):* presided over commerce; imports in the sixth century were paid for by Rome in salt, timber, and slaves. CAPITOLINE TEMPLE: platform of *cappellaccio* without mortar. The temple had flanking colonnades, unlike the "normal," smaller Etruscan temple described by Vitruvius—Jupiter, Juno, and Minerva (identified with the Greek Zeus, Hera, and Athena) had already been grouped on the Capitolium Vetus on the Quirinal (whose god Quirinus was identified with Romulus). EXPANSION OF TARQUINIUS SUPERBUS: Antium (Anzio), Ardea, and probably Lavinium seem to have accepted Roman military leadership (temporarily). Gabii guarded the eastern flank of Latium against the Sabines: treaty celebrated on a coin of Augustus. Garrisons (of allies) at Pometia (Pomezia), Circeii (S. Felice Circeo), Signia (Segni).

The Fall of the Monarchy. DOWNFALL OF SUPERBUS: ascribed to love affair (with woman), cf. downfall of Athenian Hippias (510 B.C.) (with boy). ARICIA became leader of the league of Ferentina. DESTRUCTION OF ETRUSCAN TOWN: late sixth century, S. Giovenale, near Viterbo. PORSENNA: perhaps an Etruscan title (purthna). CLUSIUM: at the southern end of the Val di Chiana. (A modern theory identified Porsena's city instead with Marsigliana d'Albegna or Orbetello, on the coast). ETRUSCAN RAIDER-SETTLERS IN ROME: Mastarna (from *magister*, "general"?) and Caeles Vibenna. CUMAE BATTLE: the Syracusan victor was Hiero I. MARZABOTTO: on flood plain of River Renus (Reno); gridiron street plan. ADRIA: gave its name to the Adriatic Sea. SPINA: built on piles amid a network of canals. ETRUSCAN WRITING IN EUROPE: Scandinavian runes in the Middle Ages were still based on Etruscan letters.

PART II   THE UNITY OF ITALY AND ROME

Chapter 3. The Unification of Italy

Rome's Hostile Neighbors. LATINS: By 500 B.C. the original 50 or more communities were reduced to 10 or 12. LAVINIUM: at least 13 altars of 500 B.C. or a little earlier, recently discovered large-scale statuary from sixth, but mainly of fifth and fourth centuries; and archaic Latin inscription to Castor and Pollux. Lavinium first developed parallel to the Alban communities, then rose as they declined. TUSCULUM: its leader Octavius Mamilius was believed to have been Tarquinius Superbus's son-in-law. TREATY WITH LATINS: (Cassian Treaty, 493 B.C.); made by Spurius Cassius Vecellinus. ARDEA: home of legendary Italian (Rutulian) leader Turnus in Virgil's *Aeneid*. Perhaps Ardea, like Lavinium, had for a time been in Roman hands at an earlier date. OSCAN: alphabet derived through Etruscan alphabet from Chalcidic (Euboean) Greek. VOLSCI: originated in upper Liris (Garigliano) valley west of the Fucine Lake, and moved across Lepini Mountains towards Rome.

They were the tribe of the legendary heroine Camilla in Virgil's *Aeneid*. ANTIUM: captured 338; the beaks of its ships were the first war prizes to embellish Rome, placed on the speaker's platform (*rostra*, "beaks") in the Forum by Gaius Maenius. LATIN COLONIES: the earliest were Cora (Cori, dated to 501), Signia (Segni, 495), Velitrae (Velletri, ca. 494), Norba 492. There were about 14 of these "old" colonies (*priscae Latinae coloniae*) by 338. The term *colonus*, from *colere*, "to cultivate," reveals an agricultural motive. SABINES: had probably begun to descend the Tiber valley in eighth century. Their towns included Reate (Rieti), Cures (near Via Salaria), Amiternum (S. Vittorino). FETIALES: presided over international relations; no war was acceptable to the gods unless in defense of Rome or its allies.

   Victory over Veii.   ETRUSCANS IN FIFTH CENTURY ROME: there are Etruscan names of consuls in Fasti 509-490 and 461-448; in 492 grain had been imported from Etruria. Archaeological evidence shows waning of Etruscan contacts ca. 475-450. FIDENAE: the tradition of a very early Latin colony (of regal date) here is uncertain. VEII: Rome had arranged for a flag to be flown on the Janiculum Hill in case of attack. Veii had a tunnel piercing a ridge leading to the Tiber valley 17 miles north of Rome, also another shortcut to the river halfway to Ostia. FABII: continuous consulships ca. 485-479/7, then ten-year gap. They shared their leading position with the family of the Licinii. CREMERA BATTLE: legendary details suspiciously similar to those of the battle of Thermopylae between the Greeks and Persians (480 B.C.). CENSORS: period of office ended with *lustrum* ("cleansing"). Censors were appointed at intervals of five years from 209 B.C. onwards. They took over the selection of senators from the consuls. CAMILLUS: reputedly dictator five times, military tribune with consular power five times, four Triumphs. EXPANSION AFTER VEII: Capena and Falerii annexed; four new rustic Roman tribes.

   The Gallic Invasion and its Aftermath.   CELTS: La Tène style (from Swiss-type site) succeeds Hallstatt ca. 500 B.C. The La Tène Celts invented horse-drawn carts. GAULS: sack of Rome mentioned by Theopompus (ca. 350) and Aristotle. Further raids in 360s, 350s and 340s, which caused the Italian peoples to turn to Rome. Subsequently the Gauls of north Italy became skillful agriculturalists. CAERE: ports: Pyrgi (Santa Severa), Alsium (Palo), Punicum (Santa Marinella). Raid by Dionysius I of Syracuse ca. 384. HOSTILITY TO VEII: Greek imports to Caere had increased from ca. 630, and those to Veii had decreased, perhaps because of Roman territorial gains from the latter. HOSPITIUM WITH CAERE: ca. 390/86 (?). Rome joined Caere in sending 500 colonists to Sardinia and Corsica. Some ascribe this to ca. 300 rather than ca. 386 B.C. WALL OF SERVIUS: (fourth century) of Grotta Oscura tufa. CIRCUS MAXIMUS: believed to have dated from regal times.

   The Romans in Latium and Campania.   LATIN COLONIES AFTER GALLIC INVASION: Nepet (Nepi) and Sutrium (Sutri) ca. 383-382, formally dependencies of Falerii. TUSCULUM: its consuls at Rome: Mamilii, Fulvii, Fonteii, Juventii, Porcii. PRAENESTE: the Via Praenestina led to Rome; Praeneste was an Etruscanized Latian town, like Satricum (Conca), Lanuvium (Lanuvio), Velitrae (Velletri). *Fortuna:* the "bringer" (from *ferre*), later identified with the Greek Tyche (Chance). CAPUA: its bronze work was praised by Cato the censor in second century B.C. TIBUR: on River Anio (Aniene); dominated Via Valeria.

The Samnite Wars. SAMNITES: belonged to Sabellian group of peoples; they were believed to have originated from Sabine Amiternum (S. Vittorino). RIGHT TO EXCHANGE CITIZENSHIP: private rights included the right to exchange citizenship on moving from the one city to the other *(ius migrandi* or *mutandae civitatis),* limited in third century B.C. (to prevent too much immigration to Rome) and abolished in second century. Latin colonies privileged in 338: Ardea, Circeii, Nepet, Norba, Setia, Signia, Sutrium—half of the *priscae Latinae coloniae.* SABINES: after revolt of 290, some were enslaved, and the rest given *civitas sine suffragio.* Cales was one of a small number of Latin colonies allowed to coin silver in the third century. Others were Suessa Aurunca (Sessa), Paestum (formerly Posidonia), Signia, and Alba Fucens (Albe). LATIN COLONIES: COSA: polygonal walls, with corbelled gateway such as also survive at Signia. OSTIA: Town wall of Fidenae tufa. TARRACINA: called Anxur by the Volsci. SAMNITE TRIBES: Caraceni, Pentri, Caudini, Hirpini. NEAPOLIS: issued coins on behalf of Rome in the later fourth century, inscribed "of the Romans" in Greek. VIA APPIA: by 244 extended to Brundisium. By the end of the third century, seven major roads led to and from Rome. THIRD SAMNITE WAR: The Lucanians had appealed to Rome. The Samnites won a victory near Luceria (Lucera) (294), and the Romans near Aquilonia (Lacedogna) (293). MANIPLE: *manipulus,* "handful," from a bundle of straw tied to a pole to act as a flag. A maniple contained two centuries of 80 men, each divided into ten mess units sharing a tent and a mule. GLADIATORS: first called "Samnites"; later they also included Thracians and Gauls. TREATIES: with peoples of Etruria, Umbria, Picenum, and N. Apulia and the Marsi. In the later third century B.C. the Romans also made truces of varying duration (instead of permanent treaties) with other Etruscan cities. 50,000 SQUARE MILES CONTROLLED BY ROME: included 10,000 square miles of Roman and 5,000 of Latin territory. The system included partial, though not necessarily always conscious, borrowings from Sparta, the Panhellenic, Thessalian, Aetolian and Achaean Leagues, and the Athenian Empire. COINAGE: *aes grave,* true coins of defined face value, developed from *aes signatum* of central Italy (of later fourth century), consisting of flat bars of varying size with a design on one side. This in turn had evolved from shapeless, unstamped *aes rude,* valued purely by weight, which had partially replaced cattle as a medium of exchange in fifth century B.C.

Chapter 4. The Class Struggle

The Early Republic. CONSULS: perhaps at first, for a time, there was only one, possibly known as the *praetor maximus.* DICTATORS: may have developed from *praetor maximus.* Nominated by a consul on the Senate's proposal with subsequent ratifying law. Only a few of the recorded early dictatorships seem to be genuine. LEGISLATION: remarkable in that it could be initiated by all three branches (magistrates, Senate, and assemblies). PATRONS: the evidence of a patron or client could not be enforced against the other.

Patricians and Plebeians. PLEBEIANS: allegedly plebeian consuls ca. 502-500 may not have been plebeians at all but patricians. PATRICIANS: out of 53 fifth-century *gentes,* only 29 still appear in fourth century; by 300 B.C. they formed less than one twentieth of the population. AGITATIONS FOR LAND: go back to ca. 486.

Livy records seven between 441 and 410. Until the Apennines were conquered, there was a lack of summer pastures. CERES: temple probably on site of S. Maria Cosmedin. The cult was looked after by two *plebian* aediles, assistants of the tribunes of the people (two patrician curule aedileships were created in 367 B.C.). TYRANTS: allegedly tried to seize power at Rome in 478, 431, 376 B.C. GREEK TRADE: Athenian commerce with Rome fell off sharply 450-400. APOLLO: temple of ca. 431 in Flaminian Fields, on site of previous shrine (Apollinar). EPIDEMICS: anthrax? FOOD: five shortages of grain reported 508-411. In about fourth century coarse emmer wheat was partly superseded by more highly evolved bread wheat; and vine- and olive-growing had been learned from the Greeks—though the need for heavy initial outlays slowed down development. DEBT: cf. problems of fourth century Greece. SECESSIONS: allegedly 494, 449, 448, 342, 287 B.C. Menenius Agrippa reputedly appeased the plebeians in 494. OATH OF PLEBEIANS: *lex sacrata,* hence probably erroneous tradition of secession to Mons Sacer (just beyond R. Anio). TRIBUNI PLEBIS: originally 2, or 4, or 5; 10 by 449 B.C. CONCILIUM PLEBIS: generally known as *Comitia plebis tributa* after ca. 287. The *Comitia populi tributa* was founded in imitation of this (it elected quaestors, curule aediles, etc.) PLEBISCITA: in ca. 449 B.C. (?) all such future measures that received the prior sanction of the patrician senators *(patrum auctoritas)* were recognized as universally binding. Unconditional validity from 339 (?) and/or 287.

The Twelve Tables.   DECEMVIRI: names of first team (execpt one) seem authentic, but not second team (including some plebeians). TWELVE TABLES: traditionally ten published by the first team of decemvirs, plus two "unjust" ones by the second. A formal procedure of appeal *(provocatio)* carrying no guarantee of admission may have existed by the time of the tables.

Social Appeasement.   LAWS OF 449: *Leges Valeriae Horatiae.* MEASURE OF 447: the two quaestors (junior financial officials), previously appointed by the consuls, were to be elected by the *Concilium plebis.* Two were added in 421 when the plebeians were admitted. It is often uncertain whether specific "measures" reported in the tradition were conceded by the patricians as having force of law or merely asserted by the plebeians as a right. RESTORATION OF CONSULSHIP: *Leges Liciniae Sextiae.* One of the tribunes, Lucius Sextius Lateranus, may have become the first plebeian consul in 366. These two tribunes supposedly limited land ownership to 300 acres (500 *iugera*), but this tradition may be a reflection of later political disputes. CENSORS: *Lex Publilia* of 339 laid it down that one must be a plebeian. It was not adhered to until 131 that both members of a pair of censors be plebeians. NOBLES: also included those descended from a *tribunus militum consulari potestate.* DEBT MEASURES: allegedly 352, 351, 342, 326 (?). The *Lex Genucia* (342) had tried to veto usury, at least temporarily. CONCORD: Camillus's temple was at the foot of the Capitol, near the Forum. LEX POETELIA: 326 or possibly 313 B.C. It also permitted mortgages on land. AQUA APPIA: followed by Anio Vetus (272) from Sabine hills, tunneled with short bridges and an inverted siphon. CNAEUS FLAVIUS: curule aedile 304 B.C. NEW NOBILITY: its hegemony was upheld by the Fabii Maximi who controlled the Senate in the early third century B.C.

PART III　ROME AGAINST CARTHAGE

Chapter 5. First Wars against Foreign Powers

The Invasion of Pyrrhus. TARENTUM: at its zenith under the philosopher-scientist Archytas, early fourth century. Its attempt to mediate in the Second Samnite War (ca. 314) had been rebuffed by Rome. VENUSIA: on upper Aufidus (R. Ofanto); probably 6000 settlers. Latin colony at Hadria or Hatria (Atri) at the same time, and Roman colony at Sena Gallica (Senigallia) a few years later. THURII: former Sybaris. GREEK HELPERS OF TARENTUM IN LATER FOURTH CENTURY: Archidamus II of Sparta, Alexander I of Epirus, Cleonymus of Sparta. PYRRHUS: capital at Ambracia (Arta); completed Hellenization of Epirus. His army included 3000 Thessalian cavalry and 2000 archers. HERACLEA: detached from Tarentum by Rome by favorable treaty (ca. 278). AUSCULUM: Pyrrhus was threatening the Latin colonies of Venusia and Luceria. BENEVENTUM: called Malventum until made a Latin colony in 268, at same time as Ariminum (Rimini); they were the two farthest colonies from Rome ever to be founded; they split Samnium in half. EGYPT: Roman treaty with Ptolemy II in 273; Rome had made an agreement with Rhodes in ca. 306. SILVER COINAGE: didrachms inscribed ROMANO, issued at south Italian mint after 280. Coins of ca. 269 issued at Rome have type of wolf and twins. CARTHAGE: Population of city (fourth century): 400,000–500,000, compared to 100,000–150,000 at Rome, 200,000 at Tarentum. CARTHAGINIAN SICILY: Panormus founded early seventh century; principal port Motya near Lilybaeum (Marsala). CARTHAGINIAN SARDINIA: recent discoveries (e.g., Monte Sirae) show importance ca. 600. Chief port Nora was much older. CORSICA: Greeks defeated off Alalia (Aleria) ca. 535 B.C. Corsica went to the Etruscans and later to the Carthaginians. CAERE: Carthaginian presence at its ports Pyrgi and Punicum. TUNISIA: fertile valley of R. Bagradas (Medjerda), beside which was the second Carthaginian city Utica (Henchir bou Chateur), traditionally older. WEST AFRICA: e.g., exploration of Hanno before 480 B.C. AGRICULTURAL STUDIES: 32-book work of Mago, translated by order of Roman Senate in later second century B.C. CARTHAGINIANS AT ROME: Perhaps the Altar of Hercules *(Ara Maxima)* beside the Tiber was founded with a view not only to Greek but to Carthaginian associations (Hercules being identified with the Semitic deity Melkart). TREATIES WITH ROME: according to one theory the first treaty was with the Etruscans, not the Romans. MESSANA: dominated since 283 by Mamertini ("men of Mars"), companion mercenaries of Syracusan Agathocles. ROMAN FLEETS: by 311 a flotilla; 267, 4 *quaestores Italici* (at Ostia, etc.) responsible for it.

The First Punic War. THE WAR: In 262 Rome took Segesta and Agrigentum (Agrigento); their capture was a turning point. QUINQUEREMES: better than obsolete triremes in which, although there were fewer rowers, every one of them had to be a skilled oarsman. Two Carthaginian warships have now been found under the sea off Lilybaeum (Marsala), including one that apparently dates from the First Punic War. REGULUS: according to legend, rather than urge the Roman Senate to make peace, he went back voluntarily to be tortured and killed by the Carthaginians. LAST PHASE: Carthaginian successes by young Hamilcar Barca (248–242), badly supplied from home. PROW: on bronze *as* from ca. 240–235 B.C. PEACE TREATY: veto on

Carthaginian presence in Italian waters was for benefit of Greek cities in south Italy. SICILIAN PROVINCE: quaestors set up at Syracuse and Lilybaeum. INDIRECT TAXES: levied by the cities expecially on imports and exports. They also derived income from monopolies. WAR OF THE MERCENARIES (TRUCELESS WAR): started at Sicca Veneria (El Kef), Liby-Phoenicians and Numidians joined; promises had been broken by Hanno the Great and landlords.

Chapter 6. The Changing Roman World

An Age of Innovations. GLADIATORS: in 358 B.C., 307 Roman prisoners had been slaughtered as human sacrifices at Tarquinii (Tarquinia). Capua (S. Maria Capua Vetere), and Puteoli (Pozzuoli, the former Dicaearchia) in Campania had the largest amphitheatres known until the Colosseum. GREEK WORKS OF ART: first seen in Triumph of Lucius Papirius Cursor, captor of Tarentum in 272. Manius Valerius Messalla showed paintings of his Sicilian victories in 264. LIVIUS ANDRONICUS: when freed, he took on his former owner's name, as was the custom. Ulysses (Odysseus) had long been regarded as an Italic hero. Livius may have become Rome's first schoolmaster. *Ludi Scaenici* were now added to *Ludi Romani* (240) [religious *Ludi Tarentini,* later known as *Ludi Saeculares,* were believed to have been introduced in 348 (or 249?)]; they purified the city at intervals of time (often, the passage of a century), by propitiatory ceremonies to the underworld deities. JURISTIC LITERATURE: its founder at Rome was Sextus Aelius Paetus Catus (consul, 198 B.C.)

The Challenge of Flaminius. PLEBEIAN COUNCIL (CONCILIUM PLEBIS, COMITIA PLEBIS TRIBUTA): based on 35 tribes by 241 B.C. GAULS: *ager Gallicus* annexed in ca. 283, after Roman defeat at Arrentium (Arezzo) in 284. Invasion by Boii, Lingones, Insubres, Taurini, Gaesati in 225.

Chapter 7. The Invasion by Hannibal

The Carthaginians in Spain. HAMILCAR BARCA: had seized hilltop Ercte or Heirkte behind Panormus [(Palermo) M. Pellegrino or M. Castellacio] as base for raids in First Punic War, and had joined with his political enemy Hanno the Great in terminating the War of the Mercenaries (Truceless War). Drowned in R. Helice in Spain. CARTHAGO NOVA: originally Mastia. SAGUNTUM: may have been recognized as a Roman ally before 226. EBRO TREATY: Romans were prepared to agree because of Gallic threat at home.

The Victories of Hannibal. ROMAN MANPOWER 218 B.C.: perhaps out of a total population of Italy of three million, with two million slaves [(?) plus population of 1,400,000 in Cisalpine Gaul], there were 270,000–300,000 adult Roman and 640,000 allied males. ALPS: crossed by Hannibal somewhere between Little S. Bernard and M. Genèvre passes (probably a pass of M. Cenis or M. Gènevre group). All his 37 elephants seem to have survived the crossing, although they then did not last long. PLACENTIA: just east of the point where R. Trebia (Trebbia), flowing down from Apennines, joins the Po. 217 B.C.: II legions were put into the field, including four to block road to Rome. Hannibal penetrated through Collina Pass, and then on between Pistoria (Pistoia) and Faesulae (Fiesole). FABIUS MAXIMUS: had held an earlier dictatorship in 221. In 217 he was duped into letting Hannibal move from Campania to Apulia. CANNAE: near south bank of Aufidus (R. Ofanto). The consuls were Lucius Aemilius Paullus and Gaius Terentius Varro, 215 B.C. Twenty-five legions were raised. CAPUA: the rebellious city, together with its dependencies Atella (Aversa) and Calatia (S. Giacomo alle Gallazze), issued coins of its own, inscribed in the Italic Oscan language. SYRACUSE: betrayed by Spanish officer to Marcus Claudius Marcellus, the "Sword of Rome," despite the skill of the great mathematician Archimedes in devising engines of war. TARENTUM: taken by Hannibal by treachery (citadel remaining in Roman hands), plundered by Romans on recapture. COINAGE: subdivisions of the *denarius* were also issued.

The Scipios in Spain. THE TWO CORNELIUS SCIPIOS (father and uncle of Africanus): Publius, who failed to stop Hannibal's departure for Spain, then was defeated at Ticinus and Trebia, and returned to Spain in 217; and Cnaeus, sent to Spain in 218, where he won a naval victory off the Ebro in the following year. The brothers defeated Hasdrubal Barca near Ibera on the Ebro in 215, but in 211 Publius was killed on the upper Baetis (Guadalquivir) and Cnaeus at Ilorci (Lorqui) behind Carthago Nova. PUBLIUS SCIPIO JUNIOR (PUBLIUS'S SON, LATER AFRICANUS): the first private citizen to be invested with proconsular *imperium*. ILIPA (206): Hasdrubal (son of Gisgo) and Mago (brother of Hannibal) were the defeated Carthaginian commanders. TAX ON SPAIN: mints for siver coinage opened at Osca (Huesca), etc. SPANISH AUXILIA: included cavalry slingers from Baleares (Balearic) islands. ITALICA: R. Baetis was navigable by sea-going vessels for 140 miles up to there, then by smaller boats up to Córduba (Córdova) plain. REBELLIOUS LATIN COLONIES: included Ardea, Cales, Alba Fucens; they were punished by a double draft in 204. The farms of Italy were so exhausted that wheat had to be imported from Egypt (208-207).

The Triumph of Scipio Africanus. SCIPIO IN AFRICA: first victory at Great Plains [Campi Magni; near Souk el Kremis, on upper Bagradas (Medjerda)]. ZAMA (REGIA): battle probably in plain of Draa-el-Metnan (southwest of Sicca Veneria). LINES OF MANIPLE OPERATING INDEPENDENTLY: Baecula, Ilipa, Campi Magni. PORTRAITURE: Etruscan portrait busts at Clusium and Caere. From third century, Hellenistic Greek portraits also gradually exerted an influence.

PART IV   THE IMPERIAL REPUBLIC

Chapter 8. "Our Sea"

The Eclipse of the Greek Kingdoms. ALEXANDER THE GREAT: son of Philip II (359-336 B.C.) The principal states of Alexander's Hellenistic successors were named after their monarchs Antigonus I, Seleucus I Nicator, and Ptolemy I Soter (founder of the Lagid house). ILLYRIANS: took Scodra (Skhöder) and Lissus (Les, ca. 260), Corcyra (Corfu, 229). ROMAN PROTECTORATE: Apollonia (ancient, rich, and strategic port in Bay of Valona) and Dyrrhachium; (formerly Epidamnus; Durazzo, Durrës; 229). The Romans relieved Apollonia in 214. MACEDONIA: had united almost all Greece by alliance with Achaean League and conquest of Sparta (222). PEACE WITH PHILIP V (205): Peace of Phoenice. AETOLIAN LEAGUE: protectorate over Delphi in third century. They made peace with Philip V in 206 because Rome had not helped them sufficiently. ANTIOCHUS III: acquired Armenia and regained Parthia and Bactria as vassal kingdoms, crossed Persian Gulf, and entered Kabul valley (212–206). RHODES AND PERGAMUM: defeated Philip V by sea off Chios (201). FORTRESSES OF PHILIP V: Demetrias (near Volos), Chalcis, Corinth. CYNOSCEPHALAE: 3,000 Macedonians killed, 5,000 captured. Philip, weak in cavalry, gave his infantry no flank guard. FLAMININUS: had been at Tarentum (205–204) where he won the goodwill of the Greeks. HANNIBAL: leading official (suffete) of Carthage ca. 196. At Antiochus's court he was rumored to be planning a fresh invasion of Italy. MAGNESIA: the Roman commander was Lucius Cornelius Scipio (who took the name Asiaticus). Antiochus had 75,000 men to face 30,000 Romans. The Roman victory was preceded by another at sea at Myonnesus (Çifitkale). The peace of Apamea in Phrygia (Dinar, 188) was concluded by Cnaeus Manlius Vulso after he had subdued the Galatians (descendants of Gaulish immigrants) in the center of Asia Minor. Subsequent Seleucid decline caused the independent development of Pontus, Armenia, Parthia, Judaea. PERSEUS: Third Macedonian War. Romans failed to dislodge him from Tempe in 171 and 170 but succeeded in 169. Two years after Pydna he died at Alba Fucens. EPIRUS: was raided for slaves by the Romans because it had not helped them effectively. REPUBLICS OF MACEDONIA: land tax reduced by half; iron and copper worked by contractors, gold and silver mines reopened after ten years. Illyria, too, was subdivided into three republics. ANTIOCHUS IV EPIPHANES: ordered to leave Ptolemy VI's Egypt by Gaius Popillius Laenas (168).

Imperialistic Policies. RHODES AFTER PYDNA: Eumenes II's brother was Attalus II Philadelphus (160–138 B.C.). DELOS: was also to gain greatly from the destruction of Corinth in 146. ACHAEAN LEAGUE: had gone over to Rome in 198 but relations had often been strained since then. SPAIN: land communications with Italy were secured by development of Po valley, 200–150 B.C. CELTIBERIANS: a major group of peoples formed by fusion of Iberian population with Celtic invaders. FATHER OF GRACCHI: Tiberius Sempronius Gracchus; founded native town Gracchuris near Ebro (179). CARTEIA (EL ROCADILLO): for sons of soldiers, was the first Latin colony outside Italy (171). VIRIATHUS: final base was among the Carpetani, northwest of Toletum (Toledo). His soldiers were settled at Valentia (Valencia, 138). NUMANTIA: surrounded by Scipio Aemilianus (consul for the second time in 134 after special legislation) with seven camps and a five-mile long, double-ring wall. A red layer of burned material shows the town was burnt to the ground. PACIFIED SPAIN: a major strategic road was built from ca. 120 B.C. from the Pyrenees to Gibraltar (in Spain the road system did not radiate but followed the periphery of the peninsula). ANDRISCUS: Fourth Macedonian War; he overran Thessaly and was caught in Thrace. MACEDONIAN PROVINCE: included Epirus and Thessaly; alliances were made with Thracian chiefs. VIA EGNATIA: from Apollonia to Thessalonica (Salonika); by 130 it was continued in Asia Minor. CORINTH: the local autocrat, Critolaus, was its commander. CARTHAGE: in 191 offered immediate payment of 40 further installments of its indemnity and gave much free grain for Roman forces in the east. MASINISSA: his empire extended from Mauretania to Cyrenaica. Rome offered adjudications in the 160s and 150s, which did not hamper him. But he was ignored in the Third Punic War and died in 148. CATO AND CARTHAGE: opposed by Publius Scipio Nasica Corculum, who regarded it as morally salutary to have an enemy to fear. THIRD PUNIC WAR: Carthage initially surrendered and handed over hostages and war material, but on hearing that the city must be destroyed decided to fight. AFRICAN PROVINCE: 5,000 square miles with capital at Utica (Henchir bou Chateur), which had joined the Romans. Seven cities were left "free." Governors went there by an extension of their year of urban office *(prorogatio)* first in 326 B.C.; by this time general practice). If the wind was right, Ostia was only a 48-hour sail.

Chapter 9. The New Society

Senate and Nobles in Charge. NEW MEN AS CONSULS: 16 out of 262 from 264 to 134 B.C., 8 out of 108 from 200 to 146 B.C. The 200 consuls between 233 and 133 B.C. included 99 from 10 families, 159 from 15 families. AGE LIMITS (MINIMUM) OF MAGISTRACIES: *Lex Villia Annalis* (180 B.C.). Possibly the same law required an interval of two years between senior magistracies. NEW CULTS: Aesculapius (Asclepius) from Epidaurus after plague in 292, Venus Erycina from Eryx (Erice) in Sicily 215, Cybele from Asia Minor in 205–204. In 139 Jews were banished by the *praetor peregrinus.*

The Rise of Latin Culture. TRAGEDIES: about Roman history and legend: *fabula praetextata.* COMEDY: owed something to rudimentary Italian song-and-dance and dramatic sketches of the past. Naevius's comedies were mainly *palliatae* (adaptions of Greek New Comedy) but also *togatae* (about Roman themes). Mime *(fabula riciniata)* was staged at Rome before 200 B.C. SLAVES: in 217 the Saturnalia was turned into a Hellenized festival in which slaves temporarily changed places with their masters. ENNIUS: Rudiae was subjected to Greek and Latin influences from Tarentum and Brundisium (Brindisi) respectively. Ennius was brought home from Sardinia by Cato the Elder (204) and was with Marcus Fulvius Nobilior in Aetolia (189). The *Annals* are in quantitative dactylic hexameters. Thirty-one lines of his four or six books of *Satires* have survived. He was the uncle of Pacuvius of Brundisium (died ca. 130), who disputed the title of the greatest Roman tragedian with Accius of Pisaurum [(Pesaro) died after 90 B.C.]. SCIPIO AFRICANUS: after the obscure "Trials of the Scipios" (137, 184?) relating to misuse of public funds, Africanus withdrew, ill, to his farm at Liternum (north of Cumae) in Campania, where he died soon afterwards. PERSONALITY CULT: from second century state officials were permitted to erect statues of themselves in public places. Delos became an important center of Greek sculpture which influenced Rome. CATO THE ELDER: his career was made by the clan of the Valerii, enemies of the Scipios. AGAINST WOMEN'S LIBERATION: *Lex Voconia* (164). In 195 Cato had opposed the repeal of the wartime *Lex Oppia* (215) restricting female dress and jewelry. In 102 B.C. there was the first public funeral ceremony for a woman. ROMAN HISTORIES IN GREEK: Quintus Fabius Pictor, Lucius Cincius Alimentus (both took part in the Second Punic War). EDUCATION: secondary schools taught by *grammatici* were opened after the Second Punic War. SCIPIO AEMILIANUS: associates included Panaetius of Rhodes (ca. 185–109), who placed a new emphasis on human individuality and (incidentally) helped to adapt Stoicism to Roman public life, and Polybius of Megalopolis (ca. 200–after 118), Greek historian of Rome. COMEDY: Caecilius Statius [d. 168 B.C., a Gaulish (Insubrian) ex-slave], rated in the following century as the greatest of Latin comic dramatists.

Roman Wealth and New Buildings. LUXURY: the taste for it spread after the public had seen the loot in the *ovatio* (minor triumph) of Marcus Claudius Marcellus (211) and the triumphs of Cnaeus Manlius Vulso (187) and Lucius Aemilius Paullus Macedonicus, victor of Pydna. Mass imports of Greek works of art (as well as the voting of divine honors to Romans in the east) had started in the later third century B.C., and much statuary came in after the sack of Corinth (146). TAXES: there may have been irregular levies of direct taxation *(tributum)* in the 180s. Italians also had to pay indirect taxes *(vectigala)* including rents on public land, mines, and salt-works, a five percent tax on freeing slaves, and customs dues *(portoria)*. Puteoli, formerly Dicaearchia (now Pozzuoli), which grew in the Second Punic War and became a Roman colony in 194, was a leading customs station and port). BASILICAS: often with galleries, *exedrae,* and clerestories; early Roman examples 184, 179, 170. Are now believed to have evolved from the porticoes of the Hellenistic Greeks [directly imitated in Rome 196 (?), 167, 146 B.C.]. There were two types: (1) with long side facing an open area (e.g., Alba Fucens, Ardea, Cosa); (2) longitudinal, with entrance at short side (e.g., Pompeii). ARCHES IN ROME: the earliest were erected by Lucius Stertinius (196 B.C.), in Circus Maximus and Forum Boarium (Cattle Market); then 190, 120. The oldest surviving arch in Italy is at Cosa (Ansedonia, ca. 150), with a triple opening. Imperial triumphal arches at Rome: of Titus, Septimius Severus, Constantine. CONCRETE IN TEMPLES: Concord (121), Castor and Pollux (117). AQUA MARCIA: built from head of Anio valley by praetor Quintus Marcius Rex who also repaired older aqueducts. ROADS: Via Aemilia (187 B.C.) continued the Via Flaminia from Ariminum (Rimini) to Placentia (Piacenza). BRIDGES: after the Pons Aemilius, the Pons Mulvius (Ponte Milvio) was built to carry the Via Flaminia (109). STONE FACINGS: marble apparently first used for Temple of Jupiter Stator (149 B.C.). POMPEII HOUSES: Italian (Samnite) phase fourth century (e.g., House of Surgeon) replaced by Hellenistic Greek phase mid-third century. INCRUSTATION STYLE OF WALL PAINTING: from *crusta,* slab of marble, which this imitates; earliest surviving examples at Pompeii and Cosa from ca. 100 B.C.

Agriculture and Slavery. SMALL HOLDERS: generally found south Italy (except Greek south coast) unattractive, though small grid units (c. 120) have been detected in Apulia. But small holdings were still extensive in the mountains and Campania and the Po valley. MALARIA: expecially prevalent in Maremma and Pomptine (Pontine) Marshes; had perhaps been introduced by Carthaginian soldiers in the Second Punic War. SOLDIER'S PAY: ca. 170–122 B.C., five *asses* a day with deductions for food, clothes, and arms. LIMITATION ON LANDOWNERSHIP: *Leges Liciniae Sextiae* (366 B.C.), though recorded details are anachronistic. GRAIN: poorer people ate either coarse bread (ground husks and all) or porridge of meal (often millet) and water. CAMPANIA: e.g., Francolise near Capua possessed *Villae rusticae* (residence with farms) at Posta (end second century) and S. Rocco (mid-first century), recently excavated. ETRURIA: e.g., farmhouse at Villa Sambuco (near S. Giovenale, end second century), now being excavated. GRAIN COMPETITION: from Sicily and north Africa, mainly felt in Roman area and some coastal towns. WINE: probably already exported ca. 230 B.C. (red Latian), later spread widely; the first known vintage dated from the consulship of Gaius Opimius (121 B.C.) VEGETABLES: turnips, beans, also fruit (especially figs). CATTLE: Italians rarely ate meat—and it was mainly pork when they did. SLAVES: there is a fourth-century-B.C. painting of a woman with a slave from Neapolis (Naples). The First Slave War provoked unrest in Delos, Laurium in Attica (silver mines), Macedonia, Pergamum. COLONIES AFTER 200: Cisalpine Gauls forced to give up half their territory. Mutina (Modena) and Parma became Roman colonies in 183, Bononia (former Felsina, now Bologna) and Aquileia Latin colonies in 189 and 181. But Latin colonies then lapsed because of unwillingness of settlers to accept the limited Latin franchise. But Roman colonies, too, ceased to be founded for many years. Roman citizens were reluctant to sacrifice rentals of *ager publicus* to go to either sort of colony. DEBTORS: if they possessed land, it could be sold up, and they forfeited many citizen rights. But there were also many poor and discontented in the towns.

PART V THE FALL OF THE REPUBLIC

Chapter 10. Reform and War in Italy

The Gracchi. REASSERTION BY TRIBUNES: successful clashes with consuls and Senate 151, 149, 138. The *Lex Aelia* and *Lex Fufia* (ca. 150?) in retaliation gave officials the right to obstruct plebeian assemblies by the announcement of unfavorable auspices *(obnuntiatio)*. LAND PROBLEMS: the amount of *ager publicus* in illegal possession was considerable, but much inflated by rumor. TIBERIUS GRACCHUS: to increase free labor, made slave labor a target for criticism. GRUDGE AGAINST SCIPIO AEMILIANUS: because Scipio had advised the Senate to reject a treaty that Tiberius, as quaestor in Spain in 137, had made to save the army of Gaius Hostilius Mancinus. TIBERIUS'S FACTION: included his father-in-law the *princeps senatus,* Appius Claudius Pulcher. Some senators supported Tiberius because they were displeased by the appointment of Scipio Aemilianus to Spain. Tiberius was also supported by a Stoic philosopher, Gaius Blossius, of a prominent anti-Roman family from Cumae. PERGAMUM: Attalus III Philometor was its last king; after his death Eudemus visited Tiberius Gracchus of whose father Pergamenes had been clients. MURDER OF TIBERIUS GRACCHUS: the physical attack was led by Publius Cornelius Scipio Nasica Serapio. LAND COMMISSION: 76,000 allotments made 132–125; number of citizens rose eventually from 319,000 to 395,000. By III B.C. all public land in Italy was allotted except rich Compania. REELECTION TO TRIBUNATE: Gaius Papirius Carbo, tribune 131, had sought to pass bill authorizing this (though it had never been legally impermissible), but Scipio Aemilianus frustrated him; possibly a subsequent law in the early 120s carried out Carbo's intention. A further measure of Carbo, extending the secret ballot to legislative assemblies, was passed and played a part in the later breakup of oligarchic power. COLONIES OF GAIUS GRACCHUS: Neptunia (Tarentum) and Scolacium (Squillace), under the toe of Italy, look like commercial sites. ALLIED GRIEVANCES: shared by Latins who since ca. 128 had lost right to move from one city to another *(ius migrandi)* in favor of a new "Latin right" by which only local officials (magistrates) became Roman citizens. LAW COURTS: the *quaestio de repetundis* was established by a *Lex Calpurnia* of 149 B.C. SENATORS DEBARRED FROM FINANCE: *Lex Claudia de nave senatorum* (218 B.C.). This was one reason why they instead seized money in the provinces. SCIPIO AEMILIANUS'S WIFE: Sempronia, sister of Gracchi. FULVIUS FLACCUS'S LAND BILL: according to one view Tiberius Gracchus, too, had intended to distribute land to Italians, though many of them had not approved of his measures.

Marius. MASSILIA: given security by Rome's occupation of Po valley 200–150 B.C. AVERNI: under Bituitus, defeated by Quintus Fabius Maximus, who also became patron of the Allobroges and took their name "Allobrogicus." The Aedui, who were the rivals of the Arverni, had taken the side of Rome. VIA DOMITIA: an ancient route, already improved before 124. MASINISSA'S SUCCESSOR: Micipsa, succeeded by Adherbal and Jugurtha. JUGURTHA BETRAYED: by King Bocchus of Mauretania. ARAUSIO: the consuls were Cnaeus Mallius Maximus and Quintus Servilius Caepio. AQUAE SEXTIAE: Roman colony since 124 B.C. For many years after the battle, there was a bumper crop on the blood-soaked, corpse-filled soil. CAMPI RAUDII: Marius was joint commander with Catulus. 120,000 Germans were killed. ARMIES OF MARIUS: standing and short-term Roman armies were now distinguishable from each other. Marius's soldiers ("mules") each carried 100 pounds of weapon rations, cooking pots, stakes for palisades, etc. CANDIDATE MURDERED: Gaius Memmius, standing for consulship of 99 against Glaucia, who supported Saturninus (and died with him).

The War with the Italians (Social, Marsian War). ITALIAN CLAIMS: *Lex Licinia Mucia* of 95 B.C., setting up inquiry into aliens illegally claiming to be citizens, was construed by the Italians as a snub. REBEL CAPITAL: moved from Corfinium to Bovianum (Boiano) and then Aesernia (Isernia). CISALPINE GAUL: a province in 91 or 89 B.C., or possibly under Sulla. LEX JULIA: followed up by other laws (Calpurnia, Plautia Papiria, Pompeia).

Sulla in the East. MITHRIDATES VI: had gained most of the seacoast from Danube to Caucasus but was resisted by King Nicomedes IV Philopator of Bithynia (ca. 94–75 B.C.). SULLA: defeated Mithridates's general Archelaus at Chaeronea and Orchomenus, and after the peace caused the Marian general Fimbria to commit suicide. MURDERED PRAETOR: Sempronius Asellio (89 B.C.). DEBT LAW: cancelling three-fourths of all debts, passed by Lucius Valerius Flaccus, who was then murdered in Asia in a mutiny caused by Fimbria.

Chapter 11. Reaction and Breakdown

The Dictatorship of Sulla. THE EARLY SULLA: he had already began to legislate against the Senate and tribunes in 88. Roman colonies whose creation had been resumed since ca. 128, after a long intermission, were now much larger; one of Sulla's veteran colonies was Pompeii, settled to punish it for siding against him in the civil war, but relations between the old and new populations were tense, as they also were at the Sullan colony of Praeneste (Palestrina), formerly strongly anti-Sullan. Quaestors were now increased to 20, praetors from 6 to 8. Sulla encouraged and regularized the current practice of sending (proroguing) men who had just held office to provincial governorships as promagistrates (proconsuls, propraetors). Consuls now ceased to be basically military officials. TRIBUNES: prohibitions of their veto in special circumstances were multiplied. Their judicial powers were also curtailed.

The Rise of Pompey. LEPIDUS (78–77 B.C.): his supporter in Cisalpine Gaul was Marcus Junius Brutus. Lepidus was defeated at the Milvian Bridge by Catulus and died shortly afterwards from grief owing to his divorce. SERTORIUS: Metellus Pius was initially sent against him. Sertorius was murdered by Perperna. POMPEY: son of Pompeius Strabo. After bringing three legions from Picenum to help Sulla, he had killed Cnaeus Papirius Carbo in Sicily and defeated Cinna's son-in-law Cnaeus Domitius Ahenobarbus in north Africa. Pompey married Sulla's stepdaughter Aemilia (d. 80), and then later a close connection of the Metelli, Mucia, whom he divorced in 62. SLAVE REVOLT: the joint leader with Spartacus until 72 was Crixus, a Thracian. VERRES CASE: Cicero defeated the leading orator of the day, Quintus Hortensius Hortalus. JURY LAW: the *Lex Aurelia* (70 B.C.) divided panels equally among senators, knights, and *tribuni aerarii,* the next class below the knights in property qualification. PIRATE WARS: Marcus Antonius (102 B.C.), Pompey under *Lex Gabinia* (67). A Cilician command (later province; Southeast Asia Minor) had been created to deal with pirates in 102; enlarged in 64. Crete was added to the province of Cyrenaica in 67. MITHRIDATIC WARS: second conducted by Murena (81), third by Lucullus (74) and Pompey (*Lex Manilia,* 66). Lucullus had reduced accumulated interest on debts of Asian cities and forbade creditors to seize more than a fixed proportion of the sums due. Pompey cancelled many tax immunities of eastern states. ARMENIA: Tigranes I the Great (after 100–ca. 56 B.C.). JUDAEA: Pompey reappointed Hyrcanus II (high priest 76–67, high priest and ethnarch [(secular prince) 63–40]. NEW MEN: the last certain *novus homo* to win the consulship had been in 94 B.C. CICERO'S FELLOW CONSUL: Gaius Antonius Hybrida. BANKRUPT NOBLES: competition for office was intense (and canvassing expensive) because only two out of the 20 annual quaestors could later become consuls. GALLIC ENVOYS: 63; from the tribe of the Allobroges. EXECUTED CATILINARIANS: included ex-consul Publius Cornelius Lentulus Sura. PISTORIA: won by Petreius (62), Gaius Antonius Hybrida remained in his tent, allegedly ill. CAESAR'S MARIAN LINKS: Caesar married Cinna's daughter Cornelia, and his father's sister had been Marius's wife. EMERGENCY DECREE CASE: trial of Gaius Rabirius (63). HOUSES OF FIRST CENTURY B.C.: the characteristic form of wall paintings of the time ("Second Style") displayed illusionistic architectural vistas (e.g., Boscoreale bedroom in Metropolitan Museum, New York, and newly discovered villa at Oplontis (Torre Annunziata). CICERO'S EDUCATION: studied philosophy and rhetoric at Rome, Athens, and Rhodes. Schools of rhetoric (higher education) had begun at Rome early in first century B.C. LAW: Quintus Mucius Scaevola Pontifex (d. 82) published the first systematic treatise on civil law. PHILOSOPHY: Zeno came from Citium in Cyprus. Cicero followed the belief of a later Stoic, Posidonius [of Apamea in Syria (Kalat-el-

Mudik); b.ca. 135-d.ca. 50 B.C.] that philosophy had been the inventor of the civilized arts, and supported the view of the contemporary New Academy at Athens (descended from Plato's Academy) that dogma must be avoided. CONCORD OF THE ORDERS: slogan used by the historian Macer, who agitated for popular rights as tribune in 73; Cicero broadened it into a general concept involving moral responsibility and embracing moderates in the country towns *(consensus Italiae)*.

Toward the First Triumvirate. LAND INTRIGUES: (63 B.C.); Cicero opposed major agrarian bill of Rullus, which may or may not have been directed against Pompey. The veterans asked for a renewal of the *Lex Valeria* of 86 scaling down debts by three-quarters. CATO'S GRAIN DOLE: 62; cf. occasional measures in Hellenistic Greece. TAX GATHERERS (PUBLICANI): had strengthened their position after the First Mithridatic War by lending money to the Asian cities to pay tax arrears and indemnities.

PART VI   CAESAR AND AUGUSTUS

Chapter 12. Caesar

The First Consulship of Caesar. LAND LAW: 59 B.C.; extended to rich Compania by hotly contested *Lex Campana*. Bibulus attempted to obstruct legislation by *obnuntiatio* (proclamation that the auspices were ill omened), under the *Leges Aelia* and *Fufia* (ca. 150). But refuse was emptied over his head in the Forum, and his official bundle of rods *(fasces)* were broken. EGYPTIAN KING HELPED BY CAESAR: Ptolemy XII Auletes (80–51 B.C.) CAESAR'S COMMAND: *Lex Vatinia.* Dalmatia was later known as Upper Illyricum.

The Gallic War. GAUL: "three parts" (according to Caesar): Belgae, Celts, Aquitani. ARIOVISTUS: of a Suebian tribe, perhaps the Triboci. He had defeated the Aedui in 61 at Magetobriga (Moigte de Broie?), and it was they who led the appeal to Caesar against him. CLODIUS: guilds or corporations *(collegia),* often composed of men practicing the same trade, were normally permitted to exist subject to senatorial sanction; they had, however, been suppressed in 64 B.C. for political action, but were revived by Clodius. He financed his grain dole out of the annexation of Cyprus organized by his political enemy Cato the Younger (58). There were 320,000 recipients by ca. 46 B.C. CICERO EXILED: in 58 by the agency of Clodius [who bore him a grudge for destroying his alibi in a lawsuit concerning Clodius's desecration of the cult of the Good Goddess (Bona Dea) in 61]; he was brought back in 57 by Pompey. PARTHIA: centered on Media (northern Iran); Ecbatana (Hamadan) was the capital of the Arsacid royal house, Ctesiphon (in Babylonia), their winter residence. The Parthians ruled from the Euphrates to the Indus and controlled the caravan routes from the Far East. SON OF CRASSUS: Publius Licinius Crassus. QUIBERON BAY: the victor was Decimus Junius Brutus Albinus. GERMAN TRIBES SUPPRESSED IN 56: Usipetes and Tencteri. BELGIC REVOLTS (54): by Treviri; and Ambiorix of Eburones (Ardennes) massacred garrison at Aduatuca. CONFERENCES (53): Samarobriva (Amiens), Lutetia (Paris), Durocortorum (Reims). VERCINGETORIX: pan-Gallic command conferred at Bibracte, capital of Aedui (52).

FINAL OPERATION (51): Uxellodunum (Pay d'Issolu in Dordogne). CONQUERED GAUL: Gallia Comata (later divided into three provinces plus two German commands); road system based on Lugdunum (Lyon), founded in 43. ARMY PAY: became 225 *denarii* per annum. CARRHAE (53): the victor was Surenas, ruler of Seistan (eastern Iran and southwestern Afghanistan) as Parthian vassal. In the battle, his horse archers were kept supplied by swift Arabian camels carrying reserves of arrows. The Parthians also employed cataphracts (heavily mailed horsemen with large spears). CLODIUS MURDERED (52): by the gangster Milo, originally pro-Pompeian but now convicted on Pompey's initiative (in spite of Cicero's defense speech) and exiled to Massilia. POMPEY'S COMMAND (49): proposed by the consul Gaius Claudius Marcellus with the support of the two consuls-designate. RUBICON: R. Pisciatello (?).

Catullus and Lucretius. ALEXANDRIANS: Greek, third century B.C.; Callimachus, Apollonius Rhodius, Theocritus, Euphorion. Their Roman followers were called the Neoterics. ATOMISTS (Greek): Leucippus, Democritus (fifth century B.C.). LUCRETIUS ON POLITICS: II, 10–13 (trans. R. Humphries).

The Civil War. CAESAR'S INVASION: second column moved on to Arretium (Arezzo). RESERVE TREASURY: in Temple of Saturn. ILERDA: the Pompeian commanders were Afranius and Petreius. ADRIATIC FLOTILLA ELUDED BY CAESAR: commanded by Bibulus, who died soon afterwards. POMPEY MURDERED: by Ptolemaic general Achillas and two Roman officers. CLEOPATRA: a remarkable linguist, but did not trouble to learn Latin; no doubt she spoke to her Roman lovers in Greek. ARMY RELIEVING CAESAR: Mithridates of Pergamum, and Jewish contingent. VICTORY IN ASIA MINOR: at Zela (Zile) against Pharnaces II. This was the occasion of Caesar's saying "I came, I saw, I conquered" *(veni, vidi, vici)*. SECOND THREAT OF MUTINY (47): the legionaries followed Caesar from Campania to Rome where he pacified them.

The Dictatorship of Caesar. CAESAR'S SETTLEMENTS: a veteran with three children usually received rather more than six acres. Colonies in provinces remained provincial soil and paid land tax. His civilian colonies included Corinth, Carthage, Urso (Osuna in Spain). Gades (Cadiz) was the first provincial city to receive the franchise without a settlement, as a *municipium*. Some colonies, notably in Narbonese Gaul and Further Spain, were given the intermediate Latin right; i.e., their magistrates became citizens. In Cisalpine Gaul the regions south and north of the Po received Roman citizenship and "Latin right" respectively. MEDICINE: the first regular school at Rome was founded by Asclepiades of Bithynia, ca. 40 B.C. DEBT: the praetor, Caelius (a correspondent of Cicero), also proposed the abolition of house rents for one year (48), and the tribune, Dolabella, urged their total abolition. Caelius started a rising with Milo and was executed at Thurii (Sybaris). Dolabella survived (until 43). CAESAR'S WEALTH: his gold coinage, issued by Aulus Hirtius, was probably the largest in Roman history. After the Gallic War the price of gold had fallen by one-quarter. CLEOPATRA'S HALF BROTHER WITH HER AT ROME IN 46: Ptolemy XIV. She murdered him in 44. CAESAR'S LIBRARIES: organized by the learned writer Marcus Terentius Varro (b.116–d.27 B.C.); by the fourth century A.D. there were 29 libraries in Rome, nine of which are known to us. CALENDAR:

reorganized by Sosigenes; adjusted by Augustus and Pope Gregory XIII (1582). PORTRAITURE: coins of the early first century B.C. had displayed idealized portraits of early Romans; the first coin portraits of the recently dead were of Sulla and his fellow consul of 88 B.C., Quintus Pompeius Rufus, on a coin of their grandson named after the latter (54 B.C.) CAESAR'S BUSTS (OF HIS LIFETIME): e.g., at Castello d'Aglie (Turin). MAGISTRATES: Caesar increased praetors from 8 to 16, aediles from 4 to 6, quaestors from 20 to 40. EASTERN EXPEDITION: 44 B.C.; 16 legions, 10,000 cavalry and archers. In anticipation of Caesar's absence all major appointments were fixed two years ahead. CAESAR'S SECRETARIES (KNIGHTS): Gaius Oppius, biographer, and wealthy Lucius Cornelius Balbus from Gades (Cadiz). BRUTUS: *praetor urbanus* in 44, Cassius *praetor peregrinus* (less important). On a coin of ca. 54 B.C. issued when he was a young moneyer, Marcus Brutus had boasted of his descent from the legendary liberators Lucius Brutus (believed to have expelled Tarquinius Superbus) and Ahala (alleged to have put down the tyrant Maelius, 440–439 B.C.). CAESAR'S MURDER: only two senators claimed to have moved to his defense: Gaius Calvisius Sabinus and Lucius Marcius Censorinus.

Chapter 13. Augustus

The Second Triumvirate. NAME: Gaius Octavius, then Gaius Julius Caesar Octavianus. LEPIDUS: at first retained Narbonese Gaul and Further Spain (assigned to him by Caesar), lost them after Philippi, was given Africa in 40. SEXTUS POMPEIUS: set up independent rule based on Sicily (43). ANTONY'S BROTHER: Lucius Antonius, captured after siege of Perusia [(Perugia), 41]. ALLIANCE: between Antony, Octavian, and Lepidus (40); Treaty of Brundisium. BRUTUS'S MOTHER: Servilia (mistress of Caesar, presided over political salon) held conference at Antium [(Anzio), 44]; Brutus's wife was Porcia, daughter of Cato and widow of Bibulus. FULVIA: formerly married to Clodius and Curio. RECONCILIATION: between Antony and Octavian (37); Treaty of Tarentum. CLEOPATRA'S EMPIRE: established 37, amplified at Donations of Alexandra (34). Its titular rulers included her son, allegedly by Caesar, Ptolemy XV Caesar (Caesarion) and her children by Antony. ANTONY'S CLIENTS: Asander (Cimmerian Bosphorus, 41–17 B.C.), Herod the Great (Judaea), Amyntas (Galatia), Polemoo (Pontus), Archelaus (Cappadocia). PARTHIAN WARS: Parthian invasion of Syria 41–40 B.C.; successful expedition by Ventidius, 38; disastrous Roman retreat, 36; Armenia occupied by the Romans 34. SEXTUS POMPEIUS'S END: fled to Asia Minor; killed, 35. ACTIUM: preceded by Agrippa's seizure of Methone.

The Principate of Augustus. VETERANS' REWARDS: paid by Octavian (Augustus) himself for nearly 30 years, mainly from civil war spoils. COLONIES OF OCTAVIAN (AUGUSTUS): mainly in west (those in Spain issued numerous local coinages), but also a few in east, e.g., in newly annexed province of Galatia (Lycaonia, Pisidia). His colonies, unlike Caesar's, were almost exclusively military. MANPOWER: by the time of Augustus's death the free adult male population of Italy, including Cisalpine Gaul (part of Italy since 42 B.C.), was perhaps one and a half million (no more than in 218 B.C.). But the total number of slaves in Italy, including women and children, may have been as high as four million. AUGUSTAN NOBLES:

the *princeps* had married Livia (38 B.C.), of a noble clan and formerly married to the member of another, Tiberius Claudius Nero, by whom she had two sons, Tiberius and Nero Drusus (Drusus Senior). AUGUSTAN 'NEW MEN': tended to become army commanders and suffect consuls, i.e., those replacing, during the course of each year, the more important "ordinary" consuls, who were still generally noble (though many upper-class families were dying out). The *Lex Valeria Cornelia* of A.D. 5 on election procedure enhanced the dignity (not power) of the upper class. SENATORS: excused attendance at age of 60. WORSHIP OF AUGUSTUS WITH THE GODDESS ROME: first at Pergamum (Bergama) in Asia and Nicomedia (Izmit) in Bithynia; provincial councils (*konia,* concilia) presided. In Rome, an altar was erected to the *numen* ("divine power") of Augustus (A.D. 13) and his *genius* was worshipped with the *lares publici,* protective deities of Rome. His image was carried with military standards and received the homage of the troops. SPAIN: Lusitania (Portugal and western Spain) became a separate province during the reign of Augustus, and Tarraco (Tarragona) became the capital of Nearer Spain (Hispania Tarraconensis). TRAVELS: Agrippa in east, Gaul, Spain (23–21, 20–19), Augustus in Sicily, Greece, Asia (22–19). In 20 Armenia was reduced to client status, amid great applause, though the arrangement did not last. MARRIAGE LAWS: *Lex de maritandis ordinibus* and *Lex de adulteriis coercendis* (18 B.C.) reinforced by *Lex Papia Poppaea* (A.D. 9) which introduced still stronger incentives to marriage. KNIGHTS: Caesar had increased their employment as chief advisers and officers. DEATH OF AGRIPPA: a fragment of Augustus's funeral oration has now come to light. BOHEMIA: center of empire of Maroboduus [Marcomanni, (who supplanted Boii ca. 8 B.C.)]. PRAETORIAN GUARD: included inner group of mounted *speculatores* (messengers and intelligence agents), and supplemented by a separate bodyguard of Germans. PREFECT OF THE CITY: temporary appointments during the reign were followed by creation of permanent post (? ca. A.D. 13). FIRE BRIGADE: vigiles; eventually of 7,000 freedmen (A.D. 6). MILITARY PENSIONS: because of financial shortage, fixed-term enlistments (20 years legionary, 25 auxiliary) often had to be prolonged. MONARCHY: easterners thought of Augustus as monarch *(basileus),* though that title does not appear on coins. EXILED BY AUGUSTUS: his daughter Julia (2 B.C.) and granddaughter Julia (A.D. 8) and his grandson Agrippa Postumus (A.D. 7) whose death in A.D. 14 was ordered either by Augustus or Tiberius. PRIMA PORTA PAINTINGS: Museo Nazionale delle Terme, Rome; cf. a branch of what is traditionally known as the Pompeian Second Style (though these designations now need recasting). Soon afterwards the Third Style (ca. 20 B.C.–A.D. 20) showed more illusionistic landscapes, and panel paintings amid fantastic architecture. TAXES: Caesar had abolished tax farming and titles in Asia and probably Sicily, substituting fixed *tributum soli. Tributum* was paid in some provinces by all adults and in others by adult males. BRIDGES: e.g., Alcantara Bridge over Tagus, with 18 arches of which 6 remain. TUNNELS: e.g., of Occeius at Cumae (three-quarter-mile), and Neapolis-Puteoli (one-half mile). WOOL: Pompeii (building for Guild of Fullers dedicated by its woman patron the priestess Eumachia), Parma, Mediolanum (Milan), Patavium (Padua).

The Economic Basis. GLASS BLOWING: recently invented in Sidon (Saida) in

Phoenicia. EARTHENWARE: of coarser variety at Mutina (Modena) and Aquileia. FOREIGN TRADE: reflected by Latin and Greek words surviving in German, Semitic, Pahlevi, Iranian, Irish, and even a few in Indian and Mongolian. LEPCIS MAGNA: founded by Carthage in sixth century B.C. to oppose the Greeks. COINAGE: brass (*orichalcum:* zinc alloy) and copper replaced discredited bronze (lead and tin alloy, terminated in 80s B.C. except for special issues) in official coinages. Local city currencies of bronze were supplemented, for a time a very few of silver. Client kingdoms had coinages of their own, in silver and bronze—and gold in the Cimmerian Bosphorus (Crimea). LAND TRANSPORT: Diocletian's Edict of Prices shows that a 1200-pound wagon load of wheat would double in price in 300 miles. FREEDMEN: priests (Augustales) of the cult in which Augustus was associated with the Lares.

Augustan Literature. MAECENAS: probably from aristocracy of Arretium (Arezzo); had played a major political part up to the battle of Actium, and therefore acted more than once as the absent Augustus's representative at Rome. He was sloppy and soft according to Seneca, but Horace described him as an active man and a keen critic. ECLOGUES OF VIRGIL: most were loosely modeled on Theocritus of Syracuse (b. ca. 300–d. ca. 260 B.C.). GEORGICS: poetical and patriotic, but contained information based on agricultural handbook of Marcus Terentius Varro (*Res Rusticae,* 37 B.C.). AENEID: romantic element cf. Apollonius Rhodius of Alexandria, *Argonautica* (third century B.C.). Latin bride of Aeneas—Lavinia. HORACE: b. 65–d. 8 B.C.; *Epodes* and *Odes* (including *Carmen Saeculare*) in lyrical meters [latter claimed Alcaeus (b. ca. 620 B.C.) as model]: *Satires* and *Epistles* (including *Ars Poetica*) in hexameters. His Sabine farm perhaps identifiable near Digentia (Licenza), 22 miles northeast of Rome. PROPERTIES: (59–47 B.C.); claimed Callimachus of Cyrene (b. ca. 305–d. ca. 240) as model. A contemporary elegist was Tibullus (b. ca. 55 or 48; d. ca. 19 B.C.), whose patron was the soldier, statesman, and orator Marcus Valerius Messalla Corvinus (b. 64 B.C.–d. A.D. 8). LIVY: alternatively his dates could be 64 B.C.–A.D. 12. His history ended in 9 B.C. OVID: his tragedy the *Medea* is lost.

PART VII   THE IMPERIAL PEACE

Chapter 14. The Inheritors of Empire

The Successors of Augustus. THE EAST: Cappadocia (eastern Asia Minor) and Commagene (northwestern Syria) annexed (A.D. 17). DEATH OF GERMANICUS: Cnaeus Calpurnius Piso, imperial governor of Syria, was accused of his murder in the Senate and although innocent of this charge (but guilty of sedition) killed himself. TREASON CHARGES: under the *Lex Julia maiestatis,* probably passed by Julius Caesar. SEJANUS: son of Lucius Aelius Strabo of Volsinii (Orvieto): for a time father and son were joint praetorian prefects. Before Sejanus become consul in A.D. 31 he had been granted the rank of praetor. SONS OF GERMANICUS AND AGRIPPINA THE ELDER: Nero Caesar (d. A.D. 31), Drusus Caesar (d. 33), and Gaius (Caligula, later emperor). GRANDSON OF TIBERIUS: Tiberius Gemellus, killed by Caligula in 38.

REVOLT IN UPPER GERMANY (39): under Cnaeus Cornelius Lentulus Gaetulicus. Also executed was Caligula's brother-in-law and heir apparent Marcus Lepidus; Caligula's sisters Agrippina junior and Julia Livilla were banished. CALIGULA'S WIFE (FOURTH AND LAST): Caesonia. CLAUDIUS: son of Nero Drusus (Drusus, the Elder, brother of Tiberius) and Antonia. REVOLT IN DALMATIA (UPPER IL-LYRICUM): One of the two provinces into which Illyricum was divided in ca. A.D. 9: Lucius Furius Camellus Scribonianus (42). BRITAIN: the invasion was prompted by the death of Cunobelinus (ca. A.D. 9-40/43; Shakespeare's Cymbeline) of the Catuvellauni, overlord of southeastern England. By 47 the frontier was the Fosse Way [Lindum (Lincoln)—South Devon]. The revolt of Cunobelinus's son Caratacus ended in 51 and veterans were settled at Colonia Camulodunum (Colchester) in 50 (also at Colonia Agrippinensis, now Köln). But the capital of Britain was later moved from Camulodunum to the much larger Londinium (330 acres). Perhaps 6,000 miles of roads were built in the first four decades of the British province. MAURETANIA: gradually pacified after murder of its client king Ptolemy at Rome in 40. THRACE: made a province after the murder of its last client prince in 46. Lycia (southern Asia Minor) was also annexed as part of province Lycia-Pamphylia (43). GAULS: nobles were brought into the Senate (by *adlectio*), and all Roman citizens in Gaul were permitted to stand for office in the capital, following a speech by Claudius, largely preserved on a bronze tablet at Lugdunum (Lyon). MESSALINA: great-neice of Augustus. Her lover executed in 48 was Gaius Silius. NERO'S NAME: originally Lucius (his father was Cnaeus) Domitius Ahenobarbus. NERO'S AMUSE-MENTS: early in his reign he associated with *pantomimi* (male ballet dancers). He was also interested not only in music but in chariot racing (of which there were four main factions). BOUDICCA: her revolt was suppressed by Gaius Suetonius Paulinus (60). TIGELLINUS'S FELLOW PREFECT: Faenius Rufus, executed in 65 with Scricca, after a plot to place Gaius Calpurnius Piso on the throne. PHILOSOPHICAL REPUBLI-CANS: Thrasea Paetus, forced to commit suicide in 66. CORBULO'S PEACE: Tiridates I of Armenia was jointly sponsored by Rome and Parthia. After these wars the Euphrates garrison was permanently increased at the expense of the Rhine and Danube. VINDEX: defeated by the eminent Verginius Rufus, commander in Upper Germany, who refused the throne for himself (as again in the following year, 69).

The Year of the Four Emperors. GALBA'S ADVISERS: Vinius, Laco, Icelus. GALBA'S HEIR: Lucius Calpurnius Piso Licinianus. OTHO: of princely family from Ferentium (Ferento) in Etruria.

Vespasian and His Sons. GALLO-GERMAN REVOLT: captured major Rhine base of Vetera (near Birten) in 70; the whole river line to Argentorate (Strasbourg) or beyond was lost, Cerialis recovered Classicus's capital Augusta Trevironum (Trier), destroyed the Gallic Empire, and drove the Batavians back home. UPPER RHINE–UPPER DANUBE REENTRANT: Agri Decumates. FIRST JEWISH REVOLT: Masada resisted until 73. VESPASIAN'S ORIGIN: from Sabine town of Reate (Rieti). SPAIN: southern province of Baetica received Latin rights, and between A.D. 74 and 84, 350 Spanish towns received municipal charters. TAXES: in provinces were in some cases doubled by Vespasian, and Greek immunities revoked. EDUCATION: Quintilian of Calagurris (Calahorra in Spain) was the first salaried professor of rhetoric. Teachers received tax rebates like doctors. OPPOSITION TO VESPASIAN: supported by Stoic and Cynic ideas. Helvidius Priscus executed. PLOT OF CAECINA (79): allied with Eprius Marcellus, leading orator and Vespasian's adviser. VESPASIAN'S DEATH: at Aquae Cutiliae (Bagni de Paterno). BERENICE: daughter of Agrippa I and sister of Agrippa II (northern Palestine and southern Syria): had supported Rome in the First Jewish Revolt. BRITAIN: Fishbourne Villa had probably been built for the old age of Cogidubnus of the Atrebates (ca. 43–75), a client king within the frontiers. FORTH-CLYDE LINE: forts at Camelon and near Cadder and Mumrills. VESUVIUS ERUPTION (79): Pliny the Elder, admiral and historian and scientist, died of suffocation on the beach (described in a letter of his nephew Pliny the Younger to the historian Tacitus). AGRICOLA UNDER DOMITIAN: advance beyond Firth of Forth (fortress at Inchtuthil) in 83, "MONS GRAUPIUS": site of Roman victory (84); probably not far short of the Moray Firth. Signal stations on road east from Ardoch may mark the frontier after withdrawal following Agricola's recall. Vindolanda (Chesterholm) is also a Domitianic fort (recent discoveries of limewood tablets). SOUTHWESTERN GERMANY UNDER DOMITIAN: by the end of his reign the frontier (*limes*) road ran from near Bonna (Bonn) down R. Neckar to meet the Danube in Raetia. DACIAN BATTLES: Oppius Sabinus, governor of Moesia, was killed in 85, and Cornelius Fuscus, praetorian prefect, in 86 or 87; then Roman victory at Tapae (Iron Gates) in 88. REVOLT IN UPPER GERMANY (89): by Lucius Antonius Saturninus. Afterwards Domitian converted the Upper and Lower German commands into formal provinces.

Trajan, Hadrian, Antoninus. TRAJAN'S ORIGINS: born at Italica (Santiponce) in Baetica (southern Spain) in 53. PROVINCIAL ORIGINS: in 90 the first known eastern consul was elected, and in 94 the first pair of consuls both to possess provincial backgrounds. ALIMENTA: at Veleia (Velleia in northern Italy) Trajan supported 245 boys and 34 girls born in wedlock and 2 illegitimate children. ADMINISTRATION: *curatores* of one or several cities, perhaps already under Domitian, then at Caere (Cerveteri, 113). Pliny, like a governor of Achaea (Greece) in the same reign, had special powers as *corrector*. There was a new distinction between civilian and military careers in the equestrian ranks of the government service. TRAJAN'S ARMY: 400,000 strong. The first cohort of each legion was doubled in size. There was also a new intelligence organization (*frumentarii*), and a mounted bodyguard of *equites singulares* (500, later 1,000), mainly German and Danubian (from Pannonia). TRAJAN'S DACIAN WARS: new Roman colony adjacent to old site of Sarmizegethusa, near Toteşti, ca. 110. On the frontier fortifications (Limes Dacicus), *castelli* (e.g., Buciumi, near Cluj) have unusually elaborate gates. The Danube bridge designed by Apollodorus, over 1,000 yards long, was built of stone piers and segmental timber arches. EASTERN FRONTIER: Arabia Petraea (Nabataea: western Jordan and Sinai) annexed 105–6; Bostra (Bosra) replaced Petra as capital. Later in the century Gerasa (Jerash) became an increasingly important town. JEWISH DISPERSION REVOLTS: Cyrene, Cyprus, Egypt; the aim in the first two was the extermination of the Greeks. Henceforward Jews were forbidden in Cyprus, Revolts were also fomented by the Parthian King Osroes in the Jewish communities of Bablonia. PARTHIAN ATTACKS IN ROMAN REAR: Mesopotamia, Armenia, Adiabene (Assyria). Was Trajan obliged

to abandon his conquests even before the Jewish revolts? PARTHIAN CLIENT KING
AT CTESIPHON: Parthamaspates. HADRIAN'S ORIGIN: born at Gades (Cadiz) in
Baetica (southern Spain) in 76; his paternal grandfather had married Trajan's aunt.
PLOT OF THE FOUR CONSULARS (118): including Mauretanian Lusius Quietus, who
had suppressed the Babylonian Jews and governed Judaea. They were executed by
the praetorian prefect Attianus. PROVINCES: a great series of coins honored individual provinces and Hadrian as their visitor (adventui Augusti) and restorer (re-
stitutori). The Temple of Divus Hadrianus (Hadrianeum) erected in the Campus
Martius after his death displayed sculptural representations of the provinces. DE-
FEAT IN BRITAIN: a legion was lost some time between 117 and 122. HADRIAN'S
ARMY: Hadrian introduced, or increased, heavy armored cavalry (cataphracts)
borrowed from the Sarmatians (nomads related to the Scythians); and he extended
the use of irregular "national" numeri. FORTIFICATIONS: Hadrian built a stone wall
on the Numidian as well as the British frontier and constructed a continuous
wooden palisade in Raetia and Upper Germany. HADRIAN'S WESTERN WARS:
minor risings in Britain and Mauretania. AELIUS CAESAR: his original name was
Lucius Ceionius Commodus. ANTONINUS "PIUS": insisted on the deification of
Hadrian, though the Senate was not enthusiastic. ANTONINUS'S WALL: in Britain
(A.D. 142); but the frontier was retracted more than once, and definitively before the
end of the century. ANTONINUS'S WARS: disturbances in 139-42 among Brigantes
(Yorkshire; some Britons were transplanted to the Agri Decumates) and organized
in numeri there, and in Numidia, Mauretania, Syria, Palaestina (Judaea), Egypt,
Dacia (partitioned into three provinces).

Chapter 15. Imperial Society

Imperial Art and Architecture.   ARCH OF TITUS: the spoils from the Jerusalem
temple include the Menorah (seven-branched candlestick), silver trumpet, and
golden table of the Shewbread. COLUMN OF TRAJAN: in colonnaded court flanked
by Greek and Latin libraries behind the basilica which occupied the north side of
Trajan's Forum; completed in A.D. 113 according to the plan of Apollodorus. POM-
PEII: a so-called "fourth" style from ca. 50 A.D. comprised a great many varied
themes, including more imaginative versions of the architectural vistas of the "second" style. Wall decorations also include stucco. MOSAICS: the favorite mosaic
pavements in Italy (first-third century) were black and white. Figured overall
designs are conspicuous, e.g., in Africa. Wall mosaics already appear on Pompeii
fountains. SLAVE ACCOMMODATION: socalled House of Menander (Pompeii), and
Villa of Agrippa Postumus (outside Pompeii), cf. Pliny the Younger's villa at
Laurentum. OSTIA: most of the apartment houses (of which more than 200 have
been identified) incorporated shops. Ostia replaced Puteoli (Pozzuoli) as Italy's
principal west coast port. OTHER HOUSING: Bulla Regia (Hammon Daradji) in north
Africa (a Roman colony for veterans under Hadrian) shows an experiment in
underground housing, to resist summer and winter climatic extremes. NERO'S
GOLDEN HOUSE: architects Severus and Celer. Separate pavilions, cf. Prytaneum of
Antigonus II Gonatas at Pella (Palatitsa) in Macedonia and Hadrian's Villa at Tibur
(and Sultans' Seraglio at Istanbul). DOMITIAN'S PALACE: architect Rabirius. HA-

DRIAN'S VILLA: adorned with masterpieces of Greek sculpture and of the Hadrianic school which it influenced. PANTHEON: made little impression in antiquity but exercised great influence on the Renaissance. TEMPLES: the buildings at Heliopolis (Baalbek) in Syria were exceptionally magnificent. ROMAN BATHS: Agrippa, Titus, Trajan (later Caracalla, Diocletian); cf. four so far discovered at Pompeii, two at Herculaneum. VESPASIAN'S BUILDINGS: Forum and Temple of Peace; he reconstructed the Capitoline temple and started work on the Colosseum. COLOSSEUM: fourth story is of blind arcading broken by windows. EARLIER AMPHITHEATERS: the building of Titus Statilius Taurus at Rome in 29 B.C. had been partly of wood and partly of stone, but there were earlier stone amphitheaters at Pompeii, etc. Pompey had built Rome's first stone theater (53 B.C.) and Augustus built the three-story Theater of Marcellus (13 B.C.). There were three imperial training schools for gladiators at Rome, also at Capua (S. Maria Capua Vetere), Ravenna, and Praeneste (Palestrina), unless this was still privately owned. Even Petuaria (Brough-on-Humber) had its amphitheater.

Economic and Social Imbalance. THAMUGADI: founded in A.D. 100 by Trajan as a Roman colony for veterans and originally designed on camp lines, later greatly expanded; the most complete African remains, next to Lepcis Magna (which was likewise colonized by Trajan). TRADE: Greeks and Syrians supplemented their virtual monopoly of the Mediterranean carrying trade by taking over a large share of the outlying routes. RHINELAND: e.g., Tres Tabernae (Rheinzabern) and Augusta Trevirorum (Trier), with Colonia Agrippinensis (Köln) as glassblowing center. SLAVES: by second century, it was ceasing to be profitable to employ slave gangs in agriculture and mining. Emperors received petitions from slaves as from every other category of the population. AELIUS ARISTIDES OF MYSIA (A.D. 117 OR 129–181 or later): *To Rome: Eis Romen.* cf. Pliny the Elder, "the immense majesty of the Roman peace." SALVIUS JULIANUS: of Pupput (?) near Hadrumetum (Sousse) b. ca. A.D. 100–d. ca. 69; also wrote *Digesta,* in 90 books. GAIUS (lawyer): born under Trajan (?), perhaps from a Greek province. HADRIAN: salaried jurisconsuls were members of his Consilium. LEGAL REFORMS: there were also improvements in the legal status of women. HUMILIORES: liable to flogging, torture, summary execution; lacked right of appeal to emperor which all *honestiores,* not only citizens, possessed. The dichotomy was already to some extent recognized by the time of the leading jurists Labeo (d. A.D. 10/11) and Ateius Capito (d. 22).

From Seneca to Apuleius. SENECA: his father was Seneca the Elder (b. ca. 55 B.C.–d. ca. A.D. 37/41). The younger Seneca was the author of a scientific work, the *Natural Questions.* His alleged correspondence with St. Paul is a fourth century forgery. PETRONIUS: plausibly identified with Titus Petronius Niger, consul ca. A.D. 61. His poems seem, in part at least, to be derisive parodies of Lucan and Seneca, on whose retirement Petronius became prominent. Set pieces: also "The Widow of Ephesus." His writing is ignored by Tacitus (who describes him as *arbiter elegantiae*), and fiction is not included in Quintilian's survey of Latin literature. MARTIAL: from Bilbilis (Calatayud). Other Domitianic poets were Statius *(Thebaid, Silvae),* Silius Italicus *(Punicia),* and Valerius Flaccus *(Argonautica).* TACITUS: his name appears to have been Publius Cornelius Tacitus. It is disputed whether the *Annals* were published late in Trajan's reign (as is usually believed) or early in Hadrian's. LUCIAN OF SAMOSATA (Samsat in southern Turkey, ca. A.D. 120): his works, in Greek, developed a special variety of the dialogue, based on Cynic and other antecedents. SOPHISTS OF SECOND CENTURY A.D.: the Second Sophistic" (the First was in the fifth century B.C.). ARCHAIC REVIVAL: the New Speech *(Elocutio Novella)*, sponsored by Fronto (b. ca. A.D. 100–d. ca. 166), the tutor of Marcus Aurelius and leading Roman orator of his day. ASTROLOGY: in vogue in eastern Mediterranean since second century B.C.; spread to Italy late in the following century. SCIENCE: virtually its last figure was Galen of Pergamum (b. A.D. 129–d. ca. 199) who summarized the ancient knowledge of medicine.

The Mystery Religions. DEMETER: her Mysteries were centered on Eleusis in Greece. DIONYSUS (BACCHUS): wall paintings in Villa of Mysteries outside Pompeii, first century B.C. CYBELE: poem on myth of Attis by Catullus. Bloodbaths of animals *(taurobolium, criobolium)* originated in Asia Minor and first appeared in the west in second century A.D. Before Cybele, the Mystery cult of Asclepius (Aesculapius) had been imported to Rome after a plague (293 B.C., from Epidaurus). ISIS: the Egyptian gods gained the imperial cachet under Hadrian.

Chapter 16. The Jews, Jesus, and Paul

The Jews. ISRAEL (kingdom): fell to Assyria 721 B.C. JUDAH: fell to Babylonia 597–586 B.C. PROPHETS: the "major" prophetic books are those of Isaiah (multiple authorship), Jeremiah, and Ezekiel (and Daniel in the English Bible). TEMPLE: Antiochus IV Epiphanes set up a statue of Olympian Zeus in the Holy of Holies (168 B.C.). The temple was reconsecrated by Judas Maccabaeus (165–164 B.C.) and rebuilt in 22–18 B.C. by Herod the Great (37–34 B.C.) whom Antony had placed on the Judaean throne to succeed the Hasmonaean Mattathias Antigonus (40–37), a client of Parthia. JESUS'S BIRTH: misattributed to A.D. 1 by Dionysius Exiguus [from Scythia (southern Russia), ca. A.D. 500–60). NON-CANONICAL GOSPELS: e.g. of *Thomas, Eve, Mary, James, John, Judas, Matthias, Peter, Philip.* JUDAEA: ruled by prince (ethnarch) Archelaus B.C. 4–A.D. 6 by Roman prefects (knights) from A.D. 6–41; then (after interlude under King Agrippa I, A.D. 41–44) by Roman procurators (knights) from A.D. 44 until First Jewish Revolt; thereafter by senior (senatorial) governors. SON OF MAN: *bar nasha.* QUMRAN: Dead Sea Scrolls of various dates up to dispersal of sect in First Jewish Revolt. APOSTLES: Peter, James and John the sons of Zebedee, Andrew, Philip, Bartholomew, Matthew, Thomas, James the son of Alphaeus, Thaddaeus (or Judas), Simon the Zealot, and Judas Iscariot (meaning "of Kerioth"). FULFILLMENT OF OLD TESTAMENT: Typology. PONTIUS PILATUS: prefect of Judaea A.D. 26–36.

Paul. DISPERSION: Ptolemy I Soter had introduced many Jews and Samaritans (dissident Jews from northern Palestine) into Alexandria, and Antiochus III the Great settled 2,000 Jewish families in Asia Minor. EARLIEST LETTERS (EPISTLES) OF PAUL: probably *I* and *II Thessalonians* (ca. A.D. 50), though some place *Galatians* in ca. 49. ACTS OF THE APOSTLES: perhaps written towards A.D. 90. PETER: supposedly martyred in Rome under Nero, though his career after the first years following Jesus's death is uncertain. JAMES THE JUST: put to death by the Jewish high priest Ananus II in A.D. 62. PAUL AND PAX ROMANA: cf. rabbinical story that God had created the Roman peace simply so that Jews might study the law undistracted. PROCURATORS OF JUDAEA WHO DETAINED PAUL: Antonius Felix (52–ca. 60) and Porcius Festus (ca. 60–62). JEWISH CHRISTIANS: their decline was accelerated after the Second Jewish Revolt under Hadrian. The smaller sects into which they split included the Ebionites. GOSPELS: written for Gentile Christians, though Matthew possibly envisaged a Jewish readership as well. MARCION: of Sinope (Sinop) in northern Asia Minor, came to Rome ca. A.D. 137.

PART VIII TOWARDS A NEW WORLD

Chapter 17. Collapse and Recovery

Marcus Aurelius and his Son. AURELIUS AND VERUS: originally Marcus Annius Verus and Lucius Ceionius Commodus respectively. Antoninus Pius had adopted them at Hadrian's wish in 138 (Verus was the son of Aelius Caesar). EPIDEMIC: exanthematous typhus or bubonic plague? NORTHERN ENEMIES OF AURELIUS: Marcomanni (German) and Sarmatians (or Jazyges, non-German) to their southeast. The Germans burned Opitergium (Oderzo in northern Italy) in 170. REVOLT IN EAST (175): Avidius Cassius. DEATH OF MARCUS AURELIUS: at Vindonissa (Windisch) or Sirmium (Sremska Mitrovica). HEIR OF MARCUS AURELIUS: he passed over Pompeianus married to his daughter Lucilla. She conspired against Commodus in ca. 182 and was exiled and killed. COMMODUS'S PRAETORIAN PREFECTS: Perennis 182–85, Cleander 186–89, Laetus 191.

The Dynasty of Severus. DIDIUS JULIANUS: won throne at auction against Sulpicianus, city prefect. SEVERUS: from Lepcis Magna, which he splendidly rebuilt. Just over half the senators were now provincials, and about one-third of these provincials were north African. CITY TROOPS INCREASED: Severus also trebled the watch *(vigiles)*. "CARACALLA": a Celtic or German tunic; his original name was Bassianus; later officially called Marcus Aurelius Antoninus. PARTHIAN WAR: but Severus twice failed to take the desert fortress of Hatra. BRITISH WAR: Severus built a new legionary fortress at Carpow on the r. Tay (above Abernethy). CARACALLA'S WIFE: Plautilla. NORTHERN WARS: Alamanni (mentioned for first time) defeated, and Chatti (?) bought off in 213. ELAGABALUS: his original name was Varius Avitus Bassianus (after his father Varius Marcellus); later officially called Marcus Aurelius Antoninus, like Caracalla. ELAGABALUS'S MOTHER: Julia Soaemias. SEVERUS ALEXANDER: his original name was Alexianus. His father was Gessius Marcianus. NORTHERN FRONTIER: garrison weakened by Severus Alexander's eastern wars.

The Disintegration of the Empire. MAXIMINUS I: elevated by a Danubian unit at Moguntiacum (Mainz). SEVEN CAESARS IN 238: Maximinus I, Maximus Caesar (his son), Gordianus I and II Africanus (in Carthage), Balbinus and Pupienus (known as Maximus) (in Rome), Gordianus III Pius (238–44, prefect Timesitheus d. 243/4). Gordianus III fought in the east but was murdered at Zaitha near the Euphrates, probably at the instigation of his successor Philip. MILLENNIUM: Secular Games (Ludi Saeculares) A.D. 248. DECIUS: from southern Pannonia; he assumed the name of Trajanus. EPIDEMIC: continued until at least 270. SONS: promoted by Severus, Maximinus, Philip, Decius, Valerian, Carus. PHILIP'S FATHER: Marinus in Trachonitis (southeast of Damascus). VALERIAN: followed brief reign of Aemilianus (253). ZENOBIA: her son Vaballathus Athenodorus was made Augustus. Her chief minister was the Syrian philosopher Longinus. LAST PARTHIAN KING: Artabanus V. SASSANIANS: after Sasan, grandfather of Ardashir. Their holy city was Istakhr, ancient residence of the Achaemenids. SHAPUR I'S INVASIONS OF ROMAN EMPIRE: 242/4, between 250 and 256, 259–60. GOTHIC INVASIONS: as far as Marcianopolis (Provadiya, west of Varna, 248) and as far as Ephesus (Selçuk) and Pessinus (Balhisar, 253). FRANKS: plundered Tarraco (Tarragona), capital of Nearer Spain (Hispania Tarraconensis). HERULI: originally from Scandinavia. Some had migrated to Rhine area, most to Black Sea.

The Military Recovery. MOBILE FORCE: the first commander Aureolus, a Dacian, revolted against Gallienus but surrendered to the next emperor Claudius II Gothicus, who killed him. NAISSUS: probably the victory was won by Gallienus rather than after his death by Claudius II Gothicus, to whom it was also attributed by later historians. ALAMANNI: had been defeated by Gallienus in ca. 258–60 but settled in the Agri Decumates, which the Romans permanently evacuated. CLAUDIUS II'S BROTHER: Quintillus (270). ZENOBIA'S DEFEATS: Zabdas defeated at Antioch and Emesa (Homs) in 271. AURELIAN'S WALL AT ROME: 12 miles long, with 16 gates and 381 rectangular towers; originally 20 feet high. Built by civilian labor. AURELIAN'S SUCCESSOR: Tacitus (275–76), an elderly senator; defeated the Goths in Pontus but was killed by his troops or committed suicide. CARUS: defeated Germans (Quadi) and Sarmatians on Danube and captured Ctesiphon. He was the first emperor to omit to request senatorial approval of his accession.

The Collapse of the Economy. AURUM CORONARIUM: gold crowns had been offered to eastern and Hellenistic conquerors and Roman generals of second century B.C. COMPLAINTS: e.g., from Burunum (South-el-Khmis, Tunisia) to Commodus, from Lydian tenants probably to Severus (both these were from imperial estates), Scaptopare (Kyustendil in Bulgaria) in 238, Aragueni (Phrygia) to Philip; and many protests on Egyptian papyri. Probably the later practice of taking refuge on the great country estates had already begun; e.g., Kaua (Mauretania), cf. a great third century peristyle house near Colonia Agrippinensis (Köln), with grain warehouse. But private munificence towards cities largely ceased in the later third century.

Chapter 18. The Climax of the Pagan Empire

The Stoicism of Marcus Aurelius. EPICTETUS (b.ca. 55–d.ca. 135): from Hierapolis (Pamukkale) in Phrygia. MARCUS AURELIUS: recognized occasional heavenly guidance. His view of the cosmopolis was partly derived from the Stoic Posidonius who held that inner tensions preserve it as a composite whole. SEVERUS'S PRAETORIAN PREFECTS: under Antoninus Pius, too, they had regularly been prominent jurists. PAPINIAN: joint prefect with Plautianus 203–05. Executed by Caracalla in 212. ULPIAN: had been Papinian's assessor. Killed by mutinous praetorians in 223. PAULUS: pupil of Cervidius Scaevola; Papinian's assessor, and may have been briefly joint prefect with Ulpian. Wrote 320 books. CONSTITUTIO ANTONINIANA: our version (a Greek papyrus) may be a policy statement, not the original *constitutio* itself. A class known as *dediticii* ("capitulants") was excluded along with slaves; perhaps it principally comprised people recently and forcibly settled within the empire (known as *laeti*), though there was also a category of freed slaves described as *dediticii*. Ostensible aim of the *constitutio:* "so that the Gods, with more worshippers, would favor the pious Roman people more." Nevertheless, the national law of the Greek past continued to assert itself against imperial law, at least until Diocletian systematically enforced the latter.

New Buildings and Portraits. BATHS OF CARACALLA: the reservoir could hold 2,688,000 cubic feet of water. MARCUS AURELIUS'S PORTRAITS: some show blank, Antonine classicism, but a few are in a novel, tense style: e.g., from Arch of C. 178 (vanished) celebrating Marcomannic triumph, and gold head from Aventicum (Avenches in Switzerland) at Lausanne. MARCUS AURELIUS'S COLUMN: style originally foreshadowed, in part, by reliefs from lost column of Antoninus. PORTRAITS: Commodus as Hercules in Palazzo dei Conservatori, Rome; Caracalla in Museo Archeologico Nazionale, Naples; Maximinus I in Ny Carlsberg Glypothek, Copenhagen (his coin portraits carry realism almost to the point of caricature); Philip in the Vatican; Decius in Capitoline Museum, Rome; Trebonianus Gallus in Metropolitan Museum, New York; Gallienus in Museo Nazionale delle Terme, Rome.

Plotinus, Mithras, and Mani. PLOTINUS: studied in Alexandria under the Platonist Ammonius Saccas who also taught Origen and Longinus. PORPHYRY (CA. A.D. 232–305) FROM TYRE (SUR): pupil first of Longinus then of Poltinus. SUN CULT: traditionally went back in Rome to King Numa Pompilius. Identified with Apollo as in Greece since about fifth century B.C. MITHRAS: supported the god Ahuramazda, against Ahriman. MANI: arrested by Persian king Bahram I and died at Gundeshapur (ca. 274/7). Kartir, chief Magus and architect of the state religion, prevailed.

Chapter 19. The Supreme State and Church

The New State of Diocletian. DIOCLETIAN succeeded the sons of Carus, Numerian (probably killed by his praetorian prefect Aper) and Carinus (killed after a battle with Diocletian near R. Margus (Morava). REVOLT IN BRITAIN: Carausius (ca. 287–93; he apparently controlled northeastern Gaul), Allectus (ca. 293–96; defeated by Constantius I's praetorian prefect Asclepiodotus). Some forts of Britain's Saxon shore may date from this period. OTHER NORTHERN SUCCESSES: Constantius I in Germany (302–04) and five victories of Diocletian on Danube (from 302). REVOLTS IN EGYPT: the second proclaimed the usurper Domitiius Domitianus (297–98). PERSIAN WAR (296–98): Diocletian and Galerius were defeated by Narses I near Carrhae (Haran), but Galerius seized Armenia, and then Ctesiphon, and annexed five small provinces. MAXIMIAN'S RETIREMENT: the palace at Piazza Armerina in Sicily may possibly have belonged to him, or to his son Maxentius. DIOCESES *(dioeceseis):* each under a *vicarius,* i.e., officially a deputy of the praetorian prefects, (in whose favor the power of the *vicarii* subsequently declined). PRICE EDICT *(Edictum de Pretiis):* the most complete copy is from Aezani (Emet) in Phrygia (Asia Minor). CURRENCY REFORM OF DIOCLETIAN: underestimated the value of the precious metal coinage in relation to the base metal issues, so that the price of commodities in terms of the latter rose sharply. CEREMONIAL: the name of Diocletian's imperial council was changed from *consilium* to *consistorium,* because its members no longer sat but stood in his presence. SALONAE: the palace covered nine acres. Its plan was based on a blend of Roman camps, city walls, and civil architecture. COMPANIONS OF THE GODS: Commodus had displayed Hercules as his companion *(comes)* on coins and medallions.

The Growth of Christianity. CLEMENT OF ALEXANDRIA: "how may a rich man be saved"? ORIGEN: taught by Leonides (his father), Pantaenus, Clement, and Ammonius Saccas (also the teacher of Plotinus). His numerous works included a refutation of the pagan Celsus. TERTULLIAN: born in or near Carthage. He joined the extreme, ascetic, Montanist movement. CYPRIAN: executed in 258 during Valerian's persecution. JEWS: began to be outnumbered by Christians in second century A.D. Although Severus forbade proselytism by Jews (as by Christians), their good relations with Rome were cemented in Syria Palaestina (the former Judaea) by the recognized national leader (patriarch) Judah I ha-Nasi, "the prince" (A.D. 135–219). There was extensive synagogue building in Galilee (Chorazin, Capernaum, Kefr Bir'im): cf. at Dura Europus on the Euphrates. Exilarchs, the counterpart of the Palestinian patriarchs, presided over flourishing communities of Babylonian Jews in third century (Nehardea, Sura, Pumbeditha, Machuza near Ctesiphon). DECIUS'S PERSECUTION: Pope (bishop of Rome) Fabian was executed. DIOCLETIAN'S PERSECUTION: neo-Platonist Hierocles, governor of Bithynia and Egypt, was one of its leaders and also wrote against the Christians. SUCCESSORS OF DIOCLETIAN: Constantius I (305–36), Galerius (305–11), Severus II (306–7). Maximian (second reign 306–8, third attempt 310), Maximinus II Daia (308–13; nephew of Galerius), Constantine I (the Great) (312–37), Licinius (312–24; from the new Dacia, south of the Danube); but Constantine and Licinius had first been declared Augusti in 306 and 308 respectively.

Constantine the Great. HIS MOTHER: St. Helena, a barmaid from Bithynia; she became a pious Christian (at an uncertain date) and died in ca. 328. GERMAN WARS OF CONSTANTINE: against Franks, Alamanni, etc. (306–13). CONSTANTINOPLE: did not have a large population until ca. 360. By the end of the century it had 4,388 private residences. For church buildings, see below. CHRISTIANIZATION: in the latest edition of the "Edict of Serdica," the name of Licinius was omitted. The "Edict of Milan" consisted of regulations of Constantine and Licinius that were issued when the latter visited Mediolanum (Milan) to marry Constantine's half sister Constantia, and subsequently repeated by Licinius in a proclamation at Nicomedia (Izmit), (though Licinius, quarreling with Constantine, later reverted to persecution). African milestones with the Christian Chi-Rho symbol date from 317–19. A vault mosaic in the Mausoleum of the Julii under St. Peter's at Rome identifies Christ and the Sun. King Tiridates III of Armenia had joined the Christian faith and imposed it on his country soon after his restoration to its throne in 298. SUPREME DEITY (SUMMUS SANCTUS DEUS): revered by Hierocles and invoked by troops of Licinius before his victory over Maximinus II Daia at Tzirallum (near Edirne) in Thrace in 313. CHURCH FUNDS: an extension of the private wealth of the emperor rather than of state funds. CHRISTIAN COMMUNITIES: the best organized and biggest were at Antioch and Alexandria. DISSIDENT CHRISTIANS: e.g., the Donatists of northern Africa condemned all who had sacrificed to pagan deities in Diocletian's persecution and were eventually persecuted by Constantine (316–21). He built an important church at Cirta, renamed Constantina (now Constantine). CHRISTIAN CATACOMBS AT ROME: St. Callixtus, Sebastian, Domitilla, etc. JEWS: catacombs at Rome (some to be opened before long to the public); Via Appia Pignatelli, Villa Torlonia, Vigna Rondanini. Roman treatment of the Jews deteriorated under Constantius II (337–61), expecially after the rebellion of Patricius in Palestine. HOUSE-CHURCHES: church at Dura-Europus on Euphrates (232) was built to succeed a place of worship in a private house. But purpose-built churches preceded Diocletian's persecution. BASILICAS: Trajan's timber-roofed Basilica Ulpia was widely imitated; cf. fine Basilica of Severus at Lepcis Magna. LATERAN: from family of Plautii Laterani. It may not have become the papal cathedral immediately. ST. PETER'S: built over shrine of St. Peter which the surviving structure dates from ca. A.D. 160–70. Constantine also transformed the *cella memoriae* of St. Paul into the Basilica Ostiensis (St. Paul outside the Walls). His great Roman churches were all located outside the walls so as not to offend the pagans. HOLY APOSTLES, CONSTANTINOPLE: under its conical roof, the remains of Constantine the Great, the "thirteenth apostle" lay for a time. GOLDEN OCTAGON, ANTIOCH: forerunner of palace-church of Aquisgrana (Aachen), etc. PALESTINE (SYRIA PALAESTINA): in addition to the Holy Sepulcher there were further great churches of Constantine at Jerusalem (on the sites of the Nativity and the Ascension, initiated by his mother Helena, as well as at Bethlehem and Hebron). Such combinations of centralized and longitudinal designs reached their climax in Justinian I's Santa Sophia (Aya Sofya) at Constantinople. ALLEGED PLOT OF 326: by Constantine's wife Fausta and eldest son Crispus (by his previous wife Minervina; Caesar since 316): both executed.

The Successors of Constantine. HIS HEIRS: sons: Constantine II (337–40), Constantius II (337–61) and Constans (337–50), and nephews (both killed immediately after his death). Delmatius and Hannibalianus (made King of Kings in Armenia). CONSTANTIUS II'S PERSIAN WARS: Shapur II (309–79) thrice attacked the fortress of Nisibis in Mesopotamia (Nüsaybin, southeastern Turkey) without success but was then diverted by a nomad threat on his eastern frontier. REVOLTS AGAINST CONSTANTIUS II: Magnentius, Vetranio, Nepotianus (all in 350; Magnentius reigned until 353); Silvanus, 355; Julian, 360. GALLUS (CONSTANTIUS): put down revolts in Syria Palaestina (Patricius) and Isauria (southern Asia Minor) but was recalled and put to death at Pola in Istria (Pula in northwestern Yugoslavia). JULIAN'S GERMAN VICTORIES (356–59): over Alamanni, whom he defeated at Argentorate (Strasbourg) in 356, and over Franks. REBELLION OF JULIAN (360): at Lutetia (Paris). JULIAN'S EDUCATION: by eunuch Mardonius and pagan philosopher Maximus (at Ephesus); also at Athens. RESTORATION OF JERUSALEM TEMPLE: ostensibly abandoned because of inflammable gases. JULIAN'S ADMINISTRATION: bureaucracy and bodyguard and secret policy *(agentes in rebus)* were greatly reduced, and he attempted to revive the cities and their councils. PERSIAN WAR: Julian was killed while marching to meet a reserve army. JOVIANUS: originated from Singidunum (Belgrade). He surrendered Nisibis and Singara (on Jebel Sinjar) and Galerius's gains in the east.

PART IX THE TRANSFORMATION OF EUROPE

Chapter 20. The Fall of the Western Empire

Valentinian I and Theodosius I. VALENTINIAN I'S ORIGIN: from Cibalae (Vinkovci in Yugoslavia). HIS NORTHERN CAMPAIGNS (365–73): successive headquarters at Lutetia (Paris), Ambianum (Amiens, formerly Samarobriva): to deal with attacks by Saxons, Picts, and Scots on British provinces), Treviri, and Sirmium (Sremska Mitrovica) (with interlude to crush revolt of Firmus in Africa, 373–75; there was also a later African revolt under Gildo, 398). GRATIAN: and Valens had to give Italy, Illyricum, and north Africa to Gratian's brother Valentinian II, hailed emperor at Aquincum [(Budapest) 375–92]. THEODOSIUS I'S ORIGINS: from Cauca (Coca) in Spain. REVOLTS AGAINST THEODOSIUS I: Magnus Maximus (383–88), a Spaniard, in Britain, Gaul, and Spain (he overthrew Gratian); Eugenius (392–94), a protégé of Arbogast who had Valentinian II murdered but was killed in battle of Frigidus (R. Vipacco or Wippach, tributary of Isonzo).

The Frontiers Broken. STILICHO'S WIFE: Serena. ALANS: nomadic pastoralists from between R. Volga and R. Don. USURPERS AFTER INVASION: e.g., Constantine III (407–11), elevated in Britain, established capital at Arelate (Arles). Honorius had probably settled Saxons in Britain as *foederati,* in exchange for military service. Its communities were still economically linked to the continent in ca. 420–30. ALARIC'S DEATH: at Consentia (Cosenza), buried in R. Busento. BURGUNDIANS: kingdom based on Borbetomagus (Worms) (ca. 406); transplanted to Sabaudia (Savoy) in 443. WESTERN USURPER (423–25): Johannes. CATALAUNIAN PLAINS: Theodoric I, the first Visigothic leader to be truly regarded as a king, was killed. HUN DEFEAT BY GERMANS: on R. Medao (unidentified). Germans pressed forward near Lake Constance.

The Last Emperors of the West. BRIEF FINAL REIGNS: Olybrius (472), Glycerius (473–74), Julius Nepos [(474–75); d. 480 in Dalmatia], Romulus Augustus ("Agustulus," 475–76). LOYAL REMNANT OF CENTRAL GAUL: Auvergne, with its capital at Arverna (Clermont-Ferrand; formerly Augustonemetum), lost by Julius Nepos to Visigothic king Euric (474). Arelate fell in 476. FATHER OF ROMULUS: Orestes, a Roman who had been Attila's secretary. "FALL": the term "Middle Ages" (from 476 or 395, 406, 610, 800, 842?) was first used by Professor C. Kellner of Halle in 1688. Abbe Ferdinando Galiani (1744): "The Fall of empires: what can that mean? Empires, being neither up nor down, do not fall." GERMAN APPROVAL OF "FALL": Beatus Rhenanus (fifteenth-sixteenth century); cf. the Dutch jurist and historian Hugo Grotius (sixteenth-seventeenth century).

Chapter 21. The Fatal Disunities

Social Catastrophe. GREAT ESTATES: e.g., Burgus Julius near Carthage (on mosaic in Bardo Museum, Tunis); cf. Burgus of Leontius at confluence of Dordogne and Garonne; and earlier three-storied fortress at Pfalzel (fourth century). DEFENDERS OF PEOPLE: Letter of Valentinian I to his praetorian prefect Petronius Probus. BAGAUDAE: Tibatto (435, raised slaves), physician Eudoxius (440s, fled to Huns); also in Spain, where they were crushed by Aetius in 454. THEIR PEOPLE'S COURTS:

Mentioned in verse drama *Querolus* ("the Protester"). GAULISH LANDOWNER AS EMPEROR: Avitus (455) at Arelate; coronation attended by Visigothic king Theodoric II (453–66).

Uncooperative Attitudes. ATAULF: on German-Roman cooperation, reported by a citizen of Narbo (Narbonne) to the chronicler Orosius. SIDONIUS APOLLINARIS: (b. ca. 430–d. ca. 488) of Lugdunum (Lyon); praised the Visigothic monarchs Theodoric II and Euric (having fought against the latter in 471–75). DISLOYALTY OF FEDERATES: in 409 they failed to prevent other Germans from crossing into Spain, and in 422 they deserted to the Vandals there.

Christians and Pagans. MONASTICISM: first made famous by St. Antony (born in Upper Egypt ca. 251), who organized his followers into groups during the persecution of Galerius (305–6). MONASTERIES of St. Martin of Tours: Ligugé near Pictavi (Poitiers; formerly Limonum) ca. 360, and then Marmoutier near Civitas Turonum (Tours; formerly Caesarodunum). Martin who came from Savaria in Pannonia (Szombathely in Hungary), followed St. Antony's ideal of partly eremitical and partly communal life. After 400 Honoratus established a monastery at Lerin near Cannes. JEROME: numerous works include translation of Bible into Latin (the Vulgate). JOHN CASSIAN: writer of *Institutes* and *Conferences* which exercised great influence on St. Benedict of Nursia (Norcia), abbot of Monte Cassino (died ca. 547). CHURCH IS IN THE STATE: Bishop Optatus of Milev (Mila in Algeria). MEDIOLANUM (MILAN) IN LATER FOURTH CENTURY: five huge churches: SS Nazaro, Simpliciano, Giovanni in Conca, Tecla, Lorenzo. Ambrose, bishop of Mediolanum, unearthed two pairs of saints there and one at Bononia (Bologna). FORCIBLE CONFORMITY: based on interpretations of texts of Luke's Gospel and Paul's Epistles. VICTORY DEBATE (384): between Ambrose and the pagan aristocratic Roman orator and writer Symmachus (b. ca. 340–d. ca. 402). AUGUSTINE'S BACKGROUND: his parents were Patricius and Monica, and he was educated at Thagaste, Madaurus, and Carthage. He was then in Rome for one year as a teacher before going to Mediolanum in 386. SURVIVAL OF PAGANISM: gladiatorial combats may have continued until 439–40, duels of men against wild animals until 498, and contests between wild animals until 681. AUGUSTINE ON "OPPORTUNITY": to Vincentius, Donatist bishop of Cartennae (Tenes). "YOUR" VIRGIL: letter to Nectarius of Calama. "INVICTA ROMA AETERNA": e.g., on gold medallion of client Priscus Attalus. RUTILIUS NAMATIANUS: poem, *De Reditu Suo* ("On his Return"). POPES AGAINST GOVERNMENT SERVICE: Siricius (385–99), Innocent I (401–17). PELADIUS: died after 419. He wrote commentary on Pauline epistles. Seventy tracts supporting his viewpoint are the work of his followers. AUGUSTINE DISSOCIATES CHURCH FROM STATE: under influence of lay Donatist theologian Tyconius, author of *Rules* and interpreter of St. Paul.

Chapter 22. The Aftermath

The Successor States in the West. CLOVIS: son of Childeric I, ruler of a tribe of Salian Franks. He had remained loyal to his treaties with the Romans, but won the battle of Vouille against the Visigoths, whose king Alaric II, son of Euric, was killed. Clovis had defeated a last west Roman outpost at Suessiona

(Soissons in northern France) in 486. CHARLES MARTEL: threw back a Moslem invasion from Spain (732). CHARLEMAGNE: the Holy Roman Empire disappeared only in 1806. HISPALIS (SEVILLE): its bishop Isidore (b. ca. 560–d. ca. 636), a prolific writer, was one of the principal links between the ancient world and the Middle Ages. NORTH AFRICA: the Islamic armies started their advance westwards from Egypt in 640 and had conquered the whole of north Africa by 711. OSTROGOTHS: took one-third of Italian land for their own use. The populations were kept apart. Theodoric the Ostrogoth, like the Burgundians and Visigoths, placed the head of the Byzantine emperor Anastasius I on his coins. BOETHIUS (b. ca. 480–d. 524): held high office but was then imprisoned and executed by Theodoric. He wrote *On the Consolation of Philosophy* in prison. CASSIODORUS (b. ca. 490–d. 583): senator, consul, encyclopaedist, theologian, founded religious community at Vivarium (Coscia di Staletti) in his native Calabria. BELISARIUS: occupied Carthage and captured Vandal king Gelimer (533); then in Italy 533–40 and 546–49. NARSES: Pers-Armenian eunuch; completed conquest of Italy 550–54, then administered it from Ravenna to 567. Justinian's generals also recaptured parts of southern Spain.

The Survival of Byzantium. ARCADIUS'S ADVISERS: Rufinus Eutropius, Anthemius. THEODOSIUS II: bought off Huns, 422; sum increased 434, 443. EASTERN EMPEROR LEO I: given the throne by Aspar the Alan. ZENO: from Isauria in Asia Minor; his original name was Tarasicodissa. At first for a few months co-emperor with his son Leo II (474). ANASTASIUS I: from Dyrrhachium (Durrës in Albania). His major reform of the coinage marked the beginning of the Byzantine system. JUSTIN I: from a village near Naïssus (Niš in Yugoslavia). BALKANS: Bulgars crossed the Danube and menaced Constantinople in 679. CORPUS OF JUSTINIAN I: *Digest* (50 books with 432 titles from 2,000 works); *Codex* (imperial statutes, 8 editions); *Institutes* (elementary); *Novellae* (new laws). Undertaken by a commission of 16 members, mostly presided over by Tribonian of Side [(Eski Antalya, southern Asia Minor), d. 542/5]. PERSIA: large areas of the Byzantine empire were lost to the Persian king Chosroes II Parvez (590–628). LOSS OF JUSTINIAN I'S WESTERN CONQUESTS: northern Italy settled by Lombards (568) for two centuries; Pope Gregory the Great [(590–604), the last intellectual to combine western and Greek culture] negotiated directly with them. Hopes of a united empire were further shattered by movement of Slavs into the Balkans (seventh century) separating Italy from the east, and by the loss of northern Africa to the Arabs (eighth century). CRUSADERS AT CONSTANTINOPLE: 1204–61; the "Latin Empire." TURKS: the Seljuk Turks defeated the Byzantines at Manzikert in 1071. The Ottoman Turks began to encroach on the empire under the founder of their dynasty Osman I (1288–1326). FALL OF CONSTANTINOPLE (1453): the end of the "Middle Ages" (or this has been dated to 1440, 1492, 1515, 1548). USURPERS IN EASTERN EMPIRE: Procopius (365–66, distant relation of Julian the Apostate); Basiliscus (475–76), Marcian (479), Leontius I (484–88) (all in Zeno's reign); and Vitalian (513–15).

ANCIENT SOURCES

1. LATIN HISTORICAL WRITERS

AMMIANUS MARCELLINUS, ca. A.D. 330–95, born at Antioch in Syria (Antakya in SE Turkey). History *(Rerum Gestarum libri)* of years A.D. 96–378 (Books 14–31 about A.D. 353–78 survive).

CAESAR, Gaius Julius, 100–44 B.C. Dictator, Seven books of "Commentaries" on Gallic War (eighth is by Aulus Hirtius), three on *Civil War* (the concluding books on African, Alexandrian, and Spanish wars are by other authors).

CASSIODORUS, ca. A.D. 490–583; born at Scylacium (Squillace) in S Italy, Extant examples of his numerous works include the *Chronica*, a brief summary of Roman history to A.D. 519. See also Jordanes.

EUTROPIUS, Fourth century A.D. Survey *(Breviarium)* of Roman history from beginning to A.D. 364.

FLORUS, ANNAEUS (?), second century A.D.; born in North Africa. *Epitome* of Roman history to wars of Augustus.

HISTORIA AUGUSTA, ostensibly the work of six authors (probably pseudonyms); apparently of the later fourth century A.D. Partly fictitious "biographies" of Roman emperors, Caesars, and usurpers from A.D. 117 to 284 (gap for 244–59).

ISIDORE, bishop of Hispalis (Seville), A.D. 602–36; numerous works included history to his own times *(Chronica Majora)* and *History of the Goths.*

JEROME, SAINT (Eusebius Hieronymus), ca. A.D. 348–420; born at Stridon in Dalmatia. His historical works include a *Chronicle* of ancient events and short biographies of Christian writers *(De Viris Illustribus).*

JORDANES, mid-sixth century A.D.; probably a Goth from the Lower Danube. Summaries of Gothic and Roman history, former summarizing the *Gothic Histories* of Cassiodorus (q.v.)

LIVY (Titus Livius), 59 B.C.–A.D. 17 or 64 B.C.–A.D. 12; born at Patavium (Padua in N Italy). History of Rome (*Ab Urbe Condita;* to 9 B.C.) in 142 books, of which 35 are extant, covering the periods 753–243 and 219–167 B.C. From the lost books we have fragments and excerpts, and there are two sets of abridgments.

NEPOS, Cornelius, ca. 99–24 B.C.; born in North Italy. Out of various works 24 short biographies survive.

OROSIUS, Paulus, early fifth century. A.D.; probably born at Bracara Augusta

(Braga in Portugal). *Christian Chronicle (Historiae adversum Paganos)* in seven books from the Creation to A.D. 417.

SALLUST (Gaius Sallustius Crispus), ca. 86–35 B.C.; b. Amiternum (San Vittorino in central Italy). Monographs on Catilinarian conspiracy *(Bellum Catilinae)* and Jugurthine War *(Bellum Iugurthinum)* in addition to lost *Histories*.

SUETONIUS (Gaius Suetonius Tranquillus), ca. A.D. 69–104 (?); probably from Hippo Regius (Annaba in Algeria). Writings include biographies: *De Vita Caesarum (The Twelve Caesars), De Viris Illustribus* (including *De Grammaticis et Rhetoribus), De Poetis* (at least three survive), *De Oratoribus* (15, summary of one survives), *De Historicis* (one of six survives).

TACITUS, Publius Cornelius, ca. A.D. 56–before or after 117; probably of Gallic or North Italian origin. *Histories* of the years A.D. 69–96 (?): out of 12 or 14 books, 4 and part of the fifth survive (on the Civil Wars, A.D. 69–70). Then *Annals* covering the years A.D. 14–68; out of 18 or 16 books, 10 (minus parts of 3) survive (on Tiberius, part of Claudius's reign, and most of Nero's). Previous works included a biography of his father-in-law, *Agricola,* and the *Germania* and *Dialogue on Orators (Dialogus de Oratoribus).*

VALERIUS MAXIMUS, wrote in 30s A.D. Moral and rhetorical history *(Facta ac dicta memorabilia)* in 9 books.

VELLEIUS PATERCULUS, ca. 19 B.C.–after A.D. 30; of Campanian origin. Compendium of Roman history *(Historiae Romanae)* to A.D. 30.

2. GREEK HISTORICAL WRITERS

APPIAN, 2nd cent. A.D.; probably born at Alexandria in Egypt. History of Roman conquests to Trajan, in 24 books of which nos. 6–9 (mostly) and 11–17 are complete.

DIO CASSIUS (Cassius Dio Cocceianus), ca. A.D. 155–235; from Nicaea (Iznik in NW Turkey). Roman history to A.D. 229, in 80 books of which nos. 36–54 (68–10 B.C.) are preserved; 55–60 (91 B.C.–A.D. 46) exist in abbreviated form; 17 and 79–80 in part. Xiphilinus (eleventh century) epitomized from book 36 onwards, and Zonaras (twelfth century) gives the gist of 1–21 and 44–80.

DIODORUS SICULUS, lived under Caesar and Augustus; from Agyrium (Agira) in Sicily. World history *(Bibliotheke)* in 40 books to Caesar's Gallic War, of which 1–8 and 11–20 are fully preserved and the remaining books fragmentary.

DIONYSIUS, worked under Augustus; from Halicarnassus (Bodrum in SW Turkey). His writings included *Roman Antiquities* to outbreak of First Punic War, in 20 books of which the first 10 survive.

EUSEBIUS, ca. A.D. 260–340; of Caesarea Maritima (near Sdot Yam in Israel). His writings included *Church History,* extended in latest edition to A.D. 324, and eulogistic life of Constantine the Great.

HERODIAN, early third century A.D.; from Syria. Roman History from A.D. 180–238 in 8 books.

JOSEPHUS, FLAVIUS, A.D. 37–38–after 94; of Jewish, Pharisaic origin. *Jewish War* (about the First Jewish Revolt), Greek translation in 7 books of lost Aramaic original; *Jewish Antiquities* in 20 books, a history of the Jews from the Creation to just before the First Revolt; His *Life,* an autobiographical defense; and *Against Apion,* a two-book work attacking anti-Semitic writers from the third century B.C.

NICOLAUS, later first century B.C.; from Damascus in Syria. Court historian of Herod the Great (37–4 B.C.); his works included a *Universal History* to Herod's death of which portions are preserved.

PLUTARCH (Lucius (?) Mestrius Plutarchus), before A.D. 50–after 120; of Chaeronea in Greece. Numerous writings include 23 pairs of "parallel lives" of Greeks and Romans, and lives of the Caesars, of which only *Galba* and *Otho* survive.

POLYBIUS, ca. 200–118 B.C.; of Megalopolis in Greece. *Universal History* of the years 220–144 B.C. in 40 books, of which we have the first 5, a large part of book 6, substantial portions of 7–16, and smaller extracts from most of the others, comprising altogether nearly a third of the whole work.

PROCOPIUS, ca. A.D. 500–after 562; born at Caesarea Maritima (near Sdot Yam in Israel). *History of the Wars of Justinian* in 8 books and censorious *Secret History.*

THEODORETUS, ca. A.D. 393–466; bishop of Cyrrhus (Kurus in SE Turkey). Writings included *Church History* from Constantine the Great to A.D. 428, and *Religious History* containing biographies of ascetics.

ZONARAS, Johannes, twelfth century A.D.; monk at Hagia Glyceria in the Princes' Islands (Kizil Adalar). *Universal Epitome of Histories* to A.D. 1118, now in 18 books, excerpting Dio Cassius, Plutarch, etc.

ZOSIMUS, ca. A.D. 500; a pagan, possibly from Ascalon (Ashkelon) or Gaza in SW Palestine. *Historia Nova* from Augustus to A.D. 410.

OTHER SOURCES

(1) Other historians and biographers, whose works in this field are now lost or mainly lost but detectable through intermediaries. Of particular importance (among very many) are the Latin writers Cato the Elder (234–149 B.C.), Licinius Macer (d. 68 B.C.), Pliny the Elder (A.D. 23–79), Pollio (76 B.C.–A.D. 4), Valerius Antias (1st cent. B.C.), and Varro (116–27 B.C.), and, in Greek, Cincius Alimentus (late second century B.C.), the emperor Claudius (10 B.C.–A.D. 54), Fabius Pictor (late second century B.C.), and Posidonius (ca. 135–50 B.C.).

(2) Other Greek and Latin authors of a primarily nonhistorical character whose works nevertheless contain historical information, notably Augustine, Cicero, Lucan, Salvian, Seneca the Younger, Sidonius Apollinaris, Virgil, etc.

(3) Inscriptions.

(4) Papyri, mainly from Egypt.

(5) Graffiti, especially at Pompeii.

(6) Coins, of the Roman state and local communities and client kingdoms, and of the neighbors and enemies of the Roman Empire.

(7) Commemorative medallions of the Roman state and local communities of the empire.

(8) Works of art and architecture and engineering.

(9) Remains of agricultural and commercial and industrial activities.

BIBLIOGRAPHY

AFRICA, T. W. *The Immense Majesty: A History of Rome and the Roman Empire*, New York, 1974.

ALFÖLDI, A. *Early Rome and the Latins*, Ann Arbor, 1965.

ANDRÉ, J. M. *Le siècle d'Auguste*, Paris, 1974.

ARNOTT, P. D. *An Introduction to the Roman World*, London, 1976.

BADIAN, E. *Roman Imperialism in the Late Republic*, 2nd ed., Oxford, 1968.

BAILEY, C., ed. *The Legacy of Rome*, Oxford, 1924.

BALSDON, J. P. V. D. *Life and Leisure in Ancient Rome*, London, 1969.

————. *Roman Women*, London, 1962.

————, ed. *The Romans*, London, 1965.

BANTI, L. *Il mondo degli etruschi*, 2nd ed., Rome, 1969 (*Etruscan Cities and their Culture*, London and Berkeley, 1973).

BENGTSON, H. *Einführung in die alte Geschichte*, 6th ed., Munich, 1974 (*Introduction to Ancient History*, London and Berkeley, 1975).

BIANCHI BANDINELLI, R. *Rome: le centre du pouvoir*, Paris, 1969 (*Rome the Center of Power: Roman Art to A.D. 200*, London, 1970).

————. *Rome: la fin de l'art antique*, Paris, 1970 (*The Late Empire: Roman Art A.D. 200–400*, London, 1971).

BLOCH, R. *Les origines de Rome*, Paris, 1959 (*The Origins of Rome*, London, 1960).

BOAK, A. E. R., and SINNIGEN, W. G. *History of Rome to A.D. 565*, 5th ed., New York, 1965.

BOETHIUS, A. AND WARD-PERKINS, J. B. *Etruscan and Roman Architecture*, Harmondsworth, 1970.

BONNER, S. F. *Education in Ancient Rome*, London, 1977.

BRAUER, G. C. *The Age of the Soldier Emperors*, Park Ridge, 1975.

BRILLIANT, R. *Roman Art from the Republic to Constantine*, London, 1974.

BRISSON, J. P. *Carthage ou Rome*, Paris, 1973.

BORCH, H. C. *Roman Society: A Social, Economic and Cultural History*, Lexington (Mass.), 1977.

BRUNT, P. A. *Social Conflicts in the Roman Republic*, London, 1971.

CALABI, I. *L'uso storiografico delle iscrizioni latine*, Milan, 1953.

CAMBRIDGE ANCIENT HISTORY. Vols VII–XII, Cambridge, 1928–39.

CARCOPINO, H. *La vie quotidienne à Rome a l'apogée de l'empire*, Paris, 1939 (*Daily Life in Ancient Rome*, Harmondsworth, 1956).

CARSON, R. A. G. *Coins of Greece and Rome*, 2nd ed., London, 1970.

CARY, M., AND SCULLARD, H. H. *A History of Rome,* 3rd ed. (of Cary's *History*), London, 1975.

CASSON, L. *Travel in the Ancient World,* London, 1974.

CHARLESWORTH, M. P. *The Roman Empire,* Oxford, 1951.

CHEVALLIER, R. *Les voies romaines,* Paris, 1972 (*Roman Roads,* London and Berkeley, 1976).

CHRIST, K., ed. *Hannibal,* Darmstadt, 1974.

CHRIST, K. *Römische Geschichte: Einführung, Quellenkunde, Bibliographie,* Darmstadt, 1973.

CLARKE, M. L. *The Roman Mind,* London, 1956.

COARELLI, F., etc. *Le città etrusche,* Milan, 1973 (*Etruscan Cities,* London, 1975).

COWELL, F. R. *Everyday Life in Ancient Rome,* London, 1961.

CROOK, J. A., *Law and Life of Rome,* London, 1967.

CUNLIFFE, B. *Rome and the Barbarians,* London, 1975.

DILKE, O. A. W. *The Ancient Romans: How they Lived and Worked,* Newton Abbot, 1975.

DOREY, T. A., and DUDLEY, D. R. *Rome against Carthage,* London, 1971.

DOWNEY, G. *The Late Roman Empire,* New York, 1969.

DUDLEY, D. R. *The Romans,* London, 1970 (*Roman Society,* 1975).

EARL, D. *The Moral and Political Tradition of Rome,* London, 1967.

ERRINGTON, R. M. *The Dawn of Empire: Rome's Rise to World Power,* London, 1972.

FERGUSON, J. *The Religions of the Roman Empire,* London, 1970.

FINLEY, M. I. *The Ancient Economy,* London, 1973.

————, ed. *Slavery in Classical Antiquity,* London, 1960.

FOWLER, W. W. *Rome,* 3rd ed., Oxford, 1967.

FRIEDLÄNDER, L. *Darstellungen aus der Sittengeschichte Roms,* 10th ed., Leipzig, 1922 (*Roman Life and Manners under the Early Empire,* London, 1965 ed.).

GABBA, E. *Esercito e società nella tarda republica romana,* Bologna, 1973 (*Republican Rome: the Army and the Allies,* Oxford, 1977).

GAGE, J., *Enquêtes sur les structures sociales et réligieuses de la Rome primitive,* Brussels, 1977.

————. *Les classes sociales dans l'empire romain,* Paris, 1969.

GARZETTI, A. *L'impero da Tiberio agli Antonini,* Rome, 1960 (*From Tiberius to the Antonines,* London, 1974).

GENTILI, B., etc. *Storia della letteratura latina,* Rome, 1976.

GIBBON, E. *History of the Decline and Fall of the Roman Empire,* London, 1776–1788.

GRANT, M. *The Climax of Rome,* 3rd ed., London, 1974.

————. *The Fall of the Roman Empire,* Radnor (Pennsylvania), 1976.

————. *The Jews in the Roman World,* London, 1973.*

————. *Roman History from Coins,* 2nd ed., Cambridge, 1968.

————. *Roman Literature,* 3rd ed., Harmondsworth, 1964.

————. *The World of Rome,* 3rd ed., London, 1974.

GRIMAL, P. *La civilisation romaine,* Paris, 1960 (*The Civilization of Rome,* London, 1963.)

————, etc. *Der Hellenismus und der Aufstieg Roms,* Frankfurt-am-Main, 1965 (*Hellenism and the Rise of Rome,* London, 1968).

GRUEN, E. S., ed. *The Image of Rome,* Englewood Cliffs, 1969.

HADAS, M. *A History of Rome,* New York, 1956.

---

*See also *Jesus* (1977) and *Saint Paul* (1976) for short bibliographies.

HAMMOND, M. *The Antonine Monarchy,* Oxford, 1959.

HAYWOOD, R. M. *Ancient Rome,* New York, 1967.

HEICHELHEIM, F. M., and Yeo, C.A. *History of the Roman People,* Englewood Cliffs, 1962.

HEURGON, J. *Rome et la mediterranée occidentale jusqu'aux guerres puniques,* Paris, 1969 (*The Rise of Rome,* London, 1973).

HEUSS, A. *Römische Geschichte,* Braunschweig, 2nd ed., 1964.

HIGHET, G. *The Classical Tradition,* Oxford, 2nd ed., 1967.

HOMO, L. *Le haut-empire,* Paris, 1941.

JOLOWICZ, H. F. *Historical Introduction to the Study of Roman Law,* 2nd ed., Cambridge, 1972.

JONES, A. H. M. *The Decline of the Ancient World,* London, 1966.

————. *A History of Rome through the Fifth Century,* London, 1968.

————. *The Roman Economy,* Oxford, 1974.

————. *The Later Roman Empire,* Oxford, 1964.

KAEHLER, H. *Rom und sein Welt,* 2nd ed., Munich, 1968–70 (*Rome and her Empire,* London, 1963).

KELLY, J. M. *Roman Litigation,* Oxford, 1966.

KENT, J. P. F. *Roman Coins,* London and New York, 1978.

KIENAST, D. *Augustus,* Darmstadt, 1977.

KJELLBERG, E., AND SÄFLUND, G. *Grekisk och Romersk Konst,* Stockholm, 1958 (*Greek and Roman Art,* London, 1968).

KRAFT, H., ed. *Konstantin der Grosse,* Darmstadt, 1974.

KUNKEL, W. *Römische Rechtsgeschichte,* 6th ed., Köln, 1971 (*An Introduction to Roman Legal and Constitutional History,* 2nd ed., Oxford, 1973).

LE GALL, J. *La religion romaine de l'époque de Caton l'ancien au règne de l'empereur Commode,* Paris, 1975.

LEVI, M. A., and MELONI, P. *Storia romana dagli etruschi a Teodosio,* 4th ed., Milan, 1968.

LEWIS, N., and REINHOLD, M., *Roman Civilization: A Sourcebook,* New York, 1955.

LOT, F. *La fin du monde antique et le début du moyen age,* Paris, 1927 (*The End of the Ancient World,* 2nd ed., London, 1966).

LUTTWAK, E. N. *The Grand Strategy of the Roman Empire,* Baltimore, 1977.

MCDONALD, A. H. *Republican Rome,* London, 1966.

MACDONALD, W. L. *The Architecture of the Roman Empire,* New Haven, 1965.

MACMULLEN, R. *The Roman Government's Response to Crisis A.D. 235–337,* New Haven, 1976.

————. *Roman Social Relations 50 B.C.–A.D. 289,* New Haven, 1974.

MANSUELLI, G. *Etrurien und die Ansänge Roms,* Milan, 1963 (*Etruria and Early Rome,* London, 1966).

MARKUS, R. A. *Christianity in the Roman World,* London, 1974.

MAROTTI, I. *Litteratura latina,* Bologna, 1976.

MARROU, H. I. *Histoire de l'éducation dans l'antiquité,* 2nd ed., 1948 (*History of Education in Antiquity,* London, reprint 1977).

MARSH, F. B. *A History of the Roman World from 146 B.C. to 30 B.C.,* 3rd ed., London, 1963.

MARTIN, J. P. *La Rome ancienne: 753 avant J.C.–395 après J.C.,* Paris, 1973.

MASSON, G. A. *A Concise History of Republican Rome,* London, 1973.

MATTINGLY, H. *Roman Coins,* 2nd ed., London, 1960.

————. *Roman Imperial Civilization,* London, 1957.

MAZZARINO, S. *La fine del mondo antico,* Milan, 1959 (*The End of the Ancient World,* London, 1966).

MILLAR, F. *The Emperor in the Roman World,* London, 1977.

————, etc. *Das Römische Reich und seine Nachbarn,* Frankfurt-am-Main, 1966 (*The Roman Empire and its Neighbors,* London, 1967).

MOMMSEN, T. *Römische Geschichte,* 1854–56, 1886, ed. K. Christ, Darmstadt, 1976 (*History of Rome,* London, 1913, abridged ed. 1960).

NASH, E. *Pictorial Dictionary of Ancient Rome,* 2nd ed., New York, 1968.

NICOLET, C. *Le métier de citoyen dans la Rome républicaine,* Paris, 1976.

————. *Rome et la conquête du monde Méditerranée 264–27 B.C.,* Vol. I, *Les Structures de l'Italie romaine,* Paris, 1977.

OGILVIE, R. M. *Early Rome and the Etruscans,* London, 1976.

————. *The Romans and their Gods,* London, 1969.

OXFORD CLASSICAL DICTIONARY, 2nd ed., Oxford, 1970.

PALANQUE, J-R. *Le bas-empire,* Paris, 1971.

PALLOTTINO, M. *Etruscologia,* 7th ed., Milan, 1972 (*The Etruscans,* Harmondsworth, 1975, from 6th ed.).

————, etc., eds. *Popoli e civiltà dell Italia antica,* Rome, 1974.

PALMER, R. E. A., *The Archaic Community of the Romans,* Cambridge, 1970.

PAOLI, U. E. *Vita Romana,* 10th ed., Florence, 1967 (*Rome: Its People, Life and Customs,* London, 1963).

PARKER, H. M. D. *A History of the Roman World from A.D. 138 to 337,* 2nd ed., London, 1958.

PASSERINI, A. *Linee di storia romana in eta imperiale,* 2nd ed., Milan, 1972.

PAYNE, R. *Ancient Rome,* New York, 1970.

PEROWNE, S. *The End of the Roman World,* London, 1966.

PETIT, P. *Histoire générale de l'empire romain,* Paris, 1974.

PICARD, G. *Empire romain (Architecture universelle),* Fribourg, 1965.

PIGANIOL, A. *L'empire chrétien,* 2nd ed., Paris, 1972.

————. *Histoire de Rome,* 5th ed., Paris, 1962.

RADICE, B. *Who's Who in the Ancient World,* 2nd ed., London, 1973.

RAFFALT, R. *Grosse Kaiser Roms,* Munich, 1977.

REMONDON, R. *La crise de l'empire romain,* Paris, 1964.

ROSTOVTZEFF, M. *Social and Economic History of the Roman Empire,* 2nd ed. (P. M. Fraser), Oxford, 1957.

ROULAND, N. *Clientela: Essai sur l'influence des rapports de clientèle sur la vie politique romaine,* Aix-Marseille (diss.), 1977.

SALMON, E. T., *A History of the Roman World from 30 B.C. to A.D. 138,* 6th ed., London, 1968.

SCHMIDT, J. *Vie et mort des esclaves dans la Rome antique,* Paris, 1973.

SCULLARD, H. H., *The Etruscan Cities and Rome,* London, 1967.

————. *From the Gracchi to Nero,* 4th ed., London, 1976.

————. *A History of the Roman World from 753 to 146 B.C.,* 3rd ed., London, 1961.

SHERWIN-WHITE, A. N. *The Roman Citizenship,* 2nd ed., Oxford, 1973.

SIMON, M., AND BENOIT, A. *Le Judaisme et le Christianisme antique,* Paris, 1968.

SMALLWOOD, E. M. *The Jews under Roman Rule from Pompey to Diocletian,* Leiden, 1976.

STARR, C. G. *Civilization and the Caesars,* Ithaca (N.Y.), 1954.

————. *The Emergence of Rome,* 2nd ed., Ithaca (N.Y.), 1965.

STRONG, D. *Roman Art,* Harmondsworth, 1976.
SUTHERLAND, C. H. V. *Roman Coins,* London, 1974.
SYME, R. *Roman Papers,* Oxford, 1977.
————. *The Roman Revolution,* Oxford, 1939.
TEMPORINI, H., ed. *Aufstieg und Niedergang der antiken Welt,* Berlin, 1972 (many parts).
THOMAS, J. A. C. *Textbook of Roman Law,* Amsterdam, 1977.
TOYNBEE, J. M. C. *The Art of the Romans,* London, 1965.
————. *Roman Historical Portraits,* London and New York, 1978.
TURNER, E. G. *The Papyrologist at Work,* Durham (N. Carolina), 1976.
VOGT, J. *Die römische Republik,* 6th ed., Freiburg, 1973.
————. *Der Niedergang Roms,* Zurich, 1965 (*The Decline of Rome,* London, 1967).
WALBANK, F. W. *The Awful Revolution,* Liverpool, 1969.
WATSON, A. *Rome of the Twelve Tables,* Princeton, 1975.
WATSON, G. R. *The Roman Soldier,* London, 1969.
WHEELER, R. E. M. *Roman Art and Architecture,* Rome, 1964.
WHITE, L., ed. *The Transformation of the Roman World,* Berkeley, 1966.
WILKINSON, L. P. *The Roman Experience,* New York, 1975.
ZANKER, P., ed. *Hellenismus in Mittelitalien,* Göttingen, 1976.

TABLE OF DATES*

---

*Until the 4th cent. B.C., Italian dates are only approximate.

B.C.

340–338	Latin and Campanian War.
339	Publilian laws.
[334–323	Conquests of Alexander the Great.]
328–302	Second Samnite War.
321	Defeat by Samnites at the Caudine Forks.
312	Censorship of Appius Claudius. Via Appia and Aqua Appia.
298–290	Third Samnite War.
297	Hortensian Law.
295	Samnites defeated at Sentinum.
280–275	War with Pyrrhus.
[ca. 274–232(?)	Rule of Asoka in India.]
264–241	First Punic War.
241	Victory off Aegates Islands. Annexation of Sicily.
241–238	War of Mercenaries (Truceless War) against Carthage.
238	Annexation of Sardinia and Corsica.
237	Hamilcar Barca goes to Spain.
232	Flaminian land law.
226	Ebro treaty with Hasdrubal Barca.
225	Gauls defeated at Telamon.
218–201	Second Punic War.
218–216	Defeats at R. Ticinus, R. Trebia, L. Trasimene, and Cannae.
215–209	Revolts of Capua, Tarentum, Syracuse.
207	Hasdrubal defeated at R. Metaurus.
206	Victory of Scipio Africanus at Ilipa.
[206 B.C.–	
A.D. 220	Han Dynasty in China.]
202 B.C.	Victory of Scipio Africanus at Zama.
200–196	Second Macedonian War.
197	Philip V defeated at Cynoscephalae.
192–189	War against Antiochus III.
190	Antiochus III defeated at Magnesia.
171–68	Third Macedonian War.
168	Perseus defeated at Pydna.
149–46	Third Punic War.
146	Destruction of Carthage and Corinth.
139–132	First Slave Revolt in Sicily.
133	Scipio Aemilianus captures Numantia.
133–129	Pergamum left to Rome and annexed as province of Asia.
133 & 123–	
122	Tribunates of Tiberius and Gaius Gracchus.
121	Defeat of Arverni and Allobroges in Gaul.
112–105	Jugurthine War.
104–100	Second Slave Revolt in Sicily.
102–101	Marius defeats Teutones and Cimbri.

B.C.

91	Tribunate and murder of Marcus Livius Drusus the Younger.
91–87	Social (Marsian) War.
90	Julian Law conferring rights upon Italians.
88	Sulla marches on Rome.
88–84	First Mithridatic War.
81	Second Mithridatic War
81	Dictatorship of Sulla.
81–72	Revolt of Sertorius in Spain.
74–63	Third Mithridatic War.
73–71	Slave revolt of Spartacus.
70	Consulships of Pompey and Crassus.
67	Gabinian Law gives Pompey pirate command.
66–63	Manilian Law gives Pompey Mithridatic command. Eastern settlement.
63	Consulship of Cicero. Conspiracy of Catiline.
60	"First Triumvirate" of Pompey, Crassus, and Caesar.
59	First consulship of Caesar.
58–51	Caesar's Gallic War.
53	Crassus defeated and killed by Parthians at Carrhae.
49–45	Civil War. Caesar's victories at Pharsalus (followed by death of Pompey), Thapsus, Munda.
44	Perpetual dictatorship and assassination of Caesar.
43	Second Triumvirate of Antony, Octavian, and Lepidus. Death of Cicero.
42	Deaths of Brutus and Cassius, defeated at Philippi.
36	Octavian eliminates Sextus Pompeius and Lepidus.
31	Octavian and Agrippa defeat Antony and Cleopatra at Actium.
30	Deaths of Antony and Cleopatra. Egypt annexed.
27 B.C.– A.D. 14	*Augustus (Octavian)*
25	Annexation of Galatia.
19	Death of Virgil.
16–9	Annexations to Danube and Elbe.
8	Death of Horace.
[6–4(?)	Birth of Jesus.]
A.D. 6–9	Revolts in Pannonia and Illyricum.
9	Arminius defeats and kills Varus at Teutoburg Forest.
14–37	*Tiberius.*
19	Death of Germanicus.
[ca. 30 or 33	Crucifixion of Jesus.]
31	Execution of Sejanus.
37–41	*Caligula (Gaius).*
41–54	*Claudius.*
41–46	Annexation of Mauretania, SE England (Britannia), and Thrace.

A.D.

[ca. 45–58	Missionary journeys of Paul.]
54–68	*Nero.*
61	Revolt of Boudicca (Boadicea) in Britain.
63–66	Settlement of Armenian question with Parthia.
65	Pisonian conspiracy and deaths of Seneca and Petronius.
66–70	First Jewish Revolt (First Roman War).
68–69	*Galba, Otho, Vitellius.* Civil Wars.
69–79	*Vespasian.*
79–81	*Titus.*
79	Destruction of Pompeii and Herculaneum by eruption of Vesuvius.
80	Inauguration of Flavian Amphitheatre (Colosseum) at Rome.
81–96	*Domitian.*
96–98	*Nerva.*
98–117	*Trajan.*
106	Annexation of Dacia.
113–17	Trajan's eastern campaigns.
115–ca. 118	Revolts of Jewish Dispersion in Cyrene, Cyprus, and Egypt.
117–38	*Hadrian.*
122	Hadrian's Wall in Britain.
132–35	Second Jewish Revolt (Second Roman War).
138–61	*Antoninus Pius.*
142	Antonine Wall in Britain.
161–80	*Marcus Aurelius and Lucius Verus* (d. 169).
162–66	Parthian War.
166–72, 177–80	Marcomannic and Sarmatian wars.
180–92	*Commodus.*
193	*Pertinax, Didius Julianus.*
193–211	*Septimius Severus.*
194	Defeat of Pescennius Niger at Issus.
197	Defeat of Clodius Albinus at Lugdunum.
197–99	Parthian War.
208–11	British wars.
211–17	*Caracalla and Geta* (d. 211 or 212)
212	The Constitutio Antoniniana conferring general citizenship.
212	Death of jurist Papinian.
217–18	*Macrinus.*
218–22	*Elagabalus.*
222–35	*Severus Alexander.* Rule of Julia Mamaea.
223	Deaths of Julia Maesa and jurist Ulpian.
ca. 226	Persians (Sassanians) overthrow Parthians.
235–38	*Maximinus I. Thrax.*
238	*Gordianus I* and *II Africanus* proclaimed in Africa; *Balbinus* and *Pupienus.*

A.D.

238–44   *Gordianus III;* rule of Timesitheus (d. 243).
241–72   Sapor I. Sassanian King of Persia.
244–49   Philip the Arabian.
248   Millenary Games in Rome.
249–51   *Trajanus Decius.* Persecution of Christians.
251   Decius defeated and killed by Goths at Abrittus.
251–53   *Trebonianus Gallus.* Epidemic begins.
253   *Aemilian.*
253–60   *Valerian and Gallienus.* German and Persian invasions.
257   Renewed persecution of Christians.
259–73   Usurpation of Postumus and successors in western provinces.
260   Valerian captured by Persians. Sole reign of *Gallienus.*
261–67   Odenathus viceroy of the east.
267   Zenobia independent ruler in the east.
268   Goths defeated at Naissus.
268–70   *Claudius Gothicus.*
269   Decisive victories over Goths.
ca. 270   Death of Plotinus.
270–75   *Aurelian.*
270   Dacia abandoned.
271   Wall of Aurelian started at Rome.
273   Zenobia defeated. Capture of Palmyra.
274   Tetricus, emperor in Gaul, defeated at Catalaunian Plains. Temple of
            Sun god at Rome.
275–76   *Tacitus.*
276–82   *Probus.*
277–79   Victories on Rhine and Danube.
277   Death of Mani.
282–83   *Carus.*
283–84   *Carinus and Numerian.*
284–305   *Diocletian and Maximian (286).*
286–96   Usurpations of Carausius (d. 293) and Allectus in Britain.
293   Constantius I (d. 306) and Galerius (d. 311) appointed Caesars.
297–98   Persian War.
301   Edict on Prices.
303–11   Great Persecution of Christians.
311   Edict of Serdica (Sofia).
312   Constantine I the Great defeats Maxentius at the Milvian Bridge.
312–37   Constantine I the Great and Licinius (d. 324)
313   Edict of Mediolanum (Milan) in favor of Christians.
324–30   Foundation of Constantinople.
325   Council of Nicaea.
326   Execution of Fausta and Crispus.
337   Accessions of *Constantine II (d. 340), Constantius II (d. 361),* and *Constans (d. 350)*

INDEX